All the Pasha's

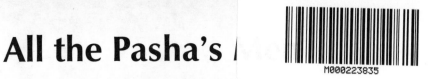

All the Pasha's Men

Mehmed Ali, his army and the making of modern Egypt

Khaled Fahmy

The American University in Cairo Press
Cairo New York

First published in paperback in 2002 by
The American University in Cairo Press
113 Sharia Kasr el Aini, Cairo, Egypt
420 Fifth Avenue, New York, NY 10018
www.aucpress.com

Second printing 2004

Dar el Kutub No. 16706/01
ISBN 977 424 696 9

Printed in Egypt

For
my parents and
Kouross Esmaeli,
with respect and gratitude

Contents

Illustrations

Preface

Although this book is a study of the army that was founded in Egypt in the first half of the nineteenth century, it does not offer a straightforward account of military history. While dealing with Egypt's history during the reign of Mehmed Ali Pasha (1805–48) by closely studying the army the Pasha founded midway through his long career, it does not follow the generals and officers of this army whilst they trained their men in camps, commanded their troops in battle, or basked in their military victories. Rather, this is a book that is primarily interested in the men who did most of the "dirty work" of this army, those thousands of Egyptian peasant-soldiers who were conscripted to serve in this army: it follows the soldiers from the time they were recruited, to the time they were sent to the training camps, then to the bloody sites of pitched battles, and finally back to their barracks where they recuperated from past battles and prepared for future ones.

The purpose of following the soldiers of this army so closely is not only to document their unprecedented experience and to check their reactions to what were novel and unfamiliar practices and institutions; it is also, and primarily, to check the validity of the common belief that this army was instrumental in raising Egyptian national consciousness and, indeed, in founding modern Egyptian nationalism specifically by giving these thousands of men the opportunity to bear arms and to defend their nation, a "right" that they were denied for centuries, if not millennia.

By closely studying this army – how it was fed, supplied, and medically cared for, and more importantly, how its soldiers were conscripted and trained, how they reacted to their officers' commands, and how they resisted the military authorities – this book argues that this army was, indeed, instrumental in founding the modern Egyptian nation. This it did, though, not by enlightening Egyptians regarding the essential truths of the "nation," but by instituting novel practices of surveillance, control and management that radically altered the nature of the government in Cairo and fundamentally changed the manner in which it dealt with the Egyptian population. This army was also a crucial element in changing the ethnic and linguistic configuration of Egypt's middle and upper classes in a manner that unwittingly gave rise to "nationalist" sentiments among the soldiery who were mostly Arabic-speakers and who resented being ruled and dominated by a Turkish-speaking military/bureaucratic elite.

This book, then, is not a biography of Mehmed Ali; it does not follow him from the time he arrived in Egypt in 1801 till his death nearly half a century later, tracing his wonderful deeds; nor does it give an account of this long period as if seen from his perspective. Rather, its subject is the army he founded and the men who fought in it. Instead of looking at the army as *the* national institution that gave those conscripts the "right" to bear arms and to defend their nation, or of writing its history in a manner that the Pasha himself would have liked, this book sees it as an institution of power that forced these tens of thousands of men to carry arms and to fight for Mehmed Ali and his family, and in the process changed the nature of Egyptian society and affected the lives of the men who served in it. The book tries to investigate how these men resisted and/or accommodated this most powerful of the Pasha's institutions, an institution which was unrivaled in the way in touched their bodies and sought to control their minds.

Besides being a study of nationalism and nationalist historiography, therefore, this is a book on power and resistance. Looking at the army as the modern institution of power *par excellence* this book attempts to see how power with its modern manifestations and institutions is perceived, accommodated and resisted by its subjects. While finding Michel Foucault's notions of power useful and insightful, this book critiques a particular reading of his work that stresses the monolithic nature of the institutions of power and accepts the inevitability of its forms. Instead of an impressive and consistent picture of how modern power objectifies its subjects, what is offered below is an attempt to present a more complex, and – intentionally – more blurred picture of power, one that can incorporate fractures, dissonance and resistance. By highlighting the small acts of defiance and resistance undertaken by the soldiers in this army, the intention is to undermine the impressive representations of power and its unceasing desire to silence its subjects. These small, every-day acts of resistance, while not grand or heroic, were still effective in challenging the attempts of power to control and manipulate the soldiers' lives and bodies, and alarmed the military authorities precisely by showing them that, through these small acts of resistance the soldiers managed to distance themselves from the Pasha and his grand projects.

This obviously leads to the question of whether it is feasible to write a history of an institution of power in a manner that not only avoids reproducing its own narrative but which can also incorporate the dialog that it constantly has with resistance. Given that the overwhelming majority of the people with whom this book is concerned were illiterate and did not leave behind written accounts which could inform us of what it was like to be objectified in this insistent manner, the question is whether it is still possible to include them as subjects and not merely as objects of power. Fortunately, the documents that this book relies upon made possible the incorporation of the soldiers' perspective in narrating the history of Mehmed Ali's army.

While some of the British Foreign Office documents housed in the Public Record Office, London, were of some value in understanding how the army functioned, these offer mostly an outsider's view of the events and personalities touched upon in this study and, therefore, they have been used only minimally. Similarly some accounts by contemporary travelers and military observers are used, but again only to give further descriptions to material gathered elsewhere. More substantially, this book relies on material collected from the Egyptian National Archives and, to a lesser extent, from the Egyptian National Library, both in Cairo. Broadly speaking, these are of three different kinds. On the one level, there are the numerous letters and regulations issued by the Pasha and his top officials. These include the correspondence between Mehmed Ali and the Commander-in-Chief of his forces, his son Ibrahim Pasha, letters to and from the Sublime Porte and various notables in Istanbul, as well as the numerous letters of the top officials issuing regulations to make sure that the army was well trained, well fed and regularly paid. The various military laws and training manuals which were the earliest publications of the Būlāq Press and which are housed in the Egyptian National Library make up the second group of contemporary documents that this study relies upon. In contrast to the very monolithic picture of power that comes across from reading these sources, the Archives, fortunately, also contains very valuable information in the form of the "journals" (*yevmiyyet*, lit. daily accounts) from the military camps and war fronts that include such documents as roll calls, inventory lists, courts martial, pay rolls and descriptions of marches and of battles. By relying on this diverse array of official documents it is possible to present an integral view of the army which not only avoids the usual concentration on the person of Mehmed Ali that often characterizes the historiography of Egypt during his reign, but also allows one to have a closer look at the every-day performance of that army and the manner in which the soldiers reacted to their officers' commands and orders. While this book does not claim to have "captured the voice" of the soldiers, given that the sources it relies on are still the sources of power itself, it attempts to challenge the monolithic picture that is usually offered of the performance of such an impressive institution of power and provides instead a more fractured, and, for this reason, a more telling image of that army.

Acknowledgements

This study is the result of several years of work in Cairo, Oxford and Princeton and has benefited greatly from the help and guidance of various people to whom many thanks are owed. Foremost are my professors at the American University in Cairo, and especially Galal Amin and Enid Hill to whom I am grateful for their unmatched generosity with their time and assistance as well as for showing me an example of dedication to teaching and encouragement of young scholars that I have rarely seen elsewhere.

At Oxford I was most fortunate in having Roger Owen as my supervisor. His help, advice and supportive comments were very valuable in guiding me throughout the difficult task of writing my D.Phil. dissertation. His insistence on rigorous scholarship and his love of, and dedication to, his students will always be most inspiring. Michael Gilsenan, although not supervising my work in an official manner, gave freely of his time and assistance in guiding me through writing my dissertation. During numerous walks in the beautiful gardens of Magdalen and St. John's Colleges I came to develop a friendship that added considerable warmth to my "Oxford experience."

For valuable comments on the present text and its earlier drafts I would like to thank, first and foremost, my D.Phil. examiners Eugene Rogan and Sami Zubaida who read the dissertation carefully and critically. Tim Mitchell, too, was most generous with his insightful comments and criticisms. I extend my thanks also to the many friends who have read parts of the text; these include: Nadia Benabid, Elliott Colla, Arthur Denner, Mine Ener, Jan Goldberg, Shamil Jeppie, Ussama Makdisi and Letitia Ufford. Both Youssef Nabil and Andy Shanken helped me with the illustrations, and Mrs. Virginia Catmur of Cambridge University Press copy-edited the text with care.

There are many persons who have contributed in more than one way to this project: Reem Saad by her unfailing support and most lively company has added much joy and richness to my stay in Oxford. Her perceptive comments and often deserved criticisms of the text were most valuable in helping me revise it. I would also like to thank my friends who were kind enough to tolerate me over the years with my burdensome companion, Mehmed Ali: Iman Hamdi, Hager Hadidi, Hania Sholkamy, Manal Fouad, Nadia Kamel, Naira Ijja, Randa Shaath, Sohail Luka and Ziad Bahaeldine.

I owe a very special debt to every individual member of the Egyptian National Archives, especially to Mr. Ibrahim Fathalla, Ms. Afaf Ragab, Mrs. Nadia Mostafa and, of course, Madame Sawsan Abdel-Ghani. The staff of the Radcliffe Camera of the Bodleian Library, Oxford, of Dar al-Kutub, Cairo, of the Firestone Library, Princeton, and my former colleagues at the Library of the American University in Cairo were all very helpful.

Last, but in no manner least, I wish to offer my deepest thanks to my sister, Rania, and her husband, Hany, for their support and understanding, and, above all, to my parents who have given me all their love and care and who encouraged me throughout my academic career.

Note on transliteration, dates and references

Both Arabic and Turkish words are transliterated using the conventions of the *International Journal of Middle East Studies*. Names of Arabic-speaking persons are transliterated as if they were Arabic names, while those of Turkish-speaking persons are transliterated as if they were Turkish.

Hijri dates mentioned in the notes are always cited with their Gregorian equivalents. The Ottoman abbreviations for the names of the months, which were used in the original documents, have been adopted here. These are:

M: Muharrem (Arabic Muḥarram)
S: Safer (Ṣafar)
Ra: Rebiülevvel (Rabīʿ al-Awwal)
R: Rebiülahir (Rabīʿ al-Thānī)
Ca: Cemaziyülevvel (Jumādā al-Ūlā)
C: Cemaziyülahir (Jumādā al-Ākhirā)
B: Receb (Rajab)
Ş: Şaban (Shaʿbān)
N: Ramazan (Ramaḍān)
L: Şevval (Shawwāl)
Za: Zilkade (Dhū al-Qiʿda)
Z: Zilhice (Dhū al-Ḥijja)

As mentioned in the comprehensive bibliography at the end of this study, material from Dār al-Wathāʾiq al-Qawmiyya, the Egyptian National Archives, are either from *sijillāt* (bound registers) or *maḥāfiẓ* (boxes). The latter are referred to in the notes by name of the archival heading, then box number, followed by the document number within that box. For example, Sham 2/45 is document no. 45 of the 2nd box of *Maḥāfiẓ al-Shām*. References from the *sijillāt*, on the other hand, use the system devised by Dār al-Wathāʾiq in its mimeographed subject heading list, *Qawāʾim bi-Niẓām Tartīb Sijillāt al-Dār*. Accordingly, S/5/51/2/4 refers to letter no. 4 of the 2nd *sijill* (register) of the 51st sub-division of

Sijillāt ʿĀbdīn, which is given the code S/5. S/1: Maʿiyya Saniyya (Viceregal Department), S/2: Dīwān Khedewī (Department of Civil Affairs) and S/3: Dīwān al-Jihādiyya (Department of War) are some of the other codes.

In both the *maḥāfiẓ* and the *sijillāt*, the documents were overwhelmingly Ottoman and it is to these originals, rather than to their Arabic translations, that reference is made.

Introduction

On 25 November 1826 Mehmed Ali Pasha, the Ottoman Governor of Egypt, received in his palace Mr. John Barker in order to accept his credentials as the new British Consul in Alexandria. In a sign of deference, the Pasha stood up to greet the new consul, but ignored the official papers containing his credentials that he had in his hand. After a brief discussion of Mr. Barker's predecessor who, the Pasha said, never contradicted "his will, or dispute[d] his opinions," the Pasha then embarked upon a monolog that lasted for more than half an hour in which he told his British visitor a story about his childhood in Albania.

"I was born in a village in Albania and my father had ten children besides me, who are all dead; but, while living, not one of them ever contradicted me. Although I left my native mountains before I attained to manhood, the principal people in the place never took any step in the business of the commune, without previously inquiring what was my pleasure. I came to this country an obscure adventurer, and when I was yet a *Bimbashi* (captain), it happened one day that the commissary had to give each of the Bimbashis a tent. They were all my seniors, and naturally pretended to a preference over me; but the officer said, – "Stand ye all by; this youth, Mohammed Ali, shall be served first" and I advanced step by step, as it pleased God to ordain; and now here I am" – (rising a little on his seat, [Barker comments] and looking out of the window which was at his elbow, and commanded a view of the Lake Mareotis [to the south of Alexandria]) – "and now here I am. I never had a master," – (glancing his eye on the roll containing the *Imperial firman*).[1]

This was a strange introduction indeed: having received the Ottoman Sultan's approval to represent British interests in Alexandria, and going to present himself with the Sultan's firman in hand, the British Consul was surprised to be received by a story of Mehmed Ali's childhood in Albania. As strange as this reception might have appeared to the British Consul, this first encounter with the Pasha was full of political intent which was too obvious for the Consul not to notice. Besides referring to

[1] FO 78/147, Barker, 25 November 1826.

Plate 1 "Mehemed-Aly"

Barker's predecessor as having the wisdom not to contradict the Pasha in any of his opinions "which, he observed, was very easily done, because they were always founded on reason and justice," and thus insinuating that he expected the same from him, it was clear to Barker that the Pasha had also intended to pass on to him the message that "he was as little awed by the power of the Sovereign of Great Britain as that of the Sultan."[2]

As much as Mehmed Ali wanted to impress upon his visitor that he was an independent ruler, technically and legally he was only a vali of an

[2] *Ibid.*

Ottoman province, which meant that he had the right to receive consuls (and not ambassadors) of European countries but was denied the right to appoint political representatives to their capitals. Keen on improving his image in Europe, however, and interested in affecting public opinion there, the Pasha was left with few tools to do so. One such tool, though, was the interviews he was in the habit of giving to European visitors some of whom, he was well aware, would proceed to write and publish their accounts of their encounters with him. As such, the *coup de théâtre* that Barker was audience to in his first interview with Mehmed Ali, far from being strange or atypical, was a "very characteristic anecdote"[3] and it was not entered upon accidentally or unintentionally. Rather, it constituted part of a repertoire of stories and performances that were meticulously performed to influence the views of these European visitors.

For their part, these visitors were interested in meeting the famous Pasha who had been vali of Egypt since 1805, making him one of the longest serving provincial governors in the Ottoman Empire. These tourists, who would mostly be visiting Egypt as part of a longer trip that included a visit to the Holy Land, would typically disembark in Alexandria, sail down the newly dug Maḥmūdiyya Canal linking the port city to the Nile, and from there proceed all the way to Cairo. While visiting that most colorful of cities, they would make a point to visit the Pasha himself, who already by the 1820s had become "one of the curiosities of Egypt"[4] owing to the reforms he had introduced in Egypt and his efforts in making the country safer for tourists. From these accounts one can have a glimpse not only of how the Pasha was seen by his contemporaries, but also of how he intended to be seen.

"The old spider in his den"

In December 1836, a British nobleman, Lord Lindsay, paid the Pasha a visit in his palace in the Citadel in Cairo.

> We visited the old spider in his den, the citadel [he began] . . . Ascending a broad marble passage on an inclined plane . . . and traversing a lofty antechamber crowded with attendants, we found ourselves in the presence-chamber, a noble saloon . . . but without an article of furniture, except a broad divan, or sofa, extending round the three sides of the room, in one corner of which

[3] James Augustus St. John, *Egypt and Mohammed Ali* (London: Longman, 1834), I, p. 543.
[4] A. A. Paton, *History of the Egyptian Revolution* (London: Trubner, 1863), II, pp. 82–3.

squatted his highness Mohammed Ali. Six wax-candles . . . stood in the center, yet gave but little light.[5]

This excerpt is typical of descriptions given by foreign visitors to the Pasha in his palace. The themes of light and darkness, of shadows and hypnotic gazes, figure prominently in their accounts of the encounter with the enigmatic Pasha. Two years after this visit, for example, another British traveler on visiting Mehmed Ali's palace commented on "a score of yellowish-brown candles [that were hung from the chandelier] . . . by their light we could only indistinctly see to the extremity of the apartment."[6] When ʿAbdallah Pasha of Sidon, whom Mehmed Ali's forces had besieged for more than six months in his formidable fortress of Acre, finally gave in, he was brought on board an Egyptian vessel to Alexandria where he was received magnanimously by the Egyptian Pasha. Here is the contemporary newspaper account of the encounter of these two bitter enemies.

People had gathered in masses to see [ʿAbdallah Pasha] and a larger number of statesmen [*arbāb al-dawla*] were waiting on shore to receive him. On disembarking . . . he was escorted to the palace . . . and when he entered the audience chamber he found among those waiting for him His Highness, Mehmed Ali Pasha, *and the place was badly lit.* Smilingly, the Pasha stood up to receive him and to calm him down. ʿAbdallah Pasha lowered his head and threw himself at His Highness's feet kissing his cloak and asking for forgiveness.[7]

Besides light and shadows, it was the Pasha's eyes that provided the other theme that visitors regularly commented on. Mr. Ramsay, Lord Lindsay's friend who accompanied him on his trip to Egypt, had the following to say about the Pasha's eyes.

He did not address any of his subjects, but I observed his sharp cunning eyes fixing itself on every one. The light was not strong enough to remark minutely, but I can agree with former travellers as to the vivid expression of his eye, and, for the rest . . . it is absurd to talk of, or have any idea of his face.[8]

At around the same time that this account was written another British traveler, a certain Dr. Wilde who was attending a "gentleman [making] a voyage for the benefit of his health"[9] made a point of visiting the Pasha's other palace in Shubra, in the outskirts of Cairo.

5 A. W. C. Lindsay, Lord, *Letters on Egypt, Edom, and the Holy Land* (London: Henry Colborn, 1938), I, p. 34.

6 Anon., "Interviews with Mehemet Ali," *Tait's Edinburgh Magazine*, 5(1838), p. 696.

7 Ḥaidar al-Shihābī, *al-Ghurar al-Ḥisān fī Akhbār Abnāʾ al-Zāmān*, ed., Asad Rustum and Fouad al-Bustānī (Beirut: The Catholic Press, 1933), pp. 860–1. The newspaper, which is not named, is dated 5 June 1832. Emphasis added.

8 Mr Ramsay's Journal, quoted in Lord Lindsay, I, p. 35n.

9 W. R. Wilde, *Narrative of a Voyage to Madeira, Teneriffe and Along the Shores of the Mediterranean Including a visit to Algiers, Egypt, Palestine, etc.* (Dublin: William Curry, 1844). p. v.

Seeing a company of Franks [in his garden, the Pasha slackened his] pace to salute us; thus affording us a view of this extraordinary character. He is a fine-looking old man, now [September 1837] upwards of seventy (1769 was, I believe, the birth year of Napoleon, Wellington and M. Alee [sic]) with a very long silver beard . . . Slight as was our view of him, it did not pass without making us feel the power of an eye of more brilliancy and penetration than I ever beheld.[10]

Another traveler who had visited Egypt fifteen years earlier was surprised by how the Pasha, in spite of his old age, still managed to mesmerize his audience by his looks. "[T]he energy of his mind, the vivacity of his features, and the piercing lightning of his glance have undergone no change since I first saw him in the year 1825, nearly 15 years ago."[11] Still another traveler was disconcerted by the Pasha's "piercing eye [which was] incessantly rolling about."[12] These descriptions were valid not only for the old-aged Pasha: as early as 1823 it was noted that although "the Pasha has a vulgar low-born face, [he has] a commanding intelligent eye."[13]

Even those visitors who saw the Pasha as "undignified and ridiculous" could not help but comment on the "glance of his bright and restless eye," noting that "as his unquiet eyes glided incessantly from one to the other of the party around him, or glanced stealthily at the door beyond, [they] could trace, in their workings, the restless and ever-watchful spirit of Mehemet Ali."[14] Shortly after his death A. Paton, one of the shrewdest observers of mid-century Egypt, admitted that the Pasha's "features were remarkable neither for beauty nor the reverse; but, [he hastened to add] if ever a man had an eye that denoted genius, Mohammed Ali was that person. Never dead nor quiescent, it was fascinating like that of a gazelle; or in the hour of storm, fierce as the eagle's."[15] Charles Murray, the last British Consul-General during the Pasha's long reign, summed it up well when he said

his eyes were of that peculiar grey which seems especially to belong to remarkable men; they were bright and set deep in the head. A strange wild fire gleamed in them at times, and they shot forth ireful glances, which few could withstand; but when in a mirthful mood they twinkled with a droll, malicious fun. Sometimes anger and humour were so quaintly blended in their expression that it was difficult to know which predominated.[16]

10 *Ibid.*, p. 232.
11 Richard R. Madden, *Egypt and Mohammed Ali* (London: Hamilton, 1841), p. 11.
12 H. P. Measor, *A Tour in Egypt, Arabia Petræa and the Holy Land in the Years 1841–2* (London: Francis and John Rivington, 1844), p. 119.
13 Sir Frederick Heniker, *Notes During a Visit to Egypt, the Oases, Mount Sinai and Jerusalem* (London: Murray, 1823), p. 63.
14 "Interviews with Mehemet Ali," p. 697.
15 Paton, *History*, II, pp. 165–6.
16 Charles A. Murray, *A Short Memoir of Mohammed Ali* (London: Bernard Quaritch, 1898), p. 58.

Staging the gaze

At first sight, these stories woven around the person and gaze of Mehmed Ali appear anecdotal and marginal in the writings of contemporary European travelers, intending to add flavour to their accounts of what was already an exotic, unfamiliar and fascinating oriental tour. On the other hand, one can already detect some common themes and even expressions in this rich repertoire of stories concerning the great Pasha, suggesting perhaps that these European travelers were aware of each others' writings and that they had come to Egypt having read each others' work. The "I-was-born-in-a-village-in-Albania" story, for example, besides being told twice by Barker in his dispatches to London,[17] was reproduced in St. John's published book.[18] Furthermore, one occasionally comes across an allusion to the effect that what is being watched had already been seen before: "I can agree with former travelers . . ."[19]

Alternatively, the remarkable common features in these accounts might suggest that what these European travelers were audience to constituted part of a scene/act that was well rehearsed and carefully produced. It is perhaps no accident that nearly all visitors start their accounts by describing the busy, loud and ornamented antechamber full of officials and members of the public coming mostly to present petitions to the Pasha. Then they give an account of the "presence-room", a grand hall "belle dans sa nudité"[20] and bare of everything but a sofa in a corner of which sat a figure shrouded in shadows. During the ensuing conversation they were surprised to discover that the mysterious figure was none but the great Pasha himself, but since they could not see his face nor "detect the expression of his countenance," they were left literally in the dark. This feeling of mystery and suspense was amplified by the impression that the source of light had on them: the chandeliers that were brought in, oddly enough, "gave but little light."

During the conversation with the Pasha a climactic point was usually reached when he suddenly leaned forward or pushed back his turban from above his eyebrows to allow the light to fall on his eyes. This final act of haunting theatricality was brought about by

> a peculiarity in his mode of wearing the turban – close down over his eyes – [which] takes off much from the fine character of his countenance, concealing

[17] FO 78/147, Barker, 25 November 1826, and FO 78/170, Barker, 19 January 1828.

[18] St. John, *Egypt*, I, pp. 543–4. It was also published in the book that Barker's son edited from his father's letters, John Barker, *Syria and Egypt Under the Last Five Sultans of Turkey* (London: Samuel Tinsley, 1876), II, p. 48–49.

[19] See note 8 above.

[20] Nubar Pasha, *Mémoires de Nubar Pasha*, ed. Mirrit Botros Ghali (Beirut: Librairie du Liban, 1983), p. 5.

his handsome forehead, compressing the eyebrows, throwing the eyes into shade, and giving them a sinister expression.[21]

But having seen the final act in this staged encounter, the visitor discovered that what he visibly saw did not "illuminate" him to the extent of understanding this enigmatic character. In fact, listening to his laugh and seeing his gaze, he felt a chill of terror pass through his body and, failing to demystify it, ended up alluding to previous descriptions of the Pasha ("an expression I have read somewhere . . . came suddenly into my head")[22] thus reinforcing the "textual" approach to the person of Mehmed Ali, and perpetuating the awesome, enigmatic side of his character.

The encounter with the Pasha, thus, besides being a tourist stop in the itinerary of European visitors, was a highly theatrical one: in it the Pasha comes across clearly as being aware that he is being seen, reflects this awareness and catches us, the readers of accounts of these encounters, unawares. Few visitors managed to escape the effect of that spell that Mehmed Ali would cast on his audience; most of them felt that the Pasha was in control of not only Egypt but even the encounter that they were part of. They were consciously aware of the Pasha's piercing gaze seeing through them, and they often quoted the Pasha saying, "The only books I ever read . . . are men's faces, and I seldom read them amiss."[23] As such, they, too, come across as accomplices in this haunting theatricality, and by transcribing their encounter into their published memoirs they made sure that the Pasha's powerful, enigmatic aura would perpetually live on.

One visitor, though, came very close to avoiding that piercing look of the Pasha; he was James Augustus St. John, who visited Egypt in the early 1830s and met the Pasha on 21 November 1832. His description of the encounter with the Pasha starts off as most other accounts do:

arriving at the entrance [of the palace, we] found a number of janissaries, and other attendants, in their costly and gorgeous uniforms, lounging about the grand flight of steps which leads to the divan. Having ascended these stairs, we crossed several spacious halls . . . and, making our way through crowds of courtiers of all nations, arrived at the audience-chamber . . . [There the Pasha had] placed himself as usual [!] in a corner of the room; where, his whole body being involved in shadow, it was extremely difficult to detect the expression of his countenance, or the uneasy rapid motion of his eyes.[24]

Yet, in the discussion that ensued St. John soon realized that he was

21 C. R. Scott, *Rambles in Egypt and Candia* (London: Henry Colborn, 1837), I, pp. 178–79.
22 See note 8 above. 23 Murray, *Short Memoir*, p. 4.
24 St. John, *Egypt*, I, pp. 49–50.

involved in a game of gazes and manipulations, and that the Pasha, knowing that his British visitor was about to write a book on His "Highness's government, and the present state of the country," was clearly trying to impress him. Rather than give in to Mehmed Ali's manipulation, the shrewd visitor set out to demystify the mysterious Pasha and instead of starting his account with a description of the Pasha's physical features, he ends with it:

> Mohammed Ali is a man of middling stature . . . His features . . . are plain, if not coarse; but they are lighted up with so much intelligence, and his dark eyes beam so brightly, that I should not be surprised if I found persons familiar with his countenance thought him handsome. In dress he differs but little, if at all, from any other Turkish gentleman; he has, however, a certain dignity in his manners which . . . borders upon majesty. But this dignity seems almost inseparable from the possession of power: the man who can do much good or harm, whatever may be his stature, form or features will always appear to exhibit it; as the scorpion, in size no larger than a snail, is viewed with awe, because he is supposed to carry death in his sting.[25]

In other words, instead of proceeding to give an account of the Pasha's rule in Egypt that would border on being a dictated autobiography (the way most other accounts were), St. John realized that the Pasha's mesmerizing presence is ultimately connected with the power he holds; and that this power is essentially an effect not of the Pasha's inherent genius, but of the elaborate mystique of his court ceremonials that attempt to impress the spectator into thinking that what goes on there is "not merely important but in some odd fashion connected with the way the world is built."[26]

Taking its lead from St. John, this book attempts to see if it is possible to write the history of Egypt in the first half of the nineteenth century without being stung by the Pasha or hypnotized by his gaze. The reason it opened with an account of his body and his gaze is to introduce a theme, or more precisely a technique, that runs throughout this book: each of the chapters that follows, with the exception of chapter 5, opens with a spectacle that is intended to be evocative and mesmerizing, but which, it is argued, is still possible to see through and deconstruct. In one sense, then, this is a book about spectacles of power: how they are staged and watched. It deals with numerous such spectacles mostly staged by a man who, as we have seen and as we shall see further, was a

[25] *Ibid.*, pp. 58–59.

[26] Clifford Geertz, "Centers, kings, and charisma: Reflections on the symbolics of power," in Sean Wilentz, ed., *Rites of Power: Symbolism, Ritual and Politics Since the Middle Ages* (Philadelphia: University of Pennsylvania Press, 1985), p. 15.

master of the art of staging spectacles and of influencing audiences. Another reason for opening with a glimpse of the Pasha in his palaces is to warn the reader about the Pasha's gaze and to stress the fact that while attempting to avoid it, this book is still written with the knowledge that his controlling gaze continues to exert its influence.

The army, the economy and society

Only after warning the reader by introducing the "old spider in his den" and seeing him manipulating his audience can one feel safe in stepping back to narrate Mehmed Ali's story and to place him in a wider historical context. This narration will not start at the beginning, as he would have liked, with his childhood in Albania or with his arrival in Egypt, or at the end, as some nationalist historians would have preferred, highlighting his showdown with Great Britain, but in the middle of his long career as governor of Egypt, and precisely in the year AH 1236/AD 1820–1. This is the year that Mehmed Ali started to found a modern army in Egypt, an army which was based on conscription and which relied on the institutions of the modern state that he founded mainly to serve that army. It is this army, rather than Mehmed Ali's character or his person, that is the subject of this book, and it is this central institution that is studied below in order to analyze the nature of Egyptian society in the first half of the nineteenth century.

By the time Mehmed Ali started to found this army in 1820 he had already been occupying the prestigious and lucrative post of governor of Egypt on behalf of the Ottoman Sultan for fifteen years. During this long period he had managed to tighten Cairo's control over the provinces by fighting corruption in the local bureaucracy,[27] by conducting a cadastral survey (1813–14) that was crucial in abolishing the tax farming system (*iltizām*) and in the cancellation of the immunities on agricultural land belonging to mosques and pious foundations (*awqāf*),[28] and, most importantly, by getting rid in the infamous Massacre of the Citadel (1811) of the power of the military landlords, the Mamluks, who had been in effective control of the province for

[27] For the founding of the new bureaucracy and its characteristic "household" nature, see Robert Hunter, *Egypt Under the Khedives, 1805–79* (Pittsburgh: University of Pittsburgh Press, 1984).

[28] On Mehmed Ali's agricultural policy, see Helen Anne Rivlin, *The Agricultural Policy of Muḥammad ʿAlī in Egypt* (Cambridge, Mass.: Harvard University Press, 1961); ʿAlī Barakāt, *Taṭawwur al-Milkiyya al-Zirāʿiyya fī Miṣr, 1813–1914 wa Atharuhu ʿala al-Ḥaraka al-Siyāsiyya* [Development of Agricultural Property in Egypt, 1813–1914 and its Effects on the Political Movement] (Cairo: Dār al-Thaqāfa al-Jadīda, 1977); and Kenneth M. Cuno, *The Pasha's Peasants: Land, Society and Economy in Lower Egypt, 1740–1858* (Cambridge: Cambridge University Press, 1992).

centuries in spite of Ottoman legal suzerainty.[29] Centralization of political and administrative control was also enhanced by a rapid increase in agricultural productivity based on an expansion of the cultivated area and an increase in the area of perennial irrigation. Having done away with the power of middle-men in the shape of former *multazims*, religious men who were managing the *awqāf*, or the Mamluks, more and more revenue was funneled to Cairo and into the Pasha's coffers. In addition, the Pasha introduced a wide-ranging policy of monopolies whereby staple goods as well as cash crops were to be sold only to government warehouses and at prices fixed by the Pasha. As a result of these measures annual revenue increased from 8 million francs in 1805 to 50 million francs in 1821,[30] allowing the Pasha to undertake projects that were not even conceivable in the long period of Ottoman rule.

The digging of the Maḥmūdiyya canal offers a graphic example of the degree to which the Pasha had managed to secure his control over the province of Egypt and is a testimony to his ability to undertake huge infrastructural projects that none of the Ottoman governors before him had managed to undertake. Started in April 1817, the project lasted for three years and was aimed at linking Alexandria to the western branch of the Nile. The ambitious project involved coercing thousands of men and women from all the provinces of Lower Egypt to work on it. During the month of March 1819 the number of laborers working on the project was said to have been as high as 300,000. After its completion the canal was 72 kilometers long and had cost 35,000 purses (around 7.5 million francs).[31] Although contemporary reports stress the appallingly high rate of casualties (estimates range from 12,000 to 100,000) and the highly improvised manner in which the canal was excavated,[32] still, the sheer size of the labor force involved as well as the cost and duration of the project testify to the ability of the Pasha's administration in Cairo to tap and control the human and material resources of his province.

By the early 1820s, then, the Pasha had managed to undertake what every Ottoman governor before him for the previous three centuries had tried but failed to do, namely, to organize the economy of the province

[29] The standard account of the massacre is in ʿAbdel-Raḥmān al-Jabartī, *ʿĀjā'ib al-Āthār fi'l-Tarājim wa'l-Akhbār* (Cairo: Būlāq, AH 1297/AD 1880), IV, pp. 127–32.

[30] Georges Douin, ed., *La Mission du Baron de Boislecomte, L'Egypte et la Syrie en 1833* (Cairo: Royal Egyptian Geographical Society, 1927), p. 126.

[31] Rivlin, *Agricultural Policy*, pp. 216–21.

[32] *Ibid.*, pp. 221, 353 n. 15, and al-Jabartī, *ʿAjā'ib al-Āthār*, IV, pp. 301–304. On al-Jabartī's figures, which form the basis of Rivlin's assessment, see Cuno's cautionary remarks; Cuno, *The Pasha's Peasants*, pp. 121–22.

of Egypt and to reap its considerable potential wealth. Had the Pasha died in 1820, he would have been fifty years old and he would have already secured for himself a distinguished place in the history of Egypt and of the Ottoman Empire. He would have been known as the longest serving Ottoman governor of the province of Egypt, one who had managed to make its economy more efficient and to improve the performance of its bureaucracy. He would also have secured for himself the reputation among Egyptians of being one of the most brutal of the Ottoman governors who, through monopolies and corvée, had pushed them to unprecedented levels of poverty and misery. For by the early 1820s labor shortages were already in evidence, resistance to the corvée was acquiring an alarming momentum, resentment to the Pasha's monopolies system had forced the government to amend its policies and, most significantly, "the rural society was pushed to the limit of its ability to produce and pay taxes."[33]

Yet instead of being the beginning of the end of government oppression or a marker of the apogee of the Pasha's rule, the years 1820–1 constitute a watershed, dividing the Pasha's rule into two periods of nearly equal length. For the Pasha had the good fortune to live for nearly another thirty years, during which time he introduced institutions and ushered in policies that make the already impressive policies of 1805–20 and the suffering they caused the Egyptians to fade by comparison. Two developments in particular assume gigantic proportions and mark 1821 as a crucial year in the Pasha's career, namely the successful experimentation with the cultivation of long-staple cotton and the founding of a modern conscription-based army. While both these developments took place in the same year, there was no causal link between them. Nonetheless, from that time onwards very strong links existed between these two developments of the Pasha's policies which proved to be the cornerstones of his entire regime: through cotton cultivation, which grew exponentially in the 1820s, the Pasha managed to reap unprecedented profits from its sale, which he then monopolized and used to construct his army, build his navy, establish his factories and construct numerous schools, hospitals and palaces.

Together, these two developments, the introduction and cultivation on a large scale of long-staple cotton and the building of a modern army, formed the twin pillars of the Pasha's regime and none of the other institutions that Egypt witnessed during the first half of the nineteenth century parallels their importance. While cotton cultivation radically changed the nature of Egyptian agriculture, altered Cairo's

33 *Ibid.*, p. 117.

relationship with the provinces, increased Egypt's link to the European economy and significantly increased the government's budget,[34] the army had an unparalleled impact on society since besides conscripting Egyptians for the first time in centuries, it triggered the need to found more and more institutions which together radically transformed the face of Egyptian society. The army occupied central stage among the Pasha's numerous institutions and was the *raison d'être* of various other impressive institutions. For example, the many factories that were founded were intended mainly to produce commodities for the use of the army, which was their most important market. Similarly, most of the schools that were opened were aiming at graduating officers for the army. Likewise, the earliest modern hospitals to be built in Egypt were essentially military hospitals that were constructed near camps with high troop concentration. Moreover, the army, since it was a conscript army, changed the lives of thousands of Egyptians who were dragged into its service and radically changed the lives of their families who were often left behind trying to do their best after losing an important, if not also the primary, bread winner. Moreover, using this army Mehmed Ali managed, albeit for a short period of time, to extend his control over wide areas of the Middle East including the Hijaz, the Sudan, Syria and parts of southern Anatolia, and naturally Egypt's relationship with these areas changed radically.

Mehmed Ali: the "founder of modern Egypt"

Owing to the introduction in Egypt of so many novel institutions in the first half of the nineteenth century Mehmed Ali is commonly believed to be "The Founder of Modern Egypt."[35] Through his various public projects – the opening of schools, the building of hospitals, the founding of factories and the creation of a modern army – the Pasha is seen not merely as having improved the finances of Egypt or as having enhanced the efficiency of the bureaucracy of Cairo, but as having laid the very foundation for a "national" take-off. These efforts at "modernization" on the part of the Pasha are usually portrayed as being part of a master-plan, a well-integrated scheme of development that was aimed not only at "modernizing" Egyptian society and transforming its economy, but also at gaining independence from Ottoman control from which it was believed to have been suffering for nearly three centuries. As said above,

[34] Roger Owen, *Cotton and the Egyptian Economy, 1820–1914* (Oxford: Clarendon Press, 1969).

[35] Henry Dodwell, *The Founder of Modern Egypt* (Cambridge: The University Press, 1931).

not only did the Pasha found a modern army, he also founded countless educational, medical and infrastructural bodies to serve it. Yet in spite of these co-ordinated efforts on the part of the Pasha to reactivate the Egyptian economy after centuries of stagnation and even decline, the "experiment" failed. Even before the Pasha's death a large number of the factories, schools and other establishments that he had founded were either closed down or were abandoned and neglected. European, especially British, intervention is usually identified as the cause of the failure of this ambitious, well-planned and impressive "experiment," and two episodes are often mentioned as examples of how Europe managed to frustrate Mehmed Ali's ambitious policies. The first was the 1838 Balta Liman commercial treaty between Great Britain and the Sublime Porte, aimed at abolishing commercial monopolies throughout the Ottoman Empire at large but targeted specifically at Mehmed Ali's monopolies. These monopolies were believed to have been the backbone of the Pasha's economic policy and to have given his industries the protection they needed to compete with European goods. Having lost that protection, the infant industries and the services connected to them fell to ruins. The second incident that is usually highlighted to stress how European efforts were most instrumental in aborting this impressive "experiment" in development was the firman of 1841 which was passed by the Ottoman Sultan but which was a result of European pressure. This firman stripped Egypt of the territorial possessions that it had managed to acquire during the preceding two decades and, of equal significance, reduced the size of its armed forces to 18,000 men during peacetime, only a small fraction of its original size.

Having been deprived of its "colonies," and losing the army which constituted a large market for its products, the Egyptian factories found it difficult to produce commodities that could compete with foreign, mostly British, goods. In Egypt itself, local industries were closed down after losing their protective tariff barriers. At the same time foreign merchants flooded the Egyptian market with their cheap goods after the collapse of the Pasha's monopoly system. Soon afterwards they established financial houses and started extending numerous loans to members of the ruling family as well as to the rural population that triggered a debt spiral that forced Egypt to become more and more economically dependent on the West. Nearly thirty years after the death of Mehmed Ali a severe financial crisis offered a pretext for foreign intervention which eventually led to an invasion by British troops, thus effectively reducing Egypt to the position of a British protectorate and ushering in a period of military occupation that lasted for seventy years.

In this way one of the earliest, most ambitious development plans outside Europe came to a dramatic end. After being one of the first countries to promote industrialization outside Europe in a manner that "partly prefigured the models of state-induced growth championed by Japan and Czarist Russia during the latter half of the 19th century,"[36] Egypt was reduced to something like a mere colony of the British Empire. Not before another century had passed would Egypt witness any establishments of the size of those founded by Mehmed Ali. By that time, however, it would be too late, and Egypt would be strongly entrenched as a Third World country with the gap separating it from the leading industrial nations of the world widening more and more.

Briefly put, this is how the history of Egypt during the first half of the nineteenth century is written about by most Egyptian nationalist historians.[37] They see in Mehmed Ali's "experiment" an interesting "chapter" in the long history of Egypt, a chapter that was supposed to witness the lifting of Egypt from the pre-modern, feudal rule under the Ottoman Empire to "catch up" with modern, capitalist Europe. In effect they argue that if it were not for European intervention Egypt would have continued her ambitious modernization efforts, efforts that were begun in earnest by Mehmed Ali from as early as the first decade of the nineteenth century and before any other country outside Europe.

The Sphinx, the Pasha and the Egyptian nation

Yet in spite of his frustrated efforts and his aborted projects (and probably precisely because of them) Mehmed Ali occupies a unique place in modern Egyptian nationalist historiography. In him Egyptian nationalists see the prototype of a national hero who, through determination and good work, attempted to resurrect his country from the brink of total collapse under the Ottomans and deliver her into the modern age. Let us listen to the Sphinx himself describe the career of the Great Pasha in a letter he sent to his beloved Cairo on the centenary of Mehmed Ali's death.

I have been harboring overflowing feelings that I can no longer contain, passionate feelings that pull me towards you, in spite of being tied here to my place with the Pyramids behind me. The Sphinx today will speak, but with no

[36] Jean Batou, "Muhammad-'Ali's Egypt, 1805–48: A command economy in the 19th century?" In Jean Batou, ed., *Between Development and Underdevelopment: The Precarious Attempts at Industrialization of the Periphery, 1800–70* (Geneva: Droz, 1991), p. 182.

[37] Most notably, see 'Abdel-Raḥmān al-Rāf'ī, *'Aṣr Muḥammad 'Alī* [Mehmed Ali's Reign] (Cairo: Maktabat al-Nahḍa al-Miṣriyya, 1951); M. Sabry, *L'Empire égyptien sous Mohamed-Ali et la question d'Orient (1811–49)* (Paris: P. Geuthner, 1930); and 'Abdel-Raḥmān Zakī, *al-Tārīkh al-Ḥarbī li-'Aṣr Muḥammad 'Alī al-Kabīr* [Military History of the Reign of Mehmed Ali the Great] (Cairo: Dār al-Ma'ārif, 1950).

voice to be heard. He will unveil his secrets in this letter to you, Cairo, and to you alone. You might have thought that I am nothing but a piece of solid stone . . . but have you ever thought that this solid mass might have a heart like other living hearts? It is time that this heart speaks its buried love . . . I have seen days and years pass by and you have always remained my beloved and my passion for you has always kept its purity. I can recount how you remained for a while an Arab girl, in your bedouin Fusṭāṭ . . . Then Djawhar the Sicilian came bestowing on you the treasures of the Maghreb . . . until you became, indeed, the Conqueror of the Hearts [*Qāhirat al-Qulūb*] . . . In this Fatimid glory you put on your best garments . . . and people's hearts came seeking you from all corners of the world . . . Yet, with your wisdom and sagacity you . . . were a patron of the Faith, and on your bright cityscape the minaret of al-Azhar could be seen proclaiming the Word of God, and at your gates multitudes came seeking knowledge and bounty . . . Times, however, changed, and after your wealth and glory, you saw misery and weakness . . . My heart was bleeding for you, and how could I remain still seeing you suffering under the tutelage of this Mamluk eyeing you like a tiger eyes his prey? Yet even in your difficulty and frailty you were noble, and in due time the power of this tyrant was eclipsed and you came out Victorious [*al-Qāhira*] again. And how couldn't you when God has sent you this genius, the son of Kavala? I could see him in his distant place of origin sitting for long hours fixing his eye on you, penetrating with his piercing insight the layers of time . . . and listening to your imploring plea. He then could not but jump to your rescue, saying "Here I come, here I come." I saw him descending on you stretching his arms wide open and you threw yourself into his embrace, with a trembling heart and overflowing yearning, as if this embrace would last forever. He disappeared in you and you in him and together you became one indivisible person. Can anyone mention Cairo without the phantom of Mehmed Ali leaping to his mind? Doesn't he, till this day, hover high above you from his citadel, defending and protecting you?[38]

This is how Maḥmūd Taymūr, the famous Egyptian novelist, commemorated the centenary of Mehmed Ali's death. This love letter from the Sphinx to his beloved city is "translated" by Taymūr from the original Hieroglyphics, "my own native language," the Sphinx explained, "for in spite of all the different languages that my soul has been carrying for ages, Hieroglyphics is my favorite. I cannot part with it." In the modern Egyptian collective consciousness – in novels, films, cartoons – it is the Sphinx more than any other monument that stands for Egypt; his massive solidity symbolizes her endurance, his faint sarcastic smile refers to her subtle way of answering her enemies, and his silence is believed to be more eloquent than the hefty tomes written

[38] Maḥmūd Taymūr, "Abū al-Hawl yunājī al-Qāhira" [The Sphinx confides in Cairo], *al-Hilāl*, 57 (August 1949), pp. 36–39. "Fusṭāṭ" is the name of the first settlement that the Arabs founded in Egypt from which they ruled the province; "Djawhar" was the military commander who led the Fatimid invasion of Egypt from the east; and "Kavala" is the home town of Mehmed Ali in modern-day northern Greece which was then part of the Ottoman Empire.

by the numerous sages who dwelt there and more effective than the adventures of all the conquerors who have passed though her lands. Yet Taymūr is now making him speak. The Sphinx's words are worth listening to, for, as Taymūr would have us believe, if ever one wants to listen to Egypt's true voice and her own self-perception, one would not find a purer, more authentic voice than that of the Sphinx.

So what did Taymūr read in the Sphinx's letter written in 1949? In that most telling letter he read a concise nationalist version of Egypt's long history in which she appears as having a clear unadulterated identity that goes as far back as her pharaonic past, hence the language in which the letter is written and the Sphinx's insistence that it is the dearest to his heart. But Egypt, personified in the city of Cairo, also has an Islamic component that is constitutive of her identity and which is here represented by al-Azhar and its minaret dominating the cityscape. Conspicuously absent from Taymūr's version of Egypt's history is a long period of over three centuries of Ottoman rule. Having avoided any explicit reference to this period by name, he conflates it with Mamluk rule to which he alludes when he has the Sphinx refer to the tutelage of the "Mamluk." Echoing a widely believed notion, Taymūr refers to this period as one of oppression and tyranny. With all her past glory and previous power behind her Egypt could not deliver herself from this oppression; she had to await a Savior, a Prince, who would appear as in an Epiphany to deliver her from her misery and restore her previous glory and prominence. This Deliverer finally appeared in the person of Mehmed Ali who, as soon as he heard Egypt's pleas to be saved, descended literally from the sky to lift her from her misery and sorrow.

In a nutshell this is how Egyptian historiography of Mehmed Ali is written, although never so passionately and seldom so eloquently. In a sense it calls to mind Marx's comment on the place of Napoleon in French historical consciousness. "Historical tradition," he said, "gave rise to the belief of the French peasants in the miracle that a man named Napoleon would bring all the glory back to them. And an individual turned up who gave himself out as the man . . ."[39] Marx could very well have been referring to the Egyptian fascination with Mehmed Ali. Like Napoleon III, Mehmed Ali "turned up" ("*es fand sich*" are Marx's untranslatable words), mysteriously appearing on the Egyptian historical landscape. Answering Egypt's pleas, the Great Pasha descended from heaven to deliver her from oppression, and to lift her from the dark recesses of centuries of Ottoman neglect and misery into the bright sunlight of dignity and national independence.

[39] Karl Marx, *The Eighteenth Brumaire of Louis Bonaparte* (New York: International Publishers, 1984), p. 124.

This book offers a critique of this particular reading of Egyptian history. While not concentrating on the person of Mehmed Ali Pasha, it investigates his career closely to see how it is read in a manner that makes the three centuries preceding it appear as tyrannical and foreign. More fundamentally, it deals with Mehmed Ali's long career as a way of explaining how "Egypt" came to be seen as a nation with a purposeful, clear identity. Rather than taking "Egypt" as referring to a nation with an unadulterated identity inhabiting a territory with distinct borders that sharply distinguish it from other nations, this book argues that "Egypt" came to refer to a nation so defined only in the nineteenth century and mostly as a result of Mehmed Ali's policies.

The belief that "Egypt" refers to a pre-existing nation, i.e. that it is an eternal, primordial entity, so characteristic of nationalist historiography, can probably best be detected by reviewing how Mehmed Ali's army has traditionally been written about. In discussions of the Pasha's army, three assumptions, central to the nationalist argument, are usually reiterated. The first supposes that the soldiers of this army were fighting in what they believed to be national wars, wars that were waged to defend "Egypt" or to expand its borders. In spite of some isolated acts of resistance to the novel practices of the modern army, these peasant-conscripts, it is commonly argued, came to realize that by participating in these wars they discovered their true sentiments, *viz.* that they were Egyptians first and foremost, and not Muslims or Ottoman subjects, for example. In this manner the nationalist argument assumes that the army was only a catalyst that helped Egyptians discover their true identity – something that was bound to happen, but which in the absence of that "national" army might simply have taken a longer time to materialize.

Having assumed that the army taught those innocent and naive peasants the essential truths of the nation, its unadulterated personality and their umbilical attachment to it, the nationalist argument proceeds with a second assumption, namely, that any problems that this army faced were not the result of "any shortcomings on the part of Egyptians," but were due to "external" malice and conspiracy. In this sense, the failure of Mehmed Ali's entire "experiment" and not only his military establishment, was the result of British machinations aimed at frustrating the Egyptian nation's attempts at development, independence and dignity.

The third assumption that is repeatedly reiterated in nationalist accounts of Mehmed Ali's army is the unproblematic characterization of the Ottomans as the "enemy." Having stressed the pure personality of Egypt that could be traced back in its pristine form to pharaonic times, fighting the army of the Ottoman Sultan is seen as the ultimate sign of nationalism, since the Ottomans have already been identified as the "other" – a backward, stubborn and dogmatic enemy, one that had been occupying Egypt for long, dark centuries causing her to "lag behind" the humanist and scientific developments that were taking place in Europe.

The Pasha and his men

The army that the Pasha founded is seen as giving the "fellahin" of Egypt the chance to bear arms, to defend the fatherland and thus to come to discover their true identity, i.e. that they were essentially and truly Egyptians and that their identities as Muslims or Ottoman subjects were either artificial or secondary. It is commonly argued, for example, that the fellahin "who for centuries had been tied down to the land and cheated of their liberties, were at last to be resurrected from oblivion and to be taught for the first time since Saladin the fundamental lessons of citizenship and nationalism."[40]

The problem with this argument insofar as it pertains to the army, besides the obvious one of lumping together the entire rural population of Egypt under the general rubric of "fellahin," is that the population of Egypt, far from enthusiastically flocking to serve in the army, was in fact very resentful of military service and strongly resisted serving in the army. Recognizing that the scale of this resistance was alarming, that it was not localized but was widespread throughout Egypt, and that the rural population went out of their way to make this resistance obvious, it is still commonplace to argue that this was only a temporary reaction caused above all by "the fellah's strong attachment to his land and the unfamiliarity of military life to him."[41] The opposition to the service in the "national" institution, therefore, something that might have appeared somewhat paradoxical, is explained away by insisting that this opposition was caused by the "fellahin's" strong attachment to the land, a sentiment that proves their "nationalist" feelings. Once the "fellahin" came to appreciate the benefits of military life and that serving in the army was the most truthful way of defending the lands they loved so much, they ceased to resist it and ultimately even became proud of

[40] M. A. Rifa't, *The Awakening of Modern Egypt* (London: Longman, 1947), p. 38.

[41] Jamīl 'Ubaid, *Qiṣṣat Ihtilāl Muḥammad 'Alī lil-Yūnān* [The Story of Mehmed Ali's Occupation of Greece] (Cairo: General Egyptian Book Organization, 1990), pp. 79–80; Aḥmad 'Izzat 'Abdel-Karīm, *Tārīkh al-Ta'līm fī 'Aṣr Muḥammad 'Alī* [History of Education in the Reign of Mehmed Ali] (Cairo: Maṭba'at al-Nahḍa al-Miṣriyya, 1938), pp. 36–37.

belonging to it.[42] The rural population of Egypt was, accordingly, taught that serving in the army, while requiring their abandoning their much beloved lands, was in fact the best way to express their loyalty to them and to defend them with their lives if need be, and the Pasha's army was seen as the "school" in which they were "taught" how to identify themselves as "Egyptians." This identity now appeared as natural and more essential than any local or religious identity that they might have adopted. Being a Muslim or an Ottoman subject was suddenly seen as either "artificial" or secondary compared to this more "primordial" identity. In that sense the army that Mehmed Ali found is seen as "the prime pillar of Egyptian independence."[43]

This book challenges this powerful, monolithic discourse of Egyptian nationalism. It argues that the Pasha's army did indeed turn the population of Egypt into loyal and devoted citizens of Egypt. This it managed to do, however, not by "opening their eyes" to their true identities, or helping them to discover their hidden sentiments, but by subjecting them to a rigorous and tight disciplining regime whereby their bodies and minds were minutely controlled so that the Pasha and his elite could accomplish their own ambitions. In that sense the Pasha's army was crucial for "educating" the population of Egypt to believe that fighting for Mehmed Ali and his family was tantamount to giving one's life for the sake of the "nation," a nation that was now thought to have always already existed and which, moreover, demanded the sacrifices of its own citizens. In other words, this book tries to critique that powerful discourse of nationalism by challenging the assumptions on which it is based and specifically by arguing that the "Egyptian nation" was not a primordial, pre-existing entity waiting to be realized as argued in the nationalist discourse which claims to be only describing it, but that it was a product of that very same discourse which attempted to write it into being.

More concretely, this book attempts to argue that the nation was brought into being through the agency of a multiplicity of "national" institutions, the army being the prime example of them, which together worked to homogenize the nation, to coerce and discipline its citizens, and to silence and exclude its minorities, its "deviants" and its "outcasts." As such, and concentrating on *the* national institution, the army, this book takes acts of resistance (to conscription and to other policies of the various national institutions) not as showing their true and umbilical attachment to their lands, but as testifying to the conscripts' aversion to their officers' elitist policies and as showing their resistance to having their bodies used for causes that were not theirs.

42 al-Rāfʿī, *ʿAṣr Muḥammad ʿAlī*, p. 331.

43 *Ibid.*, p. 321.

The Pasha and Palmerston

It is here that we come to the second assumption of nationalist historiography, namely, that the Egyptian nationalist project of gaining independence from the Ottoman Empire and of establishing the basis of an independent, self-sustaining "take-off" failed not through "any shortcoming of the Egyptians" but because of European intervention. Having seen "Egypt" as a clearly defined nation and given the honest, unceasing efforts of "her children," and after stressing the consistent policies of Mehmed Ali, the reason Egypt did not "take off" during the first half of the nineteenth century and become one of the leading nations of the world is always attributed to European intervention. Protective of their privileged position and determined to prevent latecomers from joining the highly competitive race to modernity "European powers, at Britain's instigation, joined forces against Egypt and denied her the fruits of her [military] victory."[44]

The argument that foreign, mostly Western forces are primarily to blame for the "wrong" turn taken by Egypt during the nineteenth century is clearly represented by M. Fahmy's *La Révolution de l'industrie en Egypte et ses conséquences au 19e siècle*.[45] In a typical manner Fahmy plays down the significance of the problems that the Pasha faced with his "factories," and the inherent bureaucratic complications which accounted for the fact that when a director of a factory, for example, needed "a pound of grease the whole process [could] take up to four days"[46] receive no mention in his study. Nor does he allude to the fact that the Pasha's industrialization plan had faced enormous difficulties to start with, not because of competition with the West, but because Egypt lacked any substantial sources of motive power or trained labor. Fahmy, furthermore, is satisfied to call a manufacturing scheme in a country that had only six steam engines[47] a "revolution in industry." In his mind there is no doubt that it was mostly due to opposition by the West that this consistent industrialization program failed.[48] In a similar fashion a recent study of the history of health care in nineteenth-century Egypt effectively dismisses the serious problems that the Pasha and his top medical advisors faced when they attempted to found a modern medical

44 *Ibid.*, p. 13.

45 Moustafa Fahmy, *La Révolution de l'industrie en Egypte et ses conséquences au 19e siècle (1800–50)* (Leiden: E. J. Brill, 1954).

46 St. John, *Egypt*, II, pp. 419–20.

47 Fahmy, *Révolution*, p. 53.

48 *Ibid.*, p. 98. It has to be stated that this book is not a rigorous attempt to study Mehmed Ali's economic policy, a study that would require consulting the documents of *Divan-ı Fabrīqāt*, the Factories Department, housed in the Egyptian National Archives, which have only recently been cataloged.

institution. These problems, it is argued, were practically and perceptively ironed out thanks to the Pasha's determination and genius; the study concludes by saying that it was only the advent of the British in 1882 that destroyed the indigenous health establishment by forcing it to shift from treating the local population to serving the much smaller and essentially elitist colonial community.[49]

It has to be admitted, however, that not all nationalist historians are so dismissive of the inherent problems encountered by the Pasha's "experiment" and some of them do highlight the significant obstacles that were faced in founding the modern army with its related institutions of hospitals, schools, "factories," etc. Nevertheless, after pointing out the serious problems that his various educational, military, "industrial," and irrigation projects encountered, they nevertheless insist that the Pasha eventually surmounted them by his characteristic energy and skill. In effect, they argue that the failure of Mehmed Ali's "experiment" stemmed not from any inherent problems in how it was run but could be attributed to such things as the Pasha being "ahead of his time,"[50] or his successors' not finishing the job he started.[51] Or else it is claimed that, all problems notwithstanding, he succeeded in putting the country on the right path for its "renaissance and development."[52]

The clearest representative of this line of argument is A. L. Marsot's *Egypt in the Reign of Muhammad Ali*.[53] While recognizing that the Pasha faced significant problems in his attempt to develop Egyptian society and economy, Marsot argues that he managed to overcome them with characteristic tact and skill. The main problem, she insists, lay with European opposition which was championed by Britain and was personally led by Lord Palmerston, the British Foreign Secretary. Palmerston, Marsot argues, took a very strong dislike to Mehmed Ali whom he used to compare to a coffee shop waiter "seeking to be commander of the faithful,"[54] and succeeded in rallying the European powers behind him to bring about the "undoing" of Mehmed Ali and his reform program in Egypt. The reason why Palmerston was so adamantly opposed to Mehmed Ali, Marsot believes, was the Pasha's economic policies which Palmerston viewed with suspicion since British

49 Amira el-Azhary Sonbol, *The Creation of a Medical Profession in Egypt, 1800–1922* (New York: Syracuse University Press, 1991).
50 Sabry, *L'Empire égyptien*, p. 580.
51 Abūl-Futūḥ Raḍwān, *Tārīkh Maṭba'at Būlāq* [History of the Būlāq Press] (Cairo: Būlāq, 1953), pp. 342–43.
52 'Abdel-Karīm, *Tārīkh al-Ta'līm*, pp. 655–64.
53 Afaf Lutfi al-Sayyid Marsot, *Egypt in the Reign of Muhammad Ali* (Cambridge: Cambridge University Press, 1984).
54 *Ibid.*, p. 235.

goods were barred from Egyptian markets as well as from other areas under the Pasha's rule. In other words, while enumerating other potential reasons for Palmerston's opposition to Mehmed Ali, Marsot argues that it was mostly the fear that "Muhammad Ali could well become a tiresome [commercial] rival"[55] to the British that caused Palmerston's venomous hostility to the Pasha leading to the latter's eventual "undoing." Her study of the Pasha concludes by saying that "[i]ndustrialization was doomed to fail in Egypt, not through the shortcomings of the Egyptians, but because of external European pressures which used Ottoman legal control over Egypt to kill off any potential rivalry to their own industrial ventures."[56]

The present book, while accepting the assumption that Britain did indeed view Mehmed Ali's activities suspiciously and that her policies as represented and pursued by Lord Palmerston were, in fact, instrumental in curbing Mehmed Ali's power, does not unproblematically assume that the reason for this hostile stance was its fear of the Pasha's industrial schemes. Rather, it argues that Mehmed Ali's imperialist expansion over wide areas of the Ottoman Empire seriously challenged Britain's more ambitious imperialist designs and was regarded in London and Bombay as a threat to Britain's possessions in Asia, her communications with India and her influence in Istanbul. While this point is dealt with separately in chapter 7 below, it is important to point out at the outset that this book does not try to ascertain whether it was external opposition to Mehmed Ali's policies or some inherent difficulties that caused the frustration of the Pasha's ambitious "experiment." Indeed, this book brings into question this very distinction between "internal" and "external" factors and will argue that it is an outcome of the Pasha's policies and, significantly, of the manner in which they have been written about, and is not something that Mehmed Ali confronted at the outset of his long career.

The Pasha and his Sultan

This brings us to the third assumption of the Egyptian nationalist discourse, the assumption that the Ottoman context of the Pasha's rule could be easily dismissed as a mere pretext that allowed Palmerston to fight Mehmed Ali and to frustrate his policies. As noted above in reference to Taymūr's translation of the Sphinx's letter, the easy dismissal of three centuries of Ottoman control as a backward, oppressive period that represents Egypt's "dark ages" is characteristic of

[55] *Ibid.*, p. 242. [56] *Ibid.*, p. 259.

the general amnesia that afflicts all nationalist discourses. Having assumed the primordial, unadulterated existence of the Egyptian nation and insisting on its inherent, essential qualities, it becomes easy to view three centuries of Ottoman rule as "foreign" and "alien." In other words, the nationalist argument not only starts from the assumption that "Egypt" was a distinct national entity but further insists that she kept her pristine nature pure and uncontaminated even after three centuries of Ottoman control.[57] Accordingly, these three centuries of Ottoman control that began in 1517 with the Ottoman victory over the Mamluks who had based their empire in Cairo are seen as a period of foreign occupation, and Ibrahim Pasha's successive victories over the Ottoman Sultan's armies in the 1830s as a long overdue revenge for that earlier defeat.[58]

It is Marsot's book that offers the clearest recent example of the view that the Ottoman rule was not only oppressive but also alien and foreign, and that Egypt's position within the Ottoman Empire was similar to that of an occupied country seeking deliverance from foreign, oppressive rule. Throughout the book Marsot claims that Mehmed Ali was despite his "foreign" origins a nationalist hero who "drew the outline of a nation-state."[59] While acknowledging that the Pasha "despised the Egyptians and . . . would only speak Turkish [and adding that] to deny that [he was an Ottoman] would be a denial of his roots and being,"[60] she still concludes that his policies "inevitably put Egypt on the path of independent statehood and self-recognition as having a separate identity distinct from other Muslims and Ottomans . . . [and] without his efforts it might have taken Egyptians much longer to be able to call Egypt their own."[61]

Realizing that Mehmed Ali had "foreign" origins that might have compromised his position as a leader of an Egypt that is otherwise assumed to be ethnically pure and uniform, Marsot attempts to resolve this apparent contradiction by resorting to the argument that the personality of Ibrahim Pasha (the Pasha's eldest son) complemented that of his father in this respect. "Ibrahim [,she argues,] had no problems of self-identity; he liked the Egyptians and hated and despised

57 It is common to argue, for example, that all the invaders who passed through Egypt, far from changing her true and pure character, were themselves affected by her. Invaders were always "Egyptianized," therefore, and Egypt constantly proved herself capable of "digesting" her occupiers; see for a recent example of this line of argument Yūnān Labīb Rizq, "al-Jabartī wa'l-shakhṣiyya al-Miṣriyya" [al-Jabartī and the Egyptian identity] in Aḥmad 'Izzat 'Abdel-Karīm, ed., *'Abdel-Raḥmān al-Jabartī: Dirāsāt wa Buḥūth* (Cairo: General Egyptian Book Organization, 1976), p. 124.

58 Jamāl Ḥamdān, *Shakhṣiyyat Miṣr* [The Identity of Egypt] (Cairo: 'Ālam al-Kutub, 1981), II, p. 638–39.

59 al-Sayyid Marsot, *Egypt*, p. 21.

60 *Ibid.*, p. 97.

61 *Ibid.*, p. 264.

the Turks . . . Together these two men and their associates were to carve out an empire for themselves out of Ottoman territories . . ."[62] Nevertheless, the same characteristic problem of nationalist discourse remains: Marsot assumes the pre-existence of national sentiments, arguing that they simply needed a great reformer to rekindle them, even if that figure was of a different ethnic, linguistic and cultural background from his subjects and even if he was not explicitly fighting for their sake and, moreover, despite their ostensible opposition to him. In other words, Mehmed Ali is a national hero in spite of himself.[63]

The problem with this line of reasoning lies not in the difficulty of clearly identifying the true sentiments of the Pasha but in the underlying assumptions of a pre-existing Egyptian nation that was waiting for a hero to deliver it from the heavy Ottoman yoke. For it is the nationalists' taking for granted the uncontaminated presence of an Egyptian nation that forces Marsot to find a problem with Mehmed Ali's ethnic background and to try and resolve it by adding Ibrahim's personality to it. The root of this problem ultimately lies in the nationalists' insistence on looking at the nation as undivided, homogenous and, above all, ethnically pure entity. Consequently the discovery that there was a "foreigner" leading the nation towards autonomy and independence in its struggle against its equally "foreign" enemy becomes very disturbing. In a number of places this insistence on drawing clear boundaries around "Egypt" and on seeing it as a clearly identifiable entity within the Ottoman Empire when none existed leads Marsot to interpret certain documents in a most peculiar way as when, for example, she translates a key letter that Mehmed Ali sent to his agent in Istanbul, Najib Efendi, in 1827 at the height of the Greek War. In this letter the Pasha was contemplating the efforts he had made so far in helping his Sultan and was gloomily thinking of the prospect of fighting a combined European naval force that he would have little chance of defeating. "Here I am at a loss," he said: "shall I be grieved at the calamity of the Sublime State (*devlet-i aliyye*) or at my own lost effort?"[64] Instead of

62 *Ibid.*, p. 97.

63 See in this respect the Pasha's own words quoted by Madden where he says, "I was compelled again for their [i.e. these fellahs'] own sakes, to force them to work, and without the whip they would do nothing": Madden, *Egypt*, p. 38. The same author writes shortly afterwards that ". . . one thing I am certain of, that whenever Mohammed Ali dies, he will go down to the grave lamented by some fifty or sixty individuals, none of whom are of his country, and execrated by some two millions of his subjects, who are the natives of it": *ibid.*, p. 44; see also Waghorn's comment that "[i]t has been insisted that Mohamed Ali has done nothing to better the condition of the Fellah. I reply, he has done everything he can do, not, perhaps, for them, but for their sons": Thomas Waghorn, *Egypt in 1837* (London: Smith Elder, 1837), p. 15.

64 Bahr Barra 12/7, on 14 Ra 1243/6 October 1827.

translating *devlet-i aliyye* as "the Sublime State," the conventional term for the Ottoman Empire, Marsot in her citation of that letter translates it as "*my country*."[65] This particularly skewed reading of an important and telling document is partly due to the fact that Marsot seems to have been relying on an Arabic translation rather than the original Turkish text of the document.[66] However, it is mostly due to a particular reading of Egyptian history and specifically of Mehmed Ali's career, a reading that sees his reign as a chapter in the never-ending saga of Egypt's struggle to express her true identity.

Rather than viewing Mehmed Ali as a national or proto-national hero, the present book argues that the Pasha did have ambivalent feelings towards both his Egyptian subjects and his Ottoman Sultan not because he was suffering from an identity crisis caused by the fact that he was an Albanian who "had no cultural identity other than the Ottoman one," causing him to have a "love–hate relationship with the Ottomans and [to fear] a loss of identity,"[67] but because of his untenable position within the Ottoman Empire. For it was the Pasha's desire to carve out an empire for himself at the expense of the Sultan's own empire, an act that could only be seen as one of rebellion and aggression, and *at the same time* his desire to be forgiven by the Sultan that caused the Pasha's conflicting "psychological" problems.

This book, however, and as mentioned above, is not a study of the Pasha and his psyche, important and interesting though a psychological profile of the Pasha would surely be. It seeks, instead, to challenge the nationalist argument that sees the Ottoman background of the Pasha's career as a mere pretext that Palmerston, for example, was clever enough to have used to bring about the "undoing" of Mehmed Ali and his "empire."[68] Instead, this book looks at the Pasha's career in an Ottoman context and starts from the assumption that three hundred years of Ottoman rule must have had a significant impact on the legal, cultural and economic position of Egypt, and that only if "Egypt" is

[65] al-Sayyid Marsot, *Egypt*, p. 215. For a full translation of this telling letter, see chapter 1 below. For an extant French translation, see Georges Douin, *Navarin, le 6 Juillet–20 Octobre, 1827* (Cairo: Royal Egyptian Geographical Society, 1927), pp. 243–45.

[66] It should be noted that most of these translations were done at the explicit order of King Fouad (r. 1923–36), Mehmed Ali's great-grandson. Having recently won the title of King, Fouad was keen not only in portraying the history of his family in a positive light, but also in highlighting the fact that his was an independent royal family right from his great-grandfather's time. He thus invited a number of historians to come and work on a highly selected group of his family's papers, which became the nucleus of the Royal Archives of Egypt that was housed in ʿAbdīn Palace, the precursor of the present Egyptian National Archives. Not only was this a selected group of documents, they were also slightly edited on being translated from the original Ottoman Turkish to Arabic.

[67] al-Sayyid Marsot, *Egypt*, p. 32.

[68] *Ibid.*, pp. 232–48.

taken to refer to a nation with a clearly defined identity could these three centuries be seen as foreign and alien.

In contrast to the nationalists' insistence on the pure essence of the Egyptian nation that led to the easy dismissal of three centuries of Egypt's history as unworthy of study, scholars are now taking this long period more seriously, seeing in it a lively and vibrant society.[69] A good example is Ehud Toledano's *State and Society in Mid-Nineteenth-Century Egypt* which seeks to challenge the notion that Egypt constituted a distinct entity within the Ottoman Empire and instead stresses the Ottoman nature of Egypt during the nineteenth century.[70] Toledano argues that under Mehmed Ali's successors and even more so during the Pasha's reign, occupiers of the highest positions in the military and the bureaucracy and holders of large land estates formed a distinct group that he calls the "Ottoman–Egyptian" elite. These people were marked off from the non-elite members by the fact that they "spoke Turkish; shared the values and heritage of Ottoman culture . . . came from various parts of the [Ottoman] empire . . . [and] were committed to serve in Egypt under an Ottoman–Egyptian dynasty . . ."[71] Toledano rightly points out one of the most important characteristics of the upper echelons of Egyptian society in the nineteenth century, namely the fact that its members had more in common with the urban elite members of other provinces of the Ottoman Empire than with the Arabic-speaking inhabitants of the province they were ruling. Also useful is his description of Egyptian society as essentially composed of two clearly demarcated groups, the first being the Turkish-speaking elite and the second composed of the Arabic-speaking masses.

Useful as this welcome reminder is, however, Toledano's picture of Egyptian society in the "middle decades" is heavily influenced by the views of these Turkish-speaking elite and although he attempts to get

[69] See, for example, André Raymond, *The Great Arab Cities in the 16th–18th Centuries: An Introduction* (New York: New York University Press, 1984); 'Irāqī Yūsuf Muḥammad, *al-Wujūd al-'Uthmānī al-Mamlūkī fī Miṣr fī al-Qarn al-Thāmin 'Ashr wa Awā'il al-Qarn al-Tāsi' 'Ashr* [Ottoman–Mamluk Presence in Egypt in the Eighteenth and the Beginning of the Nineteenth Centuries] (Cairo: Dār al-Ma'ārif, 1985); Layla 'Abdel-Laṭīf Aḥmad, *al-Mujtama' al-Miṣrī fī al-'Aṣr al-'Uthmānī* [Egyptian Society During the Ottoman Period] (Cairo: Dār al-Kitāb al-Jāmi'ī, 1987); Muḥammad Afīfī, *al-Awqāf wa'l Hayā al-Ijtimā'iyya fī Miṣr fī al-'Aṣr al-'Uthmānī* [Awqāf and Social Life in Egypt During the Ottoman Period])(Cairo: General Egyptian Book Organization, 1991); Nelly Hanna, *Habiter au Caire: La maison moyenne et ses habitants aux XIIe et XIIIe siècles* (Cairo: IFAO, 1991); and Jane Hathaway, "Years of Ocak Power: The Rise of the Qazdugli Household and the Transformation of Ottoman Egypt's Military Society, 1670–1750" (Unpublished Ph.D. Dissertation, Princeton University, 1992).

[70] Ehud Toledano, *State and Society in Mid-Nineteenth-Century Egypt* (Cambridge: Cambridge University Press, 1990).

[71] *Ibid.*, p. 16.

closer to the non-elite members of Egyptian society it is difficult to see clearly from his narrative how these two groups interacted with each other. While he argues, for example, that "[t]he socio-cultural process of boundary drawing and redrawing was constantly acted out in mid-nineteenth-century Egypt,"[72] and that the peripheral zone between these two groups was "the twilight zone where limits are blurred, where boundaries overlap,"[73] the very form the book takes – being divided in two parts, one devoted to the study of the elite and the other of the non-elite, and having a separate chapter on the "Great social divide in Egyptian society" – makes it difficult to see how exactly these social barriers and boundaries were crossed or negotiated.

More problematic is the insufficient attention given in Toledano's account of the people at these uneasy peripheries, these borders separating the two groups one from the other. Scribes, guards, lower-ranking government bureaucrats, non-commissioned officers, nurses and servants: these are examples of people who stood at the peripheries of these two groups and facilitated the communication and the interaction between their respective members. Instead of highlighting the roles of these people as negotiators of boundaries and facilitators of the dialog between the two groups, Toledano in fact highlights the distinctiveness of both groups and the near impossibility of a dialog. Consider, for example the case of Mutawallī, an Egyptian servant of a member of the Ottoman–Egyptian elite who was involved in a fight with a certain Hasan Efendi, a middle-level bureaucrat. Toledano relies on police records to reconstruct the story of that fight whereby Hasan Efendi accused Mutawallī of beating him in the street at night. Mutawallī answered by denying the charges and said that he only got involved in a fight that Hasan Efendi had had with another Turkish-speaking man, a certain police guard by the name of Salih. He said that he could not understand the reason for the brawl since they were speaking Turkish. Toledano appreciates the implausibility of this allegation, since, as a servant in a Turkish-speaking household Mutawallī must have had some knowledge of Turkish. And so he writes, "Servants were addressed by their Turkish-speaking masters in Arabic when service was needed. Otherwise, they were excluded from the Turkish-speaking world around them by the sheer barrier of language. Whether true or invented, Mutawallī's story had to make sense if he had any chance of being believed." He then underscores his point by saying, "[t]he picture of these two linguistically segregated worlds coexisting in

[72] *Ibid.*, p. 17. [73] *Ibid.*, p. 69.

the same place was very much a reality in Egyptian cities and towns at mid-century."[74]

The problem with Toledano's reading of that telling case is that, in stressing the mutual exclusivity of the two cultural groups, Toledano seems to have accepted Mutawallī's allegation that he could not, in fact, understand any Turkish and hence could not ascertain what the original fight was about. Mutawallī had to make this allegation so that his claim of having became involved in the fight only to separate the two men could be believed. As it turned out from further questioning (which Toledano does not reproduce), Mutawallī had been lying and it seems that he was engaged in the fighting in a much more active manner than he had claimed. It follows that his claim of ignorance of Turkish should have been as questioned by Toledano as it must surely have been by the investigating authorities. Toledano, however, accepts Mutawallī's claim of his inability to speak or understand Turkish, thus reinforcing his point of the mutual exclusivity of these two linguistically segregated worlds. Be that as it may, what is more significant was that the case, as preserved in the police records, was recorded by a scribe who was obviously bilingual: while set down in the same Arabic script, the report is in fact written in two different languages, Arabic and Ottoman Turkish, Turkish being the language of the elite-member plaintiff and Arabic that of the non-elite-member accused. The fact that the scribe could move so easily from one language to the other testifies to the fluidity and facility with which certain people navigated their way between these two groups and so could and did lubricate their interactions with each other. In short, these two worlds could not have been as mutually exclusive as Toledano has pointed out and the various intermediaries of guards, scribes, servants, etc. must have played a crucial role as social lubricants.

While finding Toledano's main argument of the Ottoman character of Egypt's elite culture convincing and useful in grasping the nature of Egyptian society in the first half of the nineteenth century, his depiction of the relationship between elite and non-elite members of this society is somewhat rigid and fails to show the dynamism that must have characterized it. Ultimately, a true assessment of how fluid Egyptian society was in the nineteenth century would have to show the Turkish-speaking elite members interacting with the Arabic-speaking natives, intermarrying with them, starting using Arabic in their every-day lives, acquiring agricultural land, settling permanently in Egypt, taking Alexandria rather than Izmir, for example, as their favorite summer

74 *Ibid.*, p. 159.

resorts, etc. Such an assessment, however, would require following the interaction of these two groups over a time period much longer than the reign of Abbas (1849–54), the period that Toledano confines his focus to. Although Toledano argues that "[o]n the peripheries, in the absence of the artificial line separating elite from popular culture, a form of socio-cultural negotiation occurred,"[75] the evidence he adduces has the effect of showing how this artificial line became a real one rather than being challenged or negotiated. The net result is the enforcing, rather than the blurring, of the distinction between elite and non-elite members, a distinction that, he insists, was a "vivid aspect of daily life."[76]

However, given the shorter period of time, one can still show how these two groups interacted with each other, not by highlighting the essential, legal and semantic differences between both groups, but by stressing the role played by intermediaries who occupied the crucial roles at the boundaries separating one group from the other. By concentrating on Mehmed Ali's army what is offered below is an account of not only how its Turkish-speaking officers were ethnically, linguistically, legally and economically distinct from their Arabic-speaking soldiers, but also of how this essential conflictual relationship was often mediated by people occupying the uncomfortable positions separating the two groups. For Mehmed Ali's army did not function only through the insightful command of its commanders or the heroic sacrifices of its soldiers; it also functioned with the help of hundreds of scribes and officials who manned the bureaucracy that supplied and fed it, through the efforts of the often bilingual non-commissioned officers who mediated between the officers and the men they commanded, of the hundreds of nurses who administered to the health of the sick and wounded and who translated the commands of their doctors to them, and finally of the numerous sentries who guarded the gates and fences of the barracks and camps to make sure that military discipline was enforced as intended by the senior officers. These people occupying the uneasy position at the often negotiated barriers and frontiers had been neglected from most of the accounts of the Pasha's army and his reign in general, and this book attempts a closer look at the important roles they played in greasing Mehmed Ali's war machine.

The Pasha and his *nizam*

The aim of stressing the role of these crucial intermediaries, therefore, is not only to argue that communication was possible between the

[75] *Ibid.*, p. 250. [76] *Ibid.*, p. 155.

Turkish-speaking elite members and the Arabic-speaking masses they ruled, but also to elaborate on the discrepancy that often existed between the laws and regulations issued by this elite and the way they were implemented on, or understood by, the "masses." For it was these "social lubricators" who helped to translate the often inaccessible laws and regulations issued by Mehmed Ali and his military authorities into a language and into practices that would be understood by the "masses." This discussion of laws and their implementation brings us to Timothy Mitchell's *Colonising Egypt* which offers, among other things, a rigorous attempt to deal with the complicated question of Egyptian nationalism.[77] Mitchell criticizes the traditional view that saw the appearance of nationalism in the second half of the nineteenth century in Egypt as an "awakening," an unproblematic coming to terms with the "singular truth about 'the nation' [which is] waiting to be realised." This view, he argues, sees nationalism as "something discovered, not invented."[78] Drawing on the ideas of French postmodern theories, specifically those of Michel Foucault and Jacques Derrida, Mitchell offers a radically different approach to understand how the modern Egyptian nation-state came into being. From Foucault, and specifically from his *Discipline and Punish*,[79] he draws on the new notions of "disciplinary power" of how bodies were counted and surveyed, spaces created and organized, activities monitored and classified. From Derrida, he draws the notion of representation, that is, the effect of this new system of disciplinary power that helped it in being perceived as "a structure standing apart from things in themselves, a separate realm of order and meaning."[80]

The net result is a work that offers an original way to view Egyptian history in the nineteenth century and one that challenges the traditional manner in which it has been viewed. For the novelty of Mitchell's *Colonising Egypt* lies in its ability to show the peculiarity of the process of introducing "modern" institutions in Egypt, a process that has been taken so much for granted and mistaken so often as humanist, progressive reform, and in showing how these "reforms" were a result of a modern conception of power that was both corporal and disciplinary (in the Foucauldian sense) and which was also metaphysical and representational. For him the colonization of Egypt is not to be understood in the traditional manner of the process of structuring

[77] Timothy Mitchell, *Colonising Egypt* (Cambridge: Cambridge University Press, 1988).
[78] *Ibid.*, p. 119.
[79] Michel Foucault, *Discipline and Punish: The Birth of the Prison*, trans., Alan Sheridan (New York: Vintage Books, 1979).
[80] Mitchell, *Colonising Egypt*, pp. 153–54.

Egyptian society after the British military takeover in 1882. Rather, it was a process that had started much earlier and which entailed the complete restructuring of Egyptian society – the government bureaucracy, the military, the schools, cities, towns, streets, houses, families and the body of the individual – in such a way that made Egypt not only more profitable, more productive, but also *represented* the country in a manner that produced the same division of the world into two domains that had been accomplished earlier in Europe and which made it more accessible to European control.

What is offered below is an attempt to engage with Mitchell's argument by questioning, not his characterization of what preceded the introduction of modern "reforms,"[81] but by elaborating on his analysis of how they did in fact work in the Egyptian context. For Mitchell, in his attempt to uncover the logic of these modern institutions of power and their physical representations, is not interested in showing how they actually worked in the specific case of Egypt. While recognizing the fact that there often existed a discrepancy between the blueprints he studied and their implementation, arguing, in fact, that the whole process of "colonization" was to effect this discrepancy, Mitchell's main task remains, however, to see how these "enframing devices" (laws, blueprints, maps, plans, etc.) were drafted and conceived of, rather than how they were implemented and executed. For example, while ostensibly showing how Egyptian schools were refashioned towards the end of Mehmed Ali's reign, Mitchell confines his analysis to explaining the rationale behind the new schooling system without in fact studying the actual implementation of that system in its new locale. In 1843, he says, a model school fashioned along the Lancaster system was opened in Cairo. It was a school "in which the exact position and precise task of each individual at every moment was coordinated to perform together as a machine." While admitting that it "is not known how faithfully [the school] was modeled on the English original," Mitchell implicitly assumes that the actual performance of this school could be "read" from the blueprint that was set down in England since "the Lancaster school was actively promoted . . . as a model [which] could be exactly reproduced abroad . . ."[82] What we are offered here is a concise history of the *idea* of discipline as formulated by British (and Egyptian) educationalists and not a historical account of the performance of

81 For an interesting critique of Mitchell along these lines see Sami Zubaida, "Exhibitions of power," *Economy and Society*, 19(1990), p. 359–75, where he specifically criticizes him for "running a contrast between a modernity identified with an aggressive colonial order, and an older order which had been read and misunderstood, and as such re-read by [Mitchell] often in rosy light": p. 360.

82 Mitchell, *Colonising Egypt*, p. 71.

Egyptian schools, which, while they attempted to follow the Lancaster system in all its Foucauldian details, could not be expected in all probability to have done so in the neat and automatic manner assumed by Mitchell.

This book seeks to understand the nature of the discrepancy between the plan and its execution, between the law and its implementation that Mitchell takes to be due only to the very nature of modern institutions of power and their representations. By looking at the specific Egyptian context where these modern devices were applied and basing itself on an imposing and impressive institution of power, this book offers alternative explanations of the nature of this gap that separated model from reality. Specifically, it is concerned with the question of whether discrepancies arose as a result of misreadings of the law by government officials, scribes or bureaucrats, whether they were caused by internal contradictions in the letter of the law itself that could only (or more easily) be detected on implementation, or whether they were the result of resistance by those on whom the law was applied. This book, then, tries to complement the imposing picture that Mitchell offers of nineteenth-century Egyptian society as it comes across in the official blueprints which he studied with the every-day accounts of how these laws and blueprints were in fact implemented, negotiated and resisted. The army that is studied below, besides representing in as pristine a form as could be expected an ideal model for society to follow, was also an army whose soldiers, NCOs, army scribes, and occasionally its officers themselves came to subvert and challenge this oppressive order.

These then are the main questions that this book is interested in. To recapitulate: What was the nature of Egyptian society in the first half of the nineteenth century insofar as its national identity was concerned? How did the Pasha and his elite identify themselves: as a Turkish-speaking elite that ruled an Arabic-speaking province of the Ottoman Empire or as a proto-national elite that attempted to deliver Egypt from the heavy burden of the Ottoman yoke? How did the non-elite members of Egyptian society react to their rulers' struggles against the "men from Istanbul," as the officials of the central administration of the Ottoman Empire were referred to? And, finally, given the importance of the modern disciplinary and representational devices in transforming Egyptian society and introducing a new colonial order in it, how were these devices "read" and reacted to by the people on whom they were applied?

The modern army: the *nizam-i cedid*

Before summarizing the broad lines of the arguments pursued in the chapters to follow, a word is in order regarding the reason for choosing the army to answer the questions raised so far. First, and as argued in nationalist historiography, this army offered the rural population as well as the townspeople of Egypt the opportunity to bear arms and presumably gave them the right to defend their country for the first time in centuries, probably in millennia, and thus allows one to check the validity of the nationalist assumption that by doing so it helped nationalistic feelings to spread among the Egyptians during the first half of the nineteenth century. It has been argued that wars are essential for the creation of the nation,[83] and that "to make the citizen a soldier is to give him a sense of duty to the country and the consciousness of doing it which, if spread through the whole population, will convert it into . . . a nation."[84] Being a conscript army and one that fought a number of victorious battles, Mehmed Ali's army offers a good opportunity to check the validity of the Egyptian nationalists' claim that the army allowed the population of Egypt to come to terms with the essential truth of the "nation," i.e., that it is there waiting to be awakened.[85]

Second, all modern armies are a microcosm of their larger societies in a crucial sense: by erecting and maintaining clear distinctions (in dress, pay, rights and duties) between soldiers and officers and in sharpening distinctions within each group by an elaborate hierarchical structure, armies reflect the class divisions within society at large. This sharp stratification was even more apparent in the case of Mehmed Ali's army than with most other contemporary armies since the officer corps was ethnically and linguistically different from the overwhelming majority of the soldiery. Studying the internal relationship between soldiers and officers within that army, therefore, allows us to see how a representative proportion of the masses dealt with members of the elite and how these conflictual boundaries between the Turkish-speaking elite and the Arabic-speaking lower classes were constantly fought and challenged.

Third, the army, being the institution of power *par excellence*, is a suitable institution for observing the process of state formation in nineteenth-century Egypt. Similar to the role played by eighteenth-century armies in the creation of the rising European nation-states, Mehmed Ali's army could be said to be "one of the instruments with which [the state's] political power [was] originally created and made

83 Michael Howard, *War and the Nation State* (Oxford: Clarendon Press, 1978), p. 9.
84 Spenser Wilkinson, *Britain at Bay* (London: Constable, 1909), p. 191.
85 al-Rāfʿī, *ʿAṣr Muḥammad ʿAlī*, p. 331.

permanent."[86] European nation-states came into being not only through the spread of nationalist feelings and sentiments but also through the states' monopoly of means of violence and their amassing of administrative and military measures that enabled them to extend their authority and control over remote regions in a permanent and stable manner. Studying Mehmed Ali's army offers a good opportunity to verify whether a similar process could be detected in the Egyptian case, and if the growing power of the Egyptian state in the first half of the nineteenth century could be attributed to its effective monopoly of means of violence.

Finally, being an institution of order and discipline, the army is a good place to see how this new "colonizing" order played itself out in the specific Egyptian context and how it was received, accommodated and/or resisted by those on whom it was applied. Specifically this book follows the army not only to see how this novel idea of "order" was "written" and drafted by senior officers and generals, but also to check how it was "translated" and implemented by middle-ranking officers and scribes, how it was imposed by guards and sentries, and, finally, how it was "read" and resisted by the young conscripts.

Since this book is not a study of the Pasha's military career but an investigation of how his army functioned, it does not review all the campaigns that this army waged. It concentrates on the Syrian campaign (1831–40), being one of the Pasha's best organized military ventures. Chapter 1 argues that this campaign differed from other campaigns both in its causes and in the manner in which it was conducted. Accordingly, and given its importance in understanding how the army functioned, the second half of the chapter is devoted to reviewing how the campaign started and how its major battles were fought. This chapter concludes by analyzing the ambivalent "Peace of Kütahia" that ended this first round of military confrontation between Mehmed Ali and Sultan Mahmud II.

Having seen the Pasha in his palace at the beginning of this Introduction and having placed his military career in a wider context in chapter 1, chapter 2 takes a step back in time, as it were, and tries to uncover the origins of the idea of creating a modern army. The chapter proceeds with a review of the earliest steps taken to create the army, namely the training of what was to become the nucleus of the officer

[86] Peter Paret, *Understanding War* (Princeton: Princeton University Press, 1992), pp. 10–11. See also Otto Hintze, "Military organization and the organization of the state," in Felix Gilbert, ed., *The Historical Essays of Otto Hintze* (New York, 1975), pp. 178–215.

corps and, more importantly, the beginning of the conscription policy as initially applied to Upper Egypt. It also reviews the initial problems encountered in collecting the men from their villages and in securing their delivery to the training depots. Since this book is more interested in the soldiers who fought in the Pasha's wars than in their commanders or in the Pasha himself, this chapter marks the beginning of the main story that this book is concerned with: the story of a hypothetical soldier whose connection with the army starts with conscription then proceeds to training, then follows him to the battle scene, and from there to see how he recuperated from the aftermath of the battle. The subsequent chapters proceed along these lines.

Chapter 3, therefore, follows from where the previous chapter left off and reviews the process of training the new, young and often reluctant conscripts. It starts with an analysis of the regime of isolation and surveillance that was intended to mark off life on the training camps from civilian life outside the camps. It also seeks to contrast the new military legal codes that were intended to discipline the new recruits with civil laws that were applied in the countryside and to see how the army could be looked to as the kind of model for society to follow. Finally, it gives a brief review of the training manuals that symbolized in a pristine manner the machine-like image of the military and that reflected the new modes of authority, the continuous monitoring of behavior and the meticulous control of every movement and gesture of the trainees. Besides continuing with the story of the young reluctant conscript, this chapter, therefore, introduces the Foucauldian notion of power and presents in a pure form the logic of that power as detectable from the military manuals and military laws that attempted to regulate all details of military life.

Chapter 4 opens with a description of a key battle that Mehmed Ali's army fought, the battle of Konia against the Ottoman army (December 1832). Although the Egyptian army had a decisive victory in that battle, it was discovered that serious mistakes were committed by a leading brigadier who participated in the battle and whose performance comes somewhat as a surprise after reading the laws, regulations and training manuals reviewed so far. The chapter takes its lead from this particular incident and seeks to contrast the cohesive, machine-like manner in which the army was supposed to perform as has been described in the previous chapter with various accounts of the manner in which the army did actually perform. This serves to introduce a theme that is further elaborated upon in the following chapter, that of the discrepancy that separated the various military laws from the manner in which they were actually applied.

Chapter 5 follows on from there and attempts to offer a view of the soldier not on the battle scene where he is probably conditioned to act in the manner depicted in the training manuals, but on the camps and the barracks where he lives recuperating from past battles or preparing for future ones. One particular aspect is highlighted to draw a picture of the daily lives of the soldiers in the camps, namely, the manner in which the authorities attempted to control the health and hygiene of the soldiers, and how the soldiers, in turn, attempted to evade this tight system of control. Besides attempting to get as close as possible to the soldiers and trying to see how they led their daily lives on the camps, this chapter seeks to see how the monolithic picture of the army that comes across from reading its laws and regulations (a picture that is presented in chapter 3) contrasts sharply with the less impressive, but arguably more interesting (and also more blurred) picture of the soldiers evading this tight control over their bodies. Put differently, while chapter 3, and to a lesser degree, chapter 4, are interested in the notion of power and use the discourse of law to analyze it, chapter 5 is concerned with the notion of resistance and approaches it through studying the practice of medicine.

Chapter 6 raises the central question of the role the army played in the creation of Egyptian nationalism during the first half of the nineteenth century. By analyzing how the Pasha, his officers, and his soldiers viewed the army and the battles they were fighting in, the chapter re-examines the common allegation that by being allowed to bear arms for the first time in centuries the population of Egypt came to think of itself as forming a distinct people with a different identity and group personality. The chapter then ends the story of the hypothetical soldier's connection with the army, that is, with desertion. After that the chapter proceeds to answer a perplexing question of how an army whose soldiers were reluctant conscripts, dragged into it against their wishes, could still manage to produce the spectacular victories that the Pasha's army accomplished. In an attempt to answer this question it compares the performance of the Pasha's army with that of the Ottoman Sultan. It also offers a comparison with Napoleon's army which was the first army to use conscripts on a national scale and along whose lines the Pasha's army was partially modeled.

Throughout this study the army that the Pasha founded and indeed his entire regime are put in a wider Ottoman context. Chapter 7 closes then with an account of what the career of Mehmed Ali might look like if placed in this larger context, and specifically seeks to view Mehmed Ali's encounter with Palmerston from that Ottoman perspective. The aim of this final chapter, then, is not to restore Mehmed Ali to center stage by closing the book with him, but to offer one last challenge to the nationalist account of the Great Pasha and of Great Britain's hostility towards him. In contrast to the nationalist view according to which Mehmed Ali's efforts were frustrated by Great Britain, this final chapter argues that the Pasha's career was a highly successful one: he fought for hereditary rule for himself and for his sons who were to follow him, and this is precisely what he managed to accomplish.

1 Between Sultan and vali: Syria and the nature of Mehmed Ali's military expansion

In 1825 in a frank and candid interview with one of his French military advisors Mehmed Ali is reported to have said

> I am now the most important man [*l'homme du jour*] in the entire Ottoman Empire. I have returned the Holy Cities [of Mecca and Medina] to the true believers; I have carried my victorious armies to places where the power of the Grand Signor [i.e. the Ottoman Sultan] was not known, and to places whose people had still not heard of gunpowder. My right arm, my son Ibrahim, will conquer Morea and the moment his mission is crowned with success, I shall call him back and return these lands to their legitimate master. I will call back my forces, raise [new] conscripts, complete my regiments and then grab the pashalıks of Damascus and Acre . . . I will organize *une grande armée* and I shall not stop except at the Tigris and Euphrates.

Startled at the frankness and seriousness of this monolog, the French visitor said that the Pasha, in addition, confided in him his desire to invade Yemen and the Strait of Bāb al-Mandab, occupy the Port of Sawākin on the western coast of the Red Sea, "cover the entire Arabian peninsula with his troops and plant his banners in el-Katif on the Persian Gulf."[1]

Less than ten years later these words would prove to be most prophetic. In 1833, indeed, Mehmed Ali appeared as the most important vali in the Ottoman Empire, his strength and resources favorably competing with those of the Sultan himself. By the mid-1830s the Pasha had carved a small empire for himself at the expense of the Sultan's own dominions. After firmly entrenching himself in Egypt he extended his control to Syria, the Hijaz, the Sudan, Crete and most of Yemen and Eastern Arabia, that is, most of the Sultan's Arabic-speaking lands and some of his wealthiest provinces. Having wiped out two huge armies that the Sultan had mustered to confront him with, his forces then penetrated the heartland of the Ottoman Empire, Anatolia, and threatened the capital itself.

[1] Georges Douin, ed., *Une mission militaire française auprès de Mohamed Aly* (Cairo: Royal Egyptian Geographical Society, 1923), pp. 79–80.

Before seeing how these spectacular campaigns were conducted a word is in order as to the reasons behind Mehmed Ali's undertaking this extensive, unprecedented military expansion. Studies of Mehmed Ali almost invariably proceed in a chronological order following him as he conducts one campaign after the other, starting with his early expedition against the Wahhabis in the Hijaz (1811–18), then tracking him to the Sudan (1820–22), from there to the Morea (1824–27), and ending with his climactic confrontation with the Sultan and the European powers in his most ambitious and significant campaign in Syria (1831–41).[2] Portrayed in this chronological manner Mehmed Ali's career immediately seems consistent, purposeful and progressing teleologically towards a climactic, well-thought-out goal, which Egyptian historians have consistently argued to be the seeking of independence from the Ottoman Empire. At the heart of these narrations and occupying central stage (sometimes literally as was shown in the Introduction above) Mehmed Ali appears as a solitary, romantic hero who was ahead of his time, little understood by his own people and betrayed by his allies, but who, through perseverance, persistence and insight was determined to fulfill his civilizing mission of pushing Egypt into the modern age and of lifting her out of what is perceived as centuries of Ottoman stagnation, tyranny and oppression.

Looking at Mehmed Ali in this light most historical accounts that follow his military career chronologically share a number of assumptions which are sometimes explicitly, at other times implicitly, stated. One is that right from the beginning of his career Mehmed Ali was never content with ruling Egypt alone; and that he was set on extending his control over neighboring provinces, taking Egypt as a base for further expansion. In other words, this chronological narration implicitly assumes that Mehmed Ali, in addition to working stoically and persistently towards achieving independence for Egypt from the Ottoman Empire, also had a "master plan" that guided him in his efforts in achieving this goal.

This chapter attempts to check whether Mehmed Ali did in fact have such a "master plan" for expansion, and if he did, whether achieving independence was the motive force behind his incessant activities. It proceeds with a brief review of how Egypt's military expansion in the first half of the nineteenth century has been explained by various historians. Then it seeks to place this military expansion within a wider

[2] This is true not only for a straightforward military history as that of Maxime Weygand, *Histoire militaire de Mohammed Aly et de ses fils*, 2 vols. (Paris: Imprimerie Nationale, 1936), but also for such accounts as that of Dodwell and, more recently, Fred Lawson, *The Social Origins of Egyptian Expansionism During the Muhammad ʿAli Period* (New York: Columbia University Press, 1992). For examples of Egyptian historians who follow the same pattern see al-Rāfʿī, *ʿAṣr Muḥammad ʿAlī*, Sabry, *L'Empire égyptien*, and al-Sayyid Marsot, *Egypt*.

Ottoman context. For reasons that are mentioned below, the Syrian campaign is reviewed in some detail to show how Mehmed Ali was responding to, and was influenced by, developments in the Ottoman Empire at large.

Understanding the Pasha's military expansion

In dealing with the different campaigns that Mehmed Ali engaged in individually rather than as episodes that could fit in a grand strategy most historians acknowledge the fact that every one of these campaigns was dictated by unique historical causes. The Hijaz campaign, for example, besides being a response to the Sultan's order to subdue the Wahhabi rebellion,[3] is seen as serving a number of the Pasha's own aims. Among these were the desire to get rid of the turbulent and undisciplined mamluk and Albanian troops in his army,[4] the hope to get Syria as a reward for helping the Sultan in his war against the Wahhabi rebels,[5] and the desire to win fame and prestige in the Muslim world for capturing the holy cities of Islam from the rebellious Wahhabis who were seen in Istanbul as heretics and whose rising power in Arabia had allegedly caused the annual pilgrimage to cease.[6]

The Sudan campaign is considered to have provided the Pasha with an opportunity to rid himself of even more of the undisciplined and quarrelsome Albanian troops who had survived the Wahhabi wars. The Pasha might also have been lured by the alleged abundance of rich gold mines in Sinnār. More important was the need to conscript the black Sudanese in the army he was contemplating and which he had already undertaken the first steps to create. Finally, Mehmed Ali was also eager to be rid of the remnant of the mamluk forces who had taken refuge in Dongola and whom he considered a constant source of menace.[7]

3 In 1804 the Pashas of Syria and Baghdad were ordered by the Sultan to undertake a campaign against the Wahhabis. Such a campaign never took place: J. B. Kelly, *Britain and the Persian Gulf, 1795–1880* (Oxford: Clarendon Press, 1968), p. 105.

4 Dodwell, *Founder of Modern Egypt*, p. 41; Kelly, *Britain and the Persian Gulf*, p. 128.

5 al-Sayyid Marsot, *Egypt*, p. 199; Kelly, *Britain and the Persian Gulf*, p. 129; Sabry, *L'Empire égyptien*, pp. 44–45.

6 Dodwell, *Founder of Modern Egypt*, pp. 41–42; Kelly, *Britain and the Persian Gulf*, p. 105. al-Jabartī, however, sees this as only an excuse to fight the Wahhabis who, far from being heretics, he argues, were only forbidding the pilgrims from carrying weapons or musical instruments while performing the Ḥajj: al-Jabartī, *'Ajā'ib al-Āthār*, VI, p. 85 (events of Dhū al-Ḥijja, 1223). In addition to this cause of the campaign, al-Rāf'ī says that as early as that time, the Pasha was thinking of asking for independence from the Ottoman Empire and saw this war as an opportunity to force the Sultan to treat him as an equal or an ally and not as a mere vassal: al-Rāf'ī, *'Aṣr Muḥammad 'Alī*, p. 119.

7 For different reasons for the Sudan campaign see Edouard Driault, ed., *La Formation de l'empire de Mohamed-Ali de l'Arabie au Soudan (1814–23)* (Cairo: Royal Egyptian

The Greek campaign, like the Hijaz campaign, is seen as a response to an order by the Sultan to subdue the rebellion that erupted among some of his subject population and to his inability to deal with such a challenge by relying solely on the forces of the central government. Like the previous two campaigns, this one is seen as having its specific reasons as well. The most important of these was the desire on the part of the Pasha to mask his true intentions of invading Syria,[8] a desire to increase his own influence in the Ottoman capital,[9] and also to revitalize Egypt's Aegean trade, disrupted by the Greek revolt.[10]

The Syrian campaign, the most important of the Pasha's wars, is seen to have a number of interrelated causes. On the one hand, Mehmed Ali felt that after all the help he afforded to the Porte in subduing both the Wahhabi and Greek revolts he was entitled to a handsome reward,[11] and during the Morean war he had, in fact, asked for the four pashalıks of Syria to be given to him as that most coveted reward. Once the Morean war was over, however, it became clear that the Sultan (under the influence of Mehmed Ali's arch-enemy, Husrev Pasha)[12] decided to turn down the Pasha's request and Mehmed Ali was determined to take by force what, by then, he considered to be rightly his.[13] Other reasons are cited for this most important of Mehmed Ali's campaigns. Among them was his desire to create a buffer-area between the heartland of his dominions in the Nile valley and the center of Ottoman power in Anatolia,[14] as well as his realization that the Ottoman Empire was decaying and his wish to fill the gap that would ensue from the decline of its dominion by engaging in a "delicate diplomatic balance between England and France by playing one against the other."[15] Pretexts abounded, the most important of which was a quarrel with ʿAbdallah Pasha of Acre whom Mehmed Ali had accused of giving refuge to some 6,000 Egyptian fellahin who, in an attempt to evade taxes, had fled across the borders to neighboring Syria.[16]

Geographical Society, 1927), pp. xxxv-xxxvii; al-Rāfʿī, *ʿAṣr Muḥammad ʿAlī*, pp. 168–9; al-Sayyid Marsot, *Egypt*, p. 205; Sabry, *L'Empire égyptien*, p. 68; Dodwell, *Founder of Modern Egypt*, p. 50.

8 P. J. Vatikiotis, *The History of Egypt* (London: Weidenfeld and Nicolson, 1985), p. 64.

9 al-Rāfʿī, *ʿAṣr Muḥammad ʿAlī*, p. 215.

10 Stanford J. Shaw and Ezel K. Shaw, *History of the Ottoman Empire and Modern Turkey*, vol. II, *Reform, Revolution and Republic: The Rise of Modern Turkey, 1808–1975* (Cambridge: Cambridge University Press, 1977), p. 18.

11 Kelly, *Britain and the Persian Gulf*, p. 271.

12 For the tense and turbulent relationship between the two men see chapter 7 below.

13 al-Sayyid Marsot, *Egypt*, p. 220; Dodwell, *Founder of Modern Egypt*, p. 108.

14 al-Rāfʿī, *ʿAṣr Muḥammad ʿAlī*, pp. 217–18.

15 Vatikiotis, *Egypt*, p. 64.

16 Sulaymān Abū-ʿIzzeddīn, *Ibrāhīm Bāshā fī Sūriyya* [Ibrahim Pasha in Syria] (Beirut: al-Maṭbaʿa al-ʿIlmiyya, 1929), pp. 48–51. See also Rustum's interesting analysis of this

Most historians, therefore, highlight the different causes behind the various campaigns that the Pasha was engaged in. Nevertheless, they are in agreement in arguing that he had always desired to extend his dominions out of Egypt and that he was seizing the various opportunities that he was offered to achieve this goal. The clearest in expressing this idea is Dodwell who argued that "[f]rom the day when the idea of seizing the government of Egypt first occurred to him as a practical measure he had probably always nursed the thought of ruling, not on behalf of another but as an independent sovereign."[17] In a similar fashion Driault says that the Pasha undertook this huge military expansion because he "had the dream and the desire to be grand."[18] In another place he argues that after the Pasha had succeeded in founding a modern army and a formidable navy, and after he had significantly enhanced the productivity of Egypt, the Pasha "wanted to deliver [Egypt] from the guardianship, that is, the economic domination of an outside power. Was this not pardonable?"[19]

Egyptian historians are, for the most part, similarly fascinated by the great Pasha. For them there is little doubt that his greatness is due, most of all, to his unceasing effort to attain independence for Egypt from the Ottoman Empire. al-Rāfʿī, for example, argues that the struggle of the Pasha against the Sultan was a struggle for national independence and that "all the wars that Egypt entered during Mehmed Ali's rule paved the way for its independence and enhanced its position among other nations."[20] That Mehmed Ali was fighting for the independence is so blindly taken for granted by most Egyptian historians that while basing their argument on the need for Egypt to get rid of the "Ottoman yoke," the same right is denied other provinces that were also supposedly suffering under Ottoman suzerainty. These arguments with strong imperialist overtones are best represented in recent studies by two Egyptian historians. The first is J. ʿUbaid's study of Mehmed Ali's expansion into Greece. In it he argues that the reason why Mehmed Ali expanded out of Egypt was to protect the economic and military reforms that he had succeeded in introducing in Egypt "with the help of its people" and his wariness of the Sultan's attempts to depose him. He was thus, ʿUbaid continues, constantly looking for guarantees that would entrench his position in Egypt, "guarantees that could only be

pretext: Asad J. Rustum, *The Royal Archives of Egypt and the Origins of the Egyptian Expedition to Syria* (Beirut: The American Press, 1936), pp. 31–2; Dodwell, *Founder of Modern Egypt*, p. 108; al-Sayyid Marsot, *Egypt*, p. 222.

17 Dodwell, *Founder of Modern Egypt*, p. 39.

18 Driault, ed., *Empire*, p. xxxviii.

19 Edouard Driault, ed., *L'Egypte et l'Europe; la crise orientale de 1839–41* (Cairo: Royal Egyptian Geographical Society, 1930), I, p. xx.

20 al-Rāfʿī, *ʿAṣr Muḥammad ʿAlī*, p. 117.

secured if he extends his control [not only] over Egypt but also to Syria, the Arabian coast [of the Red Sea], and Iraq, if possible. The reason [for annexing these areas] is that they complement each other economically, making the task of defending them militarily easier."[21] More glaringly, another Egyptian historian, in referring to Mehmed Ali's expansion in Syria, says

> Egypt undoubtedly had a civilizing role, since she had always embraced civilization and was generous with it . . . She therefore extended her hands magnanimously to its neighbors at a time when she was filled with a feeling of strength and leadership. She believed that her duty was to work on a new wide-sweeping renaissance especially since the area that she had her eyes on was deficient and faulty.[22]

The question of whether the wars that the governor of Egypt waged during the first third of the nineteenth century were dynastic wars of imperialistic expansion or national wars of independence is central to understanding the whole of Mehmed Ali's career and, indeed, of the history of Egypt during his reign. If, as Toledano argues, Egypt was very much an Ottoman province, ruled by an Ottoman–Egyptian elite,[23] then Marsot's claim that, unlike contemporary Ottoman notables "who had merely sought quasi-independence for their provinces but were content to remain within the empire, Muhammad Ali sought independence,"[24] has to be qualified. For even if it is granted that Mehmed Ali was seeking to get rid of the "Ottoman yoke" right from the beginning of his career, the question remains as to the nature of this independence. Could it be viewed as similar to the independence sought by the Greeks during their War of Independence when large sections of the population rose against their Ottoman rulers? Or is it more plausible to link Mehmed Ali's wars, as Shaw does, with a series of internal wars within the Ottoman Empire that were waged by local governors against central government control? If so, Mehmed Ali would appear, like Ali Pasha of Janina, Davud Pasha of Baghdad, or Amir Bashir of Lebanon as a local governor of an Ottoman province who seized the opportunity of the difficulties that the Ottoman Sultan was facing both internally and externally to try and expand his own local dominions.[25] The reason why he succeeded where most of these local governors failed is seen as stemming from the fact that he managed to prepare for his military ventures by a complete and thorough reorganization of the province's

21 ʿUbaid, *Qiṣṣat Iḥtilāl*, p. 158.

22 Laṭīfa Sālim, *al-Ḥukm al-Miṣrī fi al-Shām, 1831–1841* [Egyptian Rule in Syria, 1831–41] (Cairo: Madbūlī, 1990), p. 7.

23 Ehud Toledano, "Mehmed Ali Paşa or Muhammad ʿAli Basha? An historiographical appraisal in the wake of a recent book," *Middle Eastern Studies* 21(1985), pp. 141–159.

24 al-Sayyid Marsot, *Egypt*, p. 196.

25 Shaw and Shaw, *History*, pp. 14–34.

economic, administrative and, above all, military systems. In doing so, the Pasha enlarged "the scope of the state . . . beyond that traditionally accepted by the Ottomans . . . [and he did this] with a severity far in excess of other Ottoman reformers."[26] This still begs the question of how precisely Mehmed Ali succeeded where other reform-oriented valis in the Ottoman Empire failed, and how the reforms he introduced within his province enabled him to expand at the expense of neighboring valis and, indeed, at the Sultan's own expense.

Marsot, in contrast, does not see that Mehmed Ali was blindly driven toward expansion, and argues that his expansionary policy could best be understood in economic terms. "The value of conquest [did not lie] in conquest itself. It was always posited in terms of what conquest could add to Egypt's financial situation . . . Expansion was economic planning carried out by other means."[27] This argument, however, raises more questions than it seeks to answer. Although it is true that the economic growth that Egypt witnessed during Mehmed Ali's reign required finding markets, the Egyptian market, as Marsot herself states, was far from saturated.[28] That there were economic benefits to be gained by military expansion does not necessarily mean that these economic benefits were the reason behind such expansion.[29] It might be true, for example, as Lawson argues, that the Hijaz campaign was influenced by the Pasha's desire to redirect some of the profits of the Red Sea trade towards Egypt; that the Pasha was lured by the alleged gold mines in the Sudan; that the Greek war was entered into partly to re-establish the Egyptian trade with the Aegean; and that Syria provided the Pasha with badly needed sources of timber necessary for his navy, and coal for the production of gunpowder. But to argue that these considerations were decisive in shaping Mehmed Ali's policy of expansion is to ignore the fact that two of these campaigns were ordered by his Sultan, and that Mehmed Ali agreed to comply with these orders only reluctantly and after considerable hesitation. Moreover, that some economic benefits could be reaped from annexing a certain province does not mean that military occupation was cost-free, and neither Marsot nor Lawson show anything resembling a calculated economic assessment done by Mehmed Ali or Ibrahim weighing the costs and the benefits of military annexation. In fact, when something resembling this assessment was carried out it was to show that the costs of maintaining the army in the annexed provinces far outweighed the revenue accruing from them. With regard to the economic benefits of the occupation of Syria, for example, which was arguably the wealthiest and most productive

[26] *Ibid.*, pp. 11–12. [27] al-Sayyid Marsot, *Egypt*, p. 197. [28] *Ibid.*, p. 196.
[29] For an exposition of such an argument see Lawson, *Egyptian Expansionism.*

province that Mehmed Ali annexed, it was eventually realized that there were serious problems in reaping the economic fruits of the occupation. It was suggested, for example, that in an attempt to "increase the productivity" of the province the local peasants should be given the freedom to plant whichever commodities they wanted.[30] Towards the end of the occupation when these problems were still being strongly felt, Ibrahim suggested to his father that taxes be reduced so as to encourage people to be more productive. Mehmed Ali responded by saying that "to increase our revenues we should [encourage the population to] work harder rather than lower our taxes." He added that he could not accept that the tax burden on the Syrians was heavy since "what we have taken is like an ear from a camel. We should have done as the Europeans do and collected [a flat rate] of 5 percent."[31] This was after he had received conclusive and clear reports confirming what has been feared all along, namely, that the cost of maintaining the army in Syria was not covered by the revenue raised there.[32]

Similarly, to argue that these wars did benefit a number of interrelated social forces within Egypt who were able to use foreign military expansion tactfully in their struggle for survival and hence that these wars must have been dictated by these social groups is tantamount to putting the cart before the horse. The fact that the coalition of state bureaucrats and urban merchants, for example, in their fight against *multazims* and urban artisans, stood to benefit from the resumption of the trade with the Aegean[33] does not necessarily mean that this particular coalition was behind the dispatch of Egyptian troops to Morea, and Lawson does not clearly show how the Pasha might have been pressured by them or how their interests were foremost in his mind.

In explaining Egypt's military expansion during the first third of the nineteenth century one has to bear in mind a number of general points. First, one has to make clear how and when the different campaigns were conducted. Traditional accounts of Mehmed Ali, by following him chronologically from one campaign to the other, ignore important distinctions that differentiate these campaigns from each other and portray them as if they were all fought by the same army. The fact remains, however, that the Pasha started building his modern army only in the middle of his career – *after* he had already conducted his Arabian and Sudanese campaigns, thus marking them off distinctly from the

[30] S/5/47/1/110 on 22 Za 1249/3 April 1834.
[31] S/5/47/2/236 on 11 B 1255/20 September 1839.
[32] S/5/47/2/220 on 19 C 1255/31 August 1839.
[33] Lawson, *Egyptian Expansionism*, pp. 83–116.

Morean and Syrian campaigns in so far as the size and nature of the military forces engaging in them are concerned. The way the Hijaz campaign was conducted, for example, with serious logistical problems[34] and a badly trained soldiery which was a mixture of Maghribis, Sudanese, Greeks and Armenians,[35] contrasts sharply with the superb logistical organization and the well-trained, disciplined troops under the command of Ibrahim Pasha in the Morean and the Syrian wars.

Second, a thorough analysis of the links between the military and the economy should be carried out. To explain how the Syrian war differed from the Sudan campaign, for example, one has to explain how it was possible to create the economic infrastructure that enabled a fifty-thousand-troop army[36] stationed hundreds of miles away from home to be well fed, adequately clothed and regularly paid. This, in turn, necessitates understanding how the economy was run and knowing what links existed between economic needs and military expansion.

Third, and most importantly, one has to bear in mind that Egypt for all practical purposes was an Ottoman province and that Mehmed Ali was an Ottoman governor who received an annual investiture firman from the Sultan in Istanbul. Without bearing that in mind it would be difficult to explain why Mehmed Ali agreed to comply with the Sultan's orders to help him in the Hijaz and Greek wars. Having said that, however, it should also be pointed out that Egypt had always had a unique position within the Ottoman Empire, that its wealth far surpassed that of most other provinces within the Empire (with the exception of the Balkans and Anatolia),[37] and that it always had an influence on its neighboring provinces in Syria and the Hijaz.[38] Similarly, Mehmed Ali was not a mere vali among other Ottoman valis; he was "the most famous modernizer in the nineteenth-century Middle Eastern history" whose reforms in Egypt "served both as a model and an incentive" for what the Sultan himself was later to do in the Empire at large.[39]

Given the Pasha's legal position within the Empire and given the

[34] Dodwell, *Founder of Modern Egypt*, p. 48; al-Rāfʿī, *ʿAṣr Muḥammad ʿAlī*, pp. 137, 140, 157. Years later Mehmed Ali could still remember the difficulties encountered during this campaign; see his letter to Müharrem Ağa dated 14 S 1251/12 June 1835, in Amin Sāmī, ed., *Taqwīm al-Nīl* [Chronicle of the Nile], Vol. II, *ʿAṣr Muḥammad ʿAlī* [Mehmed Ali's Reign] (Cairo: Dār al-Kutub, 1928), p. 438.

[35] Dodwell, *Founder of Modern Egypt*, p. 44.

[36] This is the figure that Baron de Boislecomte gives of the size of the army in Syria; Douin, ed., *Boislecomte*, p. 113.

[37] Stanford J. Shaw, *Ottoman Egypt in the Eighteenth Century* (Cambridge, Mass.: Harvard University Press, 1962), p. 3.

[38] Daniel Crecelius, *The Roots of Modern Egypt* (Minneapolis: Bibliotheca Islamica, 1981), p. 12.

[39] Shaw and Shaw, *History*, p. 9.

ambivalent feelings he had towards his Sultan it is therefore crucial to place his military activities within the larger Ottoman context. Mehmed Ali might have had desires to expand his dominions out of Egypt, but he certainly took his legal position as a vali very seriously. The question that should be asked in this respect is why Mehmed Ali agreed to fight along with the Sultan against the Wahhabis and the Greeks and then turn against him in 1831.

In all the points mentioned above, Syria holds the key. It was in the Syrian war that the modern army was fully employed, an army only at its infancy during the Morean campaign and virtually non-existent in the Arabian and Sudanese campaigns. Furthermore, it was only by the late 1820s that the finances of Egypt had been sufficiently restructured and its productivity sufficiently increased to sustain a military expedition with the size and organization of that of the Syrian campaign.[40] Above all it was in the Syrian war that the Pasha fought his Sultan, Mahmud II, hence marking it as distinct from earlier wars in which he was helping the Sultan. The remainder of this chapter therefore concentrates on the Syrian campaign first by explaining the reasons for the Pasha's desiring Syria. Second it attempts to trace the steps that ultimately led to that blatant act of rebellion by Mehmed Ali against the Sultan and argues that it was the Pasha's growing dislike of the Sultan and the demands he was putting on him during the Morean campaign that finally forced him to defy his sovereign when the opportunity presented itself. Third, it proceeds to follow the army into Syria and attempts to draw a rough sketch of how it conducted the campaign there. The chapter then concludes by reviewing the so called "Peace of Kütahia" and questions the allegation that it was Europe's and specifically Britain's machinations that frustrated Mehmed Ali's efforts at achieving independence from the Ottoman Empire at the end of the first round of confrontation with Istanbul.

Syria: the cornerstone of the Pasha's "empire"

Unlike other provinces that Mehmed Ali conquered, there are various incidents that show the Pasha's very early interest in Syria, and there is enough evidence to show that out of all the provinces he eventually occupied, Syria was the one he most coveted and that he had his eye on it, as it were, right from the beginning of his career. Indeed, one can

[40] See, in particular, Cuno, *The Pahsa' Peasants*, table 6.3 (p. 118) where he shows how 1829 witnessed the highest revenue that Mehmed Ali managed to collect since the late 1810s. See also pp. 104–05 for the Pasha's ability to finance military expansion from increased agricultural output.

view the enormous military build-up since the early 1820s as preparing the way for the invasion of Syria, an operation that, by its own nature, had to wait for the opportune moment to be launched.

As early as 1810 Mehmed Ali showed his interest in the neighboring province and his willingness to interfere in its internal affairs, as well as his ability to influence developments there to suit his interests. Capitalizing on the enmity between Süleyman Pasha, the vali of Sidon, and Yusuf Genç Pasha, the vali of Damascus, Mehmed Ali decided to side with the latter and mediated with the Sublime Porte to reinstate him in his pashalık.[41] He wrote various letters to the Sublime Porte and to his agent in Istanbul, Najib Efendi, insinuating that he would not dispatch his almost ready campaign to the Hijaz unless Yusuf Genç were reinstated in his post, and adding that he was insisting on this demand "not out of personal reasons but to facilitate the Hijaz affair."[42] Mehmed Ali finally succeeded in his demands and his friend was pardoned although he was not reappointed to his pashalık. He spent the last six years of his life in Egypt.[43]

Mehmed Ali still had his eye fixed on Syria, though, and on several occasions he asked to be given the eyalet of Damascus in addition to that of Egypt. In 1812, for example, he spoke to the British consul about his designs on the area.[44] The following year while his forces were having difficulties trying to subdue the Wahhabis in Arabia, he wrote to the Sadrazam telling him that he could offset the reverses suffered by his army in Arabia only if he was given the eyalet of Sham (i.e. Damascus) in addition to Egypt.[45] Two years later he repeated the same request. When his supply lines got longer and longer in his war against the Wahhabis and in order to prepare for the final attack on the Saudi capital, Dar'iyya, it was realized at least 20,000 camels were required, only 3,000 of which had been secured from Syria in spite of repeated promises of help from the vali of Damascus. He again wrote to Nagib Efendi in Istanbul telling him to try yet another time to convince senior officials in the capital to bestow on him the eyalet of Damascus.[46] In

[41] He had fallen out of the Sultan's favor and the Sultan secretly appointed Süleyman Pasha as vali of Damascus. For a brief background to this rivalry see Sālim, *al-Ḥukm al-Miṣrī*, pp. 22–3.

[42] Sāmī, ed., *Taqwīm al-Nīl*, II, p. 231, letter dated 1 Ra 1226/27 March 1811. See also Asad J. Rustum, *A Calendar of State Papers from the Royal Archives of Egypt Relating to the Affairs of Syria* (Beirut: The American Press, 1940), I, pp. 4–5, docs. no. 10–17.

[43] Mehmed Ali had given him a palace in Azbakiyya to live in; al-Jabartī, *'Ajā'ib al-Āthār*, IV, pp. 121, 132, 228 and 266–9.

[44] Dodwell, *Founder of Modern Egypt*, p. 107.

[45] Sāmī, ed., *Taqwīm al-Nīl*, II, p. 244, letter dated 21 s 1228/20 August 1813. The Sadrazam was the Grand Vizier of the Ottoman Empire.

[46] Bahr Barra 4/138, on 15 S 1230/28 January 1815.

1821 he again showed a keen interest (and influence) in Syrian affairs when ʿAbdallah Pasha, the vali of Sidon, requested his mediation with the Porte to reinstate him in his pashalık after falling out of favor with the Sultan. He agreed to play the role of mediator and, thanks to his efforts ʿAbdallah Pasha was pardoned and reinstated in his post.[47]

Long before the actual invasion of Syria the Pasha of Egypt, therefore, had had a strong influence there. In an interview that Henry Salt, the British Consul-General, Mehmed Ali showed not only how influential he was in Syria, but also how conscious he was of his own power. When asked by the Consul-General what he would do if it was true that a certain Yusuf Pasha was sent to Aleppo with 10,000 men to fight him, he answered,

> The man is an ass, he cannot maintain [his men] and has sent already to me for supplies. He wished to make a figure for his own no doubt or perhaps to please me as he might imagine, but I want no great men for my friends . . . As to doing anything against me if that should be his idea, it only shows his folly; if I were to send against him 2,000 of my disciplined troops only they would destroy him. ʿAbdallah Pasha is with me, the Druses are on my side. I can command the Arabs of the desert. The man is a fool . . .[48]

This old and deep seated interest in Syria and Syrian affairs had its reasons. In the first place, Syria was famous for its raw materials, most importantly, its wood and timber that was in abundant supply in the woods of its northernmost regions. The Pasha, very conscious of the fact that Egypt lacked wood,[49] took various measures to encourage the fellahin to plant trees.[50] However, he was also aware that no matter how successful he was in this respect, the quality of wood grown in Egypt was not as good as that imported from abroad.[51] He thus undertook to import wood from any place he could find it, be it from the Sudan,[52] Cyprus,[53] Greece,[54] Anatolia, or Europe.[55]

47 For a brief review of the history of this dispute, see Sālim, *al-Ḥukm al-Miṣrī*, pp. 23–25; and Rustum, *Origins*, pp. 18–20.

48 FO 78/160, Salt, 20 January 1827. The Druses are a sect in Mount Lebanon.

49 S/1/50/1/178 on 29 B 1236/3 May 1821.

50 See, for example, S/5/51/1/107 on 28 Ş 1242/28 March 1827, and Sāmī, ed., *Taqwīm al-Nīl*, II, p. 411, letter dated 3 Za 1248/25 March 1833. See also *ibid.*, p. 379 for a table of the number and type of trees that are believed to have been planted in Egypt in the years 1828–30.

51 S/1/50/5/69 on 9 R 1239/14 December 1823. This is a letter in which it is obvious he realized that the wood produced locally was damp and could not be used either as fuel or to make wagon wheels for the cannons. See also S/1/50/1/106 on 25 R 1239/28 December 1823.

52 S/1/50/2/10 and S/1/50/2/11 both on 12 M 1237/10 October 1821.

53 Dhawat 1/91, on 11 Ş 1238/24 April 1823.

54 S/5/51/1/119 on 6 N 1242/5 April 1827.

55 Bahr Barra 10/54, on 26 Ra 1241/9 November 1825.

This desperate need for wood was necessitated by the need to build a formidable fleet and, to a lesser extent, to provide the "factories" with a reliable supply of fuel. Given its large wooded areas, Syria was an attractive region, especially in light of its proximity to Egypt which reduced transportation costs.[56] Furthermore, because it had extensive forest lands Syria was producing different kinds of wood that were suitable for the Pasha's various needs.[57] In a clear reference to its importance in this respect Ibrahim wrote to his father in the wake of the negotiations that eventually led to the "peace of Kütahia" in 1833 telling him that out of all lands in their possession they must not give up the three districts of Alaiye (Alanya), Adalia (Antalia) and Içel (Cilicia), all on the south coast of Anatolia.

As for demanding these regions [he explained,] it is based on the fact that they are well-wooded regions, and verily the nation that possesses no timbered land will find excessive difficulty in maintaining her fleet. All this is self-evident. As you know, England is a poorly wooded country, and when it sought to obtain timber from Austria, the latter country rejected the request. Indeed, Egypt is in the same position. In confirmation of my suggestion is the instruction I previously received from you in which you said, "My son, give as much care to the matter of timber as you would to crippling the army of Constantinople."[58]

Secondly, Syria also promised to be a good source of manpower for the Pasha. Although Egypt was one of the most populous provinces in the area, the Pasha's conscription policy as well as the different wars his forces were engaged in meant that there was a very real danger that the agricultural fields would be left unattended.[59] The Pasha was also concerned about the effect that wars could have on his economically productive population.[60] He is reported to have once said, "Countries with no subjects are no countries."[61] In that respect, too, the Pasha had every reason to look to Syria. With a population said to be around two million people,[62] it was very attractive for the Pasha to contemplate using its manpower. As early as 1825 he is said to have had in mind the

56 For analysis of this point by John Barker (the British Consul-General who succeeded Salt) and the cost of building the new fleet after the battle of Navarino, see FO 78/170, Barker, 5 July 1828.

57 S/1/50/6/285 on 26 L 1241/4 June 1826; and S/1/50/6/397 on 30 Za 1241/6 July 1826. See also Rustum, *Origins*, pp. 64–67.

58 Sham 18/85, on 13 N 1248/5 February 1833. This translation is from Rustum, *Origins*, pp. 58–59.

59 There was a clear realization that conscription might affect agricultural production; see, for example, S/1/48/1/2 on 13 N 1238/25 May 1823; and S/1/48/1/49 on 15 M 1239/22 November 1823.

60 S/5/51/1/37 on 11 B 1242/10 February 1827.

61 S/1/50/4/363 on 5 N 1239/5 May 1824.

62 Henri Guys, *Beyrout et le Liban* (Paris, 1850), I, pp. 275–6; II, pp. 209–10; quoted in Rustum, *Origins*, p. 69.

possibility of conscripting the inhabitants of Mount Lebanon who were reputed to make brave and strong soldiers.[63]

It is clear, therefore, that the Pasha had always desired Syria and that he had various reasons for wanting it so dearly. He, however, dared to annex it only in 1831, i.e. twenty-six years after he had secured for himself the governorship of Egypt. Why did he do so only then and not before? What events prompted him to undertake this bold move? Acknowledging that there were deep-seated reasons for Mehmed Ali to contemplate invading Syria this chapter attempts to argue that what finally prompted him to do so was the feeling of hostility and mistrust that he felt toward Sultan Mahmud II personally, and the "men in Istanbul," i.e. the Ottoman viziers and courtiers in Istanbul in general.[64] It was during the Morean war and specifically the years 1825–27 that this feeling of animosity was intensified and proved decisive in turning the Pasha against his Sultan. This was the period that witnessed Mahmud's success in abolishing the old Janissary corps, thus strengthening his control over the capital and making Mehmed Ali wary of his Sultan's increased military power; and it was also the period that witnessed the Sultan's ever increasing demands on Mehmed Ali to help him in his fight against the Greeks.

Mehmed Ali was constantly aware that his position as vali of Egypt rested more on his personal strength than on the Sultan's consent and satisfaction with him. The possibility of the Sultan expelling him from his post by force was therefore a likely one and if it were to happen, Syria would most probably be the place from which such an attack would be conducted.[65] The reason for this mutual mistrust and apprehension goes back to the very early years of Mehmed Ali's governorship. The previous Sultan, Sultan Selim III, did not forget the

63 Douin, *Mission militaire*, p. 79. For this reputation of the Lebanese *deli* warriors see al-Jabartī, *'Ajā'ib al-Āthār*, IV, p. 226 (events of Ramaḍān, 1230). See also Marshal Marmont, Duc de Raguse, *The Present State of the Turkish Empire*, trans., Colonel Sir Frederic Smith (London: Thomas Harrison, 1854), p. 244.

64 This is how Mehmed Ali referred to them. See, for example, S/5/47/2/10 on 17 B 1251/ 9 November 1835.

65 In 1786 the Ottoman Empire dispatched a naval expeditionary force led by Hassam Pasha al-Jazā'irlī assisted by a land force sent via the Mamluk leaders, Murad and Ibrahim Beys, for their semi-autonomous policy towards the Sultan in Istanbul. See 'Abdel-Wahāb Bakr, *al-Dawla al-'Uthmāniyya wa Miṣr fi al-Niṣf al-Thānī min al-Qarn al-Thāmin 'Ashr* [The Ottoman Empire and Egypt since the Second Half of the Eighteenth Century] (Cairo: Dār al-Ma'ārif, 1982), p. 240; and Shaw, *Ottoman Egypt in the Eighteenth Century*, pp. 6–8. During Mehmed Ali's governorship another plan was put down in Istanbul to invade Egypt using mainly a naval expeditionary force; see Aḥmad F. Mutwallī, ed., *al-Khiṭṭa al-'Askariyya Allati Waḍa'atha al-Dawla al-'Uthmāniyya l-Istirdād Miṣr min Qabḍat Muḥammad 'Ali* [The Military Plan Put Down By the Ottomans to Recapture Egypt from Mehmed Ali's Grasp] (Cairo: al-Zahrā', 1991). From the text of this MS. it is clear that the plan was put down after 1826.

fact that Mehmed Ali was only installed in the pashalık of Egypt against his imperial wish. During the power struggle in 1803–5 Mehmed Ali proved himself to be the most capable commander among the various warring factions in that relatively remote but significantly wealthy province of the Empire, and the Sultan had to accept grudgingly the fact that Mehmed Ali did indeed control matters in Cairo whether he liked it or not.[66] Jealous of his power and afraid of his influence and the possibility of his secession, the Sultan attempted to transfer Mehmed Ali to the pashalık of Salonika in 1806 only one year after he had been invested in the eyalet of Egypt. Musa Pasha of Salonika had actually arrived in Egypt to fulfill the imperial edict to replace Mehmed Ali as vali. On his arrival, however, Musa Pasha found that Mehmed Ali had much stronger support than the Ottomans originally thought he had and the Ottoman commanders were convinced that the force that Musa had with him was inadequate to dislodge Mehmed Ali from Egypt.[67]

This attempt to depose Mehmed Ali from his power base was repeated in more cunning ways by Sultan Mahmud II in 1813. After Mehmed Ali's forces succeeded in capturing the cities of Mecca and Medina from the Wahhabis he sent one of his mamluks, a certain Latif Ağa, to Istanbul to present the keys of both cities to the Sultan as a sign of obedience and servitude. During his stay in Istanbul, however, Latif Ağa was given the title of Pasha and encouraged to rebel against his master in Egypt. On his return to Cairo rumors were circulating that he had returned armed with a firman to depose Mehmed Ali and to replace him as vali of Egypt. Mehmed Ali, who was in Arabia at this time overseeing the campaign against the Wahhabis, was informed of this conspiracy at the last moment by his friend and deputy, Mehmed Lazoğlu, and hurried back to Egypt to attend personally to that challenge to his authority. He arrived too late, however, to take personal revenge against Latif Pasha whom Mehmed Lazoğlu had summarily beheaded at the foot of the Citadel.[68] Mehmed Ali was aware of these

[66] Stanford J. Shaw, *Between Old and New* (Cambridge, Mass.: Harvard University Press, 1971), pp. 290–1. See also Shafik Ghorbal, *The Beginnings of the Egyptian Question and the Rise of Mehemet Ali* (London: Routledge, 1928), pp. 207–32.

[67] al-Jabartī, *ʿAjāʾib al-Āthār*, IV, pp. 9–20 (events of Rabīʿ al-Thānī, 1221); Georges Douin, ed., *L'Angleterre et l'Egypte* (Cairo: Royal Egyptian Geographical Society, 1928–30), II, pp. 275, 291, 295; Shaw, *Between Old and New*, pp. 290–1.

[68] al-Jabartī, *ʿAjāʾib al-Āthār*, IV, pp. 181–3 (events of Dhū al-Ḥijja, 1228); Sir John G. Wilkinson, *Modern Egypt and Thebes* (London: John Murray, 1843), II, p. 534. al-Rāfʿī, however, does not see this as a conspiracy masterminded by Istanbul to get rid of Mehmed Ali; rather, he says that it was inspired by the jealousy and hatred that Mehmed Ali's personal friends and members of his government felt towards Latif Pasha. Whatever the "true" reasons behind the plot, the fact is it was *portrayed* to Mehmed Ali as an attempt by the government in Istanbul to get rid of him: al-Rāfʿī, *ʿAṣr Muḥammad ʿAlī*, pp. 138–41.

moves and was constantly on his guard concerning Ottoman attempts to depose him.

Moreover, the Pasha held a rather negative opinion of the way the Ottoman Empire was run and would occasionally voice his contempt and disdain when referring to things Ottoman. For example, when it became clear that his nephew, Ahmed Pasha Yeğen, was not fulfilling his new job as Governor of Mecca properly and showed himself to be over-enthusiastic about pomp and ceremony, he wrote to him saying

> the ruler who is obsessed with tradition and who is oblivious of his own interests becoming the slave of tradition, such a ruler the people do not call ruler. [On the contrary], they refer to him as a madman and lunatic. It is clear to all those who can see that the Ottoman State, although once a strong and powerful state . . . is now feeble and rampant with problems because of its viziers' obsession with ceremonies and tradition.[69]

On another occasion he showed even more disdain towards the Ottomans. At the height of the Greek campaign the British Ambassador in Istanbul, Stratford Canning, asked Salt to see if the Pasha would use his influence in Istanbul to convince the Porte to accept British mediation to end the conflict. When approached by Salt the Pasha declined, explaining that "they [i.e. the viziers in Istanbul] are too unsettled, too warring in that quarter and the Grand Signor [i.e. the Sultan] too much a bigot and too much in the hands of the Ulemas [sic] ever to consent to such a proposition."[70]

Earlier in that year a certain incident happened that can be taken as a sign that the more or less amicable, ambivalent relationship that once existed between the Sultan and his vassal was nearing its end. When Mahmud succeeded decisively in getting rid of the power of the Janissaries in June of 1826 he summoned Mehmed Najib Efendi, Mehmed Ali's agent, and asked him to write to the Pasha in Cairo requesting his help in founding a new *nizami* army. He explained that it was due to Mehmed Ali, after all, "that we saw the importance of training the troops along modern lines."[71] Nagib Efendi wrote to the Pasha asking him to dispatch instructors who had been drilled in his army to train the imperial army.[72] Although the Sultan gave Mehmed Ali the credit for initiating such important reforms, the Pasha refused to help his Sultan giving such excuses as the fact that the officers in his army were better paid than Ottoman officers and that this might cause

69 S/1/50/2/84 on 1 R 1237/23 January 1822.
70 FO 78/147, Salt, 16 September 1826.
71 Bahr Barra 10/123, on 25 Za 1241/2 July 1826.
72 S/1/50/6/437, on 12 M 1242/17 August 1826. For an Arabic translation see Sāmī, ed., *Taqwīm al-Nīl*, II, p. 325.

friction and envy between them.[73] The most he did was to send a letter to the Grand Vizier congratulating him on the bold move and expressing his personal delight in it.[74] Privately, however, he harbored different opinions. In an audience he gave to the British Consul-General in Egypt the Pasha made it clear that he had other reasons to refuse to help his sovereign. "The Pasha informed me," Salt says, "that an application had been made to him for instructors but as the Grand Signor [i.e. the Sultan] had the same means open to him as himself he had evaded complying with the request – but they are too bigoted, he said, to employ Franks."[75] Having refused to send instructors from Egypt and believing that the Ottomans would not employ Europeans to train their new troops, the Pasha must have hoped that their efforts would be frustrated.

Whether or not he was contemplating the likelihood of fighting the Sultan's own forces at some time in the future cannot be ascertained, although the evidence does not rule this out as a possibility. What is clear is that from that moment onwards the latent suspicion and mutual hatred that the two men felt towards each other became more and more manifest. When in 1828 the Sultan appealed to his vassal to help him face Russian military advances into Moldovia, the Caucasus and eastern Anatolia, Mehmed Ali refused to send in troops unless the Sultan granted him a governorship in Anatolia in return,[76] a request he knew full well would not be granted.

The reason for turning down the Sultan's request was due less to differences in character than to a real clash of interests. Being an Ottoman governor himself, and realizing how serious the situation of the Empire had become in his time, the Pasha was sharing feelings with other nineteenth-century Ottoman reformers concerning the urgency of instituting an ambitious reform program in the Empire. The problem, however, lay in the fact that whereas the changes that these reformers were contemplating and which Mahmud II was spearheading meant, among other things, strengthening the central government's authority over that of the provinces, Mehmed Ali's reforms in Egypt meant exactly the opposite. For what Mehmed Ali had managed to accomplish was to create another center within the Empire that rivaled Istanbul in its ability to control neighboring provinces and, in effect, challenged its superiority as a leading political center in the Empire. And in that sense Mahmud II and Mehmed Ali were essentially rivals. As was aptly put by Asad Rustum, "Mahmud II had actually crushed the Dereh Beys of

[73] Ahmed Lutfi Efendi, *Tarih-i Lutfi* [Lutfi's History] (Istanbul, 1873), I, p. 196.
[74] S/1/50/6/402 on 16 Z 1241/22 July 1826.
[75] FO 78/147, Salt, 4 December 1826. [76] Shaw and Shaw, *History*, p. 31.

Anatolia, Daud Pasha of Bagdad, and Ali Pasha of Janina . . . Thus, in his struggle with Mahmud II Mehemet Ali Pasha fought for his wealth, for his position and prestige, and very probably for his life also."[77]

The last straw: Morea

Although it might be true that Mehmed Ali felt this fundamental incompatibility of interests right from the beginning of his career, it does seem that what finally prompted the Pasha to rebel against his Sultan's imperial wishes was the manner in which the Morean war was conducted for it is during that campaign that the seeds of rebellion were sown that ultimately led to this first clear act of defiance by the vali of Egypt against his Sultan. Specifically, it was concerning the manner of conducting the war against the Greek rebels in the Morea that the Pasha discovered that it was impossible to collaborate with the Ottomans in any future wars.

The story of Mehmed Ali's involvement in the Morean war goes back to 1824 when an imperial order was dispatched to Egypt appointing Mehmed Ali to deal with the Greek uprising.[78] Five months later the Pasha sent a force a force comprising 17,000 newly trained infantry troops and 700 cavalrymen assisted by four artillery batteries to the Morean peninsula in the south of Greece. These were four of the first six regiments that had been recently trained, and as far as the Pasha was concerned the Morean theater of operations provided a good opportunity to try them out, checking how loyal, disciplined and well trained they were.[79]

The new regiments were very successful and "caused as much alarm by defeating the Greeks as the Sultan had done by failing to do so."[80] However, being a real war and not simply a drilling ground, the Morea gradually became a source of extreme anxiety for the Pasha, and the longer the campaign dragged on, the more its effects were felt on his finances and resources. This was so not only because of the increased numbers of troops sent to the area of conflict with all that that entailed in terms of sending their pay, clothes and equipment, but more importantly because, in addition, the Sultan asked Mehmed Ali to

77 Rustum, *Origins*, p. 50. 78 S/1/48/1/167 on 4 C 1239/5 February 1824.

79 Douin, *Mission militaire*, p. xvi; J. Heyworth-Dunne, *An Introduction to the History of Education in Modern Egypt* (London: Luzac, 1938), p. 114. See also S/1/50/4/519 on 14 M 1240/ 9 September 1824 for the formation of three more regiments that were originally earmarked for the Morean Campaign. For a fuller picture of the formation of these early regiments, see chapter 2.

80 H. W. V. Temperley, *England and the Near East: The Crimea* (London: Longman, 1964), p. 53.

furnish his navy's needs as well. The imperial navy was thus sent to Alexandria to be repaired and replenished with equipment and food before it set out again to the Aegean. Ibrahim, clearly disgusted at the way the Ottomans were incapable of supplying their own navy and dependent instead on Egyptian resources, wrote to his father saying that

> they are so helpless and inefficient that they cannot even fix the masts of their frigates . . . Your Highness knows only too well the amount of supplies you were kind enough to offer them. You also know the amount of food they ate and swallowed when they were in Alexandria.[81]

Moreover, in spite of the effort and expenses that he claimed he took to supply the imperial fleet with food, equipment and ammunition,[82] Mehmed Ali was reprimanded for not doing enough to help the Sultan. When the Pasha said that his transport vessels could not ship the required equipment of both fleets and that European merchant ships refused to transport the supplies on the pretext of neutrality, Husrev Pasha, Mehmed Ali's old enemy who by then had been promoted to the position of Grand Admiral of the Ottoman navy (*Kaptan-ı Derya*), rebuked him saying it was he (i.e. Mehmed Ali) who was making up pretexts. He added that he should get down to business and that "what suits the house is not suitable for the market," in essence, that he was not talking business and was behaving as a housewife. The Pasha would not tolerate such language. In strongly worded letters to the Grand Admiral himself, to Ibrahim Pasha, to Najib Efendi, and to Husni Bey, the Bailiff of the Imperial Palace (*Divan-ı Hümayun Çavuşbaşısı*), he reminded them that he would not accept being rewarded by ingratitude and insult when he was doing his best to meet the Sultan's demands. He wondered why it was only he who was called upon to assist the Sultan in times of crisis. He specifically reprimanded the Grand Admiral for using such language with him.[83] In fact, the mere presence of Husrev Pasha in joint command of the combined Ottoman–Egyptian fleet was a source of constant irritation both to Mehmed Ali and to his son Ibrahim, and the Pasha used all his influence in Istanbul to have Husrev removed from the joint command and Ibrahim given a free hand to conduct naval operations as he saw fit. For his part, and in addition to complaining about Husrev, Ibrahim was also annoyed by the interference of Mehmed Raşid Pasha, the vali of Rumeli, in his operations on the ground, and all attempts to have an amicable working relationship

[81] Bahr Barra 10/86, on 13 Ca 1241/24 December 1825; see also Bahr Barra 10/95 on 3 B 1241/11 February 1826.
[82] S/1/48/2/308 on 17 C 1241/28 January 1826.
[83] S/1/48/2/343 and S/1/48/2/344 both on 7 Ş 1241/18 March 1826.

between the three men failed. The language that Ibrahim used to refer to the vali of Rumeli, for example, shows how uncomfortable he was with the idea of collaborating with the Ottomans. Specifically he was complaining of the impossibility of co-operating with Raşid Pasha, since the vali was constantly giving "silly pretexts [*leyt ve lealla*, lit. "if's and but's"] and unnecessarily delaying the whole affair." He added that he was sent to the Morea to fight the infidels and not the vali of Rumeli.[84] To deal with these complaints the Porte appointed two men in Istanbul (Husni Bey and Najib Efendi) to supervise the operations of the joint command of Ibrahim–Raşid–Husrev. Ibrahim, however, would not accept being supervised by men in Istanbul and would not recognize any authority except that of his father. He wrote to his father complaining:

> Everyone knows that I showed no signs of negligence or laziness in this whole affair . . . But even if I did, why reprimand me via Istanbul? Your Highness is more than capable of punishing me through your agents here, why then resort to Istanbul to accuse me of negligence?[85]

Seeing that his requests to depose Husrev went unanswered, Mehmed Ali finally resorted to threat. He wrote to the Sublime Porte saying that unless Husrev were removed from the command of the navy and unless his son were given a free hand to conduct military operations as he saw best, he would ask Ibrahim to stop fighting the Greeks altogether.[86] Fifteen days after the arrival of this "ultimatum" in Istanbul the Porte acceded to Mehmed Ali's requests and Husrev was relieved of his post as Grand Admiral, adding another grudge to the number that the old man held against Mehmed Ali.[87] Mehmed Ali then wrote to Ibrahim Pasha telling him not to obey any orders issued from Istanbul unless they were approved by him, i.e. Mehmed Ali, first. Ibrahim, naturally, was delighted to comply.[88]

In this respect Mehmed Ali succeeded in imposing his will on the Sultan and in spite of the dangers that were naturally involved in this great campaign, he continued to play the role of the helpful, albeit reluctant and complaining vali. His position as vali, however, weighed heavily on him and there is some evidence that suggests that as early as that time he was considering what it would take to rebel against the authority of the Sultan. In January 1827, for example, the Pasha had a

[84] Bahr Barra 10/74, on 21 R 1241/3 December 1825.
[85] Bahr Barra 10/85, on 13 Ca 1241/24 December 1825.
[86] FO 78/160, Salt, 20 January 1827.
[87] Bahr Barra 11/49 and Bahr Barra 11/50, both on 19 B 1242/16 February 1827; FO 78/160, Salt, 3 March 1827.
[88] Bahr Barra 11/62, on 24 Ş 1242/23 March 1827.

long conversation with Salt and touched on the difficulty of any Pasha succeeding in rendering himself independent of the Sultan. In one of his characteristic story-telling moods he told the consul

> a story of a Pasha on the borders of Kurdistan who had rebelled against the Porte with 8,000 men under his command. The Grand Signor issued his order and another Pasha went against him with only 1,500 men yet the latter soon got the better of the first Pasha, the soldiers of this one falling from him like sand from a pilgrim's feet.[89]

As much as he hoped to get rid of the "Ottoman yoke," and as much as he was getting more and more confident of his troops and their loyalty to him and that they would not "fall from him like sand from a pilgrim's feet," Mehmed Ali was "wary of Ottoman military rejuvenation"[90] and of the fact that the Sultan had military forces to be contended with. Furthermore, the Pasha knew that he also had to contend with the moral authority that the Sultan had in the land of Islam. It was one thing for Greek Christian subjects to rebel against the Ottoman authority, but quite another thing for a Muslim vali to rebel against the Defender of the Faith. Furthermore, the Pasha still had hopes of the Sultan rewarding him with his long cherished province, Syria.[91]

In 1827 developments finally soured and the Pasha had to reconsider seriously his position in the war. During the summer of that year it became clear that the European powers were united in granting the Greeks their independence from the Porte and that his involvement in the Greek campaign might lead to a head-on confrontation with Europe. He increasingly found himself (in the words of the British Consul-General) "in a very difficult position. Much was expected from him by the Porte at the same time that he was anxious not to do anything contrary to the wishes of the British and French governments." He even suggested to Salt that if the negotiations between the European powers and the Porte on the issue of Greek independence fail, then he would be looking for a pretext to get out of the war. This he suggested could be done if the French and the British sent a joint naval force to Alexandria to "make a demonstration of compelling [him] to desist

89 FO 78/160, Salt, 20 January 1827, enclosed in despatch of 10 February 1827.

90 Avigdor Levy, "The officer corps in Sultan Mahmud II's New Ottoman Army, 1826–39," *International Journal of Middle East Studies* 2(1971), p. 22.

91 See, for example, the interesting account of staging an interview with some "Jerusalem notables" in the presence of some Ottoman visitors asking Mehmed Ali to interfere in Syria. As expected, the story was transmitted to Istanbul and relayed back to the Pasha via one of his agents there. See Bahr Barra 11/31, on 5 Ca 1242/5 December 1826. After the disaster of Navarino Mehmed Ali wrote to Nagib Efendi telling him to open the subject of Syria again secretly and delicately; Sāmī, ed., *Taqwīm al-Nīl*, II, p. 333, letter dated 26 C 1243/15 January 1828.

from the war [in which case] he would immediately withdraw his troops and son from the Morea."[92]

The Porte, in contrast, did not see any reason for alarm nor did it take the assembly of European fleets in the Aegean seriously. The Grand Vizier wrote to Ibrahim telling him not to "take heed of the noise and clamor that the Europeans are making (*ayağı patırdılar*)." He added that since "victory does not depend on the number of ships but on the strength of men's hearts," he should stand fast in front of the feeble threats that the European powers had issued against the "formidable Ottoman State."[93] Neither Mehmed Ali nor Ibrahim shared the Grand Vizier's optimistic assessment of the situation, however, and they both viewed the presence of the combined British, French and Russian fleets in front of Navarino very gravely.[94] Before the naval battle of Navarino, in which he lost most of his beloved fleet, Mehmed Ali wrote a frank and rather desperate letter to his agent in Istanbul, Najib Efendi, anticipating the disaster, and saying that he was neither prepared nor willing to confront the European powers. The letter is interesting enough to merit quoting in full.

> Regarding the present situation there are two issues worth thinking of. The first is that the moves of the Europeans are merely a bluff; the second is that the fleets will, in fact, try to intercept our navies. If they are only bluffing then this is exactly what we want . . . However, you know well that when those who take charge of states and kingdoms confront such issues, they anticipate the worst outcome rather than [simply] hoping for the best. If, therefore, the Europeans are not bluffing . . . then we have to realize that we cannot stand up against them, and the only possible outcome [if we do so] will be sinking the entire fleet and causing the death of up to 30 or 40 thousand men . . . Then it will be said that Mehmed Ali Pasha was the cause of this disaster and my name will always be stained with such a disgrace . . . Taking the responsibility of wasting thirty or forty thousand lives is no easy task. I have, therefore, stopped sending letters to my son encouraging him to fight on. Wars are not won only by depending on God and trusting in Him, but also by putting all possible human effort into it. God has ordered us in His Book [not only] to stand up to the enemy [but also] to spare no effort in confronting him. This, however, necessitates a thorough knowledge of the art of war. Unfortunately, my dear friend, although we are men of war (*ehlli harbdan*), yet we are still in the A B of that art (*alif ba*), whereas the Europeans are way ahead of us and have put their theories [about war] into practice . . . [Contemplating all of this] one thinks of accepting the lesser of two evils, namely, the principle of independence [for the Greeks] and [conducting it through] Austrian mediation. This will mean unfortunately that . . . all the effort and money that I have put into this affair will have been wasted together with my soldiers and officers . . . Here I am at a loss: shall I be grieved at the

[92] FO 78/160, Salt, 30 June 1827.
[93] Bahr Barra 12/15, on 6 R 1243/28 October 1827.
[94] Bahr Barra 12/16, on 8 R 1243/30 October 1827.

calamity of the Sublime State (*devlet-i aliyye*) or at my lost effort? I am, therefore, most sorrowful and anguished.[95]

In this candid letter Mehmed Ali was clever enough to know that the Europeans were not bluffing. Moreover, besides being clear that the outcome of any confrontation would be grave, he came very close to anticipating the magnitude of the horrible disaster that befell the combined Ottoman–Egyptian fleet in Navarino on 20 October 1827.[96] In less than three hours the entire Ottoman fleet was lost and most of the ships of the Egyptian fleet were either sunk or burnt.[97] This was the fleet that Mehmed Ali had gone to great lengths to buy and improve, and it was the fleet that he used to boast about acquiring saying that the world of Islam had never witnessed anything like it.[98] And it was lost not through any negligence or misconduct on his part but because of the "obstinate and arrogant refusal of the Porte to accept European mediation" in the whole issue of Greek independence.[99] This intransigent position on the part of the Porte did not change after Navarino: the Porte refused to hear of any requests by Ibrahim to withdraw to Egypt and instead kept on pressing on him the importance of holding on to all territories under his control as well as initiating further campaigns against the Christian population in the Morean peninsula and, if need be, to burn all villages on his way.[100] Mehmed Ali refused to listen to these stubborn and unrealistic demands of the Porte and proceeded to sign a treaty with the European powers guaranteeing the safety of his son's withdrawal from the Greek mainland.[101] Moreover, and this must have been felt more heartily, the Sultan refused to give Mehmed Ali Syria as he had hoped and instead gave him the island of Crete to govern, an island he had already captured and which was in a constant state of rebellion since the start of the Greek revolution. Furthermore, its resources and importance were not to be compared to those of Syria. Never again would he accept the docile role that was expected of him and he would always be on the look-out for any pretext to take what he had been coveting for a long time: Syria.

95 Bahr Barra 12/7, on 14 Ra 1243/6 October 1827.

96 News of the disaster arrived in Egypt on 4 November 1827. See Edouard Driault, ed., *L'Expédition de Crète et de Morée (1823–28)* (Cairo: Royal Egyptian Geographical Society, 1930), p. 288.

97 For a detailed account of the battle, see C. M. Woodhouse, *The Battle of Navarino* (London: Hodder and Stoughton, 1965), pp. 110–41, and George Douin, *Navarin, le 6 Juillet-20 Octobre, 1827* (Cairo: Royal Egyptian Geographical Society, 1927), pp. 283–311.

98 S/5/51/1/202 on 30 Za 1242/25 May 1827.

99 Driault, *L'Expédition*, p. 288.

100 Bahr Barra 12/18, on 17 R 1243/10 November 1827.

101 René Cattaui, ed., *Le Règne de Mohamed Aly d'après les archives russes en Egypte* (Cairo: Royal Egyptian Geographical Society, 1931), I, p. 284.

The invasion

For two years Mehmed Ali set about repairing the damage he suffered in this Morean debacle in preparation for taking what, by then, he must have felt to be rightly his. (During this period he was approached by the French to undertake an expedition to capture the Barbary states of Tripoli, Tunis and Algiers. After some consideration and a lot of diplomatic exchange, however, the Pasha realized that the expedition was too costly to merit taking the risks involved and that it would divert him from the provinces he strongly desired.)[102] Following the destruction of his fleet in Navarino the Pasha was determined on acquiring a new fleet, this time not only by buying it from whomever would be kind enough to sell him ships, but also by attempting to build himself one in Egypt. With this end in mind he secured the services of a French engineer, M. de Cerisy, who started to construct an arsenal in Alexandria in June 1829.[103]

Two years later the preparations for the invasion of Syria were almost complete. Naturally, their true intention was not declared and throughout the summer of 1831 speculation had been going on in London, Paris and Istanbul about the purpose of the increased military activity witnessed in Alexandria and Cairo.[104] Conscription waves were intensifying at such a rate that the European powers were getting suspicious as to their true intention.[105] The naval arsenal in Alexandria also showed a frenzied increase in activity.[106] Military factories were geared to high production and the Friday holiday was canceled to meet targets set by the Pasha.[107]

Finally on 2 November 1831 the crucial hour arrived and two expeditions were given orders to move with Syria as their destination,

[102] Georges Douin, *Mohamed Ali et l'expédition d'Alger* (Cairo: Royal Egyptian Geographical Society, 1930), and Dodwell, *Founder of Modern Egypt*, pp. 94–105.

[103] For the preparations preceding the actual construction of the Arsenal see FO 78/170, Barker, 5 July 1828; and A. B. Clot Bey, *Aperçu général sur l'Egypte* (Paris: Fortin, Masson, 1840), II, pp. 236–49.

[104] Earlier, in March 1829, John Barker thought that the increased military activity in Cairo and Alexandria was in preparation for a military expedition to assist the Sultan in his war against Russia; FO 78/184, Barker, 10 March 1829. Dodwell, on the other hand, says that the Pasha had been asked to send troops to help subdue the rebellion of Mustafa Pasha Iskudarlı. When the request was dropped he "proposed to use the assembled forces to attack Abdullah Pasha of Acre"; Dodwell, *Founder of Modern Egypt*, p. 108.

[105] Georges Douin, ed., *La Première Guerre de Syrie* (Cairo: Royal Egyptian Geographical Society, 1931), I, pp. 7, 31, 61; Douin, *L'Expédition d'Alger*, p. 6.

[106] Douin, *La Première Guerre*, I, p. 27.

[107] S/5/51/2/68, on 7 Za 1247/9 April 1832; S/5/51/2/91, on 17 Za 1247/19 April 1832. These two documents are concerning the production of gunpowder.

one by land and the other by sea. (The troops were supposed to leave in the summer but their departure was delayed until autumn owing to the outbreak of cholera in Cairo which took a heavy toll on the army.)[108] Four infantry regiments[109] and a similar number of cavalry regiments[110] left by land from Ṣālḥiyya in the north of Cairo via al-ʿArīsh and finally to Jaffa.[111] In Jaffa they were met by Ibrahim Pasha who had arrived by sea on 9 November,[112] and entered the city three days later.[113] Ibrahim Pasha was heading a formidable fleet composed of sixteen ships of war and seventeen transport vessels which carried on board his staff officers[114] as well as forty small cannons and a number of siege cannons in addition to food, ammunition, fodder and medical supplies for the combined sea and land forces that numbered 30,000 men.[115]

After capturing Jaffa, Ibrahim entered the city of Ḥaifa without much effort on 17 November 1831. Immediately afterwards, Sidon, Tyre, Beirut, Tripoli, Latakia, Jerusalem, and Nablus all gave their allegiance to Mehmed Ali's son thus allowing him to concentrate his efforts on capturing the strategic city of Acre.[116] The army arrived at the outskirts of that formidable fortress in November and laid siege on it on 4 December 1831.[117]

Alarmed at the spectacular success of the advance of Ibrahim's army into Syria, the Sultan sent a special emissary to Alexandria in an

108 LaVerne Kuhnke, *Lives at Risk* (Berkeley: University of California Press, 1990), pp. 51–7. al-Rāfʿī says that the army lost 5,000 men in this epidemic, which also carried away 150,000 civilians in a little over a month: al-Rāfʿī, *ʿAṣr Muḥammad ʿAlī*, p. 222.

109 These were the 8th, under the command of Yusuf Bey Miralay, the 10th of Ahmed Bey, the 13th of Mehmed Bey, and the 12th of Yakup Bey. The general commander of the infantry regiments was Ibrahim Pasha Yeğen, Mehmed Ali's nephew.

110 These were the 3rd, under the command of Saleh Bey, the 5th of Ahmed Bey, the 6th of Halil Bey, and the 7th of Yusuf Bey. The general commander of these cavalry forces was Abbas Pasha, Mehmed Ali's grandson.

111 They arrived there on 14 November 1831; Sham 1/27, on 21 C 1247/26 November 1831.

112 Sham 1/13, on 4 C 1247/10 November 1831; Sāmī, ed., *Taqwīm al-Nīl*, II, p. 384.

113 Sham 1/23, on 18 C 1247/24 November 1831.

114 These included Osman Bey Nureddin, the Chief of Staff (*Cihadiye-i Rical-ı Reisi*); Süleyman Bey (Colonel Sèves); Nazif Bey, Commissary-General of the army (*Nüzlü Emini*); and Hanna Bey Bahari, the Chief Financial Supervisor (*Reisülküttab*).

115 Abū-ʿIzzeddīn, *Ibrāhīm Bāshā fī Sūriyya*, pp. 73–4; E. de Cadalvène and E. Barrault, *Histoire de la guerre de Méhémed-Ali contre la Porte Ottomane, en Syrie et en Asie Mineure* (Paris, 1837), pp. 62–3; Ismāʿīl Serheng, *Ḥaqāʾiq al-Akhbār fī Duwal al-Biḥār* [The True Narrations About Maritime Nations](Cairo: Būlāq, 1898), II, p. 245. Marshal Marmont exaggerates the number of regiments and puts the size of the force at "around forty thousand men"; Marshal Marmont, *Turkish Empire*, p. 245.

116 Sham 1/23, on 18 C 1247/24 November 1831; Edouard Gouin, *L'Egypte au XIX siècle* (Paris, 1847), p. 418. On the fortifications of Acre as Ibrahim found them see Asad J. Rustum, *Notes on Akka and its Defences Under Ibrahim Pasha* (1926), pp. 5–22.

117 Abū-ʿIzzeddīn, *Ibrāhīm Bāshā fī Sūriyya*, p. 79.

attempt to persuade Mehmed Ali to pull back his forces and to warn him that if he did not comply, then a huge army of newly trained *nizami* troops would be assembled against his son's forces.[118] When it became clear that the Egyptian Pasha had no intention of pulling back his forces, the Porte ordered the Syrian valis to raise men and send them to Aleppo in preparation for fighting Ibrahim's troops. Mehmed Pasha, deputy of the vali of Aleppo, was given the title of Serasker (Commander-in-Chief) of Syria and Arabia and was entrusted with heading this force that it was hoped would stop the advance of the Egyptian army.[119] Furthermore, on 3 March 1832 the annual *tevcihat* (imperial appointments to the posts of provincial governors) were announced leaving the positions of the governors of the eyalets of Egypt, Jedda and Crete vacant until Mehmed Ali and Ibrahim should respond positively to the Porte's request to withdraw. When this failed, a *fetva* (religious edict) was issued, in effect, excommunicating both Mehmed Ali and Ibrahim Pasha and appointing in their respective pashalıks Hüseyin Pasha, the destroyer of the Janissaries, who was then Governor of Edirne. In addition, the same Pasha was appointed head of the Ottoman forces in Anatolia with the task of joining Mehmed Pasha of Aleppo and preparing jointly the task of stopping Ibrahim Pasha.[120]

In the meantime the Egyptian forces were busily tightening the siege on the city of Acre, a city which had withstood Napoleon's siege thirty-two years earlier. After a period of nearly six months the city finally fell on 27 May 1832.[121] Ibrahim then proceeded northward to capture Damascus, which city he entered on 16 June 1832.[122] He then rushed further north to meet Mehmed Pasha's army before he could be joined by Hüseyin Pasha. He succeeded in doing so and met Mehmed Pasha who was heading an army composed of four infantry regiments, three cavalry regiments and 15,000 irregulars. A fierce battle took place near Ḥomṣ on 8 July 1832 and ended with the defeat of Mehmed Pasha's army. Around 2,000 of his men were killed and between 2,500 and 3,000 were taken prisoners as well as all his ammunition, tents and twenty-four cannons.[123]

118 Sham 2/60, on 13 B 1247/18 December 1831; Cadalvène and Barrault, *La Guerre de Méhémet-Ali*, pp. 80–83.

119 Lutfi, *Tarih-i Lutfi*, IV, p. 6; Cadalvène and Barrault, *La Guerre de Méhémet-Ali*, p. 83.

120 Cattaui, ed., *Mohamed Aly*, I, p. 476; Cadalvène and Barrault, *La Guerre de Méhémet-Ali*, p. 99; Lutfi, *Tarih-i Lutfi*, IV, p. 7.

121 For a contemporary account of how the city fell after hours of fierce fighting, see Asad J. Rustum, ed., *Ḥurūb Ibrāhīm Bāshā fī Sūriyya wa'l-Anāḍūl* [Ibrahim Pasha's Wars in Syria and Anatolia] (Heliopolis: Imprimerie Syrienne, n.d.), I, pp. 17–18.

122 For an eyewitness account of the entry of the army in Damascus, see the anonymous account quoted by Abū-ʿIzzeddīn, pp. 92–3.

123 Sham 9/52, on 9 S 1248/8 July 1832; Sham 9/65, on 12 S 1248/11 July 1832. For an

Plate 2 “The capture of Saint-Jean d’Acre by Egyptian troops”

Ibrahim Pasha was determined, however, to confront "the *murdar* (dirty) Hüseyin Pasha who has been appointed *sirdar* (Commander-in-Chief)."[124] Hüseyin Pasha was late in departing from Anatolia and instead of meeting Mehmed Pasha before the latter had confronted Ibrahim's army, he was met instead by the defeated remnants of Mehmed Pasha's army that had fled from the battle of Ḥomṣ.[125] Ibrahim Pasha did meet his rival, Hüseyin Pasha, however, at the famous battle of Bilan at the northernmost borders of Syria just to the south of the Taurus mountains. On 29 July 1832, the Turkish army, composed of around 20,000 men, half of them regulars, under the command of Hüseyin Pasha, met the Egyptian army totaling around 16,000 men forming four infantry regiments assisted by three cavalry regiments and four artillery batteries all under the command of Ibrahim Pasha. After three and a half hours of heavy fighting Ibrahim won a decisive victory: the Ottomans lost around 1,000 men and 1,900 were taken prisoners. In addition, twelve pieces of cannon were captured by the Egyptians. For his part, Ibrahim lost 102 men and 172 horses, and 162 men were wounded.[126]

Up until that moment the ostensible reason for forwarding these troops to Syria was to punish ʿAbdallah Pasha of Acre for giving refuge to a number of Egyptian peasants who had fled to Syria in an attempt to evade conscription and taxes levied by the Pasha's government. [127] When Mehmed Ali complained to the Sublime Porte about ʿAbdallah Pasha's refusal to hand back the peasants, the Porte replied by saying that as far as it was concerned both Egypt and Syria were imperial eyalets and the Sultan did not mind where his subjects wished to dwell

Arabic translation of this last document, see Sāmī, ed., *Taqwīm al-Nīl*, II, pp. 398–400. For descriptions of the battle see St. John, *Egypt*, II, pp. 498–500; Marshal Marmont, *Turkish Empire*, pp. 247–50; Gouin, *L'Egypte*, p. 441.

124 Sham 9/121, on 21 S 1248/20 July 1832. On his promotion to this rank, as well as a background to his military career, see Cadalvène and Barrault, *La Guerre de Méhémet-Ali*, pp. 161–2; Lutfi, *Tarih-i Lutfi*, IV, p. 7; ʿAbdel-Raḥmān Zakī, "The first and second Syrian campaigns," in *Dhikrā al-Baṭal al-Fātiḥ Ibrāhīm Bāshā, 1848–1948* [The Hundredth Anniversary of Ibrahim Pasha the Conqueror, 1848–1948] (Cairo: Madbūlī, 1990 [1948]), pp. 312–13; Abū-ʿIzzeddīn, p. 102; Shaw and Shaw, *History*, p. 33.

125 Abū-ʿIzzeddīn, *Ibrāhīm Bāshā fī Sūriyya*, p. 102.

126 Sham 10/15, on 3 Ra 1248/31 July 1832; Sham 10/30, on 5 Ra 1248/2 August 1832; Sham 10/38, on 5 Ra 1248/2 August 1832; Sham 10/105, on 13 Ra 1248/10 August 1832 (the last two documents give the detailed information about the POWs); Sāmī, ed., *Taqwīm al-Nīl*, II, p. 402; Cadalvène and Barrault, *La Guerre de Méhémet-Ali*, pp. 179–89; Marshal Marmont, *Turkish Empire*, pp. 250–2.

127 Rustum, *Origins*, pp. 17–32. Mehmed Ali had been complaining for some time to the Sublime Porte about ʿAbdallah Pasha's activities; Bahr Barra 13/69, on 14 L 1245/11 April 1830.

as long as this was within his dominions.[128] Obviously this was not the true or main reason for undertaking such a bold and dangerous expedition and the Porte knew very well that it was only a pretext.[129] However, this continued to be the official line issued from Cairo.[130]

In the meantime Ibrahim was marching northward and his army thus crossed the Taurus mountains and captured the strategic cities of Tarsus and Adana (31 July 1832). He then halted any further advance waiting for instructions from his father. There was no danger of the Ottomans attacking since their army was in no position to assume offensive action.[131] The vast territory now under Ibrahim Pasha's command, however, had to be secured and garrisons had to be distributed among the different cities. After gaps had been filled by new recruits from Egypt[132] and after new equipment and supplies had arrived, the city of Urfa was captured to control routes leading to Sıvas, Diyarbakır and Erzurum. Maraş was also captured to control possible army movements in the area of the Taurus mountains. Most communications with Egypt were by sea where the Egyptian navy had a comfortable command over the waters of the eastern Mediterranean.[133]

Confronted with these defeats Sultan Mahmud II decided to raise yet another army in an attempt to "arrest the progress of an army whose success endangered the stability of his throne."[134] He therefore summoned the Sadrazam Mehmed Raşid Pasha (an ally and protégé of Husrev) and entrusted him with raising a new army from different provinces of the Empire. Towards the end of October 1832 the Sadrazam was able to raise a formidable army composed of 80,000 men divided into four major sections. The first comprised about 20,000 men, mostly Albanians and *nizami* troops who were stationed in Scutari in Albania and was headed by the Sadrazam himself. The second section was composed of a similar number of men raised from areas around Erzurum and headed by Osman Pasha, vali of Trabzon. The third section numbered around 10,000 men under the command of

[128] Serheng, *Ḥaqā'iq al-Akhbār*, II, p. 243.

[129] As an example of the Porte's clear understanding of Mehmed Ali's true intentions *before* the initiation of military activities, see Sham 1/2 bis, on 3 Ra 1247/12 August 1831.

[130] See, for example, S/5/51/2/1 on 5 s 1247/9 January 1832, from Mehmed Ali to the Sublime Porte in which he says that he had undertaken this dramatic step only after he had repeatedly complained to the Porte of ʻAbdallah Pasha's activities and was not answered; "on the contrary I was completely forgotten (*nesyen mensiyen*)".

[131] Cattaui, ed., *Mohamed Aly*, I, pp. 534–355; Douin, ed., *La Première Guerre*, I, p. 299.

[132] S/1/48/4/30 on 16 C 1248/10 November 1832; Sāmī, ed., *Taqwīm al-Nīl*, II, pp. 407, 409, 410.

[133] Marshal Marmont, *Turkish Empire*, pp. 252–3; Douin, *La Première Guerre*, I, p. 450.

[134] Marshal Marmont, *Turkish Empire*, p. 252.

Süleyman Pasha and was stationed to the north of Ibrahim Pasha's army in the south of Anatolia. The fourth and last section was composed of 20,000 to 30,000 men who were the remnants of Hüseyin Pasha's army and these were gathered around Konia under the command of Raouf Pasha.[135] Aware of these preparations on the part of the Ottomans, Ibrahim was pressing his father to give him permission to proceed northward to deal with this troop concentration before they joined forces and formed a formidable front which would be more difficult to deal with. Finally in October he ordered his men to move northward towards the strategic city of Konia at the very center of the Anatolian plateau. Two months later, on 21 December 1832, the two armies met on the plain to the north of the city, and during the seven-hour battle Ibrahim's army managed to inflict a heavy defeat on the Ottomans who were headed by the Sadrazam, Raşid Pasha.[136]

This was the clearest victory Ibrahim had secured so far: the Ottomans lost ninety-two cannons, suffered 3,000 casualties and 10,000 were taken prisoner. Most significantly, the Egyptian army captured the Sadrazam himself who was led to Ibrahim Pasha as a prisoner. For their part, the Egyptians only suffered 262 casualties and 530 men were wounded. The remnants of the Ottoman army were gathered in Eskişehir and on hearing news of the defeat, the Sultan acceded to most of Mehmed Ali's demands. According to the official *Takvimi-i Vekayi* the Sultan "in his customary graciousness and generosity decided to send special envoys to the vali of Egypt to find a way to stop the bloodshed of His subjects."[137]

The "peace of Kütahia"

Halil Pasha, the head of the Ottoman navy, was thus dispatched to Alexandria with offers of peace to the Pasha of Egypt. This initiated a long and arduous process of negotiation which culminated in the peace of Kütahia agreed upon in May 1833. In this peace, brokered by the European powers (mainly Russia and France), the Sultan reluctantly conceded to his rebellious vali the eyalets of Egypt, Hijaz and Crete. Furthermore, Ibrahim Pasha was given the eyalets of Acre, Damascus, Tripoli and Aleppo, and after considerable hesitation, the post of

[135] A. Zakī, "The first and second Syrian campaigns," p. 340. Marshal Marmont, however, says that the combined Ottoman forces did not exceed 50,000 regulars; Marshal Marmont, *Turkish Empire*, p. 252.

[136] For a description of the battle, see chapter 4 below.

[137] *Takvimi-i Vekayi*, issue no. 49 on 19 S 1248/11 January 1833; a copy of this is in Sham 16/34, on 19 S 1248/11 January 1833.

muhassil (i.e. collector of taxes) of Adana as well.[138] It is important to note, however, that the "peace of Kütahia" was not a permanent settlement, it was not a peace treaty but an agreement between Mahmud II and Mehmed Ali to end the state of war that had existed between them for over a year. Rather than finding his position more secure than before the campaign had started, the Pasha soon discovered that his osensibly improved status was dependent on an annual renewal by the Sultan, and was thus subject to his whims and to the intrigues of various courtiers in Istanbul. For after all, Mehmed Ali was not granted an independent status that would be recognized by the European powers and hence the agreement did not secure for him "the much desired legal independence as a sovereign" that he had been supposedly fighting for.[139] As such, the agreement ending the Syrian war left none of the principal parties involved completely satisfied. "The Sultan had suffered the vexation of defeat by a contumacious pasha; Muhammad ʿAli had secured neither independent status nor a controlling influence at the Porte; the western powers were annoyed at the opening which Ibrahim's victories had offered to the Russians; while the Russians were disappointed at having been unable to entrench themselves more securely at Constantinople."[140]

While it might be true to argue that the inconclusive and ambivalent nature of the "peace of Kütahia" had its reasons not in any European conspiracy designed to deny Mehmed Ali the fruits of his military conquests, or in British attempts to thwart his efforts at gaining independence, it was also the result of Mehmed Ali's own cautious and often shifting stand during the difficult negotiations that led to that agreement. There can be various reasons for Mehmed Ali's caution. One main reason was his receiving conflicting messages from the different European powers regarding their respective possible reactions to his moves against the Sultan. During the Morean war he once wrote to Nagib Efendi in Istanbul telling him "although I may be well versed in European mercantile affairs, I am ignorant when it comes to its political situation."[141] Four years later his position was not much better and that remark was equally applicable to the new situation. In 1832 the

[138] A. Zakī, "The first and second Syrian campaigns," p. 360. For the festivities celebrating the arrival in Egypt of the firman granting these provinces to Mehmed Ali and his son, see Sāmī, ed., *Taqwīm al-Nīl*, II, p. 412, letter dated 19 Z 1248/9 May 1833 and *ibid.*, p. 413, letter dated 10 M 1249/30 May 1833. For the distribution of Ibrahim Pasha's forces in Syria after the battle see Abū-ʿIzzeddīn, p. 129; Clot Bey, *Aperçu*, II, pp. 230–2.

[139] al-Sayyid Marsot, *Egypt*, p. 231.

[140] Dodwell, *Founder of Modern Egypt*, pp. 122–3.

[141] Bahr Barra 12/7, on 14 Ra 1243/6 October 1827.

French were passing on messages that they would stand by him in his struggle with the Sultan; the Russians, for their part, sent him an envoy, General Mouraviev, only one week before Halil's arrival in Alexandria with a verbal threat that they would oppose him "with their forces by sea and by land if he persisted in advancing on Constantinople."[142] And the stand of the one European power that mattered most, Great Britain, Mehmed Ali could not figure out, partly because of his own ambivalent position towards the British (a point that will be dealt with later) and partly because of British indecision and wavering attitude regarding the Pasha's war with the Sultan. Since this is a point of considerable importance and since the European powers (especially Britain) are usually blamed for aborting Mehmed Ali's bid for independence,[143] it is worthwhile dealing with it in some detail.

Although John Barker, the British Consul-General during the Syrian campaign, "was always opposed" to the Pasha's policy towards the Sultan, the "British Cabinet did not declare its policy, and Mr. Barker did not receive from home any instructions favorable to Meh'med Ali's projects."[144] Mehmed Ali knew that the messages he was receiving from Barker were the Consul's own personal opinions and Palmerston, the British Foreign Secretary, who was later adamant in upholding the principle of preserving the integrity of the Ottoman Empire, was completely silent on the issue of his struggle with the Sultan. "There is not a single word either to Constantinople and Alexandria or to the British ambassadors at Paris, Vienna, and St. Petersburg; hardly any observation can be noticed during 1832 on despatches coming from these centers and touching on the subject of the Syrian war."[145] The hostility that Palmerston felt towards Mehmed Ali developed later and, as will be shown in chapter 7 below, had other causes.

Be that as it may, what is important to note is that independence was *not* one of the conditions set forth by Mehmed Ali when he met Halil Pasha in Alexandria; this demand was persistently demanded by Ibrahim Pasha in letters sent to his father from his camp near Konia, but was not voiced by Mehmed Ali himself until much later. When

142 J. Barker, *Syria and Egypt*, II, p. 191.

143 al-Sayyid Marsot, *Egypt*, p. 231.

144 Barker, *Syria and Egypt*, II, p. 192.

145 M. Vereté, "Palmerston and the Levant Crisis, 1832," *Journal of Modern History*, 24 (June 1952), p. 145. Vereté argues, not very successfully, it should be added, that Palmerston as early as 1832 *did* have a clear idea about where British interests lay regarding the Turco-Egyptian crisis. He fails to explain, for example, why Palmerston refused the Porte's request for naval assistance. Be that as it may, the important issue is that even if he did have clear ideas about the Levant crisis, his Consul in Egypt did not know what these might have been, and Mehmed Ali was left in the dark regarding possible British moves.

Halil Pasha arrived with an offer of peace in Alexandria on 21 January 1833, Mehmed did not intend to raise the issue of independence with him, not only because he was wondering about European reactions to this bold move, but more probably because *he could not contemplate it himself*. A look at how he received the Sultan's envoy might shed some light on how he attempted to deal with the whole arduous negotiation ahead of him. Halil Pasha

> was received by him with the greatest marks of distinction. A salute of seventeen guns was fired. On reaching the palace at the foot of the flight of stairs, Haleel Pacha [sic] was assisted by two officers of the Viceroy . . . each supporting an arm, as he advanced to ascend the steps. The Viceroy descended at the same time, and they met nearly in the middle, Haleel continually entreating His Highness not to descend. On meeting, Haleel Pacha attempted to seize the Viceroy's hand with the intention of carrying it to his lips, but the Viceroy prevented him by embracing him and kissing him on the cheek; but Haleel Pacha succeeded in imprinting a kiss on the hand of His Highness. They then made their way through a dense crowd to the Hall of Audience, the Viceroy's hand being locked in the right hand of Haleel Pacha, who had his other hand round the waist of His Highness.[146]

These are not the actions of someone who intends to pass on to his negotiating partner that his are going to be difficult terms to meet. Having won a decisive military victory this would have been the time to press with his demands for independence assuming that this was his desire and that he had been contemplating secession right from the start. However, in his negotiations with Halil Pasha, Mehmed Ali did not raise the issue of independence; again it was Ibrahim who was urging his father to do so. Mehmed Ali started asking for independence only in 1838; back in 1833 he could still not think of himself as being outside of Ottoman authority altogether. The inconclusive nature of the peace of Kütahia, therefore, was representative of the Pasha's own ambivalent feelings towards the Ottoman Sultan and towards his own military activities against him. Reviewing the Pasha's position from the time of starting hostilities until their cessation can illustrate this point further.

After sending his troops to Syria and after undertaking what could only be taken as a blatant act of rebellion against the authority of the Sultan, Mehmed Ali was still hoping to acquire Syria *and* to be pardoned by Mahmud at the same time. Documents abound showing how Mehmed Ali in 1832 still thought that he could get away with his act and that he could, in effect, both have his cake and eat it too. While besieging the fortress of Acre for eight months during which numerous

[146] Barker, *Syria and Egypt*, II, pp. 193–4.

letters were sent from Istanbul urging him to desist and warning him of the consequences if he did not, he was still pleading for forgiveness from the Sultan and asking to be given Syria without being declared a rebel. When he knew that all his pretexts for his bold military move were not accepted by the Sultan, he wrote to the Grand Vizier telling him

> I think that I have not done anything that could not be forgiven. Unfortunately, I did not think that the issue of [besieging] Acre would not be covered by an imperial pardon. This is why I undertook it without thinking that by doing so I was overstepping the limits of obedience and submission [to the Sultan].[147]

After the fall of Acre the Pasha might have felt more confident and it appears that he was harboring more negative views toward the Sultan and his viziers. (In a letter to Ibrahim Pasha, he described them as people who had been "tyrannical and treacherous for five hundred years.")[148] Yet even then he was still writing to senior officials in Istanbul asking for the Sultan's forgiveness, saying that he was approaching seventy years of age and did not want anything except to act as a "humble servant to the Faith and the [Ottoman] State."[149] Furthermore, after his armies had defeated the Ottomans in these successive battles and when the imams of various city mosques asked whose name should be mentioned in the Friday prayers, Mehmed Ali's or Sultan Mahmud's, they were answered that they should continue to use the Sultan's name.[150] This caused Ibrahim to be so distressed that he wrote a strongly worded letter to his father urging him to order the use of his name in the prayers and to start minting coins in his name.[151] Finally, after the battle of Bilan on 29 July 1832 when the *Vekayi-i Mısıriyye,* which acted as a government bulletin and which was aimed at Ottoman officials as much as at his own employees, started to drop its cautious, conciliatory tone and to become more candid and less apologetic, Ibrahim was thrilled. He wrote to his father saying, "Egypt's independence has now become evident, and I am more pleased with mentioning this matter in the *Vekayi-i Mısıriyye* explicitly and without hypocrisy (*riyasız*) than with the victories themselves."[152]

Still, it was only in 1838 that Mehmed Ali decided to get rid of the Ottoman suzerainty altogether and to ask for independence. For the seven-year period from the inauguration of hostilities and up to that

[147] S/5/51/2/5 on 24 N 1247/26 February 1832. See also S/5/51/2/2 and 3, both on 5 Ş 1247/9 January 1832, for other letters to a couple of officials in Istanbul asking them to mediate on his behalf with the Sultan.
[148] S/5/51/2/186 on 4 M 1248/3 June 1832.
[149] S/5/51/2/10 on 2 Ca 1248/27 September 1832.
[150] Sham 9/122, on 21 S 1248/20 July 1832.
[151] Sham 10/257, on 29 Ra 1248/26 August 1832.
[152] Sham 10/254, on 29 Ra 1248/26 August 1832.

time the Pasha was only claiming to be after reforming the Ottoman Empire.[153] This does not seem to have been a mere pretext on the part of the Pasha. He might not have believed in it entirely himself, but at the same time he could not think of himself as an outcast vali rebelling against the Ottoman Sultan; he needed to think of himself as doing something from *within* the Ottoman Empire and not *against* it.

This hesitation can only be explained by the Pasha's own ambivalent feelings toward the Ottoman Empire and his position within it. Rather than seeing himself as a leader of a province seeking independence from the Ottoman Empire, Mehmed Ali was only too aware of the fact that technically and legally he was still a vali appointed by the Ottoman Sultan in Istanbul to rule a province within the Empire. There are various signs that show that the Pasha did indeed take this aspect of his rule seriously and though he appears independent-minded, often taking decisions in his province without consulting his sovereign, this does not mean that he dismissed Ottoman authority altogether. For example, the annual firman of investiture re-appointing him in his pashalık was received in great pomp and splendor and a big celebration was held to read it aloud in the Citadel.[154] The Pasha himself was Turkish-speaking and as far as is known he never spoke Arabic (although it is difficult to believe that he did not understand it).[155] As a further example of his Ottoman character, when the canal joining Alexandria to the Nile was dug he decided to name it the Maḥmūdiyya, after Sultan Mahmud II.[156] The Pasha was also very well informed about developments in the Ottoman capital Istanbul. His agent in Istanbul, Najib Efendi, and other informers, updated him regularly about developments there and looked after his interests in the capital.[157] In his attempt to keep in touch with developments there as closely as possible he ordered Boghus Bey, his chief foreign advisor, to buy a brig that would be fast enough to transport mail swiftly to and from Istanbul.[158] To increase his influence in the capital he was in the habit of regularly sending "presents" to

153 For an exposition of this claim, see Sabry, *L'Empire égyptien*, pp. 152–5. For an opposing view, see Rustum, *Origins*, pp. 33–46.

154 See, for example, Sāmī, ed., *Taqwīm al-Nīl*, II, p. 284, firman for AH 1236/AD 1820–1, and S/1/47/2/280 on 27 L 1235/8 August 1820.

155 See his explicit order to have all letters dispatched to him to be written in Turkish and those that were written in Arabic to be accompanied by a Turkish translation; S/5/51/2/69 on 7 Za 1247/8 April 1832.

156 It was initially called the Ashrafiyya, after al-Sultan al-Ashraf Qaitbay, the Mamluk ruler of Egypt who re-dug it after centuries of neglect; S/1/47/1/81 on 29 Za 1233/30 September 1813. See also Sāmī, ed., *Taqwīm al-Nīl*, II, pp. 284–5.

157 See, for example, Bahr Barra 10/44, on 7 Ra 1241/20 October 1825, and Bahr Barra 11/26, on 21 R 1242/23 November 1826.

158 S/1/48/1/26 on 29 L 1238/9 July 1823.

various officials in the Ottoman government as well to members of the imperial family.[159] The Ottoman "sentiments" of the Pasha's rule and outlook is probably best shown in his ideas about culture and good manners. When he decided to educate his nephew, Ibrahim Yegen, in "good manners," it was not to London or to Paris that he sent him but to Istanbul.[160] His palaces, furthermore, were designed in an explicitly Ottoman style.[161] Similarly, the imperial- looking mosque that he built in Cairo and which dominates the city's skyline was also built in the Ottoman style. His culture and court etiquette were fashioned around his understanding of Ottoman models. In short, the Pasha's world was an Ottoman world; he understood things within that context and it made sense to him to view matters from that perspective.

The problem, however, was that the vali was too ambitious to be content with his position as a subservient vassal, and as time went on and as he grew stronger and stronger, he began to have aspirations of more independence from Istanbul. As is shown above, this inherent tension acquired momentum during the Greek debacle and surfaced in 1831 when he ordered his son to lead an expedition to invade Syria without the consent of the Sultan. Yet, as is shown above, he was still uncomfortable with his latest bold move and found it difficult to legitimate his shaky position. Given his outlook and background, it is only natural to expect him to hesitate when deciding to cast off the Ottoman garb altogether, not only because of the moral and religious issues involved in fighting the Muslim Sultan but also because by doing so he would seriously challenge the only world that he could associate with and felt, as it were, comfortable in.

Conclusion

This chapter opened with an account given by Mehmed Ali himself in 1825 expressing his intentions to spread his influence over neighboring provinces of the Ottoman Empire and to effectively create a mini-empire at the expense of that of the Sultan in Istanbul. The chapter

159 See, for example, S/1/50/4/492 and S/1/50/4/495, both on 22 Za 1239/20 August 1824. For presents received by the Valide Sultan, the Sultan's mother, see Bahr Barra 4/53, on 23 S 1231/ 14 January 1816. For presents received by the Sultan himself and rumors circulating about this in Istanbul see Bahr Barra 4/153, on 27 Z 1231/18 November 1816.

160 S/1/50/4/525 and 526, both on 14 M 1240/9 September 1824.

161 Janet Abu-Lughod, *Cairo: 1001 Years of the City Victorious* (Princeton: Princeton University Press, 1971), p. 94. Wilkinson says that his palaces were also influenced by European style; John G. Wilkinson, *Modern Egypt and Thebes* (London: John Murray, 1843), I, p. 243.

ended with events in 1833 that go a long way towards showing that the Pasha appears to have fulfilled his prophetic prediction made eight years earlier. Yet this chapter has argued that this apparently teleological progression of events hides considerable tensions, tensions that relate to the Pasha's own aims and aspirations and how to read them.

While acknowledging the fact that Mehmed Ali might have always harbored a strong desire to cast off Ottoman control and even to expand his areas of control beyond Egypt, he still thought this to be a dangerous course of action. It was dangerous not only because it invited the possibility of European hostility towards him, but also because he found it difficult to contemplate his rule outside Ottoman sovereignty altogether. Being declared a rebel weighed heavily on his soul and he found it difficult to imagine himself stripped of Ottoman legitimacy. What finally tipped the balance towards rebellion was the Greek war which the Sultan had asked him to intervene in, thinking that it would weaken his strong vassal. Instead, the Pasha used it as an opportunity to try out his new troops and by the end of it he came out more resolved than ever before not to co-operate with the Sultan in the future. As far as can be discerned from his own letters it does not appear that he had contemplated military action against the Sultan before that time.

Four years after withdrawing his troops from Morea his son marched on to Syria at the head of a mighty military machine and started a ten-year period of occupation of the Syrian provinces; during this time his forces clashed with those of the Ottomans four times, and in all of them he snatched spectacular victories. These military victories, however, were not translated into new legal realities. The peace of Kütahia reached at after the cessation of hostilities did not grant Mehmed Ali the independence he was supposedly fighting for. As has been shown above, the inconclusive nature of this verbal agreement was not due to British or European hostilities to Mehmed Ali's schemes or to their interference in Istanbul to prevent him from pressing his demands. Rather, it was a reflection of the Pasha's own confused and ambivalent feelings regarding his position within the Ottoman Empire and his inability to come to terms with the legal implications of his rebellious moves, *viz*, to be declared a rebel by the Ottoman Sultan and to have Ottoman legitimacy withdrawn from him.

Nevertheless, and on a pure military level, the fact remains that the victories his armies managed to accomplish on the battle front were swift, stunning and highly successful. One can argue that this impressive accomplishment was made possible by the relatively feeble government in Istanbul that was caught unawares and was not quick or flexible enough to face this challenge coming from unexpected quarters. Above all, however, it was made possible by relying on naked force. It was the modern army that Mehmed Ali started to build in 1820–1 that enabled him to expand his sphere of influence to cover such wide areas of the Ottoman Empire. How Mehmed Ali was able to create that army and have it trained, paid and supplied in a manner that made these successive victories possible is the story of the following chapters.

2 The birth of an army: conscription and resistance

During a visit to a local village market in Banī Suwayf in 1832, an English traveler described a scene of poor peasants, men and women, squatting, selling such humble products as water-jars, pots, pans and mats. Suddenly, he says,

> in the midst of these, as if to "shame the meanness" of their humble dress, we observed a number of cavalry officers, in their rich variegated costume, mounted on superb horse, galloping up the steep mounds, then down again, checking their fiery steeds in mid-gallop. Their principal commander, dressed in a magnificent scarlet cloak, embroidered dress, and costly shawl, with a fine horse and sabre, appeared from his luxuriant carroty mustachios, to be some German renegade.[1]

What is interesting about St. John's description of the descent of the new cavalry troops on this peaceful village is the way he brings together these two worlds, the civilian and the military. The appearance of the "rich, variegated costume" of the officers is contrasted sharply with the humbleness and simplicity of the peasants, their dress and their products. Juxtaposed in this manner, a great difference appears between the two worlds with the old setting suddenly looking traditional, backward and mediocre, and the new appearing as dynamic and vibrant. One finds very little connection between the humble peasants in their peaceful little village and the galloping cavalry officers in their magnificent scarlet cloaks and the only way they appear together in the same scene is by "imposing" one on top of the other.

In a similar way the career of Mehmed Ali during the first half of the nineteenth century in Egypt is usually described as the "superimposition" of badly needed reforms on the traditional, stagnant and backward Egyptian society. At center stage appears the solitary figure of Mehmed Ali as a sole reformer who was determined to "pull" Egypt out of her misery, and rarely are we given an explanation of how it was precisely

[1] St. John, *Egypt*, I, p. 217.

that this seemingly illiterate,[2] uninformed tobacco merchant who lived in a small town in northern Greece came to understand the importance of such things as modern medical science, the disciplining of troops and the new schooling system. "The founder of Modern Egypt," therefore, appears as a towering figure who is closer to a prophet than he is to an Ottoman reformer and whose failure lies in the unfortunate fact that he was ahead of his time and that his people did not understand him.[3] While acknowledging how important and impressive Mehmed Ali's military reforms were, most historical accounts of Mehmed Ali make little attempt to explain how these reforms were linked to developments in Egypt before he appeared on the scene, how they relate to other contemporary reforms, or, even, how Mehmed Ali himself came across such ideas. ʿAbdel-Raḥmān Zakī, the Egyptian military historian of Mehmed Ali's reign, for example, when describing the early stages of forming the modern army, alludes to nothing but the character of the Pasha. He says that from his arrival in Egypt as an officer in the Ottoman contingent that was sent to evict the French from the country Mehmed Ali had always harbored the idea of forming a "disciplined army which would be his tool for founding his new rule. From the day he was installed as a vali in Egypt he did his best to create a national army . . . He had to keep this idea as a secret, however, waiting for the opportune moment to put it into practice."[4]

There is no doubt that the creation of a modern standing army that was disciplined, well trained and regularly paid was the creation of the Pasha and that his close advisors did not receive the idea with much enthusiasm.[5] However, little is known about the origins of this idea and how it gradually developed in the Pasha's mind, or, indeed, how it was eventually made possible by the help and collaboration of his assistants and advisors.

It is the intention of this chapter to attempt to unravel the origins of the idea of founding a modern, disciplined army, and to suggest what

[2] It is fairly certain that Mehmed Ali did not learn to read and write until he was aged about fifty; accordingly his letters were dictated to scribes and written down on the spot (a fact that explains the very spontaneous and immediate nature of many of them), and the books with which he was familiar and to which he often referred had been read to him.

[3] Dodwell, *Founder of Modern Egypt*, pp. 240–1, Sabry, *L'Empire égyptien*, p. 580.

[4] Zakī, *al-Tārīkh al-Ḥarbī*, p. 158.

[5] When he informed Mahmud Bey, one of his closest advisors and later Director of the War Department (*Cihadiye Nazırı*) about his intention to create a modern army, he was so adamant in his rejection of the project and alarmed at its expected dangers that Mehmed Ali remembered the incident ten years later; S/1/48/3/161 on 1 Ra 1243/22 September 1827; see Rustum, ed., *Calendar*, I, pp. 95–7, doc. 232, for an Arabic translation.

influences might have prompted the Pasha to undertake this bold step. As such this chapter serves two purposes. First, having seen in the last chapter how Mehmed Ali succeeded in using his military force to capture his long-coveted province, Syria, this chapter and the following ones try to see how he managed to muster this military force in the first place. As said in the Introduction above, the story told here is not that of the great Pasha, his ambition or his designs; it is a story of an army and of the thousands of men from all over Egypt who served in it. The story therefore proceeds not chronologically following the Pasha waging one campaign after another, like most military history accounts do following great commanders in their glorious exploits. Rather, we follow a hypothetical soldier in the Pasha's army from the time he is conscripted, and we trace him to the training camp, then to the battle, and finally we watch him during the aftermath of the battle. This chapter starts the story and deals with the first of these processes, namely conscription; the following chapter will pick up where this one leaves our soldier and will deal with training. Subsequent chapters will proceed likewise.

Second, this chapter has another intention – that of explaining the connection between the army and the modern state that was created in Egypt in the first half of the nineteenth century. Specifically, it introduces a main theme that will be picked up later, namely, that of seeing how the army completely changed the nature of the Egyptian state and fundamentally transformed its relationship to the population of the country. Besides being an army that relied on conscription, the Pasha's army was novel in its reliance on the central government for its provisions and supplies. This was an army whose soldiers were issued uniforms designed, tailored and distributed from Cairo, and which had, among other things, an unprecedented medical establishment catering for it. It was an army that also depended on the central bureaucracy for its food, ammunition and supplies. Moreover, it was an army which triggered, through its reliance on conscription, considerable opposition from the population. In dealing with this opposition, the state resorted to various policing and surveillance practices and institutions that together changed the manner in which the state controlled society and altered the relationship that the population had with the government. It is the intention of this chapter to investigate this novel aspect of the army and to see how it was a crucial stimulus behind the formation of the modern state in Egypt.

First, though, what follows is a short survey of the early steps of founding this army and of how it came to rely so squarely on conscription.

Origins of the idea of a disciplined army

No one living at the turn of the nineteenth century could evade the effect of Napoleon and his armies that swept the entire European continent and the devastation and havoc that they caused in their wake. Being a military man himself and living on the fringes of this continent, Mehmed Ali must have been curious to know more about these armies that were the talk of the day. Indeed, the Pasha was a great admirer of the Emperor and even during his lifetime his flatterers used to "persuade him that he is a second Napoleon."[6] Later in his life he ordered a biography of Napoleon to be translated into Turkish and to be printed in the government press at Būlāq.[7]

Moreover, on his landing in Egypt in 1801 he had a chance to see Napoleon's army for himself. Although Napoleon had left Egypt two years earlier in search of greater glory in France, and although this act had a significant effect on the morale of his troops who stayed behind in the hostile lands of Egypt, it would be wrong to assume that the *Armée d'Orient* had completely disintegrated after the departure of its charismatic leader. Furthermore, in spite of the short period during which it stayed in the country, the French Army did make a noticeable impact on Egypt. Though they did not try to enlist the Egyptians at large into their *Armée d'Orient*, the French nevertheless did form a regiment of some 2,000 Copts who were trained by French officers, clad in French uniforms and attached to the French army. A number of mamluk youths were also drafted in the French army and were said to make very good soldiers. Furthermore, some Maghribi soldiers were also organized according to the French system and drilled along French lines with the words of command issued in French.[8]

Immediately after the departure of the French army from Egypt Husrev Pasha, the new Ottoman Vali (whom we have already seen in the previous chapter and who would later become Mehmed Ali's life-

[6] Scott, *Rambles in Egypt*, II, p. 113.

[7] S/1/48/4/241 on 25 B 1249/9 December 1833. The book was translated under the title of *Bonapart Tarihi* (Cairo: Būlāq, AH 1249/AD 1833–4). For a list of books printed by the Būlāq Press, see John Bowring, "Report on Egypt and Candia," *Parliamentary Papers, Reports from Commissioners*, 21 (1840), pp. 142–3; Richard N. Verdery, "The publications of the Bulaq Press under Muhammad ʿAli of Egypt," *Journal of the American Oriental Society* 91(1971), pp. 129–32. Mehmed Ali was also interested in Machiavelli, although he did not give the final approval for publishing an already finished MS of *The Prince* since, as he said, "it had nothing to teach us"; see Jamāl al-Dīn al-Shayyāl, *Tārīkh al-Tarjama wa'l-Ḥaraka al-Thaqāfiyya fī ʿAṣr Muḥammad ʿAlī* [History of Translation and the Cultural Movement During the Reign of Mehmed Ali] (Cairo, n.p., 1951), pp. 80–2.

[8] Athanase G. Politis, *L'Hellénisme et l'Egypte moderne* (Paris: Félix Alcan, 1929), I, p. 123.

long nemesis) set out to train some of the mamluk soldiers along French lines after enlisting in his service all those French officers who stayed behind when their army left Egypt. Husrev also formed a Sudanese regiment and trained it in the French style after tailoring for them "tight" French uniforms. These he formed into a private escort guard for himself, and he appointed an officer to "teach them the positions of the French."[9]

These attempts at borrowing from the French, crude as they were, must have struck Mehmed Ali when he first came to Egypt in 1801 and, as will be shown below, they influenced him when he tried to introduce new tactics and training drills to the Albanian troops that formed the backbone of his military force in the 1810s. When in the early 1820s he resorted to building a new army by gathering slaves from the Sudan and then by conscripting the fellahin of Egypt the Pasha came to depend heavily on French advisors to run his army and train his soldiers. Chief among these advisors was "Colonel" Sèves, more famously known as Süleyman Pasha, who was employed by Mehmed Ali in 1820[10] and who eventually became second-in-command of the army ranking only below Ibrahim Pasha. Furthermore, when Mehmed Ali wanted to establish a "strong and consistent order along which [his] soldiers [were] to be trained" he decided to ask the assistance of M. Drovetti, the French Consul-General, who suggested the name of General Boyer, a French officer who had previously been to Egypt among Napoleon's expedition.[11] In due course General Boyer arrived in Egypt at the head of a military mission which it was hoped would be able to "arrange the administration of [the Pasha's] new disciplined troops."[12]

It is therefore clear that the Pasha was informed about Napoleon's army and that he was influenced by it when he came to organize his own army. However, Mehmed Ali's fascination with western models of reform, and French ones in particular, seems to be overstated. As obvious as it is that he was borrowing from the French, it is clear that he was equally influenced by the Ottomans who themselves had been borrowing from the French and adopting their models to suit their own

9 al-Jabartī, *ʿAjāʾib al-Āthār*, III, p. 222 (events of Muḥarram, 1217).

10 S/1/47/3/82 on 29 S 1236/6 December 1820. It is doubtful that Sèves ever reached the rank of colonel; it is more likely that he was a captain before arriving in Egypt in 1819. He had served in Napoleon's army and witnessed both Waterloo and Trafalgar. After Napoleon's exile he sought employment in various armies and was about to go to Persia to serve with the Qajar Shah when he decided to stop on the way and work for Mehmed Ali instead; see D. A. Cameron, *Egypt in the Nineteenth Century* (London: Smith, Elder & Co., 1898), p. 131; al-Rāfʿī, *ʿAṣr Muḥammad ʿAlī*, p. 326.

11 S/1/48/1/32 on 27 Za 1238/16 August 1823.

12 FO 78/126, Salt, 10 October 1824. For an account of that mission see Douin, ed., *Mission militaire*.

needs. There is some evidence that suggest that the Pasha was familiar with contemporary Ottoman reform attempts especially in the military field[13] and that he was influenced by them in his attempts to create a modern army of his own.

Most important of these Ottoman attempts to create a disciplined army was Sultan Selim's new army, the *nizam-i cedid*. Selim's formation of the *nizam-i cedid* was a phenomenal act that caused much uproar in the capital and whose reputation far exceeded the boundaries of Istanbul and spread all over the Empire. So famous were the tactics that Selim introduced in his army that when in 1802 Husrev Pasha attempted to organize his troops in Egypt along modern lines with the assistance of some French officers, he gave them the Ottoman name, the *nizam-i cedid*.[14] Moreover, some of these new *nizami* troops of Sultan Selim had a chance to come to Egypt as part of the Ottoman forces that were sent by sea under the command of the Capitan Pasha to expel the French from the country.[15] An avid defender of the new *nizami* troops had this to say about the 4,000 troops that were sent as part of a larger Ottoman force:

> It ought to be generally known that, whilst many thousands of our undisciplined forces were unable to obtain the least advantage in the war they waged in Alexandria and Cairo against the reprobates of France, our gunners and regular infantry, although few in number, bravely combated the infidels and defeated them incessantly; and the flight of a single individual of that corps was never seen nor heard of.[16]

It is not known for certain if Mehmed Ali did see for himself the performance of these new troops of the Sultan, although it is unlikely that they would have gone unnoticed by him given the fact that he was in Egypt at the same time.[17] In any case, when he was devising an organizational structure for his army Mehmed Ali clearly preferred the one put down by Sultan Selim to that of Napoleon. In 1822 he

[13] For a review of these attempts in the eighteenth century see Avigdor Levy, "Military reform and the problem of centralization in the Ottoman Empire in the eighteenth century," *Middle Eastern Studies* 18 (1982), pp. 227–49, and Stanford J. Shaw, "The origins of Ottoman military reform," *Journal of Modern History* 37 (1965), pp. 291–306.

[14] See note 9 above.

[15] Shaw, *Between Old and New*, p. 135. For a British assessment of the performance of these newly trained troops see Piers Macksey, *British Victory in Egypt, 1801* (London: Routledge, 1995), p. 155.

[16] Mustafa Rashid Celebi Efendi, "An explanation of the Nizam-y-Gedid," in William Wilkinson, *An Account of the Principalities of Wallachia and Moldovia* (London: Longman, 1820), pp. 251–2.

[17] On the arrival and performance of these new *nizami* troops, see the contemporary account by a British foot soldier: Thomas Walsh, *Journal of the Late Campaign in Egypt* (London: Hansard, 1803), pp. 146–7.

commissioned Süleyman Ağa (Colonel Sèves), Osman Efendi Nureddin (whom he had earlier sent to France on an educational mission) and Ahmed Efendi Mühendis (who was translating military and naval books from French)[18] to draw up a plan for the organization of the army; it was turned down because it was blindly copying the structure of Napoleon's army. "Although the plan that Süleyman Ağa had put down is a wonderful one," Mehmed Ali told his son, Ibrahim Pasha, "it has been implemented by Napoleon to lead an army composed of several thousand troops. Our army, however, is a new one which we have only recently begun creating."[19] Two weeks later he ordered his son to have a meeting with the same officials who had drafted the original plan and ordered them to draft a new organizational scheme for the army which he explicitly said should be along the lines of Sultan Selim's army.[20]

These then were the influences on the Pasha's mind when he decided to form a disciplined army and it is clear from other reform attempts in the Ottoman Empire at large that his was not the only attempt at founding a modern, disciplined army, and that he was not as pioneering in this respect as he might appear if developments in Egypt are studied in isolation of the wider Ottoman context. Looking at the army he created at the end of his reign, however, one thing stands out as significantly different from other Ottoman military reform attempts, namely, adopting something close to universal conscription whereby masses of peasants were drafted in the new army. Yet again, in this respect the Pasha was being more pragmatic than radical. By following the steps he took in coming to this decision it becomes clear that he did not originally contemplate conscripting the fellahin of Egypt when he was thinking of founding his new army; rather he was pushed to taking this bold step only after he had run out of other alternatives.

Massacring the Mamluks

Before he undertook to train any troops along the new lines he was contemplating, however, the Pasha had to strengthen his own position as master of Egypt. This necessitated getting rid of the power of the Mamluks who had effectively been the warlords of the country for centuries. Learning from Sultan Selim's unfortunate experience in dealing with his own old guard, Mehmed Ali knew only too well that

[18] See his short autobiographical account at the end of *Kanunname-i Bahriye-i Cihadiye* [Naval Regulations] (Cairo: Būlāq, AH 1242/AD 1827), pp. 141–2.
[19] S/1/50/2/209 on 18 B 1237/11 April 1822.
[20] S/1/50/2/235 on 5 Ş 1237/28 April 1822.

Plate 3 "Massacre of the Mamluks"

any attempt to introduce modern tactics and training drills would have been met with staunch resistance on the part of the Mamluks who would rightly see in these new military techniques an attempt to abolish the old system which they had been monopolizing for centuries and to replace it by a new system in which their privileged positions would be seriously challenged.

After years of attempting to pacify them the Pasha finally decided to get rid of their influence by expediently killing their leaders. On 1 March, 1811 a festive ceremony was held in the Citadel to celebrate the appointment of his son, Tusun Pasha, to fight the Wahhabi rebels in Arabia. Mehmed Ali saw this as a golden opportunity to execute his deadly plan. He invited the heads of all the Mamluk households to attend the festive celebration and once they were on their way up a narrow alleyway leading to his court in the Citadel, he ordered his Albanian soldiers to open fire on them. Over four hundred and fifty of the Mamluk emirs were killed in that incident. This was followed by a ferocious pogrom against any Mamluk leaders who had succeeded in escaping the massacre in the Citadel. The Pasha's Albanian troops were allowed to enter the Mamluks' houses in Cairo plundering their property and raping their women. In the event around 1,000 Mamluk emirs and soldiers died in the city of Cairo alone during the few days that followed the massacre in the Citadel.[21] This was followed a year later by a military expedition led by Ibrahim Pasha to Upper Egypt to pursue those Mamluks who had succeeded in evading the massacre in Cairo, and another 1,000 were said to have been killed.[22]

This dramatic incident is invariably highlighted in nearly every book that deals with the Pasha's reign arguing, in effect, how he was thus successful in fulfilling a "dream that Egypt had had for seven centuries [sic]."[23] However, it is important to remember that even in this incident Mehmed Ali was not as pioneering as first appears, and that there had been earlier and very similar attempts by the Ottomans to get rid of the Mamluks. The last such attempt took place after Mehmed Ali had arrived in Egypt. On 22 October 1801 Hüseyin Pasha, the Grand Admiral of the Ottoman navy (who had arrived with the new *nizami* troops to assist the British in evicting the French from the country) invited the leading Mamluk emirs to a banquet on board his flagship and confronted them with an imperial invitation to go with him to Istanbul. Seeing the "invitation" for what it was, the emirs attempted to escape the ship and in the ensuing struggle a large number of them were killed and others were arrested only to be rescued later by the British and allowed to flee to upper Egypt.[24]

[21] al-Jabartī, *'Ajā'ib al-Āthār*, IV, pp. 127–32 (events of Ṣafar, 1226).
[22] FO 24/4 letter to Misset, 6 May 1813. Quoted in Dodwell, *Founder of Modern Egypt*, pp. 35–6.
[23] Ḥussayn Kafāfī, *Muḥammad 'Ali: Ru'ya li-Ḥādithat al-Qal'a* [Mehmed Ali: A View on the Citadel Incident] (Cairo: General Egyptian Book Organization, 1993), p. 166.
[24] al-Jabartī, *'Ajā'ib al-Āthār*, III, p. 201 (events of Jumādī al-Thānī, 1216); Shaw, *Between Old and New*, pp. 276–7; Macksey, *British Victory*, p. 232.

Disciplining the Albanians

Although it is argued that by employing these "Cromwellian measures [Mehmed Ali finally managed to become the] undisputed master in the country,"[25] he still had to contend with the unruly Albanian forces. These proved more difficult to deal with than the Mamluks mainly because the Pasha was an Albanian himself and it would not have been that expedient to kill his own soldiers. This was so not because this would have been judged unethical or immoral but because the Albanians continued to be the backbone of his strength for some time. Counting nearly as mercenaries within the larger Ottoman contingent that brought them to Egypt, however, they were not a very orderly body of troops and they often revolted in small uprisings in the streets of Cairo asking for their pay or to be returned home. They also retained their tribal structure and recognized Mehmed Ali only as a "first among equals," resisting any attempt by him to impose discipline on them.

In August 1815, however, the Pasha decided to impose order on the troops by force, and "to put their pay and expenses under an organized principle (*rabita ve nizam*)."[26] Influenced by a certain Ibrahim Ağa who had recently arrived from Istanbul,[27] the Pasha gathered his Albanian soldiers in Maydān al-Rumayla at the foot of the Citadel for target practice. For over three hours the soldiers fired their guns in "successive volleys making a thundery noise like the French." The following day it was rumored that the Pasha wanted to have a count of the soldiers and "to train them according to *al-nizām al-jadīd*, copying the positions of the French. He wanted them to put on tight clothes and to change their appearance (*ughayyir shaklahum*)."[28]

The attempt failed miserably. The soldiers reluctantly complied with the Pasha's orders on the first day only to conspire to kill him the following night. The Pasha was informed of the plot in time to escape the assassination attempt, and when the rebels knew that their conspiracy was foiled, they went on the rampage in the streets of Cairo looting and damaging a considerable amount of property and Mehmed Ali was able to pacify the merchants and the populace only by returning their stolen property or compensating them for the damages.[29]

25 Dodwell, *Founder of Modern Egypt*, p. 36.

26 Bahr Barra 4/149, on 30 N 1230/5 September 1815.

27 P. N. Hamont, *L'Egypte sous Méhémet-Ali* (Paris: Léauty et Lecointe, 1843), II, p. 4.

28 al-Jabartī, *'Ajā'ib al-Āthār*, IV, p. 222 (events of Sha'bān, 1230).

29 Dhawat 1/76, on 1 N 1230/7 August 1815; al-Jabartī, *'Ajā'ib al-Āthār*, IV, pp. 223–5; Felix Mengin, *Histoire de l'Egypte sous le gouvernement de Mohammed-Aly* (Paris: Arthus Bertrand, 1823), II, pp. 49–50; J. J. Halls, *The Life and Correspondence of Henry Salt* (London: Richard Bentley, 1834), I, p. 445.

Having failed in imposing order and discipline on them, he decided to get rid of them, not in the dramatic way of massacring them like the Mamluks, but by sending them to their deaths in the Arabian desert. When the Sultan ordered Mehmed Ali to fight the Wahhabis in Arabia he was reluctant to agree to comply with the imperial order considering the amount of time and money that would have gone into fulfilling it. However, he realized that this would be a golden opportunity to get rid of many troublesome groups, foremost among whom were the Albanians. During the seven-year conflict against the Wahhabis he sent wave after wave of them to face their destiny in the barren deserts of Arabia, thus effectively ridding himself of their nuisance.[30]

Enslaving the Sudanese

The ground was now prepared for the introduction of the new tactics. Initially the Pasha did not think of conscripting the fellahin of Egypt mainly because that would have meant moving productive labor from the agricultural sector which was the main source of revenue.[31] Instead, he had his eye on the Sudan to supply him with docile, obedient soldiers for his new army, and in the summer of 1820 the Pasha dispatched two expeditions to the Sudan, one under the command of his son, Ismail Pasha, and the other under Mehmed Bey Defterdar, his son-in-law. The two expeditions numbered ten thousand soldiers and were composed of Maghribi and Egyptian bedouins as well as a force of Turkish-speaking infantry and cavalry.[32]

As said above in chapter 1, the Sudan campaign had various purposes. The exploitation of the gold mines that were alleged to be in abundance there is one of them.[33] Another reason was the desire to catch the remnants of the Mamluk emirs who had taken refuge in Upper Egypt and then in Kurdufān.[34] So was the desire to control the Red Sea trade.[35] al-Rāfʿī characteristically alleged that it was aiming at "ensuring the security of Egypt and establishing its political unity with the Sudan."[36] Although there might be some truth in these allegations[37] the main reason for invading the Sudan as far as could be detected from the Pasha's own letters to his commanders was undoubtedly to capture

30 Heyworth-Dunne, *Education*, p. 111; al-Rāfʿī, *ʿAṣr Muḥammad ʿAlī*, pp. 121.
31 See note 74 below. 32 al-Rāfʿī, *ʿAṣr Muḥammad ʿAlī*, p. 160.
33 S/1/50/1/1 on 2 M 1236/10 October 1820; S/1/50/2/240 on 7 Ş 1237/29 April 1822.
34 S/1/50/1/20 on 25 M 1236/3 November 1820.
35 Dodwell, *Founder of Modern Egypt*, p. 50.
36 al-Rāfʿī, *ʿAṣr Muḥammad ʿAlī*, p. 157.
37 al-Jabartī mentions them all as possible reasons: al-Jabartī, *ʿAjāʾib al-Āthār*, IV, p. 305 (events of Muḥarram 1235).

as many of the inhabitants there as possible and send them to Egypt to form the soldiery of the new army that the Pasha intended to create. When Ismail Pasha wrote to Mehmed Ali informing him of the amount of taxes levied in the conquered areas, his father wrote back telling him to pay more attention to collecting men not money "since the reason for incurring all these expenses and undertaking all these troubles is not to collect money, as I have repeatedly written to you, but to raise men who would be suitable for our affairs."[38] In another letter he added that "the value of slaves who prove to be suitable for our services is more precious than jewels . . . hence I have ordered you to raise 6,000 of these slaves."[39]

No sooner had the two expeditions been dispatched, however, than they started to encounter serious problems. It was soon realized that the forces sent with Ismail Pasha and Mehmed Bey were insufficient to conquer and control the vast areas of the Sudan.[40] More Hawwāra bedouins were dispatched to Ismail Pasha to assist him in keeping order in Sinnār since "it is a vast country."[41] Eventually, the army's advance had to be halted to consolidate areas already conquered and to wait for more supplies and reinforcements from Egypt.[42]

Moreover, Ismail Pasha proved to be utterly incompetent in managing the army. He was inexperienced, indecisive, stubborn and uncharismatic. His father was constantly urging him to seek the advice of older men in his company.[43] Ismail, however, did not listen to his father's advice and eventually lost the confidence of his own men. An alarming number of his artillerymen deserted him at a time when he most needed them.[44] Furthermore, the whole province of Sinnār broke out in revolt as a result of the new taxes he was levying and the manner by which he was collecting them.[45] His brutality, rashness, and

38 S/1/50/2/325 on 1 Za 1237/20 July 1822.

39 S/1/50/2/340 on 19 Za 1237/8 August 1822. See also S/1/50/4/195 on 19 M 1239/26 September 1823.

40 S/1/50/1/19 on 25 M 1236/3 November 1820.

41 S/1/47/3/696 on 4 Z 1236/2 September 1821. On Mehmed Ali's policies towards the Hawwāra tribe, see Layla 'Abdel-Laṭīf Aḥmad, *Siyāsat Muḥhammad 'Alī Izā' al-'Urbān fī Miṣr* [Mehmed Ali's policy Towards the Bedouins in Egypt] (Cairo: Dār al-Kitāb al-Jāmi'ī, 1986), pp. 25–42.

42 S/1/50/2/23 on 3 S 1237/30 October 1821.

43 S/1/50/1/85 on 12 Ra 1236/18 December 1820. See also S/1/50/1/82 on 10 Ra 1236/16 December 1820; S/1/50/1/117 on 9 R 1236/14 January 1821 and S/1/50/1/172 on 19 B 1236/22 April 1821. These are all letters from Mehmed Ali to his son complaining about his style of leadership, specifically his indecisiveness. Ismail was twenty-five years old at that time.

44 S/1/47/2/480 on 16 Z 1235/24 September 1820; and S/1/47/2/510 on 18 Z 1235/26 September 1820.

45 Bahr Barra 19/21, on 1 B 1237/24 March 1822.

impetuous nature ultimately cost him his own life in a tragic incident: he was burnt alive during a banquet that Nemr, the King of Shindī, ostensibly held in his honor. This was in revenge for Ismail having previously humiliated him by slapping him on the face.[46]

As serious as Ismail's bad command was, the main problem facing the army was how to secure the transportation to Egypt of the slaves who had been rounded up. The first consignment of these unfortunate beings totaling 1,900 men, women and children arrived in Isna north of Aswan in August, 1821. Those who were suitable were selected for military service; the others were to be sold in slave markets in Cairo.[47] Later these slaves were sent to Aswan where a special barracks was built specifically for the purpose of receiving them.[48] However, a large number of the Sudanese slaves perished on the way before reaching the Aswan depot. Mehmed Bey Defterdar, Mehmed Ali's son-in-law, who assumed control of the campaign after the death of his brother-in-law, Ismail Pasha, wrote to Mehmed Ali in Egypt telling him that the slaves could not stand the trip they had to endure from Kurdufān to Ḥalfa to the south of Aswan and suggested that ships be built to transport the slaves down the Nile.[49]

The same problem was encountered when the slaves arrived in Egypt: a large number of them perished on the long march from Aswan to Cairo. Mehmed Ali soon ordered that they be transported by Nile boats,[50] and orders were issued to build forty such vessels every month.[51] He also ordered all the warehouses in Aswan and Manfalūṭ to be replenished and ready to feed the slaves that were arriving there in larger and larger numbers.[52] Moreover, he sent a senior official (Kasem Ağa, Governor of Qina) to supervise the whole process of transporting the slaves "without losses".[53]

It had earlier been realized that the army sent to the Sudan was much larger than the number of slaves captured, which defeated the purpose for which it was sent in the first place, and so it was decided that for every 1,000 men sent 3,000 slaves must be collected.[54] However, even this principle now did not make sense, since those who had been collected were in very poor health and were dying "like sheep with the

46 al-Rāf'ī, *'Aṣr Muḥammad 'Alī*, pp. 166–7.

47 S/1/47/3/647 on 14 Za 1236/14 August 1821.

48 Dhawat 5/78, on 12 M 1238/29 September 1822.

49 Bahr Barra 8/89, on 3 Ra 1238/18 November 1822.

50 S/1/50/2/14 on 27 M 1237/25 October 1821; S/1/47/4/106 on 28 M 1237/26 October 1821; S/1/50/2/361 on 9 Z 1237/27 August 1822.

51 S/1/50/2/283 on 9 L 1237/29 June 1822.

52 S/1/48/1/121, 122, and 123, all on 8 Ca 1239/9 January 1824.

53 S/1/48/1/183 on 19 C 1239/20 February 1824.

54 S/1/50/2/64 on 23 Ra 1237/19 December 1821.

rot."[55] In desperation Mehmed Ali wrote to Boghus Bey, his Armenian advisor on foreign affairs, ordering him to hire a number of American doctors to treat the slaves. These were preferred to European physicians since they had experience of dealing with "this race" (*bu tayfa*).[56]

Conscripting the Egyptians

It soon became obvious to the Pasha that something was going drastically wrong with his plans to raise an army of these Sudanese men. When, for example, he knew that out of 2,400 slaves arriving in Aswan only 1,245 managed to reach Cairo, he said "My wonder! We spend so much energy to fetch these slaves, healthy and capable of work, from remote areas only to perish in our midst and in front of our eyes!"[57] To add to his problems, the Turkish and Albanian soldiers that were sent to the Sudan were not accustomed to the weather there and soon fell victim to dysentery and other fevers.[58] The troops also started to grumble and to demand to be sent back to Egypt. It was then that the Pasha thought for the first time of conscripting the natives of Egypt in order to relieve his Turkish soldiers from this task. In a letter dated 18 February 1822 to the Governor of Jirja, Ahmed Pasha Tahir, he said

> It is obvious that we are sending troops under the command of our children to the Sudan so as to fetch us blacks to use in the affair of the Hijaz [campaign] and other similar services . . . However, since the Turks are members of our race, and since they must remain close to us all the time and should be saved from being sent to these remote areas, it has become necessary to gather a number of soldiers from Upper Egypt. We thus saw fit that you conscript around four thousand men from these provinces.[59]

This is the earliest decree by the Pasha ordering the conscription of the fellah population of Egypt to the army, and it is clear from it that nothing of the nature of the *levée en masse* was contemplated. Rather, the idea was to replace those Turkish soldiers who for one reason or another objected to being sent to the Sudan. The new conscripts were to be drafted only for three years at the end of which time they were to be given a stamped certificate and allowed to go back to their villages.[60]

For the time being, however, the slaves that were gathered from the Sudan continued to form the bulk of the soldiery. These Sudanese slaves together with the limited number of Egyptian fellahin who were

[55] Dodwell, *Founder of Modern Egypt*, p. 64.
[56] S/1/48/1/68 on 1 R 1239/5 December 1823.
[57] S/1/50/5/375 on 30 L 1239/27 June 1824.
[58] Dodwell, *Founder of Modern Egypt*, p. 51.
[59] S/1/50/2/145 on 25 Ca 1237/18 February 1822.
[60] *Ibid.*

conscripted from Upper Egypt were sent to a training camp in Aswan that was directed by Mehmed Bey Lazoğlu, the Pasha's trusted deputy.[61] At the same time the nucleus of the officer corps was being formed by training a number of mamluks of Mehmed Ali and Ibrahim Pasha in addition to a number of mamluks donated by key officials.[62] These mamluks were sent to Upper Egypt to be trained where two special schools were built for them, one in Aswan and the other in Farshūṭ slightly to the north of Aswan. As a rule Mehmed Ali's slaves were trained in the Aswan school, while Ibrahim Pasha's mamluks were trained in Farshūṭ.[63] In addition to these mamluks other young Turkish-speaking soldiers from the old army were sent to the Farshūṭ school for training, although the mamluks were given priority over them when it came to assigning the graduating cadets their new officer ranks.[64]

In an attempt to secure staff for the new schools the Pasha had already sent to his agent in Istanbul, Najib Efendi, asking him to despatch an engineer and two teachers fluent in both Turkish and French.[65] The principal teacher, however, was to be Sèves who was also responsible for supervising the training of both the cadets and the soldiers. Specifically, he was to co-ordinate the activities of the various schools so as to form new battalions from the recently trained soldiers to be headed by the new cadets.[66]

While both the officers and soldiers were being trained consultation was going on among top officials to devise an organizational structure for the new army.[67] People involved in these consultations were Ibrahim Pasha, Süleyman Ağa (Sèves), Ahmed Pasha Tahir (Governor of Jirja), Mehmed Bey Lazoğlu (head of the military school established in Aswan, and later to be appointed as Director of the War Department)

[61] Sāmī, ed., *Taqwīm al-Nīl*, II, p. 294, letter dated 2 Ca 1237/26 January 1822. Lazoğlu was later appointed as Director of the War Department; John Wilkinson, *Modern Egypt*, II, pp. 534–5.

[62] al-Rāfʿī, *ʿAṣr Muḥammad ʿAlī*, p. 327. For the training of Ismail Pasha's mamluks, see S/1/48/1/195 on 29 C 1239/1 March 1824; and S/1/48/1/215 on 19 B 1239/20 March 1824. Although all mamluks were technically slaves, there were sharp differences among them. The leaders of the households are referred to as "Mamluks," and it was these who were the target of the massacre of 1811. Their followers who later joined Mehmed Ali's service as well as other white slaves who were bought by him and by other dignitaries are referred to as "mamluks."

[63] S/1/50/2/210 on 18 B 1237/11 April 1822. Douin says that the Pasha's personal mamluks that were sent to Aswan numbered between 300 and 400; Douin, ed., *Mission militaire*, p. xiii. al-Rāfʿī puts the total number of cadets at around 1,000; al-Rāfʿī, *ʿAṣr Muḥammad ʿAlī*, p. 327.

[64] S/1/50/2/377 on 13 M 1238/30 September 1822.

[65] Sāmī, ed., *Taqwīm al-Nīl*, II, p. 288, letter dated 5 Ra 1236/12 December 1820.

[66] S/1/50/2/122 on 14 Ca 1237/9 February 1822.

[67] See, for example, S/1/50/2/258 on 25 Ş 1237/18 May 1822; and S/1/50/2/260 on 26 Ş 1237/19 May 1822.

and, of course, Mehmed Ali himself. At issue were the following points: the size and internal division of the regiments, the ratio of officers to soldiers, and the ethnic composition of the officer corps, in addition to the pay of the different ranks.

The consultations reflect a big degree of flexibility and pragmatism and decisions were often taken only to be repealed after discovering that in application they proved to be faulty. Mention had been made, for example, of adopting Sultan Selim's model rather than Napoleon's because it was seen as more appropriate to a small army which was still in its formative phase. Similarly, the names of the military ranks used in Sultan Selim's army were changed since they were unfamiliar to the cadets. Moreover, although according to an initial plan it was possible to promote *evlad-ı Arab*, (lit. sons of Arabs, i.e. Arabic-speaking Egyptians) to the rank of *Binbaşı Mülazimi*, Mehmed Ali insisted that no fellahin should be promoted beyond the rank of *bölükbaşı* "commanding twenty-five soldiers."[68]

Furthermore, during this early training of the new troops a number of problems were spotted and action was taken to remedy them. For example, Ibrahim Pasha wrote to his father that some of the exercises looked good on paper but turned out to be inconsistent and self-contradictory in practice. In addition, it proved difficult to instill in the new cadets the idea of military hierarchy and some of the younger officers had still not got the habit of obeying their senior officers. On investigating the reasons behind some of the early cases of desertion of soldiers, it was discovered that it was caused more by "following their own whims" and not standing their officers' punishment rather than by their low pay. He, nevertheless, suggested that the salaries of the soldiers and of the NCOs be raised, the private's to 18 piasters, the corporal's to 25 piasters, the sergeant's to 30 piasters, and the sergeant-major's to 40 piasters. Mehmed Ali approved all of these recommendations suggested by Ibrahim except the one concerning the increase in the soldiers' pay. He added, however, that if he, i.e. Ibrahim, had already announced to the soldiers that their pay was going to be increased, then he should not go back on his word. He explained that he would have preferred the officers, not the soldiers, to get this pay rise.[69]

By working closely together, both father and son managed to come up with solutions to most questions that were raised. The size of the

[68] S/1/50/2/209 on 18 B 1237/11 April 1822. The names of these ranks were eventually changed. However, according to the old Ottoman terminology, a *bölükbaşı* was equivalent to a corporal; Stanford Shaw, "The established Ottoman army corps under Sultan Selim III (1789–1807)," *Der Islam* 40 (1965), p. 145. For the limit to which the *evlad-ı Arab* could be promoted, see chapter 6 below.

[69] S/1/50/4/86 on 30 Ş 1238/11 May 1823.

regiment (*alay*), for example, was initially fixed at 4,000 troops divided into five battalions (*orta*) with 800 men per battalion.[70] It was later decided that the regiment should be composed of four instead of five battalions, each containing 816 men with their officers thus bringing down the number of officers and soldiers per regiment to 3,264 men. It was also decided upon the names to be given to the different ranks.[71]

Formation of the first regiments

After settling these questions pertaining to the structural organization of the army and the composition of the officer corps Mehmed Ali still had one major problem to contend with, namely, the performance of the Sudanese troops. The Sudan campaign had so far yielded mixed results. While Ismail Pasha, and later Mehmed Bey Defterdar, were able to gather a significant number of slaves and send them to Egypt, a lot of them either perished on the way or proved incapable of bearing arms.[72] Out of 20,000 slaves gathered between 1820 and 1824 only 3,000 remained alive in 1824.[73] Moreover, the campaign itself was facing significant problems and had cost the Pasha a lot of money and one of his sons.

As the option of training his Albanian soldiers had failed, the alternative was to depend totally on the Egyptian fellahin and go beyond the 4,000 troops that he had conscripted early in 1822. As was shown above, these peasants were to be conscripted only for three years after which time they would be returned to their villages. Moreover, the main purpose of conscripting them was to relieve the Turkish soldiers in the Sudan from the main task of gathering Sudanese slaves. Any attempt at gathering more Egyptian fellahin carried with it the danger of moving significant numbers of laborers out of the agricultural sector.[74] Moreover, the Egyptian fellahin had not been used to military service and

70 S/1/50/4/84 on 29 Ş 1238/10 May 1823.

71 Heyworth-Dunne says (*Education*, p. 114) that the regiment was composed of five battalions with 800 soldiers each. See, however, the organizational chart put before the letters of the first page of the register S/1/48/1 which clearly shows the regiment composed of four and not five battalions. The chart is not dated but the first letter in the register is dated 13 N 1238/25 May 1823. See also S/1/48/1/152 on 24 Ca 1239/27 January 1824. For the names and salaries of each of the different ranks, see Douin, ed., *Boislecomte*, p. 114.

72 Zakī, *al-Tārīkh al-Ḥarbī*, p. 160.

73 FO 78/126, Salt, 8 February 1824.

74 There are various letters from the Pasha that show that this was a prime concern of his; see, for example, his letter of 23 June 1823 in which he was referring to the initial conscription order on Lower Egypt when it was decided that Buḥhaira province be exempted from conscription to allow it to grow the rice needed for the army, S/1/47/131 on 6 Za 1240/23 June 1823.

during Ottoman rule were, *de jure*, forbidden to bear arms.[75] Nevertheless, the Pasha had no other option and was determined to try things out. In a frank letter to Ibrahim he referred to the problems he might encounter if he decided to conscript more peasants. He said that although European governments were conscripting their own peasants

> the people of Egypt are not as accustomed to military service as the people of Europe. Moreover, our government is not as strong as theirs. This being the case . . . we have to accommodate our needs to our capabilities and . . . to advance one step at a time putting things right as we go along. We also have to be realistic and remedy our deficiencies as time goes by.[76]

Having made up his mind to rely on the peasants of Egypt, conscription waves spread throughout the country and less than a year later 30,000 troops were already being trained in a new camp that was established in Banī ʿAdī near Manfalūṭ in Middle Egypt.[77]

Testing the new troops

In the meantime, however, ten battalions of 800 men each were formed in the camps in Aswan and Farshūṭ. These were made up of the Sudanese slaves in addition to the Egyptian fellahin who were initially conscripted from villages in Upper Egypt.[78] On hearing that a new Wahhabi revolt had occurred in ʿAsīr in the south of Hijaz, Mehmed Ali decided that it was time to try out his new troops. In July 1823 he wrote to Ibrahim Pasha telling him to form a regiment out of the newly formed battalions and to dispatch it immediately to Arabia even if the soldiers had not yet finished their proper courses of training.[79] A certain Mehmed Bey was appointed in command of this force and was ordered to receive his orders from Ahmed Pasha Yeğen, Mehmed Ali's nephew, who was then governor of Mecca.[80] In addition, Mehmed Ali decided to form two more regiments out of the newly trained troops and to dispatch them to help the forces already in the Sudan.[81]

[75] Heyd says that during Ottoman rule Egyptians found possessing arms were punished by death; Uriel Heyd, *Studies in Old Ottoman Criminal Law* (Oxford: Oxford University Press, 1976), p. 261. According to Toledano Arabic-speaking Egyptians were still legally barred from carrying weapons during the reigns of Abbas and Said; Toledano, *State and Society*, pp. 163–6.

[76] S/1/48/1/20 on 8 L 1238/19 June 1823.

[77] Driault, *Empire*, p. 299.

[78] *Ibid.*, p. 285.

[79] S/1/48/1/34 on 2 Z 1238/11 July 1823.

[80] S/1/48/1/39 and 40 both on 18 Z 1238/26 August 1823.

[81] S/1/50/4/255 on 4 Ra 1239/8 November 1823. In the event, and because of the Sultan's appointment of Mehmed Ali to deal with the Morean revolt, only one regiment, under the command of Osman Bey, was sent; S/1/48/1/70 on 1 R 1239/5 December 1823. Osman Bey eventually became governor of Sudan after taking over from Mehmed Bey Defterdar. He died in Khartoum and was buried there in May 1825; ʿAbdel-Raḥmān

In November 1823, while waiting for news of these new troops to arrive, the Pasha went to Banī ʿAdī to oversee the process of training himself. He invited both the British and French Consuls-General to accompany him to the camp.[82] The results were more than satisfactory and the new troops made a great spectacle that the Pasha was certainly pleased to watch. Both Consuls, moreover, were greatly impressed by the new troops. Drovetti, the French Consul-General, said that they had "reached such a degree of precision that gives honor to the French officers who were in charge of training them."[83] "Pride, pomp and circumstances of glorious war," wrote Salt, the British Consul-General. "Every other day," he adds, the Pasha "has a grand Review and four regiments are exercised in the plain [to the west of the camp] not as an ordinary Review but as a 'petite guerre' and it really is astonishing the figure they make."[84] While staying in the camp, the Pasha decided to invite various provincial governors from different parts of Egypt, ostensibly to report to him about the problems of conscripting soldiers as well as other administrative and financial matters.[85] Having seen how impressive the new troops looked, the Pasha also wanted to impress his governors with his assembled troops so that "a true report of them might circulate through the country."[86]

While the Pasha was still in Manfalūṭ news arrived of an impressive victory that his new troops had won against the Wahhabi rebels in ʿAsīr: a contingent of only 2,500 Egyptian infantry soldiers had succeeded in defeating a Wahabbi force ten times its size.[87] It had become obvious that no matter how semi-trained these troops might have been, even the ferocious Wahhabis were no match for them. A short while later the new *nizami* troops had another chance to prove themselves to the Pasha. On 22 March 1824 a big explosion took place in a powder magazine inside the Citadel in which more than 4,000 people were killed. There were rumors that the explosion was caused by some of the old troops of Albanians and mamluks who were not pleased at the Pasha's introduction of the *nizami* troops. This posed a grave danger to the Pasha whose position was being compared to that of Sultan Selim when he attempted to get rid of the Janissaries seventeen years before.[88] A single

Zakī, "The governors of the Sudan," *al-Majalla al-Tārīkhiyya al-Miṣriyya* 1 (1948), p. 429.

82 Driault, ed., *Empire*, p. 296.

83 *Ibid.*, pp. 299–300.

84 FO 78/126, Salt, 20 January 1824.

85 S/1/48/1/95 on 18 R 1239/23 December 1823; and S/1/48/1/147 on 20 Ca 1239/ 23 January 1824.

86 FO 78/126, Salt, 20 January 1824.

87 S/1/50/4/327 on 14 B 1239/15 March 1824; and Driault, ed., *L'Expédition*, p. 10.

88 From Drovetti to Chateaubriand, 30 March 1824, in Driault, ed., *L'Expédition*, pp. 11–12.

battalion of the new troops, however, rushed to the scene, isolated the powder magazine, and quickly brought the situation under control.[89]

The following month, i.e. April 1824, the new troops had yet another chance to show how loyal, disciplined and reliable they were. A big revolt erupted in Upper Egypt against the Pasha's conscription and tax policies. Over 30,000 men and women joined this rebellion which was headed by a certain Shaykh Raḍwān who claimed himself to be the *mahdi* and declared Mehmed Ali to be an infidel. In various incidents the local population marched to the residences of local governors and took them prisoner.[90] The rebellion seemed to be very serious and was starting to spread to neighboring provinces in Middle Egypt where conscription had already been applied earlier in the year. The authorities attempted to subdue the rebellion using various means of intimidation and terror[91] but when such measures proved ineffectual and the rebellion showed no signs of abating, it was finally decided to send some of the newly trained troops to fight the rebels. This was a serious decision, indeed, since most of the soldiers at that time were conscripted from villages in Upper Egypt, the same provinces to which they were being sent to quell the uprising. Initially, the troops met fierce resistance from the villagers and some officers were attacked and killed.[92] There were even rumors that the rebellion spread to the army itself and that some 700 of the soldiers joined the rebels. The Pasha ordered an immediate investigation warning the culprits that they would be executed. In the event, forty-five officers were shot in front of their soldiers.[93]

Eventually the rebellion was brought down by Osman Bey, the colonel of the first regiment, which was on its way to the Sudan. Heading a force of 500 cavalrymen and 3,000 infantrymen of the newly trained troops, he attacked the center of the rebellion near Qina where the "lunatic Raḍwān" was hiding. The shaykh fled to the desert and arrest warrants were issued to all provinces to catch him. In two weeks' time the rebellion was completely put down with more than 4,000 people killed.[94]

This was the clearest proof yet of the loyalty of the new troops and the Pasha was greatly impressed by them knowing that they did not hesitate to fight the rebels who were sometimes their own neighbors or

[89] *Ibid.* [90] S/1/48/1/236 on 7 Ş 1239/7 April 1824.
[91] S/1/47/7/306 on 13 Ş 1239/14 April 1824.
[92] S/1/48/1/239 on 8 Ş 1239/8 April 1824.
[93] S/1/47/7/331 on 2 N 1239/1 May 1824.
[94] S/1/48/1/236 on 7 Ş 1239/7 April 1824; S/1/48/1/242 on 13 Ş 1239/13 April 1824; S/1/48/1/255 on 25 Ş 1239/24 April 1824; FO 78/126, Salt, 28 April 1824; and FO 78/126, Salt, 18 May 1824.

relatives.[95] In one incident it was reported that one of the sergeants of Osman Bey's regiment, when attacking a certain village found his own father among the rebels, and failing to convince him to give in peacefully, proceeded to kill him. On being informed of this incident Mehmed Ali wrote to the Director of the War Department, Mehmed Bey Lazoğlu, praising the soldier and promoting him to the rank of lieutenant.[96]

All these spectacular accomplishments of the new troops "completely hypnotized Muhammad Ali and he now set the machinery going for the development of his fighting services on as large scale as possible."[97] Seeing how difficult it was to transport the Sudanese slaves and how miserably they fared once they arrived, and having tested his fellah troops on more than one occasion, Mehmed Ali eventually put aside any hesitations he might have had regarding the conscription of the fellahin, and from that time onwards conscription waves francticallly followed each other so that by the mid-1830s the number of conscripts had already reached 130,000.[98] Given a population figure of around five million[99] this means that the army made up 2.6 percent of the population, a high percentage, indeed, and one that caused significant disruption to family and village life.[100]

As large as this figure might seem, the importance of conscripting the fellahin into Mehmed Ali's army does not only lie in its size. Given the Pasha's imperial designs on Syria and his effective, albeit reluctant, assistance to the Sultan in his wars in Arabia and Greece, his reign cannot be viewed in isolation of conscription; as such, it was a cornerstone of his regime and his survival depended on it. Moreover, conscription, like corvée, was an important link between Mehmed Ali and his government

95 S/1/48/1/277 on 15 N 1239/15 May 1824.

96 S/1/48/1/253 on 25 Ş 1239/25 April 1824. In the same letter he said that the new troops had an impressive impact on those who had witnessed or heard about them.

97 Heyworth-Dunne, *Education*, p. 114.

98 This is the figure cited by most contemporary observers; Clot Bey: 130,300 (Clot Bey, *Aperçu*, II, p. 232); Dr. Bowring: 127,150 (Bowring, "Report on Egypt," p. 51); Barker: 125,143 (FO 78/231, 18 February 1833); al-Rāfʿī: 130,202 (al-Rāfʿī, *ʿAṣr Muhammad ʿAlī*, p. 358). St. John arrives at the figure 193,932 only by including the bedouin irregulars, the workmen in the Liman of Alexandria and the students in the military schools (St. John, *Egypt*, II, pp. 478–9).

99 This is the figure that Panzac arrives at; Daniel Panzac, "The population of Egypt in the nineteenth century," *Asian and African Studies* 21 (1987), pp. 11–32. For earlier estimates see G. Baer, "Urbanization in Egypt, 1820–1907," in W. R. Polk and R. L. Chambers, eds., *Beginnings of Modernization in the Middle East* (Chicago: University of Chicago Press, 1968), pp. 155–69; J. McCarthy, "Nineteenth century Egyptian population," *Middle Eastern Studies* 3 (1976), pp. 1–39; and Rivlin, *Agricultural Policy*, Appendix VI.

100 Rivlin arrives at 4% by estimating the population at 2,500,000 in the 1830s which appears to be far too low; Rivlin, *Agricultural Policy*, p. 211.

machinery, on the one hand, and the peasant population of Egypt, on the other. As will be shown below, conscription and the population's reaction to it ushered in a new relationship between the government and the governed. Gone were the days when an Ottoman vali or a Mamluk emir could issue an order or declare a wish and be practically ignored, cannily evaded, or met by cold indifference and a calculated lack of interest on the part of the population. Conscription was to transform the face of Egyptian society and to drastically alter the relationship between the government and the populace.

Given the singular importance of conscription for Mehmed Ali's regime, the remainder of this chapter describes the methods employed by the authorities to gather men from their villages and attempts to trace how this policy developed over time. No accurate account of conscription will be complete without incorporating the population's reaction to it; the remainder of this chapter therefore attempts to describe how the fellahin dealt with this novel and often brutal encroachment of the state on their lives. In doing so the aim is to draw attention to the fact that conscription and the military institution in general were to transform the nature of the government in Cairo drastically by introducing new techniques of control and surveillance that had not been tried in Egypt before.

Conscription methods

As was said above, the first attempt at conscripting the Egyptian fellahin stemmed from the desire to relieve the Turkish soldiers in Mehmed Ali's pay from serving in the remote and hot lands of the Sudan. The 4,000 peasants who were gathered from villages in Upper Egypt to replace them were to be conscripted for only three years at the end of which they would each be given a stamped certificate and allowed to return to their villages and resume their normal, civilian lives. The conscripts would also be exempted from the head tax (*firda*) and other financial liabilities that the fellah population was subjected to. More importantly, these early conscripts were to be collected not by the village shaykh, but by a conscripting officer sent from Cairo for that purpose. The shaykh was only to assist him in finding men in his village who were suitable for military service. The conscript had to be from the same village from which he was drawn and not "from those who roam around from one village to the other . . . His name has to be registered in a special register (*defter*), together with the name of his village, his father's name, and their titles."[101]

[101] S/1/50/2/145 on 25 Ca 1237/18 February 1822.

In issuing the conscripting officers their orders Mehmed Ali tried to impress upon them that they had to handle this important task delicately. He wrote to Ibrahim Pasha telling him that he had been informed that the conscripting officers were gathering men from the villages in the same manner as collecting men for corvée. He told him that this method had to be stopped at once.

> Since the fellahin are not used to military service, [he explained], they should not be dragged into the army by force. We have to attract their minds to it . . . This can be done by employing some preachers who should convince the fellahin that [serving in the army] is not like corvée . . . Alternatively, we can remind them of how easy it was for the French [while they were in Egypt] to collect Copts to serve in their army owing to their eagerness to serve their faith. If that was the case with the Copts, it will certainly be more so with the fellahin whose hearts have been enflamed by their piety and their zeal in defending Islam.[102]

This was wishful thinking on the part of the Pasha. In fulfilling their duties, the conscripting officers encountered problems that were much more serious than could be solved simply by appointing preachers to attract the minds of the fellahin to military service. In addition to lacking any detailed information about the population, the authorities also did not as yet have a reliable medical system to screen the conscripted. This is something that had to wait till 1830 after Clot Bey had managed to create the Abū Za'bal medical school (later to be moved to Qaṣr al-'Ainī) and to use its graduates to examine the conscripts.[103] Moreover, unlike the recruiting officers of the French Revolutionary and Napoleonic armies,[104] for example, the officers sent from Cairo to conscript the fellahin had no guidelines with regards to the age, marital status or number of brothers of the men they should conscript. Lacking this vital information, the conscripting officers, on receiving their orders, would descend upon any given village and seize as many men as could be found "without any order, arrangement, inscription, or lot-drawing."[105] These men would then be tied together with ropes around their necks in groups of six or eight.[106] They would

102 S/1/50/2/186 on 6 B 1237/29 March 1822.

103 Moḥammad F. Shukrī, "Ba'tha 'askariyya Būlūniyya fī Miṣr fī 'ahd Muḥammad 'Alī" [A Polish military mission during Mehmed Ali's reign,] *Majallat Kulliyyat al-Ādāb, Fouad I University* 8 (1946), p. 29.

104 Isser Woloch, "Napoleonic conscription: state power and civil society," *Past and Present,* 111 (1986), pp. 102–5; and Alan Forrest, *Conscripts and Deserters: The Army and French Society During the Revolution and Empire* (Oxford: Oxford University Press, 1989), pp. 27, 47.

105 Bowring, "Report on Egypt," p. 52.

106 Jules Planat, *Histoire de la régénération de l'Egypte* (Paris, 1830), pp. 76–7.

then be marched off to the training camps escorted by the "conscription gang," leaving behind a "heart-stricken, sorrowful group" of wives, mothers and children wailing and screaming and hopelessly trying to prevent the soldiers from taking away their men.[107]

All attempts to persuade the fellahin that serving in the army was a religious duty and that being drafted was not like corvée labor fell on completely deaf ears. Even before the Pasha had turned against the Ottoman Sultan, the call to arms in defense of the faith, against the Persians,[108] the Russians or the Greeks,[109] was a completely alien and meaningless call with little or no emotional appeal. "A recruiting party with all the allurements of drums, ribbons, and promises, might march from Rosetta to Assouan without picking up a single volunteer . . ."[110] Anxious about the lot of their families left behind and the land that would necessarily lie fallow, the peasants found little incentive to join the colors, and given the illogical, "most arbitrary and unsparing" method of conscription,[111] they attempted to resist it through all means possible.

Resistance to conscription

It is here that we come to the nub of the problem facing Mehmed Ali and his military authorities: the Pasha never succeeded in inducing the fellahin to join the colors out of their free will by employing ideological or religious arguments. Soon after the new conscription policy had become known in the countryside the fellahin employed different methods to escape the Pasha's men who were sent to press them into service. One such method was open rebellion and at least two such rebellions are known to have occurred and to have been directly connected to the Pasha's conscription policy. Mention has already been made of the big revolt in Upper Egypt in 1824 in which 30,000 people rebelled against Mehmed Ali's authorities, attacked the officials sent from Cairo, and refused to pay taxes.[112] Earlier, in May 1823, immediately after conscription had been introduced in Lower Egypt, a smaller yet significant uprising erupted in the province of Minūfiyya and

107 St. John, *Egypt*, II, p. 277. See also Hamont, *L'Egypte*, II, p. 12.

108 Mehmed Ali thought that the Sultan was going to ask him to send forces to help the Imperial army in its fight against the Persians; see, S/1/50/2/217 on 22 B 1237/15 April 1822; Driault, ed., *Empire*, p. 286; Cattaui, ed., *Mohamed Aly*, I, p. 45.

109 S/1/50/2/217 on 22 B 1237/15 April 1822.

110 Scott, *Rambles in Egypt*, II, p. 219.

111 *Ibid.*, p. 216.

112 S/1/48/1/254 on 25 Ş 1239/25 April 1824.

to quell it Mehmed Ali had to go there in person armed with his palace guards and six field cannons.[113]

Besides open revolt another tactic the fellahin often used was to desert their villages altogether to avoid being taken into the army. As soon as news of the approach of the recruiting party reached a village, "– and it spread over the country like wildfire –"[114] a wave of desertion followed with masses of families fleeing their homes and villages desperately trying to evade the conscription gangs. By the late 1830s this practice was so widespread that entire villages were found completely abandoned leaving behind sad, deplorable villages "buried in their stillness . . . where the dwellings of the poor inhabitants . . . still standing, neither blackened by fire, nor destroyed by war, nor decayed by time, but deprived of their inhabitants [who attempted to avoid the agents of the Pasha] by giving up house and home, and deserting, *en masse*, the devoted town or village."[115] Naturally this could not be tolerated by the authorities for, besides evading conscription, the fugitives would thus leave their land fallow and unattended. One of the duties of the bedouins who were in the Pasha's service was to catch any peasant who might desert his village with his family in an attempt to evade conscription.[116] Ultimately, however, it was with the village shaykhs that responsibility effectively lay in detecting and catching such village absconders (*mütesehhip*s).[117] Even when it happened that a fellah left his village for Cairo where he hoped that he would be relatively more anonymous and thus more difficult to catch, orders were sent to shaykhs of *al-ḥāra* [residential quarters] to find the strangers and send them back to "develop" their villages (*imarlık için*).[118]

Controlling the absconders, however, proved to be more difficult than initially imagined. A large number of the village shaykhs connived with the peasants instead of handing them to the authorities, and in some cases the shaykhs were accepting bribes from the fugitives in order not

113 S/1/50/4/64 on 21 Ş 1238/4 May 1823; S/1/47/5/57 on 26 Ş 1238/9 May 1823; Driault, ed., *Empire*, p. 286; Cattaui, ed., *Mohamed Aly*, I, p. 45; Rivlin, *Agricultural Policy*, p. 201.

114 St. John, *Egypt*, I, p. 189.

115 Madden, *Egypt*, pp. 41–2.

116 FO 78/184, Barker, 7 July 1829.

117 Zayn al-ʿĀbedīn S. Najm, "Tasaḥḥub al-fallāḥīn fī ʿaṣr Muḥammad ʿAli: Asbābuhu wa natāʾijuhu" [The absconding of the peasants in Mehmed Ali's reign: Its causes and effects], *al-Majalla al-Tārīkhiyya al-Miṣriyya* 36 (1989), pp. 259–316; ʿAbdallah M. ʿAzabāwī, *ʿUmad wa Mashāyikh al-Qurā wa Dawruhum fī al-Mujtamaʿ al-Miṣrī fī al-Qarn al-Tāsiʿ ʿAshr* [Village Mayors and Shaykhs and Their Role in Egyptian Society During the Nineteenth Century] (Cairo: Dār al-Kitāb al-Jāmiʿī, 1984), pp. 46–8; Rivlin, *Agricultural Policy*, p. 95.

118 Divan-ı Hidiv 1/102, on 28 Z 1243/12 June 1828; see also *Vekayi-i Mısıriyye* on 23 Ra 1246/12 September 1830; Bowring, "Report on Egypt," p. 121; Rivlin, *Agricultural Policy*, pp. 104–5.

to turn them in. Article 36 of *Qānūn al-Filāḥa* which was passed in early 1830 stipulated that any such shaykh, if found guilty, would receive 200 stripes of the whip (*kurbāj*).[119] To a lesser extent the task of catching the village absconders, i.e. those peasants who deserted their villages to avoid conscription or any of the other government demands, was one of the responsibilities of the directors of departments (the *nāẓir*s of the *qism*s). This was particularly the case when the fugitives were found in a department which originally they did not come from.[120] It appears, however, that even the *nāẓir*s were not fulfilling this task properly and some of them would not report on the fugitives found in their departments. In the case of a *nāẓir* being found to harbor fugitives in his department it was decided that he would receive 100 stripes of the bastinado as well as being imprisoned for life in Abū Qīr.[121] In spite of all these regulations to curb the desertion of the peasants from their villages, the phenomenon continued and the village shaykhs on whom the responsibility of catching fugitives squarely rested proved unreliable. Their role was thus reduced to simply reporting the presence of the fugitives rather than capturing them. Article 118 of *al-Qānūn al-Muntakhab* passed in February 1844 stipulated that the village shaykhs should search for the fugitives in their villages and instead of catching them themselves, as the earlier law had stipulated, they were now asked to report to the *mudīr* of the district. If four days had passed since the fugitive had left his village without being found, and if during that time the shaykh failed to report him, the shaykh would then be considered an accomplice of the fugitive, and in this case he would be hanged.[122]

When the fellahin saw that open revolt and group desertion were ineffectual in evading the conscription gangs of the Pasha they resorted to individual acts of rebellion. One such method was to maim themselves deliberately so as to be declared medically unfit for service.[123] The exact ways of maiming and the government response to

119 Fīlīb Jallād, ed., *Qāmūs al-Idāra wa'l-Qaḍā'* [Dictionary of Administration and Justice] (Alexandria, 1890–2), III, pp. 1326–7; hereafter referred to as Jallād, ed., *Qāmūs*. For an English translation of this law see Hiroshi Kato, "Egyptian village community under Muhammed ʿAli's rule: An annotation of 'Qanun al-Filaha,'" *Orient*, 16 (1980), pp. 183–222.

120 S/1/47/7/174 on 6 Z 1240/22 July 1825; Rivlin, *Agricultural Policy*, pp. 91–2.

121 Dhawat 5/25, on 11 L 1244/16 April 1829. For imprisonment in the Liman see chapter 3 below.

122 Jallād, ed., *Qāmūs*, III, pp. 1339–40. *Ṣalb* here should mean hanging rather than crucifixion; "Although literally meaning crucifixion, in the Ottoman *ḳānūn, ṣalb* seems to be synonymous with *asmak*, hanging," Heyd, *Old Ottoman Criminal Law*, p. 260.

123 Interestingly, this seems to have been the case when any government resorted to universal conscription. For this practice in the Napoleonic armies, see Forrest, *Conscripts and Deserters*, p. 136; for a similar reaction by Russian serfs in the nineteenth century and, significantly, self-inflicted wounds (SIW) among British troops during

it will be dealt with in chapter 6 below; suffice it to say here that the most common techniques employed were chopping off the index finger, pulling the front teeth and/or putting rat poison in one's eye so as to blind oneself hopefully only temporarily. When the extent of these practices became "very common"[124] the Pasha resolved to punish the mutilated men and their accomplices severely by sending them to prison for life, as well as conscripting their relatives instead of them.[125] Another method to avoid conscription and probably the most instinctive one was to resist the conscription officers physically. Naturally the fellahin had no chance of getting around conscription that way and even when they occasionally managed to escape one conscription gang they would soon be found by another and instead of being punished, by being sent to prison, for example, as some of them hoped, they were sent to the army instead.[126]

Nevertheless even after being taken by the conscription gang, many fellahin did not give up all hopes of evading the Pasha's military service and attempted to desert either on their way to the conscription depots from which they would be distributed among the various units, or from the training camps in which these units were being drilled. It should be noted here that desertion was a perennial problem for the authorities and as such will be dealt with in more detail in chapter 6. What is of concern here is to chart the methods employed by the authorities to safeguard the delivery of the conscripts to their training camps after they had been rounded up, a process that was considerably more difficult than conscription *per se*.

Given their "intense love of home"[127] it was often during the early days or weeks after being taken away from their villages that the young fellahin found army life most unbearable, when the memory of home and of the family left behind to its own devices was still fresh and when the new values and disciplinary methods of the army had not yet struck root in their minds.[128] Even before reaching their training camps, a large number of the conscripts managed to escape and got back to their

the First World War, see John Keegan, *The Face of Battle* (London: Penguin, 1976), p. 275n.

124 Bowring, "Report on Egypt," p. 52.

125 St John, *Egypt*, I, pp. 189–91. See also Scott, *Rambles in Egypt*, II, pp. 217–18.

126 See the case of the fellah from Ṭahṭā in Upper Egypt who dared to fire at the conscription gang which was visiting his village. He managed to escape but was later found by the shaykh of his village who delivered him to the military authorities for conscription; S/1/48/1/139 on 15 Ca 1239/17 January 1824.

127 St. John, *Egypt*, I, p. 189. For a fuller examination of "home-sickness," see chapter 5 below.

128 For a comparison with the same problem facing the French army see Forrest, *Conscripts and Deserters*, p. 64.

villages. It was soon discovered that the total number of men arriving at the conscription depots was often smaller than that originally raised from the villages. Out of a total of 14,426 men raised from the Northern Provinces (Gharbiyya, Minūfiyya, Manṣūra, Sharqiyya, Gīza, and Qalyūbiyya), for example, 428 men died just after being gathered from their villages and another 622 men either fled or were sent back because they were unfit in the first place. When Mehmed Ali was informed about this discrepancy in numbers he wrote to the Governor telling him that he had to "fill these gaps."[129] These problems were not peculiar to the Northern Provinces: out of a total of 1,960 men gathered from the Middle Provinces (Banī Suwayf, Fayyūm and Aṭfīḥ), nearly a third were not "in their places *(bulmamuş)*". Mehmed Ali wrote to the governor, Halil Bey, reprimanding him heavily and warning him that if he did not do his best to fill these gaps, he would live to regret it.[130]

As we shall see below these "gaps" were filled not simply by grabbing more men from the villages to replace those who "were not in their places." New techniques were implemented to deal with the different kinds of "gaps": the deserters, those who were medically unfit in the first place and were therefore returned to their villages, and those who died of old age after being conscripted *(firar ve murteci ve muteveffi)*.[131] Accordingly, deserters would be caught by instituting a country-wide system of policing and surveillance; the medically unfit would be treated in newly founded hospitals that would be linked to a modern medical establishment; and the problem of wrongly conscripting old men would be solved if precise information had been collected about the population of the entire country that would be broken down by age, gender, residence, occupation, etc. In short, to fill these "gaps," the Egyptian state would undertake new tasks that it had hitherto not considered to fall within its duty nor its ability to perform. Let us see how this was brought about.

Government's response

From what we have seen so far it becomes clear that the Pasha's earlier wish that the fellahin's aversion to military service could be countered simply by employing religious men to convince them that serving in his forces was tantamount to defending the faith proved to be naive and optimistic. The fellahin's reaction to conscription was as drastic and unprecedented as the Pasha's orders had been and for some time the authorities seemed to have lost control over the process of collecting

129 S/1/48/1/94 on 18 Ra 1239/23 November 1823.
130 S/1/50/4/2 on 11 C 1238/24 February 1823.
131 S/1/48/1/211 on 11 B 1239/13 March 1824.

and guarding the conscripts. Furthermore, it had become obvious that this process was far from efficient and although it succeeded in gathering a considerable number of men from their villages, this had not been without its costs. Dr. Bowring, who was against conscription as a matter of principle, also opposed it not only for the brutal means that were employed to carry it out but also because it "removes from labor a far greater number of men than are required for the army as multitudes abandon their lands, and multitudes deprive themselves of their limbs for the purpose of evading the conscription."[132] Besides the problem of the land left unattended by fugitives evading conscription, the policy applied to date produced men who were old or physically unfit for "this fine and delicate matter."[133] In the absence of any criteria as to whom to conscript the conscription gangs were eager to collect as many men as could be found without any regard to age or physical fitness. It was reported that out of 48,000 men collected throughout the 1820s and sent to the Hankah camp to the north of Cairo only 20,000 men were fit for military service. "Lame, blind, decrepid, all were sent without distinction."[134] A new technique had to be found to redress the problems arising so far as well as to replace the existing system with a tighter, more efficient, one.

Central to the success of any attempt by the authorities in Cairo to conscript the fellahin was the role played by the village shaykhs. It was realized as early as 1822 that it was the shaykhs who exclusively had the detailed information needed to implement the conscription policy at the village level. Initially, as was described above, the conscription gang would arrive in the village and would round up as many men as could be found. However, given the speed by which news of its imminent arrival would spread to the villages, a wave of desertion ensued making it impossible for the Turkish-speaking officers to ascertain if the men currently present in the village were the only men available or if others had already fled the village. It soon became evident that without the collaboration of the shaykhs the authorities could not be sure that the men actually present were all the men that could potentially be gathered from any given village. Village shaykhs were therefore asked to assist the conscription officers in their task. However, many shaykhs refused to collaborate with the authorities against their fellow villagers and often

132 Bowring, "Report on Egypt," p. 5.

133 S/1/48/1/13 on 2 L 1238/12 June 1823.

134 Scott, *Rambles in Egypt*, II, p. 216. The training camps were moved to Hankah because of the appearance of the plague in Upper Egypt in 1824 and also so that they could be more easily supplied with food; S/1/48/1/222 on 28 B 1239/29 March 1824. The camps were moved in November 1824: S/1/48/1/412 on 30 Ra 1240/22 November 1824.

resisted the pressure from above to comply with the system by employing various ways that ranged from a calculated lack of interest in government policies to deliberate attempts to frustrate such policies. The *Qānūn al-Filāḥa* that was passed in 1830 abounds with regulations that show government attempts to curb this non-compliance of the shaykhs with its policies.[135] In spite of the harsh penalties by which the authorities attempted to bring them under firm control, some shaykhs managed through various ways to side with their fellow villagers rather than act as reliable agents of the government in Cairo blindly executing its orders. This was the case not only with the village shaykhs, but also with the district governors (*ḥākim*s of the *khuṭṭ*s) and the department governors (*nāẓir*s of the *qism*s)[136] who showed their loyalty to their fellow countrymen by a tightly guarded silence and a calculated pretense at ignorance of their local environment.

In this respect the different shaykhs and governors were caught between a rock and a hard place: even if it is assumed that they were genuinely interested in fulfilling the government's orders and that they had no loyalty to the people of their administrative units, a serious problem remained: on the one hand, these orders meant moving men away from agriculture, and on the other hand, the local officials had to make sure that production did not get disrupted by the government's continuous and seemingly unsatiable demand for manpower. Nowhere was this conflict more evident than in the case of applying the conscription policy. The different local officials, from the shaykhs to the department governors, often refused to hand in the men needed for the army to the conscripting officers and instead allowed them to "disappear" in their provinces and sometimes gave them refuge by hiding them in their own houses. When Mehmed Ali was informed of this he wrote an open decree (*buyrultu*) to forty-two governors warning them of the consequences of their acts. He swore by God and His Prophet that when discovered he was going to "aim at their souls with the arrows of subjugation" and would mercilessly kill them with his own hands.[137] More cunningly, the shaykhs would sometimes meet government demands for men by conscripting peasants not from their own villages but from neighboring ones. Mehmed Ali ordered this practice to be stopped at once. Any conscript sent in this way would be asked from which village he was taken and which shaykh conscripted him and if this

[135] See Arts. 6, 8, 10, 11, 13, 19, 23, 36, 40, 45, and 53 of the *Qānūn* in Jallād, ed., *Qāmūs*, III, pp. 1323–9.

[136] For a description of the duties of these officials, see Rivlin, *Agricultural Policy*, pp. 88–104.

[137] S/1/48/2/294 on 9 C 1241/20 December 1825.

was discovered not to be his own shaykh, this latter would then have either his own son or one of his relatives taken for the army instead.[138] Another way by which the local officials attempted to deceive the authorities was to conscript men who had already been "conscripted," if not for the army, then for one of the government works. For example, three men from the department of Zifta were sent to the army only to be discovered that they were already registered as workers in the "factory" of Zifta. The same fate awaited the shaykhs who conscripted them: their sons or their relatives were sent instead of the three men.[139]

A solution had to be found for this situation in which the central authorities found themselves at the mercy of the village shaykhs, the *nāẓir*s and the *ḥākim*s and subject to their intrigues. New techniques of surveillance were introduced to enable the government to have a tighter control over the population both in the cities and in the countryside. For example, in an attempt to curb the phenomenon of fellahin fleeing their villages and escaping to neighboring ones where they might be caught by the shaykhs of these new villages, the authorities decreed that every villager should carry a stamped certificate or passport (*tezkere*) which should state his name, his father's name, his physical description, and his village. If found without this certificate he would immediately be sent back to his village. Even village shaykhs were ordered to carry such *tezkere*s when visiting Cairo.[140] More radically, the authorities resorted to tattooing some soldiers' bodies in order to facilitate catching them in case they deserted. When it was discovered that sailors were escaping from their ships every Friday, the day on which they were given leave to go ashore, it was decreed that all marine soldiers should have their arms and legs stamped with the signs of a ship and an anchor.[141] (This was also done in the case of convicts sent to prison for life: their arms were tattooed with the Arabic letter "Lām" standing for "Liman" which was the name of the infamous prison in Abū Qīr near Alexandria.)[142]

In another way of increasing their surveillance and tightening their

138 S/1/48/4/175 on 3 Z 1248/22 April 1833.

139 S/1/48/3/259 on 19 Ş 1243/6 March 1828. For a similar case, see S/1/48/3/281 on 7 L 1243/23 April 1828.

140 S/1/48/4/226 on 5 Ra 1249/23 July 1833. The idea of introducing such *tezkere*s might have had its origins in a letter from Nagib Efendi to Mehmed Ali in which he informed him that it was decided in Istanbul to introduce traveling documents for any person when moving from one area to another within the Empire; Bahr Barra 8/59, on 7 Z 1237/25 August 1822.

141 S/1/48/2/360 on 22 Ş 1241/7 October 1825.

142 There are various such cases preserved in the records of this infamous prison. See, for example, the case of ʿAlī Gomʿa al-Gammāl who was sentenced to life imprisonment after being found guilty of murder: M/14/1 p. 78 on 17 R 1263/6 April 1847.

control the authorities appointed special guards to prevent the new conscripts from escaping on their way to the conscripting depots.[143] Bedouins were also asked to hand in any deserter to the authorities.[144] Eventually this task was given specifically to special forces, the *baltaci orta*s, i.e. the sappers' regiments,[145] whose earlier tasks had included guarding the corvée laborers working to clear the Maḥmūdiyya canal.[146]

"Inscribing reality"

However efficient these new tactics might have been, the authorities continued to suffer from the critical lack of any reliable information about the population: its size, its age composition, location, professions, etc. From the early years of the "conscription waves" the authorities in Cairo knew that no consistent conscription policy could properly be implemented without such information, however vague it might be. As early as 1825, for example, it was realized that to replace the soldiers who had fled or who were sent back to their villages, local officials had to know how many men were to be conscripted from their provinces in the first place. When Mehmed Ali was informed that 7,494 men were gathered in the year 1240 (1824/5), he wrote to the Director of his War Department, telling him "we have to know in the first place the number [of men] demanded from each province and the number actually gathered [in order to know] the number still remaining."[147] A similar order was earlier issued to the same Director to prepare a register giving the names of those soldiers who had been raised so far with the information broken down to the province, department, district and village from which they were gathered.[148] Similarly, in order to replace those soldiers who had died or deserted detailed registers were drafted stating, name by name, the provinces which they had originally been conscripted from,[149] and a register of absconders (*mütesehhip*s) was compiled in 1842.[150] Various lists were compiled giving the name, physical description, village and province of the deserter so as to make it easy for the authorities to catch him.[151] Of equal importance were the

143 S/1/48/1/8 on 15 N 1238/28 May 1823; and S/1/48/1/99 on 20 R 1239/25 December 1823.
144 See note 116 above.
145 S/1/48/4/479 on 30 Z 1249/9 May 1834.
146 S/1/48/3/102 on 24 B 1242/22 February 1827.
147 S/1/48/2/102 on 9 M 1241/25 August 1825.
148 S/1/48/1/192 on 25 C 1239/27 February 1824.
149 S/1/48/1/101 on 21 R 1239/26 December 1823.
150 Awamir lil-Jihadiyya 1/236, on 6 B 1258/14 August 1842.
151 S/1/48/1/364 on 23 Ca 1239/21 July 1824; S/1/48/4/183 on 21 C 1248/12 May 1832.

registers numbering and marking houses giving the number of inhabitants in each one for taxation purposes.[152] All these registers had to be updated periodically so as to take into account births and deaths and other changes.[153] Believing that "the welfare of the people depends on a good census" the Pasha as early as 1827 ordered the drafting of a general census for the Northern Provinces.[154] Eventually, this process of gathering detailed information about the population and categorizing it under different headings culminated in 1845 in the drafting of the first national census based on the number of households.[155]

The *tezkere*, the census, and the various lists that preceded it were important tools that the government used to tighten its grip over the population and to usher in the system of strong and effective governmental control that is characteristic of Mehmed Ali's reign. At the heart of these new tools was the government's desire to control the entire population in such a way that no one would evade profitable and efficient employment. The early methods of gathering peasants from their villages have shown that reliance on naked force was not efficient enough: the fellahin had discovered ways to evade it and were assisted in this by the village shaykhs. What the desertion lists, the registers of absconders and, above all, the census, represent is a new method of control and manipulation in which the authorities aimed at always having the initiative and tried to avoid being at the mercy of the local, unreliable officials.

The importance of a *tezkera*, a register, a list, or a census does not lie only in the fact that these tools enhance the efficiency of the bureaucracy or make it capable of proper book keeping. Registers, timetables, training manuals, medical reports and other such bureaucratic, textual devices all share a common characteristic: they attempt to break time and place into similar, comparable, abstract units. As will be seen in the following chapters, once these devices were used time would no longer be measured in terms of the temporal space a given act occupies (e.g. time of harvest, or of learning the Quran), but in abstract, quantifiable units of hours, minutes and seconds. Human motion would be broken down, as described in the training manuals, for example, into uniform, measurable movements that could be standardized down to the inch. In

152 S/1/48/1/159 on 30 Ca 1239/1 February 1824.

153 S/1/48/1/482 on 24 Ş 1240/19 October 1824.

154 S/1/48/3/107 on 2 Ş 1242/1 March 1827.

155 Sāmī, ed., *Taqwīm al-Nīl*, II, pp. 535–6, letter dated 13 Za 1261/14 November 1845. This is an order to conduct the census in the countryside; for the census on urban centers which was conducted in January 1847, see Kenneth Cuno and Michael Riemer, "The Census of 1847," forthcoming article.

short, people and things would be squeezed in to fit in an "inscribed" place, a slot, imposed on them by a printed register, a map, a roll call, an inventory list or a timetable.

These new tools that the bureaucracy introduced were tools of standardization and compartmentalization, of manipulation and control, tools that ushered in what could be termed a process of "inscribing reality." This process assumed that the starting point of managing people and things would be the place they occupied not in their natural environment, but on paper, e.g. in the inventory list, the roll call, or the census. Unlike a soldier whose body had been tattooed by the authorities and whose desertion was discovered *after* he was found, a soldier whose name appeared in a village conscription register would have his desertion detected even *before* he was found. Any missing item could only be truly missing if it did not show up in the list; otherwise it was still considered present albeit only in name (*ismi var cismi yok.*: lit. having a name but no body).[156] Thus when someone presented a petition to be exempted from certain government obligations, paying taxes for example, the answer would take the form of ordering his name to be crossed out (*desid*) from the relevant register.[157] On finding that five "strangers" (*goraba*) caught in Cairo had deserted from a certain village, the shaykh of that village after handing them in was given, in exchange, a similar number of receipts and told to cross out their names from the conscription register of his village.[158]

Given this importance of inscription, of the written word and of registers, the scribe appears during Mehmed Ali's reign as an official of utmost significance. It was upon him that the government's machinery of manipulation, surveillance and control was based, and it was with him that the key to the power of its impersonal nature was to be found. A law passed in 1844 organizing the internal structure of the civilian bureacuracy explicitly stated that the pages of the bureaucracy's registers had to be clean and tidy. "The pages of the register (*defter*) have to be stamped and numbered. Writing has to be continuous with no blank pages in the middle. It has to be clear and legible, without any crossings-out or corrections."[159] The clean, blank page which was sequentially numbered and neatly bound in a register was a symbol of the new power of the state: self-assured, rational, and consistent. When words were crossed out, when gaps existed between writing, or when

156 S/1/48/1/110 on 27 R 1239/29 January 1824.
157 S/1/48/1/159 on 30 Ca 1239/1 February 1824.
158 S/1/48/4/379 on 20 L 1249/3 March 1834.
159 *al-Lāiʾḥa al-Mutaʿalliqa bi-Khadamāt al-Mustakhdimīn wa Mutaʿalliqātiha* [The Decree Regarding the Duties of the (Public) Employees and its Appendices] (Cairo: Būlāq, AH 1260/AD 1844 , Art. 11, p. 22.

the register itself was lost the whole system and machinery of the government was implicitly challenged. For example, on being informed that the scribe of the military hospital in Ḥaifa had fled taking with him the hospital's registers, Lokman Efendi, the director of hospital, was ordered by the administrative governor of Syria under Egyptian rule to set out immediately to catch him and to take even more care to find the registers at any cost.[160]

There is nothing that represents this overpowering nature of the written word and its effect on things than the term *qayd*, which in Mehmed Ali's Egypt was the term used to mean conscription. Originally the term meant nothing more than "drafting" or writing a name in the conscription registers. The Arabic origin of the word, however, implies in addition to writing or inscribing the act of binding or tying (e.g. binding an animal to a tree). Moreover, it also implies subjugation, manipulation and control (*inqiyād*). A *qā'id*, for example (which has the same root), is a leader, or a driver, i.e. a figure of power and influence. Thus, the term chosen from among many other possible terms to signify the process of conscription can hardly be described as a neutral, "objective" term. It is a term that is loaded with ideas of power and control, and connotes ideas of subjugation and bondage. Similarly and more concretely, the act of conscripting the fellahin into Mehmed Ali's army was an act that ushered them into a regime of control and bondage, and into a system in which they found themselves being inscribed upon, sometimes even literally. It was an act that ushered them into a system of organization (*tertip*),[161] manipulation and control.

Conclusion

This chapter has attempted to uncover the factors that prompted Mehmed Ali to conscript the male population of Egypt and has shown that the Pasha did not originally intend to press them into military service but was forced to do so only after his Albanians troops resisted his efforts at imposing discipline and after he failed to raise troops from the Sudan in any efficient way. It then reviewed the methods that were employed to collect peasants from their villages and showed that the authorities encountered serious resistance from the peasants in this respect and in a couple of cases the resistance took the form of massive, popular revolt. In response, the government changed its policies and instituted a new technique of accounting for the population in the first place even before conscripting the peasants, a technique of control and

[160] Sham 9/34, on 6 S 1248/6 June 1832.
[161] Interestingly, that was a term that was also used to signify conscription.

manipulation whose power lay in its ability to predict their actions and account for them even before they occurred.

On a deeper level, then, this chapter has argued that the significance of conscription in Mehmed Ali's army exceeds the sheer weight of the number of those gathered or its impact on the demographic composition of the countryside. Conscription, the population's aversion and reaction to it, and the government's attempts to counteract this resistance formed the impetus for the implementation in Egypt of a radically different system of controlling and governing the country. Resorting to physical force as represented by the conscription gang was no longer thought effective in tapping the country's human resources. Gradually a shift to more subtle, hidden techniques of power took place, represented by the *tezkere*, the register, and ultimately the census.

As effective and powerful as this system might appear, the process of founding a modern army was considerably more complicated than introducing novel techniques of conscription and of surveillance, important and crucial though these must have been. Having apparently succeeded in capturing their bodies and inscribed upon them, the next task was to discipline and train these new conscripts, a process that proved to be as difficult for the authorities as that of collecting the fellahin from their villages, if not more so. The following chapter shows how the authorities attempted to do this.

3 From peasants to soldiers: discipline and training

After landing in Alexandria in the summer of 1798, the French army started a long, tedious march to Cairo under the blazing summer sun. The soldiers were suffering from fatigue, thirst and hunger. They were also considerably frightened, and even the presence of the charismatic Napoleon in their midst could not dispel the feeling of estrangement caused by a landscape and a people that were unfamiliar, exotic and often hostile.[1] They were frightened, above all, by the prospect of the expected encounter with the Mamluks, those famous warlords who had been in effective control of the country for centuries. Every Mamluk, as one French soldier reported,

> had two big musket rifles that are carried by two of his servants, and which he uses only once. Then he uses two pistols that he carries in a belt around his waist. Then eight arrows that he carries in a quiver and which he aims with extreme precision. Then he uses a mace to smash his enemy. Finally, he carries two swords, one in each hand, and catches the reins of his horse between his teeth, and woe to him who cannot evade his blows, the strength of which can easily cut a man in two. We will fight such a sort of men.[2]

The Mamluks, for their part, were thrown into great panic and confusion upon hearing of the French landing in Alexandria. On 16 July 1798 Murad Bey, the most powerful of the Mamluk emirs, disembarked at Giza and in haste started setting up entrenchments in the area bounded by the village of Giza to the south, Imbāba to the north, the Pyramids to the west and the Nile to the east. The following day he issued a general call to arms and the people were summoned to the entrenchments. al-Jabartī, who witnessed these momentous events, describes the scene: "People closed their shops and markets, and

[1] As an example of such feelings encountered during the march see *Lettres originales de l'armée françoise sous le commandement du Général Bonaparte en Egypte* (Hamburg: Villaume, 1799), reproduced in Saladin Boustany, ed., *The Journals of Bonaparte in Egypt* (Cairo: al-'Arab Bookshop, n.d.), X, pp. 33, 40–41. See also Henry Laurens, *L'Expédition d'Egypte, 1798–1801* (Paris: Armand Colin, 1995), chapter 3.

[2] L'Adjudant-Général Boyer, on 10 Thermidor, Year 6, in Boustany, ed., *Bonaparte*, X, p. 59.

everyone was in an uproar. The noise and confusion were very great. The shaykhs, the dignitaries and the common people set out with clubs and arms."[3]

Five days later the French army was seen to the north of Imbābā "and an innumerable throng surpassing all description gathered at Būlāq [on the other side of the river]."[4] When the actual fighting began

the mob started screaming and shouting such things as "God Almighty" and "Men of God" as if they were fighting by shouting and yelling. Wise men urged them to quit this [useless mode of fighting] and told them that the Prophet and His Companions fought with swords and pikes not by shouting, yelling and barking. People did not listen, though, and neither did not desist. No one reads. No one listens.[5]

In the meantime and on the other side of the river a band of Mamluk soldiers charged upon the French who fired at them "in successive volleys." On retreating to their entrenchments and seeing that shells were still pouring down on them some of the Mamluk emirs started to cross to the other side on horseback. "They jostled with each other on the ferryboats . . . [and] sand rose in clouds which the wind blew in their faces. [The battle continued] and the rifles of the French were like a boiling pot on a fierce fire."[6]

Commenting on the battle, al-Jabartī says of the Mamluks that they were

irresolute and at odds with one another, being divided in opinion, envious of each other, frightened for their lives, their well-being and their comforts, immersed in their ignorance and self-delusion, arrogant and haughty in their attire and presumptuousness, afraid of decreasing in number, and pompous in their finery, heedless of the results of their action; contemptuous of their enemy, unbalanced in their reasoning and judgement.

Immediately after such a harsh rebuke of the Mamluks and their style of warfare, al-Jabartī describes the performance of the French during the same battle.

The French were a complete contrast in everything mentioned above . . . They never considered the number of their enemy too high, nor did they care who among them was killed . . . They follow the order of their commander and faithfully obey their leader . . . They have signs and symbols (*ʿalāmāt wa ishārāt*) which they all obey to the letter.[7]

[3] ʿAbdel-Raḥmān al-Jabartī, *Tārīkh Muddat al-Faransīs bi-Miṣr*, trans. and ed. S. Moreh (Leiden: E. J. Brill, 1975), ff. 5b–6a, pp. 18–19.
[4] *Ibid.*, ff.6a–6b, in Moreh, p. 20. [5] al-Jabartī, *ʿAjāʾib al-Āthār*, III, p. 8.
[6] al-Jabartī, *Muddat*, ff. 6b–7a, in Moreh, pp. 21–2.
[7] *Ibid.*, ff. 6a–6b, in Moreh, p. 20.

From their perspective, the French in *their* description of the battle realized that the Mamluks' reputation was completely unwarranted.

Our entrance to Cairo will certainly cause such an uproar in France [General Boyer wrote home] . . . but when the people know what kind of enemy we were fighting . . . this campaign will cease to be seen as a miracle . . . Those Mamluks, famous among the Egyptians for their bravery, have no idea about military tactics, except how to draw blood with their weapons.[8]

Describing the battle itself, he says

I have never seen soldiers who charge with such valor, depending on nothing but the speed of their horses. They were descending like a torrent on our soldiers . . . [who] stood still waiting for them until they were only ten feet away and started firing at them and, in a twinkle of the eye, 150 Mamluks fell to the ground and the others fled.[9]

This dramatic confrontation of two kinds of warfare, one disciplined and orderly, and the other characterized by reliance on the bodily strength and personal courage of the warriors was repeated thirty-three years later in the battle of Acre in 1832. This time it was the turn of the Egyptians led by Ibrahim Pasha to reveal signs of the new type of warfare: hierarchical subordination, Frederickian discipline, and machine-like order. His adversary ʿAbdallah Pasha, Vali of Sidon, had closed himself up in the formidable fortress of Acre that Napoleon himself could not take some thirty years earlier. For six months Ibrahim besieged the city and it was constantly showered with shells. The Egyptian artillerymen fired literally thousands of shells and it was said that not a single house had escaped uninjured.[10] Finally the city could stand the siege no longer and when on the night of 26/27 May 1832 the Egyptian engineers and artillerymen effectively improved their precision and succeeded in making four breaches in the wall, Ibrahim Pasha summoned his senior officers to discuss with them the plan of attack that would take place the following day. At 9:15 in the morning[11] three successive shells were to be fired as signals (*işaret olmak için*) for the troops to start the attack. The four breaches in the wall were assigned to four senior officers to storm with their soldiers: two brigadiers, a colonel, and a major. Each one was given a battalion of specially trained men to be under his command. Other units were set aside for emergencies and supplies.[12]

[8] Boyer, in Boustany, ed., *Bonaparte*, X, p. 59. [9] *Ibid.*, pp. 65–6.

[10] Edward Hogg, *Visit to Alexandria, Damascus and Jerusalem, During the Successful Campaign of Ibrahim Pasha* (London: Saunders and Otley, 1835), II, pp. 139–66.

[11] "Arabic" time. 1 a.m. is one hour after sunrise, so 9:15 is early afternoon.

[12] For Ibrahim Pasha's and Ibrahim Yeğen's reports on the preparations for the attack see Sham 7/3, on 1 M 1248/31 May 1832. The same reports are reproduced verbatim

Finally, Ibrahim had to boost the morale of his men to prepare them for the coming battle. For this purpose he wrote a lengthy letter to the soldiers which was printed in the camp press and circulated among senior officers to read aloud in front of the soldiers.

Because of what we know of your courage and valor in the previous wars that you have witnessed in the Hijaz [he told them,] we have selected you from among other soldiers for the duty [of attacking the fortress] of Acre, which is now ready and exhausted. We remind and alert you that once you receive orders of attack hold your rifles tight in your hands and storm your targets like fire . . . Do not fear the enemy, because if they come with swords, then your bayonets will be longer; and if they come with muskets, then the continuous volleys that you have been trained to perform over the past eleven years will make every one of you count as ten of the enemy soldiers. You have to remember our order: first, storm quickly and forcibly and then strengthen your footholds; and, second, listen very carefully to the orders of your commanders and execute them without using your minds in understanding what they mean [*wa lā ta'malū shai'an min 'aqlikum*].[13]

On the morning of 27 May the attack took place as planned. All the details were executed as previously laid down. Ibrahim Pasha was even capable in the midst of the three-hour battle to send 100 cavalrymen to move the wounded to the camp to be treated by the army doctors and surgeons who were waiting there.[14] Finally at sunset four notables came out of the castle asking for safe-conduct (*amān*) and when they were granted it 'Abdallah Pasha gave himself up to Ibrahim Pasha.[15]

The performance of the Mamluks at the battle of Imbāba and that of the Egyptian army at the battle of Acre more than thirty years later could hardly be more sharply contrasted. The Mamluk attitude to war and fighting shown in the 1798 battle against the French was an example of a method of warfare made obsolete by the new evolving drills and technology. al-Jabartī's and Boyer's accounts of the battle show clearly how they relied on their personal bodily strength; how important cavalry was for their army so that nearly no infantry is mentioned in the accounts of the battle; how decisions to charge or retreat were left to the personal initiative of the warriors; how their dress

together with an Arabic translation in *Vekayi-i Mısıriyye*, issue no. 391, on 11 M 1248/ 11 June 1832, p. 11.

[13] Reproduced in Asad J. Rustum, ed., *al-Uṣūl al-'Arabiyya li-Tārīkh Sūriyya fī 'Ahd Muḥammad 'Alī Bāshā* [Materials for a Corpus of Arabic Documents Relating to the History of Syria Under Mehemet Ali Pasha] (Beirut: American Press, 1930), I, pp. 132–3.

[14] Sham 7/3, on 3 M 1248/2 June 1832.

[15] Besides the documents mentioned above information concerning the battle is given in M. Weygand, *Histoire militaire*, II, pp. 25–7; Cadalvène and Barrault, *La Guerre de Méhémet-Ali*, pp. 134–6; St. John, *Egypt*, II, pp. 493–5; E. Gouin, *L'Egypte*, pp. 432–4.

in its embroidered caftans and colorful turbans was an expression of their social status not of their military ranks; and finally how out-of-date their weapons were, comprising as they did swords, pikes, maces and muskets.

Ibrahim's army was a complete contrast to all of this. Instead of relying on cavalry, there was a nearly total reliance on infantry. The successful execution of the battle drew mainly on training drills that the soldiers had been exercising literally for years prior to the battle. Personal strength, courage and valor, were supplanted by strict discipline, blind obedience to superiors and literal implementation of orders. Instead of individual initiative, hierarchical subordination became the norm. Instinctive reactions had been replaced by strict implementation of a plan that had been previously laid down and meticulously rehearsed. In short, the army started to fight as a unit with the soldiers all acting in unison, following commands, orders and signals.

In the thirty or so years that separate the battles of Imbāba and Acre something dramatic had taken place. The haphazard, instinctive "art" of warfare had given place to the planned, hierarchical "science" of war. The warrior had become an extinct species and was replaced by the disciplined, trained soldier. In less than thirty years, in fact in a little more than ten years, a "modern" army was built in Egypt, an army that was essentially different from that of the Mamluks, different not only in its size or in the method of recruiting its soldiers, but also in the manner in which its soldiers were trained and disciplined. Having seen in the last chapter how the Egyptians were conscripted from their villages, this chapter attempts to continue with the story, as it were, by reviewing the process of training and disciplining that these soldiers were subjected to after being conscripted.

What follows, however, is not only an attempt to describe the process of training the soldiers and imposing discipline on them; this chapter also tries to understand the theoretical and epistemological notions on which these new techniques of discipline and order were founded. As was briefly outlined in the previous chapter, the gradual elaboration of the tasks of the government bureaucracy that was expressed by the new position of the scribe, together with the introduction of the new system of surveillance represented by the *tezkere* system, indicates that a new system of power was introduced in Egypt, one that was more efficient and centralized than that which had been employed earlier by either the Ottoman authorities in Egypt or the Mamluk emirs. Paradoxically, it was also one that was, at the same time, more diffuse and impersonal. What the scribe's register and the *tezkere* represented was a new concept of administrative authority which was introduced in Egypt and which was based not only on the systematic collection, integration and classification of information about the population but also on the need to monitor and supervise its activities.[16]

To elaborate further on this aspect of the new regime of power this chapter describes how the military authorities attempted to turn the fellahin into disciplined, well-trained soldiers, and argues that at the heart of the new technique of training and disciplining that the authorities used was a notion of power that, as Michel Foucault has described it, "operate[s] . . . without recourse, in principle at least, to excess force or violence. It is a power that seems all the less 'corporal' in that it is more subtly 'physical.'"[17] Although Foucault's work is mostly concerned with French and European history, his ideas of power "as something which circulates [which] is never localized here or there,"[18] but as something which is constantly exercised by means of "continuous and permanent systems of surveillance"[19] seem particularly useful in understanding how Mehmed Ali's army functioned. This is so partly because, as was shown in the previous chapter, this army was partially modeled along French lines and because a lot of the instructors who trained its officers and soldiers were French officers who had earlier served in Napoleon's army and who were familiar with the European military scene, a scene that is central to Foucault's analysis of what he calls modern disciplinary mechanisms.[20] More specifically, relying on Foucault's insightful ideas about how modern regimes of power were able to create docile bodies, this chapter describes how Mehmed Ali's military authorities attempted to turn the new conscripts into manageable, docile soldiers whose discipline and training were brought about not only by severe corporal punishment or by the "physical effect of terror," but by a calculated, graded, and predictable application of force that made "punishments [function as] a school rather than a festival."[21]

Foucault's ideas have rarely been used to gain insight into nineteenth-century Egyptian history. One important exception, though, is Timothy Mitchell's *Colonising Egypt* which deals with so many of the "reforms" that Egypt witnessed in the nineteenth century, especially in the last third of it. Drawing heavily on Foucault's work and especially on his *Discipline and Punish*, Mitchell shows how so many of these "reforms"

16 For this aspect of the power of the bureaucracy of the nation-state see Anthony Giddens, *The Nation-State and Violence* (Berkeley and Los Angeles: University of California Press, 1985).

17 Foucault, *Discipline and Punish*, p. 177.

18 Michel Foucault, "Two lectures," in *Power/Knowledge: Selected Interviews and Other Writings 1972–1977* (New York: Pantheon, 1980), p. 98.

19 *Ibid.*, p. 105.

20 Foucault, *Discipline and Punish*, pp. 135–69.

21 *Ibid.*, p. 111.

were informed by ideas of power, order and progress that worked on physical bodies and material space in a minute, exact and meticulous manner, exhibiting what Foucault called disciplinary, microphysical power. In addition, and drawing from Derrida's work on language, signs and the production of meaning, Mitchell argues (and here he differs from Foucault) that the system of power and order that Egypt witnessed in the last third of the nineteenth century had a metaphysical aspect to it. "It worked [he argues] by creating an appearance of order, an appearance of structure as some sort of separate, non-material realm . . . [The modern forms of] power now sought to work not only upon the exterior of the body 'from the inside out' – but by shaping the individual mind."[22]

This merger of Foucault's ideas of the disciplinary, microphysical aspect of modern power with Derrida's work on the operation of the sign and the production of meaning is what informs Mitchell's usage of the notion of "enframing," a term that is central to his argument and one which is borrowed from Heidegger.[23] As understood and used by Mitchell "enframing is a method of dividing up and containing, as in the construction of barracks or the building of villages, which operates by conjuring up a neutral surface or volume called 'space.'"[24] This enframing is made possible through such devices as the map that was superimposed on the labyrinth of streets of old, medieval Cairo, the timetable that divided time in equal slots in the newly constructed schools, the table of contents that was attached to the new mass-circulating printed book, the inventory list, the census, the roll-call. What these devices were able to do was not only to bring about a system of power that "worked by reordering material space in exact dimensions and acquiring a continuous bodily hold on its subjects"[25]; they also had a metaphysical dimension, creating a powerful effect that made things look as if they were a representation of another realm, that of ideas. This aspect of power that these devices had is based on an essential and basic distinction that the new notion of order based itself on: the "mental" plan/model that is imposed on the "material" reality/activity. This Cartesian distinction between the ideal and the material, Mitchell argues, is an essential characteristic of the western metaphysic and was crucial in the introduction of so many of the "reforms" that Egypt witnessed in the nineteenth century.

22 Mitchell, *Colonising Egypt*, p. 94.

23 Martin Heidegger, "The age of the world picture," in *The Question Concerning Technology and Other Essays*, trans. William Lovitt (New York: Harper and Row, 1977), pp. 115–54.

24 Mitchell, *Colonising Egypt*, p. 44.

25 *Ibid.*, pp. 93–4.

> The reorganization of towns [he says] and the laying out of new colonial quarters, every regulation of economic or social practice, the construction of the country's new system of irrigation canals, the control of the Nile's flow, the building of barracks, police stations and classrooms, the completion of a system of railways – this pervasive process of "order" must be understood as more than mere improvement or "reform." Such projects were all undertaken as an enframing, and hence had the effect of re-presenting a realm of the conceptual, conjuring up for the first time the prior abstractions of progress, reason, law, discipline, history, colonial authority and order.[26]

While Mitchell's attempt to supplement Foucault's ideas on power as disciplinary and microphysical – by adding to it a "representational" aspect that, he argues, helped produce this division of the world that made Egypt look as if it were a picture in an exhibition – seems problematic,[27] this chapter does not attempt to engage with Mitchell's argument along these lines; rather it attempts to elaborate on Mitchell's use of Heidegger's notion of "enframing" by reviewing in detail Mehmed Ali's military enterprise and especially the manner in which the conscripted soldiers were trained. Although Mitchell refers to some of Mehmed Ali's "reforms," he does so only in a cursory manner, paying more attention to educational reforms in the last third of the nineteenth century and the process of the production of truth and meaning in the newly constructed schools. Yet it could be argued that it would be there, in Mehmed Ali's army, the institution of power and order *par excellence*, that his ideas of "enframing" would be most apparent. This chapter, drawing its sources mostly from the legal codes, the training manuals and the various roll-calls and inventory lists that this army used, attempts to explain how the new conscripts were trained and disciplined, to elaborate further on Mitchell's notion of "enframing" and to show how the ideas of order and power that were manifest in the army helped turn the military institution into a model for society at large to follow.

Internment

When Mehmed Ali told his officials that they had to convince the fellahin that serving in the army was essentially different from corvée[28] he was probably addressing a common perception among the potential conscripts and their families, one that equated the two institutions and

[26] *Ibid.*, p. 179.

[27] See for that matter Hirschkind's critique of this particular aspect of Mitchell's book; Charles Hirschkind, "'Egypt at the Exhibition': Reflections on the optics of colonialism," *Critique of Anthropology*, 11 (1991), pp. 279–98.

[28] See note 102 in chapter 2 above.

saw little difference between them. During the early years of the army the peasants' knowledge about it was patchy, and given the similar manner in which government officials grabbed the men from their villages, it is doubtful that the men or their families initially saw much difference between conscription and corvée. The authorities therefore felt that they had to impress on the new conscripts that what they were about to experience was to be different from corvée or anything else they might have experienced so far. The way the fellah dealt with his time, his physical environment, and above all, his own body was to be radically transformed. As will be shown below, the new military life would impose timetables, medical checks and strict surveillance systems the net effect of which was intended to impress upon the new soldier the formidable barrier that would distinguish his new life in the army from his previous civilian life.

The starting point of imposing this new lifestyle on the new recruits was to isolate them from their habitual environments and to create as big a rift as possible between their new modes of living and their lives before being recruited. One way of doing this was to prevent the new soldiers from engaging in any agricultural activities, either alone or in collaboration with others.[29] More importantly, limits were placed on time spent with their children and families. So long as the soldiers were in Egypt their wives and children were allowed to follow them from camp to camp and to build shanty-towns close to the training camp, living as best as they could by sharing the meager rations of the soldiers. An estimated 22,000 women and children, for example, are supposed to have lived on the outskirts of the Hankah camp near Abū Zaʿbal.[30] Ultimately, however, and mainly for health reasons, this practice was stopped, the shanty-towns appended to the camps were dismantled, and strict regulations were enforced preventing the soldiers from having access to their families.[31]

As severe as this measure might have appeared to the soldiers it was still not considered enough for the new military psychology to penetrate into the soldiers' minds and for the training and indoctrination process to have their full impact. The soldiers were therefore isolated from outside influences by being interned in clearly segregated training

29 S/1/50/5/45 on 11 Ra 1239/15 November 1823.

30 Scott, *Rambles in Egypt*, II, p. 216. See the map of the camp in which the lodgings of the families of the soldiers are clearly shown, in *Mémoires de A.-B. Clot Bey*, ed. Jacques Tagher (Cairo: Imprimerie de l'Institut Français d'Archéologie Orientale, 1949), Pl. III.

31 Judith Tucker, *Women in Nineteenth-Century Egypt* (Cambridge: Cambridge University Press, 1985), p. 136. See also chapter 5 below.

camps. Like most internment policies applied in European countries, housing the soldiers in barracks, training the new recruits in clearly demarcated training camps, and teaching the young cadets in the new military schools were all examples of a general policy of the state to demarcate as clearly as possible the military and isolate it from the larger society.[32] The new "army was no longer to be thought of as an occasional body, brought together for seasonal campaigns. It was to be an organized force, created out of men compelled to live permanently together as a distinct community, continuously under training even when not at war."[33] In other words, isolating the recruits in barracks, training camps and military schools was the first essential step towards the creation of the professional, disciplined soldier.

Besides insuring that the training and education of the new recruits were to be conducted with minimum disruption, this process of internment had other purposes. One was an attempt to reduce the possibility of conflict with the civilian population, especially those residing in urban centers. This might have been one of the reasons behind choosing Aswan as the site for the first training camp, because of its distance from Cairo.[34] It was outside Egypt, however, that the need for interning the soldiers was most acutely felt. Problems arising from the uncontrolled encounter with the civilian population were paramount when the army was on the march or when residing in conquered territories. For example, some of the problems the authorities had with the early army that was sent to Arabia arose out of the soldiers' mingling with the local population and the ensuing complaints that they were attacking the pilgrims and stealing their animals.[35] After the creation of the new army this disruptive mingling with the local population continued to be a problem especially when the army was outside Egypt, notably in Crete, Cyprus and Syria, and the records abound with complaints by civilians against the unruly, impetuous behavior of the soldiers. In Cyprus, for example, various reports were sent to Mehmed Ali in Egypt informing him of the unruly conduct of his troops. In one case Ismail Bey, the commander of the Egyptian forces there, wrote that a number of soldiers had stolen 20 *kise*s (purses)[36] and then, out of fear of getting arrested, had taken refuge in the French consulate. Another group of soldiers attacked the residence of the French consul (who was visiting Sidon at the time) and cut

[32] William H. McNeill, *The Pursuit of Power* (Chicago: University of Chicago Press, 1982), p. 132.

[33] Mitchell, *Colonising Egypt*, pp. 36–7.

[34] al-Rāfiʿī, *ʿAṣr Muḥammad ʿAlī*, p. 327.

[35] Bahr Barra 4/156, on 11 Ş 1231/7 July 1816.

[36] 1 *kise* = 500 *piaster*.

down the trees in his garden.[37] In Syria, the situation was not much different. During and after the siege of Acre the authorities had enormous difficulty in controlling the soldiers who often went to the nearby markets and attacked the merchants,[38] robbed the villagers,[39] got drunk and caused havoc,[40] borrowed money from the merchants and did not pay it back,[41] and even attempted to sell military supplies to the locals.[42]

These problems and others could be avoided, it was believed, if the soldiers were strictly interned in their barracks. Besides holding in check the unruly behavior of the soldiers, thereby helping to calm the civilian population, the barracks helped the authorities to keep a tighter control over the soldiers and assisted in preventing desertions. In addition, they insured that training and education were to be conducted with minimum disruption. Internment thus seems to have fulfilled several purposes at once and the need for such buildings was therefore felt from an early time.[43] However, these new institutions, like their earlier counterparts in Europe, were slow to develop;[44] even by the end of Mehmed Ali's rule not all soldiers were housed in them. Sometimes barracks were specially constructed for the soldiers;[45] more often, and to cut down on expenses, an old building would be converted to fit the amy's requirements.[46] Yet there was a determined effort to keep the soldiers in barracks and to subject them to a tight system of surveillance and a new technique of training.

Surveillance

The isolation and segregation that the soldiers were subjected to in the barracks were enforced by a strict regime of surveillance. In that respect bedouins continued to play a decisive role in guarding the recruits after delivering them to their training camps. But as happened in the case of

37 S/1/50/4/296 on 30 Ca 1239/1 February 1824.
38 Sham 1/27, on 16 C 1247/12 November 1831.
39 Sham 9/188, on 28 S 1248/27 July 1832.
40 Sham 8/130, on 20 M 1248/20 June 1832.
41 Sham 11/33, on 4 R 1248/31 August 1832.
42 Sham 2/65, on 16 N 1247/18 February 1832.
43 S/1/50/2/224 on 27 B 1237/20 April 1822.
44 M. S. Anderson, *War and Society in Europe of the Old Regime, 1618–1789* (Leicester: Leicester University Press, 1988), p. 172.
45 Sham 13/27, on 5 C 1248/30 October 1832.
46 Incidentally, in this case the building should have been exempted from the tax levied on households. However, judging from the large number of petitions presented for an exemption from a tax levied on houses used as lodgings for the soldiers, it appears that this was often not the case. See, e.g., S/1/49/2/280 on 7 M 1239/13 September 1823.

the village shaykhs reviewed in the previous chapter, relying on the bedouins was not without its problems. The 'Abbādī and Hawwāra tribesmen, for example, who guarded Ismail Pasha's troops that accompanied him in his ill-fated Sudan campaign,[47] occasionally deserted and fled back to their provinces.[48] Moreover, the different tribes were in constant rivalry with one another and when they thought that they were not treated equally by the authorities, they rebelled and attacked the countryside, the very thing the government had sought to prevent by employing them.[49] Even during the march of the army to Syria, a time when the whole military machinery was supposed to be on maximum alert and discipline, the mounted bedouins appointed to safeguard the rear of the army attacked and looted the villagers who had come out to watch the army.[50] More importantly, some tribesmen were in the habit of giving refuge to deserters rather than handing them over to the authorities.[51] In response, Art. 15 of *Qānūn al-Filāḥa* passed in 1830 stipulated that

> In the event of a fellah hiding himself among the bedouins, wearing their clothes, and being discovered among them afterward . . . the tribesman who hides him will be conscripted into the military service if he is a young man (*shabb*), and if an old man (*ikhtiyār*), he will be sent to jail (Liman) for six months.[52]

Ironically, having been employed by the government to help create a tightly supervised and controlled army, the bedouins often proved to be a menace for the authorities who frequently had to employ the army itself against various tribes to bring them under control.[53] Relying on the *baltaci orta*s (sappers' regiments) to undertake the same task, namely guarding the soldiers in their camps,[54] was not very effective since they, as much as other regiments, were rampant with desertion.[55]

The appointment of bedouin guards to patrol training camps, military schools and barracks was obviously ineffective, or at least not without its own problems, for it raised the difficult and seemingly paradoxical

47 S/1/47/3/58 on 12 S 1236/19 November 1820; S/1/47/3/696 on 4 Z 1236/2 September 1821.
48 S/1/47/3/475 on 3 N 1236/4 May 1821; S/1/47/3/561 on 17 L 1236/18 July 1821.
49 S/1/47/3/371 on 25 B 1236/28 April 1821.
50 Sham 1/27, on 18 C 1247/24 November 1831.
51 See, for example, S/1/48/4/524 on 12 S 1250/20 June 1834, in which Mehmed Ali ordered Hurşid Bey to send an entire cavalry regiment to fight the Beyālī tribe for giving refuge to the deserters.
52 Jallād, *Qāmūs*, III, p. 1325.
53 See, for example, S/1/48/4/246 on 27 R 1249/14 September 1833.
54 S/1/48/4/479 on 30 Z 1249/9 May 1834.
55 S/1/48/4/155 on 16 Za 1248/7 April 1833.

question of who was to guard the guards.[56] Gradually the authorities came to realize that what was needed was a system of control and surveillance that would be similar to that reached to circumvent the role of the village shaykhs reviewed in the last chapter. Rather than depending on sentry guards and bedouin patrols catching deserters, the aim was to imprint on the minds of the soldiers the idea of internment in the first place and to subject them to a regime of surveillance that would make obedience and discipline seem natural and be habitually practiced. That system, it was hoped, would target the minds of the recruits and not only their bodies; a system that would, in the words of an eighteenth-century French military thinker, bind them "by the chain of their own ideas" rather than "constrain them with iron chains."[57] A couple of incidents can be used to illustrate Mehmed Ali's authorities' gradual shift to a system of control that was subtle and less visible, one that did not depend on the *spectacle* of punishment but on the *idea* of order, a system that could be described as "governing at a distance."[58]

The first incident is recounted by Henry Salt, the British Consul-General in the 1820s, and concerns an officer, a certain Kurd Ali, who, after being taken prisoner by his soldiers because of a delay in the distribution of their pay, talked them into ending their mutiny and giving themselves up since "it could be of no service but only involve them in rebellion and certain ruin." After he had freed himself he "seized two of the ringleaders, cut off their heads and put some thirty of the rest in prison." The officer under his command subsequently released them from prison telling them that those who chose "to serve the Pasha and rest in obedience" might stay and return to their duties; as for those who did not want to stay they would be free to leave the camp. "On this a part of the thirty prepared to leave the camp, when an order was given to fire upon them and they were for the most part slaughtered."[59]

Admittedly, the brutality used to punish the soldiers who attempted to leave the camp in this case might be due to the fact that they had

[56] For elaboration of this problem as encountered by Mehmed Ali's military authorities, see chapter 5 below.

[57] Joseph Servan, *Le Soldat Citoyen* (1780), p. 35; quoted in Foucault, *Discipline and Punish*, pp. 102–3. Servan was minister of war in 1792 with strongly anti-royalist feelings. What won him notoriety, though, more than his republican tendencies, was this book in which he foreshadowed the French Revolution by asking for universal conscription.

[58] For an elaboration of this concept see N. Rose and P. Miller, "Political power beyond the State: problematics of government," *British Journal of Sociology* 43(1992), pp. 173–205.

[59] FO 78/160, Salt, 22 and 23 April 1827.

mutinied and had gone so far as to hold their commanding officer prisoner. This case is significant, however, for it shows that the regime of internment that was based on the actual or implicit threat of the use of force was not effective: it proved inadequate to deter the soldiers from passing out of the gates of the camp. What was aimed for was a system that would have the very idea of internment and of the impossibility of desertion imprinted on the minds of the soldiers so as to prevent them from escaping in the first place and to spare the authorities having recourse to this kind of brutal force.

The second incident took place five years later; the authorities responded to it by hitting upon a simple technique that proved to offer precisely that solution: the roll-call. Immediately after the fall of Acre in May 1832 the Egyptian soldiers we saw at the beginning of this chapter as an organized, well-trained and highly disciplined body of troops who enabled Ibrahim to accomplish what Napoleon failed to do thirty years earlier, these very same soldiers went on the rampage looting the city, attacking its inhabitants, and destroying their property. All semblance of order and discipline disappeared in the havoc that followed and a large number of soldiers seized the opportunity to desert the army altogether. Ahmed Bey, the Colonel of the 10th Regiment, who was appointed in charge of the fortress of Acre after its fall, wrote to Ibrahim Pasha complaining of the situation, and instead of requesting the dispatch of bedouin troops to catch the deserters, he suggested a simple, but effective solution: a roll-call (*tadad*), he said, should be taken twice a day; those found missing would be recorded as *firar*, i.e. as deserters, and when found a day or more later the penalty for desertion would be inflicted on them.[60]

The contrast between the brutality and, arguably, the excessive use of force that the act of the officer in the first case exhibited, on the one hand, and the more impersonal, distant and subtle means of control that the officer in the second case suggested, on the other, should not be read as a movement towards a more humane, "enlightened" application of the law. Rather, it suggests that the idea of the law itself had changed and with it a new conception of discipline and how to enforce it was brought into play. The best example of this new technique of imposing order and discipline that targeted the minds rather than the bodies of the soldiers and that attempted to imprint on them the idea that they were constantly under surveillance was, again, the *tezkere*: it was declared that once interned, the soldier could not leave the camp unless he had a stamped certificate issued by his commanding officer

[60] Sham 8/130, on 20 M 1248/20 June 1832.

specifying the nature of the leave and its duration.[61] Local Syrian workers who were performing jobs for the Egyptian authorities there were also ordered to carry such *tezkere*s "so that if any one of them does something [wrong], he can be caught."[62] Earlier in 1829 when it was feared that conscripts might escape to Cairo in the hope of finding refuge there, an order was given asking all arrivals in the city to have such stamped *tezkere*s on them.[63] Even high-ranking officers were ordered to carry stamped certificates all the time.[64]

As said above this shift from a system of enforcing order by resorting to a brutal and excessive use of force to a more subtle, distant and impersonal one should not be read as a move to a more enlightened, reformed application of the law. Rather, it testifies to what Foucault calls in his *Discipline and Punish* a shift from spectacular to representational and finally to disciplinary punishment. What informed this shift was not the humane, rational and progressive ideals of the Enlightenment as much as the need to make the power of the sovereign (in this case Mehmed Ali) tolerable and acceptable to his subjects. For "power is tolerable only on condition that it mask a substantial part of itself."[65] Hence this shift to what appears as a humane execution of the law was in fact a shift to a more cunning, cynical and hidden kind of power. To examine how this shift in the idea of power and its different respresentions was brought about and, more specifically, to see how power was instrumental in imposing discipline on the new conscripts, various examples follow of the way in which punishment was carried out in the military and in society at large. This is important since, as will be argued below, it was this shift in the meaning and manifestation of power that made the training of the new conscripts possible.

The spectacle of corporal punishment

At first glance physical, corporal punishment appears to have been a common feature of both civilian and military laws: the use of the culprit's body as the site of punishment was as common in military camps as it was outside them. In the army the frequent and extensive use of the bastinado and the whip was one such means of executing corporal punishment. For example, two soldiers were given twenty

61 S/2/30/3/218, on 2 Ş 1242/1 March 1827. See also Sham 13/4, on 1 C 1248/26 October 1832.

62 Sham 9/13, on 2 S 1248/1 July 1832.

63 *Vekayi-i Mısıriyye*, issue no. 69, on 19 Ra 1245/18 September 1829.

64 Sham 11/87, on 10 R 1248/6 September 1832.

65 Michel Foucault, *The History of Sexuality*. Volume I: *An Introduction* (London: Pelican, 1981), p. 86.

lashes each for quarreling with each other during the march of their battalion.[66] When a certain soldier was proven guilty of losing a water bucket, he was given fifty lashes in front of his battalion.[67] Another soldier was given 150 lashes also in front of his battalion for stealing some apricots from the local market.[68] As a matter of principle the physical punishment of soldiers was supposed to take place in front of their battalions in order for the spectacle to be watched by their colleagues.[69]

In this respect there was nothing unique or strange in such corporal and spectacular "liturgies of power" in Mehmed Ali's army. Indeed, a lot of army and naval laws passed in Europe in the seventeenth and early eighteenth centuries were characterized by this emphasis on brutal force in the application of punishment. The 1652 Articles of War, for example, which were applied to the British navy and which formed the basis of all subsequent naval laws, "sound exceedingly fierce in the reading, for of the thirty-nine articles one-third carry the death penalty without alternative, and in another third of them death looms as a possibility."[70] In the first half of the eighteenth century the regimental courts martial of the British army often meted out "such unmerciful corporal punishments which have made even Death more desirable."[71] The Russian army in the first half of the nineteenth century employed corporal punishments on such a scale that "desertions, deaths, immorality, evasion and fear of service [were often attributed to these] 'despotic punishments.'"[72]

In Mehmed Ali's Egypt the different orders of the Pasha and the various laws that were issued during his reign also reveal that punishment, when applied in the civilian sector, was often characterized by an excessive, and probably unwarranted, use of force. *Qānūn al-Filāḥa*, for example, which was passed to deal with offenses relating mostly to damages to public property, land cultivation and the conduct of public employees, stipulated in twenty-six of its fifty-five articles the use of the

[66] Sham 11/49, on 6 R 1248/2 September 1832.
[67] Sham 2/71, on 12 B 1247/17 December 1831.
[68] Sham 8/198, on 30 M 1248/29 June 1832.
[69] Sham 2/64, on 10 B 1247/15 December 1831.
[70] Michael Lewis, *The Navy of Britain* (London: George Allen and Unwin, 1948), p. 359.
[71] Arthur N. Gilbert, "The Regimental Courts Martial in the eighteenth-century British army," *Albion* 8 (1976), p. 51. For how soldiers understood and reacted to this system of "justice" see G. A. Steppler, "British military law, discipline, and the conduct of regimental courts martial in the later eighteenth century," *English Historical Review* (October, 1987), pp. 859–86.
[72] Elise K. Wirtschafter, "Military justice and social relations in the Prereform army, 1796–1855," *Slavic Review* 44 (1985), p. 75.

kurbāj, the whip.[73] As in military punishments the idea seems to have been to inflict pain on the body of the culprit as well as to humiliate him in public. More importantly, physical punishment was also used as a deterrent to others to show in a clear, unambiguous way the fate awaiting those who dared to transgress the boundaries of the permissible. The European consuls in Cairo and Alexandria were fond of recording such cases of public punishments. In one incident, for example, when the protracted siege of Acre caused disquiet in Cairo and rumors started spreading among the civilian population, Mehmed Ali ordered three people to be beheaded and their bodies to be hanged on one of the old gates of Cairo with labels on their breasts reading "This is the fate which awaits those who cannot govern their tongues."[74] During the Syrian uprising against Mehmed Ali's rule in 1834 a man was hanged and left hanging for a long time for spreading rumors.[75]

In this respect Mehmed Ali and his authorities were not real innovators. The *sharīʿa*, as is well known, uses the body of the culprit in a similar way to bring about some kind of connection between the crime committed and its appropriate punishment. Theft, for example, is punished by amputating the hand. Similarly, the old Ottoman criminal code introduced by Süleyman the Lawgiver (r. 1520–66) expanded on the corporal punishments mentioned in the *sharīʿa* to include such cases as "castration for abducting . . . a woman, girl, or boy . . . and for sodomy; . . . the branding of the forehead for procuring and for fraud . . . the branding of the vulva of a woman or girl who voluntarily elopes with a man; the slitting of the nose or cutting off of the ear of an army deserter, and . . . the cutting off of the nose of a professional procuress."[76] The intention of all these punishments that exhibited itself so spectacularly on the body of the culprit was, in one sense, to make the body of the culprit a book to be read, as it were, by the illiterate spectators, urging them to draw connections, however vague, between the crime committed and what was believed to be its appropriate punishment.

There is, moreover, another logic behind these spectacular punishments, one which could be detected by seeing the reaction of the Pasha to the particular incident of a certain local governor who cut off the ears of a man and slit his nose after hanging him because he was caught trading in goods monopolized by the Pasha. When Mehmed Ali heard about this he was so furious that he expelled this governor from public

73 Jallād, *Qāmūs*, III, pp. 1323–9. 74 FO 78/213, Barker, 29 March 1832.
75 S/5/47/1/358 on 21 Ca 1250/25 September 1834.
76 Heyd, *Old Ottoman Criminal Law*, p. 265.

service. He explained that he did so not because of the brutality of the punishment, but because he was not authorized to do so by the Pasha in person.[77] Here we come at another logic of these "inhumane," severe corporal punishments. They were seen as acts of retribution exacted by the Sovereign against someone who dared to violate his wishes. Again the Old Ottoman Criminal Code offers a good example of how certain acts were punishable because they were seen as infringements of the Sultan's rights, e.g. forging decrees and legal certificates and counterfeiting currency. In Egypt Mehmed Ali approved some severe corporal punishments by his market inspector because he considered the acts of the merchants a direct attack on his sovereignty. "I have extended my authority to lands far and distant, he is reported to have said. "I am feared by the bedouins, by highwaymen and by others. Except the rabble of Cairo: they are not deterred by what [my] market inspectors do to them. They deserve to have a new market inspector (*muḥtassib*) who will show them no mercy and give them no reprieve."[78]

There is more than a desire to establish law and order in this statement; what we see is a hint of revenge depicted here. The Pasha is saying that he takes these offenses very seriously because he considers them an attack on his sovereign person. It is his "momentarily injured sovereignty" that had to be avenged and the public punishment was seen as a way of reconstituting this sovereignty. It does so "by manifesting [that sovereignty] at its most spectacular . . . [O]ver and above the crime that has placed the sovereign in contempt [public punishment] deploys before all eyes an invincible force. Its aim is not to re-establish a balance [as much] as to bring into play, as its extreme point, the dissymmetry between the subject who has dared to violate the law and the all-powerful sovereign who displays his strength."[79]

In other words, what informed the logic of the public punishment and its spectacle was not only the need to terrify the spectators into submission, nor the need to bring about an association of crime and punishment but also to remind them of the gulf that separates the vulnerable, expendable body of the culprit from the sanctified, central corpus of the Sovereign. This is why Foucault said that one should see public, spectacular punishments as making up one side of the equation of rituals of power; the other is made up of rituals in which the Sovereign spectacularly portrays his body in its magnificent glory in front of his subjects, e.g. coronations, submission of rebellious subjects, entering conquered cities, etc.[80] Mehmed Ali was aware of the power

[77] S/2/29/1/11 on 1 B 1242/29 January 1827.
[78] al-Jabartī, *ʿAjā'ib al-Āthār*, IV, p. 278 (events of Ramaḍān, 1232).
[79] Foucault, *Discipline and Punish*, pp. 48–9. [80] *Ibid.*, p. 48.

that these rituals had and, as was shown in the manner he received European visitors, he used his own body as the focal point of these rituals to express the juridical aspect of his political power. That his body *was* the law and hence was central and essential for the maintenance of order in the realm, and, in contrast, that the body of the criminal was to be used to remind people not only of its redundancy and its expendability, but also of the central importance of Mehmed Ali's body, is what lies behind a lot of the spectacular punishments that were carried out in the streets and squares of Cairo.This is best expressed by contrasting the following examples of how the Pasha staged these two diametrically opposed rituals of power: staging his own body and exhibiting the body of his nemesis – the criminal.

Those "rabble of Cairo," the merchants who were cheating in weights or prices,[81] were punished in a manner that was hoped would not only set an example for others who might be thinking of doing the same but also remind the onlookers of the ever-presence of the Pasha. A counterfeiter of coins was hanged from Bāb Zuweila, one of the gates of medieval Cairo, with a coin hanging from his nose. The market inspector slit the noses of some butchers and hanged pieces of meat from them as a punishment for selling meat at a price higher than those fixed by the government. The *kunāfa* merchants cheating in weight and prices were punished by being forced to sit on their hot pans while they were still on fire.[82] That what informed these kinds of punishment was not only an attempt to link crime to its appropriate punishment but also to bring about the idea of the expendability of the body of the criminal and to remind onlookers of the huge gap that separated the body of the criminal from that of the Pasha is further illustrated by the following two examples. When the extent of maiming to avoid conscription became known and when it was reported that it was the wives and mothers of the potential conscripts who were assisting them to maim themselves, Mehmed Ali ordered these women to be hanged at village entrances "so as to be an example to others."[83] Similarly, in an effort to stop the 1824 rebellion from spreading further Mehmed Ali wrote to the governor of Isna in Upper Egypt ordering him to hang some of the elderly or disabled villagers at the entrances of their villages to be a deterrent to others. The choice of the elderly and disabled was explained by saying that "they were useless and could not perform any task."[84]

[81] See note 78 above.

[82] al-Jabartī, *'Ajā'ib al-Āthār*, IV, pp. 277–9 (events of Sha'bān and Ramaḍān, 1232). *Kunāfa* is a typical Ramaḍān pastry.

[83] S/1/48/3/235 on 7 B 1243/25 January 1828.

[84] S/1/47/8/1239 on 13 s 1239/14 April 1824.

Contrast this with the manner in which the Pasha exhibited his own body when he attempted to deal with the uprising that erupted against his rule in Syria in 1834, specifically in the manner in which he disembarked in Jaffa:

> The "Marina" street in Jaffa was lined with the finest troops of the army, and a large band of music was placed in the center. At one o'clock two beautiful corvettes arrived and commenced firing a salute, which was instantly returned by the whole fleet and batteries. At four o'clock the yards were manned and with the roar of cannon from the fleet and forts His Highness Mehmet Ali Pasha disembarked.

Then comes the description of the appearance of the Pasha in person, which for a moment appears rather disappointing and anticlimactic.

> Having mounted his splendid horse, he saluted everyone, bowing gracefully to the crowd on either side. This conduct greatly surprised the people, who, when their previous pashas condescended to walk abroad, had been obliged to bend the knee, and bow the head, scarcely daring to raise their eyes, until the August presence had passed by.[85]

As disappointing as the conclusion of this impressive spectacle might appear, Mehmed Ali knew only too well that he could afford this anticlimactic appearance on center stage for there is enough evidence that suggests that even during his own time an aura of sanctity and mystique had already been formed around his own body, his name and his dwelling place. It was enough for an unarmed foreign traveler when he was close to being attacked by a local mob to utter the word "Pasha" and "Firman" for the local governor (who was leading the mob) to grow "very civil and humble."[86] Furthermore, by insisting on doing everything himself and on overseeing all the details of the government Mehmed Ali managed to convey the impression that his residence was the real center of power in his realm. As early as 1817 it was reported that "everything now is settled there [i.e. in the Citadel]. The Pashaw [sic] himself and the Kiya-Bey [i.e. *Kâhya Bey*, Mehmed Ali's deputy] – a much devoted adherent – looking into everything themselves with a scrupulous attention that baffles intrigues and [which] renders all opposition to their orders dangerous in the extreme."[87]

Moreover, the Pasha was never content to sit in the Citadel managing affairs from afar. Never completely satisfied with the reports that he was receiving regularly, he constantly went on inspection tours to investigate things for himself. His visits were rarely announced in advance, giving rise to a feeling among his officials that the Pasha was omnipresent and

[85] William Thompson, *Missionary Herald,* 1835, pp. 90–91; quoted in Rustum, *Disturbances*, p. 67.

[86] St. John, *Egypt*, II, p. 199.

[87] FO 78/89, Salt, 20 April 1817.

all-knowing. Just like the stories woven around his physical person which we read in the Introduction, those unannounced visits helped to usher in his presence and to mark the areas he visited "like some wolf or tiger spreading his scent through his territory."[88] In 1826, for example, he went in one of his typical rages, convincing himself that his governors and officials were cheating him. Feeling that he was understood by no one, he issued a general decree addressed to all of his provincial governors saying that he decided to tour the entire country and gather all those governors whom he considered to be lax and inefficient and would dig a hole in the middle of a wide field and bury them alive with his own hands for everybody to see.[89]

In the light of the power he wielded and given how his contemporaries understood and literally perceived him, and more significantly how his "presence" was felt by his officials and his subjects, it becomes easier to understand how a breach of any of his laws were considered an attack on his person. Mehmed Ali's wish was almost literally law. "So completely have [Egypt's] interests been identified with those of its ruler that to speak of the government, commerce, policy, etc. of Egypt is to speak of the character of Mohammed Ali, who may justly apply to himself the noted words of an equally despotic potentate: '*L'Egypte, c'est moi.*' "[90]

Underlying all the examples of "spectacular" punishment mentioned above is an attempt to restore the sovereignty of the Pasha which had been momentarily injured by the criminal's act. These public punishments, therefore,were

> carried out in such a way as to give a spectacle not of measure, but of imbalance and excess; in this liturgy of punishment, there must be an emphatic affirmation of power and its intrinsic superiority . . . The ceremony of punishment, then, is an exercise of "terror" . . . [which intends to make everyone] aware, through the body of the criminal, of the unrestrained presence of the sovereign.[91]

It is this necessity of proving the presence of the Pasha's body and of making the populace aware of his omnipotent, penetrating gaze that is at issue in these "liturgies of punishment."

[88] Geertz, "Centers," p. 16.
[89] Sāmī, ed., *Taqwīm al-Nīl*, II, p. 320, letter dated 13 Ca 1241, 23 January 1826. In another of his fits he became hysterical and started talking of how sick and tired he was and of how convinced he was of being deceived by everyone. He locked himself up in his quarters and denied access even to Ibrahim Pasha whom he accused of being a traitor. Finally, he said that he would pack up and go to live in Mecca; see Rivlin, *Agricultural Policy*, pp. 71–2; Paton, *History*, II, pp. 234–5.
[90] Scott, *Rambles in Egypt*, II, pp. 102–3.
[91] Foucault, *Discipline and Punish*, pp. 48–9.

The representation of the legal code

The spectacular use of the culprit's body as a deterrent or as a site of retribution, however, had its own limitations. After all, the body of the culprit can sustain only a limited amount of pain that may or may not be an effective deterrent to others from committing a similar offense. Furthermore, for this kind of deterrence to work the spectacle had to be massive and the audience great, hence the public hangings in big squares and important gathering places in urban centers. This, again, had its limitations, since only a limited number of people could be present at any one moment to watch the spectacle. And if the severity and "enchanting" nature of the spectacle of the gallows was intended to be part of a gradually expanding repertoire of stories to be circulated by the spectators to those who were absent, then more abstract means were soon to be discovered that would convey, in a more efficient way, the idea of the inevitability of the punishment and its link to the crime being committed.

Furthermore, the use of the sovereign's body had its limitations, too. For inasmuch as Mehmed Ali wanted to convey the idea that he, like God, could be at more than one place at the same time, he was, after all, only too human. Moreover, if the Pasha, by constantly roaming around looking over his officials' shoulders, hoped to produce in them the feeling that he was perpetually present, then more subtle ways were soon to be discovered which, it was hoped, would substitute for his body, represent him in his absence, and so perpetuate the feeling of his ever-powerful presence.

Above all, this was the role that the Law played, namely to "re-present" the sovereign in his absence. The state of "law and order" that so characterizes Mehmed Ali's reign and which was a feature constantly referred to by his admirers who said, for example, how "a Christian's head is as safe on his shoulders at Cairo as it is in London, and his purse safer in his pocket,"[92] and thanked him "for the perfect security with which the traveler may . . . visit the interesting ruins of Egypt,"[93] was a direct result of the deliberate use of law to represent the power of the sovereign, except that this power was now couched in juridico-legal terms.[94] This shift from the "rituals" of public punishments to the

[92] Hassanaine al-Besumee, *Egypt Under Mohammad Aly Basha* (London: Smith Elder & Co., 1838), p. 10.
[93] Measor, *A Tour in Egypt*, p. 118.
[94] This and the following section are based on Foucault's analysis of the juridico-political power of the monarchy as stated in his *History of Sexuality*, I, pp. 85–90.

"routines" of the legal code[95] was intended to overcome the limitations mentioned above that circumscribed the intimidating, deterrent effects that the spectacle of the gallows had. What was targeted now was the minds of the populace and not their "gazes." The goal was to "re-present" the Pasha in his absence and to use the law as an ever-potent symbol expressing his wish and desire. In this more subtle manifestation of power "the 'mind' [is used] as a surface of inscription for power . . . ; the submission of bodies [is brought about] through the control of ideas; [and] the analysis of representations as a principle in a politics of bodies [becomes] much more effective than the ritual anatomy of torture and execution."[96]

By defining offenses, fixing scales of punishments, identifying who in the bureaucratic–legal hierarchy is to execute the punishment, the legal code also functions as one of the ever-potent tools of power. By creating a mental association of crime and punishment, the legal code instills in the minds of people the feeling of the inevitability of punishment and its link to the crime being performed. Laws, civilian or military, owing to their abstract codification of crimes and their corresponding punishments, and to their association of the possible benefits of crime with the greater disadvantages of punishment, function as an effective deterrent to crime, and thus as a powerful means to impose discipline.

More than in other fields in the wider society, it was the army and the military institution in general that exhibited a clearer understanding of this new conception of power and it is by comparing the systems of punishment in the military and the civilian sectors that one can understand the logic that informed these new techniques of power. To see how the army differed from society at large in this respect, a number of civilian laws are compared below to a couple of military laws that were passed to regulate life in the military schools and camps. The aim of this comparison is to see how imprisonment, in particular, as the extreme case of punishment by internment, was used as a means of imposing discipline and how the military laws in general were different from civilian ones in stressing indirect, representational techniques of exhibiting power.

Qānūn al-Filāḥa

Although imprisonment is certainly less harsh and less spectacular than the scaffold, the way it was stipulated in *Qānūn al-Filāḥa* shows that it

[95] For an elaboration of this transition see Mitchell Dean, *Critical and Effective Histories: Foucault's Methods and Historical Sociology* (London: Routledge, 1994), pp. 166ff.
[96] Foucault, *Discipline and Punish*, p. 102.

still retained conceptions of revenge against the culprit rather than of using him as a deterrent to stop further crimes. The idea was not to rehabilitate him so that he could be reintroduced into society as a better citizen, but to deprive him of his freedom and control over his own body since he dared to violate one of the Sovereign's laws. Rather than meaning reform and cohabitation, imprisonment increasingly took the form of exile and banishment. The *Qānūn al-Filāḥa* mentions two such places of exile: Mount Fayzuğlu in the Sudan and the Arsenal Works in Alexandria, the infamous Liman. The offender was sent to one of these two places of exile as punishment for any number of offenses. Art. 18, for example, stipulates that any fellah or village shaykh who attempted or succeeded in burning a *jurn* (i.e. storehouse of crops) would have to pay for the cost of the damage he caused; if he could not, however, he would be sent to Fayzuğlu for one year in the case of his burning a *jurn*; in the case of his burning a house, on the other hand, he would be sent to the Liman for the same period.[97] If this offense was committed for the purpose of evading the land tax, Art. 20 stipulated that the offender be sent to the Liman for life. Art. 27 sentenced those fellahin or village shaykhs who participated in the uprising of a village against the authority of the *ma'mūr* or the *ḥākim* by sending the chief instigator (*akbar al-mufsidīn*) to Fayzuğlu for five years, the other instigators to the Liman for the same period, and any other fellahs or shaykhs who might have participated in the revolt would each be punished with 400 stripes of the *kurbāj*.[98] Art. 56 punished any official who stole public money by sending him to Fayzuğlu for a period of two to five years to be tied in iron chains, if the amount of his theft exceeded 5,000 piasters; if it was less than that amount, he would be sent to the same place for a period ranging between six months and two years; all this was to be done after the amount of money stolen was extracted from him.[99]

Furthermore, the first article of *Lā'iḥat al-Jusūr* (Ordinance of the Dykes) passed in Rajab 1258 (1842) and which functioned as an appendix to the original *Qānūn* stipulated that if negligence was proven by a village shaykh or *qāi'mmaqām* in repairing a dyke and if damage had reached the neighboring villages, those responsible would be sent to the Liman for a period ranging between six months and two years if the damage was partial; if it was total, they would be sentenced to a period ranging between two and three years.[100] The clearest example of the fact that revenge, more than reform, was what was sought is to be found in Art. 83 of *Qānūn al-Muntakhabāt* published in 1258 (1843) which stipulated that any "public employee who, on receiving an order,

[97] Jallād, *Qāmūs*, III, p. 1325. [98] *Ibid.*, p. 1326. [99] *Ibid.*, p. 1329.
[100] *Ibid.*, p. 1331.

pretends not to have understood it and writes an answer showing this . . . [and] if he repeats the offense for a fifth time, he will be sent to Abū Qīr [i.e. the Liman] for six months."[101]

In addition to the above-mentioned cases those who were sent to the Liman of Alexandria included robbers and highwaymen,[102] those peasants who dared to uproot their cotton fields and plant them with maize instead,[103] those who engaged in counterfeiting coins,[104] merchants who sold rat poison (which was banned because conscripts were using it to blind themselves to evade conscription),[105] soldiers who maimed themselves to evade military service,[106] and those who were accomplices in murder cases.[107]

The Liman of Alexandria thus became an internment house, a huge prison, housing a variety of people who were banished from their habitual locales. At one point the Arsenal had between five and six thousand people.[108] Most of those imprisoned there were interned for some offense that they had committed and were mostly kept there by the explicit wish of the Pasha: an amnesty issued by Mehmed Ali was all that was needed to free the detainees regardless of the crime that they might have committed or the danger that they were supposed to have posed to society.[109] Furthermore, the conditions of their imprisonment were far from healthy; at one time an investigation had to be undertaken to determine why a large number of the prisoners were dying.[110] Those interned in the Liman, moreover, had little control over their bodies and the authorities could use them for whatever purpose they saw fit. In 1843 the Pasha issued the following order to the Deputy of the Shūrā Al-Mu'āwana:

Owing to the arrival, lately, of a number of men from Russia who intend to undertake some experiments related to the plague, which would entail clothing

101 *Ibid.*, p. 1332.
102 Sāmī, ed., *Taqwīm al-Nīl*, II, p. 454, letter dated 12 B 1251/2 November 1835.
103 *Ibid.*, p. 449, letter dated 29 R 1251/22 October 1835.
104 Awamir lil-Jihadiyya 1/226, on 17 R 1257/9 June 1841.
105 Sāmī, ed., *Taqwīm al-Nīl*, II, p. 362, letter dated 17 Ş 1245/12 February 1830. See also chapter 6 below.
106 Sāmī, ed., *Taqwīm al-Nīl*, II, p. 365, letter dated 13 Za 1245/5 June 1830; S/1/48/3/235 on 7 B 1243/24 January 1824; S/1/48/4/365 on 14 L 1249/23 February 1834; Awamir lil-Jihadiyya 1/159, on 11 N 1253/9 December 1837.
107 Divan-ı Hidiv 2/230, on 19 S 1250/27 June 1834.
108 *Ibid.*, 2/308, on 6 M 1251/4 May 1835. St. John says that the figure was as large as 8,358; St. John, *Egypt*, II, p. 478. Owing to the fact that prisoners were sent to the Liman for hard labor, it is difficult to ascertain whether this figure refers to simple laborers or to prisoners performing hard labor.
109 Celebrating the fall of Acre, for example, the Pasha declared a general amnesty for the prisoners in the Liman; *Vekayi-i Mısriyye*, issue no. 403, on 13 S 1248/12 July 1832.
110 S/1/48/4/218 on 2 Ra 1249/20 July 1833.

> some healthy people with clothes of those who were infected . . . and since it is certain that no one would approve of doing this experiment [voluntarily], it has been decided that some convicts in the Liman be chosen for this experiment which is beneficial to mankind.[111]

The Liman of Alexandria came to represent the internment policy of the civilian authorities in a very physical way. It was a prison that was interning all kinds of people that the authorities had declared "outlaws." This undifferentiated internment of "alienated" beings is partially due to the fact that a lot of those interned were so interned not because they violated a given law but because the sovereign, Mehmed Ali, decreed so after their cases were brought in front of him. More importantly, however, the generic law that functioned as the original penal code, namely *Qānūn al-Filāḥa*, was itself an undifferentiated, ungraded, non-codified legal text that retained a lot of the features characterizing old civilian laws. The frequent use of the whip and the bastinado, as well as the type of imprisonment explained above, points to the fact that the main aim of such law and its appendices was to make the Pasha's "presence" visible precisely by highlighting the "absence" of those who dared to violate his wish as represented in the law. In this case the Liman, like Mount Fayzuğlu, was a place of banishment and exile, not a place of correction and rehabilitation. Rather than bringing about a close association of crime and punishment in the minds of the populace, civilian laws as exemplified by this one were aimed at terrifying the people into submission by resorting to the image of the prison looming above society and reminding them of the fate of those who violated the law. So impressive was the idea of that prison in the Egyptians' mentality that the word "Liman," which in Turkish means simply a port or harbor, came to be synonymous with "prison." It still retains this meaning in Egyptian Arabic down to the present time.[112]

Military codes

In contrast to *Qānūn al-Filāḥa* the various military codes passed to regulate different aspects of life in the army attempted to draw a closer link between crime and punishment. To ensure blind obedience to its regulations, Mehmed Ali's army could not rely on the blurred definition of crime or the haphazard application of punishment that characterized

[111] Sāmī, ed., *Taqwīm al-Nīl*, II, p. 525, letter dated 10 S 1259/12 March 1843.

[112] It seems that it had undergone a transitional meaning that is now lost, that of *corvée*, or forced labor; see John Wilkinson, *Modern Egypt*, I, p. 431. Mehmed Ali, he says, is to be distinguished for being "the first to substitute forced labor (*luman*) for capital punishments."

a number of laws passed to regulate aspects of civilian life. A number of laws, therefore, were passed each dealing with a specific aspect of military life and each giving detailed definitions of various offenses and the exact corresponding punishments. In order to see in detail how these laws differed from those mentioned above specifically with respect to their views of punishment, two of them are reviewed below.

The first such law is a law governing an infantry school; it was drafted in November 1834, approved by Mehmed Ali, and sent for implementation to Hurşid Bey, Deputy Director of the War Department.[113] An initial glance at this law shows clearly how different it is from the earlier *Qānūn al-Filāḥa*, for example. The first thing that strikes one when reading this law is that it was tabulated with the main divisions being those of the type of offender: students and NCOs, officers and teachers. For every one of these divisions the law is further subdivided into three divisions: the offense (*cürm ve zenub*), its corresponding punishment (*tedibat*), and the officer who is to execute the punishment (*müeddib*). The mere form the law now takes, the table, strongly leads the mind to the correspondence between crime and punishment. The law is no longer a collection of articles loosely connected to each other whose only order is the chronology of their promulgation; rather, the very form it takes shows the gradual realization that the effectiveness of the punishment stems not from its spectacular severity but from its inevitability; "it is the certainty of being punished and not the horrifying spectacle of public punishment that must discourage crime."[114] Furthermore, there is a conspicuous absence of bodily punishment and a reliance instead on imprisonment. Out of the eighty-nine articles of the law, only four articles resorted to the whip as a punishment. These were reserved for the punishment of desertion and sodomy.[115]

More characteristic of the different nature of the military laws as represented by this one is the new meaning of punishment that it embodies and which is, again, best exemplified by the regime of internment. It has to be remembered in the first place that the area of jurisdiction of this law is a military school, i.e. a place of internment in its own right. The segregation of this school must undoubtedly have

[113] The full text of the Law is in Awamir lil-Jihadiya 1/59, on 24 B 1250/26 November 1834.

[114] Foucault, *Discipline and Punish*, p. 9.

[115] Students who fled were given 200 stripes of the whip in addition to fifteen days in prison; NCOs were given 200 lashes and stripped of their rank if found committing homosexual acts; students, engaging in homosexual acts was punishable by 200 stripes and fifteen days in prison; officers caught committing the same offense were given 500 stripes and had their rank withdrawn from them. Teachers accused of engaging in homosexual acts were expelled from school altogether.

been brought about by appointing guards and patrol soldiers to catch any deserters. However, more effective was the stipulation mentioned above that any soldier who succeeded in deserting, on being caught, would be sentenced to fifteen days' imprisonment as well as being given 200 lashes of the whip.

This stipulation is strengthened by other articles that together would imprint upon the minds of the soldiers in the school the fact that they were indeed in an enclosed place, segregated from the outside world by fences and gates as well as by a legal code that created the "ideas" of outside and inside, presences and absences. Art. 12, for example, punished those soldiers who argued with the locals with eight days' imprisonment under surveillance, i.e. "house arrest" (*göz habsi*). Arts. 13–16 punished soldiers who were not present at the various roll-calls taken in the school with imprisonment as well as extra physical exercise. Furthermore, Art. 33 sentenced soldiers who absented themselves for more than twenty-four hours to eight days' imprisonment in the jail as well as deducting their pay according to the number of days they were absent.[116]

The second law, *Qānūn al-Dākhiliyya*, passed in 1834 as a generic law to organize the military camps,[117] showed a much more refined conception of imprisonment. Instead of lumping together all offenders in one place for long periods, this law specified that there were to be three kinds of imprisonment. Art. 361 stipulated that, firstly, there was "light house arrest" (*ḥabs al-ʿayn al-khafīf*) which should not exceed two months and in which the wrongdoer was kept aside in his own chamber and not allowed to be visited by anyone. Secondly, there was "heavy house arrest" (*ḥabs al-ʿayn al-thaqīl*) which was limited to one month and in which the offender was to be kept aside in his own chamber with a sentry watching him and in which he was not allowed to speak to anyone. Finally, there was imprisonment in the camp jail, the *ḥabskhāna*, which should not exceed fifteen days.[118]

It is clear that a change has taken place in the meaning and intention of punishment where it was no longer seen as a means of exacting vengeance from the offender, or a way by which the sovereign attempted to restore his momentarily injured sovereignty; rather, it became a way of making sure that no crime went unpunished. This new conception of

116 The law does not have numbered articles as such; I have numbered the lines of the law sequentially for easy reference.

117 *Qānūn al-Dākhiliyya* [Regulations for Barracks and Camps] (Cairo: Maṭbaʿat Dīwān al-Jihādiyya, AH 1250/AD 1834–5). This is the Arabic version. The original Turkish was published in the previous year as *Kanunname-i Dahiliye-i Asaker-i Piyadegân*.

118 *Ibid.*, pp. 87–8. These articles were for officers. For NCOs see Art. 371; for soldiers see Art. 376.

punishment, represented in the specific example of imprisonment and internment in general, reflected a change in the meaning of discipline and the ways to bring it about. To create a body of disciplined troops, the authorities initially relied on the use of brutal force so as to terrify the soldiers into submission. This was not without its effects and it undoubtedly succeeded in keeping a lot of the soldiers in their places. Reliance on physical force alone, however, could not ensure that the techniques of discipline had sunk deep into the minds of the soldiers. At a certain stage the effectiveness of the brutal use of force was questioned and other abstract, non-physical modes of imposing discipline were brought into play. As said above, this was a process that, it was believed, would insure that the idea of discipline had been internalized by the soldiers and that boundaries and barriers had been erected in the minds of people and not only around their bodies.

This shift to more "representational" types of control and surveillance was not unique to the Egyptian army. In Europe of the eighteenth century this gradual realization that punishment "should strike the soul rather than the body"[119] is best shown in the debates surrounding British naval discipline that followed the mutinies of 1797. Representative of the new voices of skepticism are the works of Philip Patton who wrote a number of pamphlets criticizing, among other things, the regime of punishment and the system of discipline applied in the Royal Navy. "Whatever may be the influence of [fear]," he wrote, "it has been found insufficient to produce concord . . . and it can never procure unanimity in arduous situations which integrity and the social virtues tend directly to establish in all cases whatever."[120]

In Egypt, the change in the aims and purposes of punishment and of the meaning of discipline in general is probably best represented by two things, the decline in the number of public executions and the developments in the new connotations of the word *siyaset*. Dr. Bowring, who visited Egypt in the late 1830s, said that as a result of the more efficient police surveillance in Cairo and in Egypt in general the number of public executions had been brought down to a trickle. "I have little to do now," the public executioner told him.[121] Of equal significance, the word *siyaset* started to acquire new connotations. Originally, and in its Ottoman legal context, the word denoted punishment in its most general sense. "As a technical term, however, it generally means either

119 G. de Mably, *De la législation, Oeuvres complètes*, IX, 1789, quoted in Foucault, *Discipline and Punish*, p. 16.

120 Philip Patton, *Strictures on Naval Discipline* (Edinburgh: Murray & Cochrane, n.d. [but probably *circa* 1810]), p. 9.

121 Bowring, "Report on Egypt," p. 123.

execution or severe corporal punishment or both."[122] *Siyasetnames*, therefore, originally did not mean more than a criminal code which "chiefly prescribed *siyaset*, i.e. capital punishment or severe corporal punishment (cutting off a hand, the male organ, or the nose, branding the forehead), and, in a few cases, exposition to public scorn, cutting off the beard, etc."[123]

Gradually, however, and in its specific Egyptian usages in the first half of the nineteenth century, the word came to acquire its original Arabic connotation of managing or governing. Edward Lane who also visited Egypt in the 1830s gives the following meaning to the word in his *Lexicon*: "Management, rule, government, or governance."[124] The *Siyasetname* of 1837[125] is, therefore, not a criminal code like earlier *siyasetnames* but a truly "political" law, managing and regulating the affairs of the government. This shift in the meaning of the word *siyaset* reflects a shift that had taken place in the meaning and nature of politics and power. Rather than relying on naked force the way the Mamluks used to do, for example, Mehmed Ali's government was more and more relying on other more representational tools that manipulated the minds as well as the bodies of the subjects.

Disciplinary power

Disciplining and training soldiers, however, could not be brought about only by passing laws, even if these laws differed in nature from earlier ones in that they no longer aimed at gaining retribution and intended instead to make obedience more habitual by drawing a closer association between crime and punishment. To increase the effectiveness of guards, sentry officers and patrol soldiers the legal codes designed for the army and reviewed so far were supplemented by other techniques of keeping order, imposing discipline and exhibiting power. These new techniques represent a new kind of power, what Foucault calls "disciplinary power," which, it was hoped, would not only instill the feeling of the perpetual presence of surveillant and watchful guards but also would adjust the body of the soldier so finely that its movements would be reduced to stable, standardized, comparable, and combinable units.

What prompted this shift to disciplinary power was the desire to turn

122 Heyd, *Old Ottoman Criminal Law*, pp. 259–60. 123 *Ibid.*, p. 16.

124 Edward W. Lane, *Arabic–English Lexicon* (London: Williams & Norgate, 1863, rpt. Cambridge: The Islamic Texts Society, 1984), Bk. I, Pt. I, p. 1465.

125 Reproduced in M. K. Ṣubḥī, *Tārīkh al-Ḥayāh al-Niyābiyya fī Miṣr* [History of Parliamentary Life in Egypt] (Cairo: Dār al-Kutub, 1939), V, pp. 49–75.

the "rabble" of Egypt into reliable, dependable body of troops. This was made possible not only through the vigilant and untiring efforts of people like Ibrahim and Süleyman Pashas; it was the result of the combined activities of the drill masters who attempted to execute the blueprints that these top-ranking officers had issued; of the physicians who subjected the bodies of the troops to a minute, careful scrutiny; of the quartermasters who issued calculated rations of food to the men to sustain their health and to prevent them from living off the lands that they had conquered; and finally of the legal experts who manned the military courts that tried deviations from military codes in exact, predictable manner.

In other words, what informed this new disciplinary power was a new science of government that was based on new disciplines that differentiated the healthy from the sick, the productive from the idle, the normal from the abnormal. In fact, the very notions of health, productivity and normality were by-products of these disciplines. To see how this new regime of power manifested itself in the army, with the result of properly training and disciplining the soldiers, let us follow their daily lives in the barracks and the camps as far as can be detected from the blueprints, the training manuals and the regulations that were set down by the authorities.

Numbering and labeling

For this strict regime of control to succeed the soldiers had first to be "fixed" in positions assigned to them. This was done through a number of techniques. First the soldiers were each given a number by which they were identified. It was not enough simply to register the names and physical descriptions of the soldiers in every regiment to be able to control them; each soldier came to be identified by a number he was given, i.e. the place he occupied in the bigger unit. The army payrolls were also numbered accordingly and when these registers were not properly prepared, it proved impossible to know how much every soldier was to be paid as well as how often to issue him a new uniform.[126] Low-ranking officers were also numbered in a similar fashion. When a woman merchant complained that a certain officer did not repay her money he had previously borrowed from her, it was not enough to refer to the officer in question by name; but she also had to give his number in his military/administrative unit: the first captain of the 4th Battalion of the 10th Regiment.[127] Similarly, identifying the

126 S/1/48/4/271 on 23 C 1248/23 November 1833.

127 Sham 9/171, on 26 S 1248/26 July 1832.

dead had to be done by referring to the specific regiment and even battalion of the dead soldier; his name was not enough for that purpose.[128]

This procedure of numbering the soldiers was reinforced by a finer one of labeling and registering. Art. 239 of *Qānūn al-Dākhiliyya* specified that each soldier had to have his name clearly written in big letters above the headboard of his bed.[129] (Naval officers had to be identified in a similar fashion: the cabin beds had to be marked with the names of their occupants.)[130] Furthermore, Art. 179 of the same *Qānūn* authorized the sergeant-major to order the quartermaster to "hang the required papers on the door of every chamber of the barracks giving the names and numbers of the soldiers in every battalion and company lodged therein" as well as the names and locations of their commanding officers.[131]

One of the clearest and most characteristic ways of marking the soldiers in the army was, of course, the uniform. Significantly, uniforms of soldiers not only differed from those of officers, but the law was detailed enough to specify which set of officers' uniform was to be worn at which hour of the day.[132] Furthermore, the headpiece that the soldiers had to put on during daytime had to be different from that used when going to bed. The corporal had to check this himself before taking the evening count.[133] Different kinds of soldiers had also to put on different uniforms. Those soldiers who were ordered to undertake special duties in the marketplace or in neighboring cities had to put on a colorful outfit to mark them off and they were not to put on their normal uniforms except on Fridays and during general inspection;[134] soldiers imprisoned in the jail (*kolluk*) had to wear gaiters (*tozluk*) with different-colored legs.[135]

"Fixing the soldiers" in their places takes a graphic form in the barracks as well as in the camps. Different laws and regulations were passed specifying in detail the position of every battalion and company in relation to each other, as well as the positions of every soldier within that of his company. Arts. 32–49 of *Kanun-u Seferiye*, for example, specifies the formation in which the tents of the entire regiment should be set up. The distance that separates each tent from the one next to it is given as well as the distance that separates the tents of one battalion from those of another. It goes on to specify the number of soldiers in each tent and goes so far as to specify the positions that these soldiers

[128] S/1/47/6/163 on 10 Ş 1239/10 April 1824. [129] *Qānūn al-Dākhiliyya*, p. 36.
[130] *Kanunname-i Bahriye-i Cihadiye*, Art. 18, p. 83.
[131] *Qānūn al-Dākhiliyya*, p. 17. [132] *Ibid.*, Arts. 339 and 340, p. 80.
[133] *Ibid.*, Art. 236, p. 35. [134] *Ibid.*, Art. 330, pp. 76–7.
[135] *Ibid.*, Art. 378.

should adopt during their sleep.[136] Even the shabby encampments of the women adjoining those of their husbands at the outskirts of the army camps proper had to be regulated. In a special health report by Clot Bey suggesting measures to stop the spread of contagious diseases, it was ordered that the lodgings of these women "should be lined up in two straight parallel rows with a wide road separating them. The lodgings should also be raised above the ground by a certain, unified height."[137]

Inside the barracks every soldier and piece of equipment had to be accounted for. Its exact location was specified in the law and a daily check was conducted to ensure that these regulations were carefully enforced.

> The kit (*jarabandiyya*) of every soldier has to be firmly closed and fastened in such a way that would make it possible to carry it . . . It has to be placed on the first shelf above his bed. The soldiers' cloaks (*burnus*) have to be folded according to the regulations and be put on the same shelf as well. Their clothes also have to be folded with their lining facing outward and they should be placed under the *jarabandiyya*. The fezzes (*ṭarābīsh*) have to be placed on the upper shelf. The rifles have to have their triggers released . . . The swords have to be hung from their belts on nails specified for this purpose . . . Shoes have to be cleaned and placed on the upper shelf with their soles facing upward.[138]

This attempt to control the presences of the soldiers and their equipment is further shown in the regulations ordering the march of the army from one camp to the other or, more importantly, to battle. It was during such marches that the danger of desertion was at its highest, probably because of the belief among soldiers that since the army was on the move, they were no longer as vigilantly watched as when the army was in its barracks or on the camps. To counter this feeling a strict surveillance regime was enforced. The position of every soldier and officer had to be known during the march and the army ammunition, horses and equipment had to be accounted for. At the end of the day a report had to be written recording in detail the events of the day (*vukuat*). A typical "*yol curnal*" (lit.: "Report of the Road") would begin with the dates of the start and end of the march. Then it would give details of the number of transport animals, usually camels, that the army used and how many of these were hired from the bedouins and how many owned by the government. The report would then give

[136] *Kanun-u Seferiye* [Campaign Regulations] (Cairo: Būlāq, Ramaḍān AH 1258/AD October 1842), pp. 23–39. See Appendix for the diagrams explaining these positions for cavalry and infantry regiments.

[137] A. B. Clot Bey, *Risāla min Mashūrat al-Ṣiḥḥa ila Ḥukamā' al-Jihādiyya* (Cairo: Maṭbaʿat Dīwān al-Jihādiyya, 1835), Art. 11, p. 8.

[138] *Qānūn al-Dākhiliyya*, Art. 239, pp. 36–7.

details about who was heading the march and which battalion functioned as the vanguard. Then there would be specific details of how the march itself conformed to the regulations.

The distance separating every battalion from the one following it was between fifteen and twenty steps according to the quality of the road. The soldiers mounted their horses with their boots on. Every hour of marching was followed *according to the regulations* with a half hour of rest. After resting, they marched along with their horses, putting on their marching shoes and hanging their boots as well as their swords on the saddles.

At the end of the day a count would be taken giving the number and description of broken or lost equipment as well as the number of desertions.[139] So meticulous was the control of the soldiers during the march that even going to the latrine was specified in the law: Art. 432 of *Qānūn al-Dākhiliyya* stipulated that any soldier or corporal wanting to go to the latrine during the march should give his rifle to one of his colleagues and march quickly to the latrine and be back with no delay, otherwise he should be imprisoned in the military jail.[140]

Fixing the soldiers was not only done in reference to the place they occupied, but also to the time they spent in performing whatever acts were demanded from them. The time of the soldiers was effectively dictated by timetables and schedules that aimed not only at regulating their movements and presences, but also at adjusting one soldier's time to that of others "in such a way that the maximum quantity of forces may be extracted from each and combined with the optimum result."[141] The infantry training manuals probably show this new conception of time most clearly. Art. 33 of the *Ta'līm al-Nafar wal-Bulok* stated that the forward step was to be measured from the ankle of one foot to that of the other and it should measure 24 inches; the speed of the soldier should be 76 such steps per minute.[142]

Time thus ceased to be the amount of temporal space a certain act "naturally" occupied but became a specific allotment, measured in minutes and seconds, in which that act had to be performed. Moreover, these acts were to be conducted not only within these new boundaries, but also regularly, i.e. according to the schedule imposed from above and specifying how frequent a certain act was to be performed. For example, soldiers were ordered to wash their clothes every Thursday.[143]

[139] Sham 2/39, on 2 B 1247/7 December 1831. Emphasis added.

[140] *Qānūn al-Dākhiliyya*, p. 124.

[141] Foucault, *Discipline and Punish*, p. 165.

[142] *Ta'līm al-Nafar wal-Bulok* [Training Manual for the Soldier and the Company] (Cairo: Maṭba'at Dīwān al-Jihādiyya, 1853), p. 20. This is the Arabic translation of *Talimname-i Asaker-i Piyadegân* (Cairo: Maṭba'at Dīwān al-Jihādiyya, AH 1250/AD 1834).

[143] Sham 7/22, on 2 M 1248/1 June 1832; Sham 10/172, on 20 Ra 1248/18 August 1832;

Imprisoned soldiers in the barracks were ordered to shave their heads once a week.[144] Corporals and privates had to change their uniforms every Friday.[145] During the other days of the week, i.e. Saturdays through Wednesdays, the soldiers were to do their military exercises once a day in winter and twice a day during the months of May to August. Target practice was to start on 20 April and end on 20 September of each year.[146] Bed sheets had to be changed once every twenty days during summer, and every thirty days during winter.[147] Besides regulating the life of the soldier in the barracks these manuals also made sure that the men were not to be left idle in the barracks or in the camp: their daily lives were constantly filled with numerous often trivial tasks which lacked a strictly military aspect, but which were required as a deliberate attempt to keep the men constantly engaged in useful tasks.[148]

"Presences" and "absences"

After interning the soldiers in barracks it was not enough to control their movements; a need was felt to have a close inspection and analysis of their stillness. A strict regime was established creating presences and checking them. Similarly, absences had to be known, proven and accounted for. The most powerful tool in controlling men, their activities and their bodies appeared to be no more than a piece of paper: the roll-call and the inventory list. It was through these tables that the authorities came to observe the presences of the soldiers and their absences; it was according to the inventory list that equipment was accounted for and distributed; and it was by the drawing up of hospital journals (*yevmiyyet*) that patients were distributed in hospitals, segregated from each other and their diseases systematically classified.

Kanun-u Seferiye stated that three roll-calls were to be conducted each day: the first half an hour after dawn, the second at noon and the third half an hour after sunset.[149] Such roll-calls usually gave specific details accounting for every soldier, officer and member of the administrative personnel of the regiment. It would specify the number of soldiers sent

Sham 11/205, on 21 R 1248/18 September 1832. It seems that Thursday was reserved for general sanitation; Art. 208 of *Qānūn al-Dākhiliyya* stipulated that sweeping the barracks and washing the bed sheets had to be done every Thursday, p. 25.

144 *Qānūn al-Dākhiliyya*, Art. 166, p. 12.

145 *Ibid.*, Art. 196, p. 22.

146 *Ibid.*, Art. 314, p. 69.

147 *Ibid.*, Art. 397, p. 106.

148 On the effectiveness of daily drills in turning soldiers into automatons who could form "themselves into opposing ranks a few score yards apart and fire muskets at one another, keeping it up while comrades were falling dead or wounded all around," see McNeill, *Pursuit of Power*, p. 133.

149 *Kanun-u Seferiye*, Art. 25, p. 19.

to hospitals, or to specific destinations, the dead, wounded, and most importantly, deserters (*nakis*, lit. deficient).[150]

Similarly, *Qānūn al-Dākhiliyya* stipulated that the *başçavus* (sergeant-major) was to compile a detailed register giving details about all events happening in his company. Most importantly, he should register the names of the soldiers sent to hospital, those who were discharged therefrom, the dead, and the POWs.[151] The daily journals (*yevmiyyet*) of the hospitals show clearly that the aim was not simply to intern patients there; the classification of various diseases, the segregation of the patients according to the type of disease they were inflicted by, and the calculated use of supplies, e.g. medicine, food, clothes, etc., are all a regular feature of these journals. The process of writing them was so routinized that they eventually were handed in to the various hospitals in a pre-printed table with the respective doctors simply filling in the blanks.[152]

In short, every person and piece of equipment had to be accounted for and this was best done by checking the thing itself against the place it occupied in the list. These lists had to be kept constantly updated to account for all the changes that might have occurred. Deserters leaving their equipment behind had their belongings collected by their corporals and delivered to the sergeant-majors.[153] On being informed that any soldier had had his name removed from the registers because of his desertion, death or being sent to the Liman of Alexandria, the sergeant-major had to collect his belongings immediately within forty-eight hours and send them to the government together with his registers.[154]

It was through the processes reviewed so far that it proved possible to impose order on the new recruits and to turn the peasants into disciplined soldiers. Passing laws with a strict punishment regime was not sufficient for the soldiers to internalize the different army regulations that they were asked to obey. For this to succeed these soldiers had to be interned and isolated from outside influences. Then they had to be "fixed" in their positions through such devices as the timetable and the weekly schedule.

150 See for example Sham 10/66, on 9 Ra 1248/6 August 1832 for a roll-call of an infantry regiment; Sham 7/53, on 8 M 1248/7 June 1832, for a roll-call of a cavalry regiment; Sham 9/185, on 28 S 1248/28 July 1832, for a roll-call of an artillery regiment; and Sham 10/220, on 25 Ra 1248/23 August 1832, for a roll-call of a wagoneer battalion.

151 *Qānūn al-Dākhiliyya*, Art. 173, p. 14.

152 See for example, Sham 10/128, on 16 Ra 1248/13 August 1832, and Sham 10/150, on 17 Ra 1248/14 August 1832.

153 *Qānūn al-Dākhiliyya*, Art. 233, p. 34.

154 *Ibid.*, Art. 178, pp. 16–17.

Inspection and training

This process of creating presences was intended, among other things, to subject the bodies of the soldiers to minute inspection by the army doctors so as to identify those who were capable of bearing arms and discharge the rest. Concern with the health and welfare of the new conscripts came about through the need to monitor the health of thousands of men cramped together in barracks, schools and camps with the obvious threats to hygiene that this situation entails. Specific instructions were given concerning the sanitation of the soldiers' lodgings: "The barracks has to be built on dry, high ground. It has to be well ventilated . . . and its windows have to be facing each other so that the air can pass through."[155] When these regulations failed, as indeed they had when, for example, a big rise in the cases of syphilis (*frengi*) and scabies (*cereb*) was recorded among the soldiers, Clot Bey, in another specially printed manual, ordered army doctors to inspect their men, soldiers, NCOs and officers to isolate those afflicted with either of these two diseases. This check-up was to be conducted once every week.[156] Similar inspections were conducted after battles to identify the wounded and treat them appropriately.[157] The disabled (*sakat*) were set aside to be "dealt with according to the regulations."[158] Other times, they were isolated in special localities in the desert if it was proven that they could not perform any useful job.[159] The sick were also identified and further subdivided into those inflicted with contagious diseases (*müşevveş*) and those who were not.[160] Furthermore, those inflicted with contagious diseases were treated differently after the kind of disease and the manner of its spreading were identified. Strict quarantines were imposed on places infected with the plague, be it a city,[161] a hospital,[162] or even a specific location

155 *Ibid.*, p. 3.

156 Clot Bey, *Risāla*, Item 1, p. 2. For how these two diseases were dealt with see chapter 5 below.

157 Bahr Barra 10/115, on 28 L 1241/6 June 1826.

158 S/1/48/1/376 on 19 M 1240/14 September 1824.

159 S/1/47/14/31 on 17 M 1244/31 July 1828.

160 S/1/48/1/376 on 19 M 1240/14 September 1824. See also Sham 8/125, on 19 M 1248/18 June 1832.

161 Sham 8/191, on 27 M 1248/26 June 1832. The city in question in this case was Tiberius in Palestine. For the quarantine imposed on Acre, see Sham 10/194, on 22 Ra 1248/20 August 1832; for the quarantine imposed on Sheikh Zuwaid, Sinai, see Divan-ı Hidiv 2/119, on 25 C 1248/20 November 1832.

162 Sham 9/106, on 18 S 1248/18 July 1832. Anyone attempting to escape the quarantine was ordered to be shot if he did not answer the third order to stop. Eventually a trench was dug around the hospital; Sham 9/113, on 19 S 1248/19 July 1832.

within a city.[163] Furthermore, and for sanitation purposes, bodies were not to be buried in the old cemeteries which were sometimes deemed dangerously close to the cities and, instead, special remote locations were specified for them.[164]

What we are witnessing here is more than simply an attempt to maintain a healthy sanitary environment; this is the first manifestation of a new kind of power that exhibited itself on the body of the conscript, not in the spectacular way of his being beaten in front of his battalion, but in a more subtle, diffuse and cynical way. This is what Foucault calls "disciplinary power," disciplinary not only because it attempts to manage the body (of the citizen and the conscript alike), but also in the sense that it created disciplines, discourses, that took the body of the individual to be its primary concern, e.g. medicine, psychology, criminology, etc. Out of the need to train the new conscripts and to subject them to the new techniques of discipline as will be shown below, the body of the conscript became the object, not only of manipulation, surveillance and control, but also of analysis and study. In order to have a healthy body of troops capable of bearing arms and of performing the taxing tasks set out in the training drills, let alone in battle, Clot Bey, as chief physician of the army had to give specific instructions based on "scientific" data on the amount and quality of food the soldiers should be fed, the distance they could reasonably be expected to march every day and the kind of clothing that had to be handed to them to protect them from the hot sun of the summer as well as the cold winter.[165]

The body thus became the subject of power, not in the manner it was used as its spectacular exhibit but by being the domain on which discourses and practices of power were tried out, refined and adjusted so as to render it, the body, docile, manageable and curable. Before seeing how this was specifically done with regard to the body of the conscript as detailed in the training manual let us illustrate the various shifts in the manner by which power exhibited itself and which have been reviewed so far, by following how a specific body, that of the sodomite, was dealt with in the different regimes of power reviewed so far.

In 1824 Mehmed Bey, the colonel of one of the first six regiments of

163 Divan-ı Hidiv 2/308, on 6 M 1251/4 May 1835. This was concerning the Liman in Alexandria.

164 Dhawat 6/39, on 22 Ş 1263/6 August 1846. See also Sāmī, ed., *Taqwīm al-Nīl*, II, p. 555, concerning the order to six European doctors to conduct autopsies to identify the cause of death.

165 Clot Bey, *ʿal-ʿAjāla al-Ṭibbiyya Fīmā lā Budda Minhu l'Ḥukamāʾ al-Jihādiyya* [A Short Medical Treatise Necessary for Army Doctors], trans. August Sakākīnī (Cairo: Maṭbaʿat Madrasat al-Ṭibb bi Abī Zaʿbal, 1833), pp. 4–7.

Mehmed Ali's new army, wrote to the Pasha telling him he had a problem with those who committed sodomy: should he treat them as adulterers (and thus apply the punishment for adultery on them) or should he apply a different law? Mehmed Ali responded by saying that the colonel had to consult the military regulations and apply what they said.[166] The problem was that by that time the military regulations and laws that had been translated and published in the Būlāq Press made no mention of sodomy or how to deal with it. What Mehmed Bey had at his disposal was either to apply the *sharīʿa* with its punishment of either death or *taʿzīr*, i.e. chastisement,[167] or the Old Ottoman Criminal Code which stipulated in its different versions either chastisement or castration.[168] The shift from this kind of punishment in which the body of the sodomite was made to bear the sign of his transgression to another kind of punishment in which he was punished in a manner that was supposed to *represent* the idea of law, of transgression and "outlawedness" is expressed in the law regulating the Infantry School referred to above.[169] Although homosexual offenses were dealt with in this law in a physical manner using the whip as the main kind of punishment, the law, nevertheless, by making distinctions between students, NCOs, officers and teachers gives the impression of the gradation of punishment, its predictability and its appropriateness to the crime being punished. This, as said above, was also brought about through the very form the law assumed, the table, helping to draw connections between crime and punishment. It was gradation and predictability, this connection between crime and punishment, that was aimed for and which the legal code was supposed to express and represent.

The shift to the final form of power, disciplinary power, can be detected by looking at the various letters and injunctions that Clot Bey wrote to address the issue of homosexuality in military schools. His main concern was with syphilis which, he said, was getting out of control since there was no law that forced prostitutes to be medically examined,[170] prompting men "to replace them [i.e. the afflicted

[166] S/1/48/1/434 on 1 Ca 1240/22 December 1824.

[167] There is considerable disagreement among Muslim scholars on the punishment of *liwāṭ*, i.e. homosexual activites. For contrasting views within only one school of thought, the Ḥanafīs, see ʿAlāʾ al-Dīn al-Kāsānī (d. 1191), *Badāʾiʿ al-Ṣanāʾiʿ fī Tartīb al-Sharāʾiʿ* (Cairo: al-Imām, 1972), IX, p. 4150 where he asserts that *liwāṭ* is different from *zinā*, adultery, and hence should have a different punishment. Cf. Ibn Nujaym (d. 1562), *al-Baḥr al-Rāʾiq* (Cairo: al-Maṭbaʿa al-ʿIlmiyya, n.d.), pp. 17–18, where he says that homosexual acts should be treated as adultery.

[168] Heyd, *Old Ottoman Criminal Law*, pp. 136, 265. Fines were also used as a punishment if sodomy was conducted with a male servant or minor; *ibid.*, p. 103.

[169] See note 113 above.

[170] The medical examination of prostitues had to wait till the British takeover, when

women] with a greater vice that is against human nature, by which we mean those young boys who, on the pretext of [public] dancing, commit what is improper [even] to be said."[171] What was of concern to Clot Bey, besides the affront to decency and public morals, was the cost to the government resulting from treating the syphilitic young boys, as well as the time they had to spend away from their lessons to be treated in the Qaṣr al-ʿAinī Military Hospital.[172] Eventually in the 1860s pederasty was made punishable by six months' imprisonment, and it required the collaboration of the health, educational and legal professions to detect, prove, control and ultimately punish acts of homosexuality and specifically of pederasty.[173]

In dealing with homosexual violations in the army the authorities never resorted to the spectacular way of castrating the offender that was suggested in the Old Ottoman Criminal Code. To deal with these and other violations the authorities had recourse to a different kind of power, and to a different set of tools by which they attempted to control and manipulate the body of the conscript in a subtle, more cynical manner. By viewing transgressors not as individuals who were to be spectacularly punished, banned or exiled from public space but as subjects to be studied, understood and ultimately cured, the authorities managed to transform the body of the offender from one on which punishment was exhibited to one that became the domain of scholarly, professional concern, and around which disciplines and discourses were produced. It was this regime of power that was at work in transforming the body of the young recruits into a well-trained, disciplined body of troops. Let us continue to review this process and pick up where we left off, with the soldiers being subjected to the medical examinations of Clot Bey and his authorities.

After being interned and fixed in their barracks, their daily schedules punctuated with specific, routine tasks, and their bodies examined closely for signs of disease, the new recruits were ready for training. The imprecise distribution of population in villages and towns was now eliminated; the diffuse circulation and the uncontrolled disappearance

public prostitutes had to present themselves for a weekly medical examination; see Fīlīb Jallād, ed., *al-Qāmūs al-ʿĀmm lil-Idāra wa'l-Qaḍā'* [General Dictionary of Administration and Justice] (Alexandria, 1900), III, p. 1217, Ministry of Interior Ordinance dated 11 November 1882.

171 S/3/122/2 p. 169, letter no. 143 on 7 C 1263/23 May 1847.

172 S/3/122/2, p. 182, letter no. 189 on 17 C 1263/2 June 1847.

173 This is based on information deduced from the documents of the Schools Department (e.g. Madaris, Box no. 2, "Awamir," doc. no. 15 on 11 Ca 1258/10 June 1843), the Prisons Department, the Liman of Alexandria (e.g. M/14/2, p. 126 on 23 M 1279/9 June 1862), as well as numerous cases from the registers of the Health Council, the Shura al-Aṭibba.

Plate 4 “Victory at Konia”

of the men from the barracks were properly dealt with. What remained to be done was to mold the now docile bodies of the soldiers into one unified body of disciplined troops. This was the task of training proper, a process that could best be grasped by analyzing the training manuals.[174]

When Ibrahim Pasha reminded his soldiers of their duties before storming the fortress of Acre in May 1832, he significantly urged them to listen to their commanders' orders and execute them without thinking.[175] For the unit of the army to function as a unit, be it a company, battalion, or regiment, the combined forces of the soldiers had to be carefully measured and meticulously directed. This, in turn, necessitated the formulation of a system whereby the soldiers would be trained to obey orders in a mechanical way, without pausing to think of their meaning. During battle seconds count and a delay in minutes can dramatically change the outcome. Soldiers, therefore, were trained to be attentive to orders delivered by their officers in the form of signals "whose efficacity rests on brevity and clarity; the order does not need to be explained or formulated."[176] *Taʿlīm al-Nafar*, therefore, stipulated that the command shout should be divided into two parts; the first was the "attention" order, and the second was the "execution" order. The attention order had to be loud, clear and long, especially in its last syllable. The execution order, on the other hand, had to be brisk and short.[177] The question was not whether the order was logical or sensible, but if it was clear and audible.

The orders were, furthermore, directed at manipulating very specific movements and gestures of the soldiers. The bravery and strength of the soldiers are done away with, and instead a minute and very fine adjustment of the soldiers' bodies was conducted aiming at aggregating the isolated movements of the soldiers into one, massive force, that of the battalion. To be able to add up movements necessitates, in the first place, some kind of standardization, for only similar things can be added up. The process of training the new soldiers, therefore, started with an attempt to regularize and standardize their appearance.

> Since only a minority of the new soldiers are by nature (*fī muqtaḍa al-khilqa*) similar to each other in terms of the size of their shoulders, chests or thighs, the officer training them, before giving them their weapons and teaching them how

[174] There are a large number of such manuals housed in the Egyptian National Library, Dār al-Kutub. For a nearly exhaustive list of their titles see Shayyāl, *Tārīkh al-Tarjama*, Appendix II. The *Taʿlīm al-Nafar wal-Bulok* is used here because it is the one that deals with the very early stages of the training process.

[175] See note 13 above.

[176] Foucault, *Discipline and Punish*, p. 166.

[177] *Taʿlīm al-Nafar*, Arts. 8–11, p. 14.

to stand attentively (*hazir dur*), must to do his best to rectify these defects and amend them (*iṣlāḥ al-quṣūr wa taṣlīḥahu*).[178]

Similarly, soldiers, when asked to stand still, had to be told how they were to conduct this apparently easy task in a uniform, standard manner.

The ankles of every soldier must be close to each other and be aligned on a straight line . . . and the angle between the foot and that line should be acute . . . The body must be as straight as a post. The shoulders must be held back and the elbows must touch his body. The palms must be turned outward a little, and the little finger must be placed along the plaited cord (*qīṭān*) of the pocket of the trousers. The head must be held upright with no fatigue in such a way that the chin be close to the neck, but without covering it. *The eyes have to be looking ahead at a distance of approximately fifteen feet.*[179]

All the movements of the soldiers, however small, however minute, were punctuated by the command shouts and performed according to their rhythms. "The single shout, although constituting one command, has to be divided into sections so that the soldiers can grasp the complexity of the movement and act in unison. Every single action should be performed within half a second." These actions were to be performed immediately on hearing the shouts issued by the officer.[180] For example, on hearing the second word of the command "*sağa bak*" (Eyes Right!), "the soldier has to turn his head in small uniform movements to the right until the inner corner of his left eye is aligned with the buttons of his jacket, in such a way that the eyes of all the soldiers standing in the front row should be looking in the same direction (*ʿala tartīb wāḥid*).[181]

It was in such a manner that the soldiers were trained. Every action, however complex, was broken down into its most basic constituent parts. The soldiers were then trained in how to perform these simple movements in a standard, unified way, and in unison with each other. Only after they had been thoroughly trained in these small units of movement were they allowed to move to more and more complex ones and within larger and larger formations.[182]

Training manuals thus appear to be one of the most important tools by which discipline was imposed on the soldiers. Laws, however detailed and specific, were still too general for the purpose at hand. The specific laws reviewed in this chapter and dealing with particular aspects of

[178] *Ibid.*, Art. 63, p. 28.
[179] *Ibid.*, Second Law, First Chapter, First Lesson, Art. 15, p. 15. Emphasis added.
[180] *Ibid.*, Arts. 69–73, pp. 29–30. [181] *Ibid.*, Art. 17, p. 18.
[182] *Qānūn al-Dākhiliyya*, arts. 310–12, p. 68, concerning how to form a company out of the trained privates.

army life were, admittedly, aiming at some degree of standardization among the soldiery. The aim of these laws was stated specifically to be

> to prevent absolutely and completely the officers and soldiers from acting according to their own choice and accord (*biḥasb ikhtiyārihim wa hawāhim*). [The aim is to reach such a level of uniformity] that would allow any soldier on being moved from one unit to another or on being promoted to a higher rank to still be able to recognize the same system and not encounter what he is not accustomed to (*la uṣādif . . . mā ughayyir ma'lūfiyatahu*) . . . The basis of all military strength is order and complete obedience (*al-niẓām wa kamāl al-inqiyād*).[183]

Training manuals, nevertheless, were the tools by which this goal was finally reached. By specifying the detailed manner in which the most basic acts were to be performed, these texts brought about a much stricter way of disciplining the soldiers. Through observing and controlling the most simple act (the glance) of the soldiers, and by manipulating their actions, breaking them down to their constituent units, and then ordering them to be executed according to the signals issued by the officers in the form of the command shouts, the body of the soldier was finally reduced to performing a function similar to that of a cog in a machine. The soldier ceased to be an individual, an integral human being and instead he came to occupy a unified slot, a standard position that did not, in fact, should not differ from that of any other soldier. All were soldiers in a row, numbers within a line, units that could be manipulated, moved around and articulated with each other. It was the spectacle that was aimed for, not the spectacle of the gallows, though, but the spectacle of order, regularity and intervals. The training manual, by fragmenting the soldiers and moving them around in the mobile space it created, was the most effective way of imposing discipline, exhibiting power and displaying order. The modern army became order, *nizam*, *par excellence.*

An "enframed" or an "inscribed" *nizam*?

The training manual thus helped to bring about this regime of disciplinary power that Foucault refers to in his *Discipline and Punish*. In the manual the body of the conscript is subjected to a meticulous ordering that manipulated every movement he made, no matter how small or inconsequential. Moreover, it also helped create this metaphysical effect that Mitchell refers to in his argument about enframing, for the different military laws, regulations and training manuals

[183] *Ibid.* Introduction, p. 2.

reviewed above aimed at organizing the daily lives of the troops, their activities and their drills in such a way that it offered a spectacle of order, regularity and intervals. This, as Mitchell rightly says, had the effect of conjuring up the ideas of order itself, of discipline, the law and reason.

At first glance, then (and since this chapter has been dealing with spectacles, first glances are important), the image of Mehmed Ali's army that comes across from reading the manuals that were used to train its officers and soldiers appears to be enframed as understood by Mitchell. To recall, the act of enframing involves two separate, but closely related processes. First, there is the action of the Foucauldian microphysical power that inscribes, arranges, calculates, manipulates and adjusts different spheres of modern life. This we have seen working itself out in detail in the training manual, exhibiting itself on the body of the conscript, manipulating his glance, controlling his stride, arranging his stance and adjusting his movements to fit with that of other soldiers. Second, there is the non-material, metaphysical aspect of this power that allows these acts of violence to be hidden and to present in their place the orderly, impressive image of the soldiers marching in unison, attacking together at the sound of a trumpet or a command shout from their commanding officer. This image, argues Mitchell, appears as a picture in an exhibition, having the effect of conjuring up the ideas of order and discipline.

While acknowledging the seductive appeal of viewing Mehmed Ali's army, or Egypt at large for that matter, as an enframed reality, as a picture in an exhibition, I prefer to refer to what the Pasha and his men did in Egypt as a process of "inscribing" reality rather than "enframing." This is not simply a linguistic ploy (if linguistic ploys could ever be simple); rather, it is a preference for a term that, while acknowledging the violence involved in discursive techniques of ordering and managing modern societies, still assumes an agent behind these techniques.

"Enframing," as used by Mitchell, assumes only one subject: that of the observer before whom the world appears as a picture in an exhibition, a picture whose "order occurs as the relationship between observer and picture, appearing and experienced in terms of the relationship between the picture and the plan or meaning it represents."[184] The power of the "enframing" effect of modern techniques of power, Mitchell argues, lies precisely in presenting the world as if it stands for some plan, a deeper, hidden meaning. Every time the

[184] Mitchell, *Colonising Egypt*, p. 60.

observer tries to see beyond the picture, beyond the exhibition, he/she encounters even more representations and the "real world beyond the gates [of the exhibition] turn[s] out to be rather like an extension of the exhibition."[185]

There is one main complaint to be made about Mitchell's description of how modern disciplinary techniques are supposed to work. This has to do with the confusion and helplessness that the observing subject typically (in Mitchell's analysis) experiences when confronted by these modern techniques of power which leaves him no room for resistance, accommodation or negotiation. It is true that the picture presented in this chapter *appears* to corroborate this view. But this is so because most of the sources used here were intentionally selected to present the military authorities' viewpoint and their desires regarding how the soldier was supposed to behave. So was the language used, a language of precision, discipline and order. Together, the sources and the language employed in them represent an ideal world, a world in which every action is controlled, every object accounted for and every person thoroughly manipulated.

Yet it is doubtful that this is how the soldiers viewed reality and what was happening to them. This doubt is not based only on the fact that what was produced above were training manuals, blueprints, programs that often reflected reality in a neat, abstract manner, and represented the authorities' wish of what this reality ought to be rather than how it actually was. For Mitchell's point is precisely to argue that the blueprints are not representations of mere wishes of the authorities about how best to restructure society: they lay claim to certain knowledges that are inherently powerful and do in fact have the potential of restructuring society and the way we look at it. Thus, the *yevmiyyet* (the daily report) does *already* have a slot for the number of deserters every day, the training manual does *already* acknowledge that the bodies of the conscripts are not uniform, the military law does *already* realize that soldiers might have sex with each other. The power of these devices, however, lies precisely in their ability to predict inconsistencies, to detect gaps, to acknowledge deviancy. In addition, this inherent power emmanates from the fact that such devices have an already given answer to the problems they address, whereby deserters are disciplined, law-breakers are reformed, and sodomites are cured. Ultimately the power that these different textual devices have is based on an assumption that "the real is programmable, that it is a domain

185 *Ibid.*, p. 10.

subject to certain determinants, rules, norms and processes that can be acted upon and improved by the authorities."[186]

The doubt remains, however, as to whether the soldiers did read the new military machine as such, as a machine, as an apparatus that "appeared somehow greater than the sum of its parts, as though it were a structure with an existence independent of the men who composed it."[187] There is no doubt that the new conscripts *felt* this new machine encroach on their lives, snatching them from their homes, fields and villages, subjecting them to tiring, exhausting drills, ordering them to change their daily routines and affecting their modes of talking, sleeping, eating, etc. What is less certain, however, is whether they were conditioned to *read* reality and perceive it in terms of the distinction between the material and the conceptual realms that is central in Mitchell's argument. In other words, although the material presented in this chapter gives the impression that the authorities managed not only to capture the bodies of the young men but also to control their minds and to "work from the inside out," there is considerable doubt that the young conscripts did in fact see reality in that "enframed" way.

Ultimately, the problem lies in the mutually contradictory assumptions about the nature of the observing subject implied by the notion of "enframing." On the one hand, his body and mind are subject to the meticulous, minute manipulation of disciplinary power that leaves nothing unaffected by it including the very self of this observing subject.[188] And at the same time, he is assumed to still retain the autonomy and "insight" that enables him to read through these devices some kind of inherent order, concealed plan, subterranean structure. These two kinds of subjects do not go hand in hand. "A subject on whom power operates through the incessant reading of textual inscriptions is sharply distinct from one whose mind and body themselves are nothing other than products of the workings of power."[189]

From the material presented so far we cannot tell if in fact the conscripts in Mehmed Ali's army acted in the way they were supposed to act. So far it is impossible to tell if they were able to read through, as Mitchell would assume, the various textual devices that were presented above (the training manual, the military law) the structure of power that lies underneath them. For us to see how the soldiers reacted to this new system we have to wait for the following two chapters to come as close as possible to the every-day workings of the army.

186 Rose and Miller, "Political power," p. 183.
187 Mitchell, *Colonising Egypt*, p. xii.
188 See Foucault, *Discipline and Punish*, pp. 29–30.
189 Hirschkind, "Egypt at the Exhibition," p. 292.

Conclusion

This chapter attempted to explain in detail how the young recruits (and others who were not so young, for some of the recruits were over forty) who were conscripted into Mehmed Ali's army were disciplined and trained, and eventually transformed into a reliable, well-trained, efficient body of troops. By quoting from the training manuals, the regulations and the military laws that this army habitually used this chapter aimed to see how those early recruits who had no prior knowledge or experience in military life were transformed into a well-trained and modern army that secured spectacular victories for Ibrahim Pasha and his father.

Yet on another level, this chapter also attempted to argue that this remarkable achievement was not the result of the insightful, progressive ideas of Mehmed Ali and his advisors, nor was it the outcome of the ceaseless, untiring efforts of Ibrahim Pasha and his generals. Rather, it appears to have been the product of a discursive shift that had taken place in the nature and meaning of power, a shift that was witnessed in society at large but which was most apparently manifest in the military and one that, it was argued following Foucault, displayed itself first in a spectacular, then a representative and, finally, a disciplinary manner.

Finally this chapter raised some doubtful remarks regarding the precise manner in which this disciplinary power worked itself out on the body of the conscripts. Specifically, what was raised was the question of the reliability of the various textual devices of power that the army used in allowing us to come to an understanding of the reality of that army. To know how the army attempted to apply the plans and blueprints set down for it, to understand how the men in the army felt and perceived the new disciplinary power over their bodies, we have to rely on sources other than those that this chapter has employed. The following two chapters attempt to do so.

4 Beyond the façade of order: the performance of the army

The battle of Konia in December 1832 was undoubtedly one of Ibrahim Pasha's greatest military victories. Right in the middle of Anatolia, that is, hundreds of miles away from home and in the midst of severe cold weather, he succeeded in inflicting a heavy defeat on an army that was three times as large as his own. In addition, he managed to capture the Sadrazam, Mehmed Raşid Pasha, who was leading the Ottoman army himself. After the successful conclusion of the seven-hour battle the road to Istanbul was wide open and there was no significant Ottoman military force that could have stopped Ibrahim Pasha from marching on to the capital of the Ottoman Empire. Because of its importance and centrality in Mehmed Ali's military career and that of his son, in addition to its being illuminating of the way the military machine of Mehmed Ali functioned, it is worthwhile reviewing the way in which this particular battle was conducted.

Throughout the month of December 1832 Ibrahim was busy preparing his men for battle and training them on a site to the north of Konia where he chose to confront the Ottomans. Every soldier, it was reported, had become acquainted with the exact movements he was expected to perform when the actual fighting started,[1] and the battle was said to have been exercised twenty times before it actually took place.[2] Detailed reports were regularly received about enemy movements[3] and precise information was gathered about the terrain.[4]

Finally on the morning of Friday 21 December 1832, the two armies met on the plain just north of the city of Konia in the central Anatolian

1 Sham 15/157, on 23 B 1248/17 December 1832. See also Marshal Marmont, *Turkish Empire*, p. 254; Abū-ʿIzzeddīn, *Ibrāhīm Bāshā fī Sūriyya*, p. 113.

2 Cadalvène and Barrault, *La Guerre de Méhémet-Ali*, p. 292.

3 Sham 15/148, on 23 B 1248/16 December 1832. This was the task of Kani Bey who was assistant to Osman Bey Nureddin, the Chief of Staff; see Dhawat 5/146, on 2 Z 1246/14 May 1831.

4 This was done mostly by Mostafa Mohtar who had just arrived from a student mission to Europe and was immediately sent to the front; see his report on the pass leading to Konia in Sham 11/250, on 25 R 1248/17 December 1832.

plateau. The Ottoman forces numbered 53,000 men and were headed by the Sadrazam Raşid Pasha himself. Ibrahim's army was composed of less than a third of that number, 15,000 men.[5] These were composed of five infantry regiments,[6] four cavalry regiments,[7] and the Guardia Regiment[8] under the command of Selim Bey "the Mamluk," and were assisted by six cannon batteries containing altogether thirty-six guns under the command of Selim Sati' Bey.[9] Precise orders were issued to all commanders as to their exact duties during the battle giving such detailed orders as where they were supposed to stand in relation to their respective regiments and units, as well as how to receive orders from the Commander-in-Chief, Ibrahim Pasha.[10]

Ibrahim arranged his forces in a way that clearly showed his talents as a commander. He put his forces in three rows dissected by the road leading from Konia to Istanbul. On the first row he placed two infantry regiments led jointly by Selim Bey Manastırlı. Five hundred feet behind this row he placed two other infantry regiments under the command of Süleyman Bey. The Guardia Regiment under the command of Selim Bey was placed three hundred feet behind that second line together with two cavalry brigades. Behind this third row he placed the irregular bedouin forces. As for the artillery, he placed three batteries along the first row, two with the second row and one behind the Guardia Regiment. In addition to this arrangement, and to safeguard against any attempt by the enemy to encircle his forces, only six of the eight battalions in the second infantry line were deployed in column, while the remaining two battalions were put one at each flank, and were ordered to assume the square formation.

5 Cadalvène and Barrault, *La Guerre de Méhémet-Ali*, pp. 295.

6 These were: the 12th under the command of Ibrahim Bey, the 14th under the command of Osman Bey, the 13th under the command of Raşid Bey and the 18th under the command of Hamza Bey. The 12th and the 14th regiments were put jointly under the command of Süleyman Bey Mirleva (Sèves), and the 13th and the 18th under Selim Bey Manastırlı. I could not find the name of the colonel of the fifth regiment, although it is certain that it participated in the battle; see Sham 15/187, on 30 B 1248/23 December 1832.

7 These were: the 1st under the command of Hüseyin Bey, the 2nd under the command of Sadek Bey, the 3rd under the command of Saleh Bey, and the 4th under the command of Veli Bey.

8 This was a special elite force that was handpicked by Ibrahim Pasha himself; *Vekayi-i Mısıriyye*, issue no. 172, on 13 S 1246/24 July 1831. It was disbanded by Abbas Pasha in 1849; Dhawat 5/61, on 23 S 1265/19 January 1849. It seems it was named after the French National Guard.

9 The regiments involved and the names of their commanders are all from Sham 15/157, on 23 B 1248/16 December 1832.

10 For an extremely detailed report on the conduct of the battle see Sham 23/73, on 2 S 1249/21 June 1833. See also Marshal Marmont's lucid description; Marshal Marmont, *Turkish Empire*, pp. 255–8.

At noon the battle started with the Ottomans firing cannon balls at the Egyptian side. Heavy fog, however, prevented the Ottomans from knowing the exact location of their enemy and thus this artillery bombardment was not very effective. Ibrahim Pasha, nevertheless, ordered the second row to come closer to the first one to avoid the cannon balls that were falling behind it and which were causing some casualties.

Then the Egyptian artillery started firing continuous volleys from both left and right and with minute precision in aiming until the earth was shaking on all sides . . . When the fog lifted for a brief time, Ibrahim saw that during their advance the Ottomans had created a gap of 1,000 feet between their cavalry and infantry forces and effectively isolated the left wing [i.e. the cavalry] from the army at large. Ibrahim immediately seized the opportunity and decided to lead a force himself of his cavalry and Guardia Regiments. The Guardia Regiment followed by the cavalry regiments . . . stormed northward, fiercely attacked the left wing of the Ottomans. It was assisted by the artillery batteries which showered their volleys on the Ottomans so strongly and accurately that the Ottomans' positions were badly shaken causing them to retreat northward in disarray. Thus the left wing of the Ottoman army was defeated. When [the Sadrazam] Raşid Pasha realized that his left wing had been hit by confusion and defeat, he attempted to gather its forces and encourage its men to fight back. He went there in person but lost his way in the fog before reaching his men and was captured by some Egyptian soldiers who . . . disarmed him and led him prisoner to [Ibrahim Pasha,] the son of Mehmed Ali the Great . . . Nevertheless, there was still some hope for the Ottoman commander who took charge after the collapse of the centre and left wing of the army. He saw that to succeed, he had to use his right wing . . . to encircle the left flank of the Egyptian army . . . The Egyptians faced this attack with strength and fortitude. Immediately [after the beginning of the Ottoman counter-attack] an artillery battery from the second row rushed forward to assist the left-wing battery in the front row. The combined artillery forces, both in the centre and on the left, aimed at the enemy and mowed them down. At the same time the [infantry] forces, realizing that the result of the battle rested squarely on them, courageously withstood the attack. This confrontation lasted three-quarters of an hour and resulted not only in breaking the Ottoman counter-offensive, but also in defeating them and causing them to retreat in disarray.

Such is the way that the famous Egyptian military historian, ʿAbdel-Raḥmān Zakī, chooses to narrate the battle of Konia.[11] The reason for reproducing his account of the battle more or less in full is that it represents clearly a style of writing the history of wars and campaigns that was once described by the leading European military historian, John Keegan, as "the battle piece."[12] Such accounts typically portray battles as orderly and organized events in which thousands of men are

[11] Zakī, *al-Tārīkh al-Ḥarbī*, pp. 438–41.

[12] Keegan, *Face of Battle*, pp. 35–45.

moved around on the battle plain in neat machine-like precision. Essentially bloody, tense and chaotic happenings, battles are transformed in these accounts into orderly events which are executed exactly as planned, and in which the successful commander is he who is able to conceive of the better plan and to stick to it. Confusion thus becomes the sign of the losing side and is a direct result of either bad training or deviation from the plan. It is no accident therefore that the "battle piece" is usually written from the point of view of the victorious army and hence its troops are always seen as "storming," "fiercely attacking," "facing the attack with strength and fortitude," and "showering their volleys . . . strongly and accurately", whereas the enemy is seen as "badly shaken," "mown down" and "retreating in disarray."

Graphically, this way of recounting battles is represented in the way the maps of the battles are drawn. Regiments are represented by neat and tidy geometric shapes: cavalry regiments, for example, are represented by rectangles and infantry ones by squares; troop movements are shown by straight dashed, broken lines; new positions are referred to by adding markers to the letters denoting old locations, A to A′ to A″, for example.[13] This manner of graphically representing battles is characteristic not only of some military historians recounting certain events decades or centuries later, but is often the manner chosen by the commanders themselves in describing the same events. In representing the minor skirmish that took place between the vanguards of the Egyptian and Turkish armies two days before the battle of Konia, for example, Kani Bey, assistant to Osman Nureddin, the Chief of Staff, followed the same simplistic procedure: the Egyptian units were drawn in nice and neat squares, red rectangles for the infantry, and yellow ones for the cavalry. The Turkish troops were represented by rectangles that were scattered with no order all over the map.[14]

Most significantly, "battle pieces" are always written from the viewpoint of the commanding officer. A sign of a good commander is his ability to think in abstract terms, to see units rather than individuals, to notice flags and banners rather than the men doing the actual fighting and killing, and to impose the map he so well rehearsed reading before the battle on the rugged terrain he now sees in front of him. Soldiers for him are not visible; instead what he sees are their battalions, regiments, and divisions; groups of men that he maneuvres around within the

13 For similar maps "explaining" the battle of Konia see 'Umar Tūsūn, *al-Tārīkh al-Ḥarbī li-'Aṣr Muḥammad 'Alī al-Kabīr* [Military History of the Reign of Mehmed Ali the Great] (Cairo: Dār al-Ma'ārif, n.d. [but 1930s]).

14 Sham 15/160. The map is not dated but this minor battle took place on 26 B 1248/19 December 1832.

confined arena of the battle field and in the limited time he has. The soldier appears in these classical pieces of military history following orders with "no sudden burst of undisciplined valour."[15] He obeys orders, acts in unison with his fellow soldiers and together he marches forward with them to "engage with the enemy." In other words, the "battle piece" portrays the soldier as the kind of man that the training manual we saw in the last chapter wanted the conscript to become: a man robbed of his instinctive reactions who shows no fear, feels no grief; is moved by no horror; instead he appears as a characterless, machine-like, alienated being.

Again, the language is one of order, discipline and uniformity. This is particularly so in the case of documents pertaining to the army which, by their own nature, attempt to describe things in a standardized, "recognizable and universally comprehensible vocabulary"[16] which leaves very little space for human emotions and feelings. What complicates matters further is that the fellahin of Egypt, those thousands of soldiers who made up the bulk of the fighting force of Mehmed Ali's army, were, for the most part, illiterate and did not leave us written material to tell how they felt and what they thought of this "new order" of the Pasha. What we are left with, for the most part, are documents that offer accounts of battles as experienced by officers: orderly, neat, exact.

It is very doubtful, however, that this is how the soldier actually fights. Nor is it likely that the neat and orderly account of battles such as the description of the battle of Konia mentioned above is how battles appear to the fighting soldier who sees death a few feet away and who, in order to execute the command issued to him, often has to step over the bodies of his dead or wounded comrades and also over those of the enemy. Occasionally another view of the battle, a view that is characterized by fear, confusion and horror, comes to the surface even in some official accounts that otherwise strive to portray a semblance of order and regularity. The battle of Konia, for example, is described in most of the documents in that neat and orderly manner: troop distribution, names of commanders, orders by Ibrahim to his men and actual reports of the "magnificent victory of our victorious army."[17] Five months after the battle had been "successfully" fought, however, a military tribunal was convened to investigate the reasons why the 1st Cavalry Brigade, comprising the 1st and 3rd Cavalry Regiments under the joint command of Ahmed Bey Istanbullu, did not participate at all

[15] Keegan, *Face of Battle*, p. 38. [16] *Ibid*., p. 19.

[17] See the headings summarizing these reports that the post office in Cairo gave to the letters received from the army in Syria on p. 5 of the register S/5/57/1.

Plate 5 "Ibrahim Pasha, Commander-in-Chief of the Egyptian army, 1840"

in the battle. The picture that evolves out of this single document is very different from that which is usually portrayed: "horses were trembling when the enemy fired their volleys at us," "we had to retreat here and there to avoid the fire of the enemy," "the colonel was late in ordering the trumpeter to issue the call to take the line formation." These and other statements in this single document show that what the soldiers experienced was fear, confusion, agony, a far cry from the neat and orderly impression one gets from the "battle piece." Most importantly, the account of the court martial goes on to reveal that Brigadier Ahmed Bey was not to be found in the position specified for him in the training manuals which give exact locations of every officer during battle.[18] Zakī, in his account of the battle and in an attempt to explain this rather perplexing absence, says that that brigade lost its way in the fog.[19] On investigation, however, it transpires that Brigadier Ahmed Bey had fled the battle scene with his entire brigade probably to await the result of the battle and then side with the victor. When confronted with these accusations he denied the charges and blamed Hüseyin Bey, the colonel of the 1st Cavalry Regiment, instead. Moreover, he attempted to bribe some of the soldiers and NCOs of his brigade to witness in his favor during the court martial and when they betrayed him he spat in their faces in front of the tribunal. Having proved all the charges against him, namely, violating military rules regarding his location during battle, giving a false account about it to the tribunal, and finally insulting his soldiers and NCOs, Ahmed Bey was only demoted one rank to the rank of *miralay* (colonel), "as a punishment for him and a deterrent to his peers (*kindisi tedip ve akranlarını terhip olmak*)," although the same document says that according to military law he was supposed to be executed.[20]

This particular document is interesting because it offers us an image of the workings of an army during battle that is considerably different from the one portrayed in the training manuals and military laws that were reviewed in the last chapter. The difference between the two images is not accidental: it is based on the essentially different natures of the documents portraying them. The training manual, as we have seen, describes an ideal situation in which the men and their equipment, their bodies and their minds, appear to be thoroughly manipulated, controlled and "inscribed." The court martial, on the other hand, in its attempt to identify the culprit and assign blame, describes the battle situation as actually experienced with all the confusion, havoc and panic that characterize it and distinguish it from training drills. What makes a record of a court martial interesting for our purposes, moreover, is that, besides recording the testimony of soldiers and offering a unique insight into how they might have perceived the battle, it does this always in contrast to what they were supposed to have done. A court martial is

[18] See the three charts at the end of *Kanun-u Seferiye* which give the position of senior officers in respect to their units both during battle and while on the march.

[19] Zakī, *al-Tārīkh al-Ḥarbī*, p. 440. In the map of this stage of the battle Tūsūn draws a dashed line representing the path of the brigade that disappears in the swamps to the north-west of the battle scene and then mysteriously appears again behind the infantry troops.

[20] Sham 23/73, on 2 S 1249/21 June 1833.

convened in the first place to investigate a deviation from the plan, a violation of the regulations put down in the training manual or an infringement of the regulations. The law always looms large in these accounts. The court martial is always in the shadow of the training manual, the military law. But it is the law not as neatly conceived of by the legal experts and military planners but as actually understood by the officers and practiced by the soldiers. What is interesting, moreover, about this particular court martial is that it offers a picture not only of soldiers in panic and fear, but also of a rather pathetic performance of a senior commander in a crucial battle, a battle in which all small details were supposed to have been brought together with as much machine-like precision as possible. It is also interesting for the rather lenient sentence that the brigadier in question received.

This chapter takes as its starting point these unexpected moments in the performance of a machine-like structure like that of Mehmed Ali's army. It seeks to go beyond the veneer of orderly spectacles that often characterized the army to see how it was actually functioning, as opposed to how it was supposed to function. The main question that this chapter attempts to answer is the following: how faithfully did the daily workings of that army approach the blueprints that were regularly issued to guide it and organize its functioning? Using the training manuals, penal codes and military laws that were reviewed in the last chapter can be a good way to write the *institutional* history of Mehmed Ali's army. They can also be useful in writing the history of *mentalities*, the aims and goals of those who were structuring it. However, they offer little insight into how this institution actually worked and how it was received by the society into which it was introduced. The intention, though, is not to argue that these blueprints and programs count for nothing or that they offer a simplistic picture of the performance of the army. For, as was said in the previous chapter, these programs and blueprints assume that what is out there is programmable and hence they carry within themselves an impressive element of power; the picture they offer is impressive, in spite of their simplicity, indeed, *because* of their simplicity. Rather, the intention is to explain the nature of the discrepancy between the plan and its execution, and elaborate on the gap that separated the officer's view of the battle from the soldier's manner of actually fighting it.

This chapter has a wider interest, though. This manner of writing Egyptian military history as exemplified by Zakī's "battle piece" of the battle of Konia has its echo (and a much louder one at that) in the way of writing Egyptian history at large during the Pasha's reign – not only his military career. It has to be pointed out that the Pasha, although illiterate, was constantly "writing" letters (strictly speaking, dictating them to his scribes), issuing decrees and granting interviews, a point that was not lost on his contemporaries: as the Austrian internuncio once remarked: "The Pasha has not always the virtue of silence or simulation."[21] The result is countless letters and interviews that have been used by historians to construct a history of his reign, *using his own words*. The outcome is not surprising: his rule appears impressive, orderly and neat.[22] Mistakes are corrected, crimes are punished, irregularities are standardized and inconsistencies are ironed out. In these accounts it is possible to argue how the Pasha "was capable with his genius mind [to] . . . spread education, introduce industry, improve administration . . . and build a modern army."[23]

Using the military institution as an example this chapter attempts to come to a closer and, hopefully, more critical reading of these letters. It does not start with how "insightful" the great Pasha was or how ahead of his time he might have been. Instead, it argues that the Pasha, besides issuing often impressive, orderly regulations, was also under severe time and financial constraints that frequently forced him to deviate from the very laws he was issuing. Moreover, between the "insightful" command of the Pasha in his palace in Cairo and the soldier on the field or in his barracks stood hundreds of officers and commanders. An army the size of Mehmed Ali's, dependent on the state for its upkeep and maintenance, obviously also depended on hundreds of bureaucrats and scribes for the procurement of its provisions and supplies. These men often did not form a homogeneous group and their internal feuding occasionally affected the soldiers in ways that were most probably not envisaged by the Pasha. How can one read the letters of these innumerable bureaucrats and assistants of the Pasha who helped run his bureaucracy: as reflecting keen attempts of obedient, disinterested aides to fulfill blindly and lovingly the orders of their patron, or were they also sometimes moved by their own intrigues and internal fights and quarrels as well as by their limited understanding of their paymaster's wishes? In short, whilst appreciating the inherent power implied by the training manuals and the military laws which were reviewed in the last chapter and the impressive nature of the letters and regulations of the Pasha, this chapter attempts to contrast the image that comes across from reading these documents with other less impressive, but arguably more

21 Quoted in Sabry, *L'Empire égyptien*, p. 142.

22 Amīn Sāmī's *Taqwīm al-Nīl* is the perfect example of this style of writing about the Great Pasha: a Chronicle of the Nile based on Mehmed Ali's letters.

23 *Ibid.*, pp. 566 ff.

telling, documents and to understand the nature of the discrepancy between the two pictures.

The Pasha and the spectacle of the army

On the face of it, the army offered a very impressive spectacle of order and discipline that is often said to have characterized Mehmed Ali's entire reign. Its machine-like, disciplined and orderly appearance was not something that was discovered intuitively, or on closer inspection; rather, it was one of its essential components and its visual aspect was intended to be stunning and overwhelming. It was, literally, a spectacular thing. There is some evidence that this nature of the new army that clearly distinguished it from previous armies (e.g. the Mamluk army) was already apparent to Mehmed Ali and his senior officers. We have already seen in chapter 2 how impressed he was when he saw his assembled troops for the first time in the Banī ʿAdī camp in 1824. On a number of other occasions we see the Pasha using the army to impress the spectator, whether a foreign visitor or the local population of a conquered country. When in 1827, for example, the Pasha was visited by Süleyman Pasha, the vali of Crete, orders were issued to the Director of the War Department to chose 200 of the best officers, have them wear their "ceremonial uniforms" (*kisvet-i divaniye*) and stage a small parade for the visitor to watch.[24] Shortly after the fall of Acre in May 1832, the fortress was visited by an English officer who had recently arrived from Egypt. To impress him, orders were issued to all officers and soldiers in the castle to put on their new uniforms and "to be in the most perfect order."[25] On victoriously entering cities in Syria the soldiers were ordered to put on their special uniforms and to march in an orderly way through the cities for the inhabitants to see them.[26] (When a certain lieutenant refused to put on his ceremonial uniform he was sentenced to three days' "light arrest").[27]

Beyond these spectacles of order and discipline, however, lay a different picture altogether. What one sees behind this spectacular façade is indicative of the problems that the Pasha encountered in

[24] S/1/48/3/110 on 13 Ş 1242/12 March 1827; and S/1/48/3/113 on 15 Ş 1242/14 March 1827.

[25] Sham 8/196, on 30 M 1248/29 June 1832. The detailed account of his visit to the castle is in Sham 9/5, on 1 S 1248/30 June 1832.

[26] For the entry of the army to Jaffa see Sham 1/27, events of 15 C 1247/21 November 1831; for the entry to Adana, see Sham 11/24 and Sham 11/25, both on 3 R 1248/30 August 1832. The last document describes in detail the effect that this spectacle had on the inhabitants, some of whom had climbed on the roof tops to watch the army.

[27] Sham 11/49, on 6 R 1248/3 September 1832.

building his new army: officials cheating him, corrupt officers abusing their power, inefficient bureaucrats trying only to appease the Pasha, and even the Pasha himself occasionally passing inconsistent and sometimes contradictory orders.

A good example of the problems lying behind these façades of orderly spectacles is the way the officers attempted to get around the conditions laid down by the Pasha and his military authorities. In the early years of the army Mehmed Ali could not afford to wait till all his officers learned how to read and write. He wrote to Ibrahim Pasha telling him that "although the European armies have literate officers and engineers, we cannot afford to do the same when we establish our new regiments."[28] Eventually, however, literacy, and (oddly enough) good handwriting became a condition for promotion,[29] and it was decided that all candidates should provide samples of their handwriting for the Pasha to make sure that they were indeed literate.[30]

It could be argued in this respect that good handwriting was a sign of more than knowledge of reading and writing: it "supposes a gymnastic – a whole routine whose rigorous code invests the body in its entirety, from the points of the feet to the tips of the index finger."[31] Good handwriting in that respect was another spectacle that the Pasha was interested in, a minor spectacle, probably, but one that was supposed to be a sign of discipline, and a corollary of good training. Be that as it may, when sitting for this "exam" a lot of the candidates devised easy ways to get around this stipulation for promotion. Knowing that it was their handwriting that was decisive in getting them the jobs, they would repeatedly practice only one given text and would use it as a model (*meşk*) neglecting other tasks that they were supposed to be practicing "like dictation and composition." When the Pasha heard about this trick of the students, he wrote to the Director of his War Department telling him to inform the students that he was keeping samples of their handwriting that had been previously sent to him. On arriving at the camps, he said, he would dictate an unprepared text and then compare their previous handwriting with that of the dictated text, and "whoever

28 S/1/48/1/61 on 28 S 1239/4 November 1823.

29 For literacy being a condition of appointment to civilian positions, see Sāmī, ed., *Taqwīm al-Nīl*, II, p. 427, letter dated 30 Ca 1250/4 October 1834, concerning appointment of al-Majlis al-'Umūmī.

30 A number of these letters survive; see for example, S/1/48/1/362 and 363 both on 18 Za 1239/16 July 1824; S/1/48/1/440 on 8 Ca 1240/30 December 1824 in which the Pasha approves the promotion of a certain Hüseyin Efendi because he has good handwriting (*yazısı hoş*); S/1/48/2/384 on 4 Z 1241/10 July 1826; Sham 10/251, on 29 Ra 1248/27 August 1832.

31 Foucault, *Discipline and Punish*, p. 152.

is discovered to have been cheating in the above-mentioned way will be dealt with in the appropriate manner."[32]

Another example of how difficult it was for the Pasha to insure that his new institutions functioned the way he wanted them to is provided by the operation of the postal system. In order to insure that the Pasha in Egypt was kept informed about his army in Syria, Ibrahim Pasha devised a postal system that was intended to keep his father in constant touch with the army. Ibrahim divided the distance between the army HQ in Syria and Cairo into twelve equal intervals; at the end of each a postal station was to be built. In each of these stations an official was to be appointed and given a silver watch to check if the postmen relaying the letters between the stations arrived on time or not. In implementing this new order, however, it was discovered that although the postmen to be appointed to these new stations should have been able to read and write, not enough literate officials could be found to man them. To save time, it was decided to choose some officials and teach them the numbers from one to twelve only so as to be able to check on whether the postmen arrived on time or not.[33] It is doubtful whether an illiterate official who only knew the numbers from one to twelve could use a watch, silver or otherwise, and write a report about the punctuality of mail. What appears in principle to have been a modern way to deal with time and space, with time measured in minutes and seconds and space divided up into uniform, standardized distances, turns out to have been compromised in its implementation owing to serious pressing factors. However, in choosing the timing for launching his Syrian campaign Mehmed Ali did have other considerations more important than making sure that his postmen mastered the principles of mathematics.

It was these time constraints that often forced the Pasha to deviate from the original models he was following in building his army. At the outbreak of the Syrian war, for example, Ibrahim was repeatedly urging him to send him ammunition and supplies promptly "so as not to suffer from the lack of ammunition as I used to do while in the Morea." His father answered him by saying that he was doing everything possible to meet his requests. Ibrahim replied by saying that it seemed that Engineer Cerisy, who was in charge of the Arsenal in Alexandria, was very slow in preparing ships and sending them to Syria because he was

32 S/1/48/3/25 on 4 Ra 1242/6 October 1826. It is interesting to note that the Pasha himself was illiterate.

33 Sāmī, ed., *Taqwīm al-Nīl*, II, pp. 386–7, letter dated 5 Ş 1247/9 January 1832. For other information concerning the establishment of the postal system see Katkhoda 1/66, on 8 Ca 1239/10 January 1824; Divan-ı Hidiv 2/112, on 6 C 1248/31 October 1832; Sham 18/203, on 27 N 1248/19 February 1833.

insisting on doing things the "French way." He proposed to hand over the task of preparing the ships to Hajj ʿUmar

> because we do not have time to organize our affairs along French lines. What we need now is to prepare our ships with cannons and other supplies. When we finish our business here, and His Highness becomes the [undisputed] lord of these areas, then we can prepare our ships along French and English lines. Only then will we have ample time to do this.[34]

Mehmed Ali had no problems with this kind of logic and, keen as he was to follow the models he was borrowing from, he was aware of the practical problems he had to contend with. Similarly, impressive and spectacular as he might have found his new army, he was not bound by its visual order nor was he taken in by its spectacles. For example, when in 1824 he detected signs of a serious mutiny among his newly founded army he knew that he had to take some drastic measures to deal decisively with such an alarming situation. In doing so he showed that he understood something about the effect that orderly spectacles had, but that he was not bound by the idea of order that informed them, nor by the principle of "cynical," diffuse power (in the manner used by Foucault) that is also linked to them. For he then ordered all the soldiers of the regiment in question (the 1st Regiment that was on its way to Sudan) to stand in a row and every tenth soldier to step out of line. The soldiers thus selected would then form a line of their own and be shot in front of their colleagues "to be an example to others."[35] This can hardly be described as a just or predictable application of the law, yet it is one that is understandable, given the alarming nature of the situation. The following year when another mutiny broke out among the same troops who had taken up positions in the Sudan, this time he had no such qualms with "order." He told them that at a time when their "brethren in faith" had been fighting the Greek rebels in Morea and others were engaged in subduing the Wahhabi rebels in ʿAsīr, they had been disobeying orders to march with their new leader, Moho Bey. He swore by God, the Lord of the Kaʿba, that he would severely punish them by strangling them as dogs and throwing them to their deaths in the desert.[36]

The Pasha was a practical man and finding himself faced with situations like this he often had to violate some of the very principles which at other times he was seen to stress and to punish whoever deviated from them. Even the stern stance he took against corruption

[34] Sham 3/126, on 21 Ş 1247/25 January 1832.
[35] S/1/48/1/273 on 15 N 1239/13 May 1824.
[36] S/1/48/2/108 on 9 M 1241/24 August 1825. Moho Bey had been appointed Governor of Sudan in the previous May.

amongst his officials was sometimes compromised when this was expedient. It was once reported to him, for example, that the French instructor of the 19th Infantry Regiment had stolen 30 *ardabb*s of barley. The Pasha wrote to the Director of the War Department telling him that the instructor should be expelled from government service after giving him his salary. However, since he was an expert in his job and since his services were needed, "we should forget about the matter and have the lid covered on it (*mektum kalması matlubumdur*)."[37] In another case on 2 August 1832 a court martial was convened to try two officers from the 7th and 8th Infantry Regiments which were fighting in Syria at that time. The first case concerned a certain adjutant-major of the 8th Regiment, Mehmed Efendi by name, who had deserted from his regiment during battle. Although the law stipulated that in such cases the offender should be executed, the court martial ordered Mehmed Efendi to be sent to the Liman for life. The second case concerned another officer, Raşid Ağa, a second lieutenant of the 7th Regiment, who had deserted for the third time. The court martial changed the original sentence stated in the law (execution) to lashing and a three-month imprisonment. Seeing that there was a discrepancy in the application of the law, since the offense in both cases was the same (desertion) whereas two different sentences were passed on the same day, Mehmed Ali sent a strongly worded letter to Mahmud Bey, the Director of the War Department, ordering him to tell the members of the court martial to follow the letter of the law. At the same time, however, he said that these two officers should be sent to the Liman for life, although he acknowledged that the law said that they should be executed.[38] A dead man was of no use to the Pasha, whereas a trained officer on whose education and training the Pasha had spent valuable money could, if sentenced to hard labor in the Liman for life, at least be of some value in the form of productive hard work.

Financial constraints seem also to be behind the turning of a blind eye to the law in the following case involving Mohtar Bey, the first Director of the Schools Department. The case related to a serious incident concerning one of the students of the Translations School, Captain Abdallah by name,[39] who dared to verbally abuse and hit the Director of the school, Rifāʿa Bey al-Ṭahṭāwī, himself. Owing to the seriousness of the case, a special council was convened which decided

[37] S/1/48/4/71 on 10 B 1248/3 December 1833. The *ardabb* at Mehmed Ali's time was equal to anything between five and eight English bushels; Rivlin, *Agricultural Policy*, p. 361.

[38] Awamir lil-Jihadiyya 1/39, on 11 Ra 1248/8 August 1832.

[39] All students held military rank; see ʿAbdel-Karīm, *Tārīkh al-Taʿlīm*, p. 76.

after long deliberation to punish the student by demoting him two ranks, from captain to second lieutenant. When Mehmed Ali was informed of the case he wondered why the letter of the law (which stipulated that in such cases the offender should be imprisoned for five years) has not been implemented, especially since it was Rifāʿa Bey and not an ordinary officer who was involved.[40] To this Mohtar Bey answered saying that the reason for not executing the letter of the law was that he felt that since Abdallah Efendi had previously been sent to France and given that the government had incurred considerable expense in sending him on this mission, it would not have been very wise to expel him from school. Mehmed Ali did not like this answer and said that the student in question should be given three hundred lashes and then expelled from school. He explained this harsh treatment by saying that Rifāʿa Bey had trained many people with the rank of captain; in effect, that it was more profitable to appease him than be concerned about the money spent on the student.[41]

Besides the time and financial constraints that he was under, restrictions placed on him by his having only a limited pool of experts to draw on, and the fact that he sometimes had to contravene the law to avert certain serious situations, the Pasha was also in desperate need to create an elite around himself and his family. This reciprocal dependence prompted him to bestow favors that were sometimes undeserved and occasionally to turn a blind eye to mistakes committed by members of his elite. In his attempt to strengthen his rule and found a dynasty Mehmed Ali had to play his cards delicately and avoid unnecessarily antagonizing some members of his entourage only so as to uphold the letter of the law. For example, there is the case of a certain Ali Bey who was appointed as a captain but discharged because of his "lax and loose behavior." He presented a petition to the Pasha requesting to be reappointed in the army and Mehmed Ali accepted it because "the man was the nephew of Ali Bey Maraşlı" who had been working in the War Department and "was a member of an old family."[42] A certain captain, Yakup Efendi, was once ordered to go to Cyprus to join the Pasha's forces there. He took forty-five days' leave to go to Cairo first. However, he stayed three more months in the city without permission. When the case was brought to the Pasha, he wrote to Ibrahim Efendi, the governor of Cyprus, telling him that, so long as the man had stayed in Cairo for "only" four and a half months, then the case should be dropped; if, on the other hand, it was discovered that he had stayed longer than that,

40 Madaris1/102, on 12 R 1254/5 July 1838.
41 Madaris 1/105, on 21 R 1254/14 July 1838.
42 S/1/48/4/623 on 23 Ca 1250/30 July 1834.

then he should be punished. The officer's full name was Yakup Arnavut which suggests that this exception might have been due to the fact that the man in question was, like the Pasha himself, of Albanian origin.[43] In another case Brigadier Ömer Bey held an investigation into the regiments under his command and found the regiment of Colonel Selim Bey, which was stationed at Rosetta at that time, improperly kept with "serious violations regarding the health conditions of the soldiers and in their training." During the court martial of Selim Bey, the Colonel was found guilty of negligence and sentenced to fifteen days in prison. The sentence was later reduced to only five days. Mehmed Ali wrote what was, given the gravity of the offense, a surprisingly softly worded letter to Selim Bey and told him to bear up under the sentence, that it could have been much harsher, and "warning" him that next time he would not interfere.[44] The whole incident sounds more like a nursery spanking than an attempt to impose military discipline.

The picture of the logical, consistent and predictable law offered in the last chapter need not be challenged when we compare it to these cases of how the law was actually applied and punishment orders implemented. Like other spectacles that the Pasha was fond of, legal codes, courts martial and predictable punishments were all part of a new way of imposing order and discipline on society. He seems to have believed that it was in the military that these modern methods of order and discipline could best be tried out. However, being a practical man he also understood that given his limited resources these new techniques of ordering and organizing society should function only as models to be approached as closely as possible and which could, and indeed should, be violated if need be.

Ibrahim Pasha and his officers

One of the problems that faced the Pasha in founding his army was how to create a well-trained and reliable officer corps, and it might be said that the problems he faced in creating such a group of men who would lead his soldiers in battle with efficiency and who, at the same time, would owe him respect and loyalty was as serious as the problems he faced in conscripting the peasants into the army. To a large extent, it could also be said that he succeeded in creating such a group of loyal and reliable officers. However, given the high priority he attached to their loyalty, they were often inefficient and many of them made bad

[43] S/1/48/3/62 on 12 C 1242/12 January 1827. Arnavut means Albanian.
[44] S/1/48/4/651 on 20 C 1250/24 October 1834.

officers. Moreover, given the ethnic origins of the majority of them, they were very different and distant from the men they were commanding.

The men who formed the senior echelons of the officer corps were composed of three main groups. At the heart of the officer corps and occupying the most senior military posts were the Pasha's blood relatives, his in-laws or his personal freed slaves. Even a cursory look at the composition of the top positions in the army at any moment in time will reveal this aspect of Mehmed Ali's army, namely that this was a "household army."[45] During the Morean war, for example, the head of the Egyptian navy was Müharrem Bey, the Pasha's son-in-law. Later on Mehmed Said Pasha, his fourth son, was appointed as head of the navy. The army that invaded Syria was headed by his son, Ibrahim Pasha; the head of the infantry force was Ibrahim Pasha Yeğen, his nephew (who had earlier been governor of Yemen); the head of the cavalry forces was Abbas Pasha, his grandson. After capturing Syria, Mahmud Şerif Pasha, another nephew of the Pasha, was appointed as its governor. Fourteen months after the outbreak of the Syrian war Mehmed Ali decided to replace his Director of the War Department. The new *nāẓīr* was to be Ahmed Pasha Yeğen, who had been military commander of the Hijaz but whose most important credentials for the job was the fact that he was yet another nephew of the Pasha.

As peculiar as this aspect of the army may appear it allowed the Pasha to create a nucleus of officers which by the very nature of things were closely tied to him and stood to rise or fall with him. To cement this core of officers the Pasha appointed his own personal mamluks in senior positions in the army to form the second component of the officer corps. Those were the mamluks whom Süleyman Pasha was training in the Aswan school back in 1820–3. The problem with these mamluk officers was not lack of loyalty to the Pasha but insufficient training. Although a staff college was established as early as 1825 for these mamluk cadets to be trained and although it was reputed to be one of the best of the Pasha's educational institutions,[46] it shared the same problems as the other schools, namely, students were recruited to it before they had finished their courses in the preparatory schools and were discharged from it before they had properly finished their study there.[47] This low level of competence of the new officers showed itself clearly during the Syrian campaign. One of the things Ibrahim was

[45] For the "household" nature of Mehmed Ali's government in general see Hunter, *Egypt*, pp. 22–7.

[46] St. John, *Egypt*, II, p. 399; Heyworth-Dunne, *Education*, p. 119.

[47] ʿAbdel-Karīm, *Tārīkh al-Taʿlīm*, pp. 628–9. See also Shukrī's negative assessment of the school, Shukrī "Baʿtha ʿaskariyya Būlūniyya," p. 30.

constantly complaining about to his father was that whereas his soldiers showed "exceptional signs of bravery and courage,"[48] the same could not be said about his officers. When the siege of Acre was prolonged and the city did not fall immediately as expected, Mehmed Ali wrote to Ibrahim suggesting that he should offer the besieged some money so as not to waste time and proceed to fight the Ottomans before they amassed their troops against him. Ibrahim answered by saying that he had yet to learn that cities were taken by money and that he intended to reduce it to a heap of rubble until it surrendered.[49] The problem he was facing, he insisted, was not lack of money or soldiers, but of trained officers. This was the reason he gave for the prolonged siege of the city.[50] Finally when the city did fall Ibrahim could not but admire the courage and fortitude of the soldiers attacking the city and said that he had yet to see other soldiers who could match them. He had no such complimentary words for his officers.[51]

The problems of the composition of the officer corps are compounded, moreover, when we add its third component. In addition to the students whom the Pasha had sent to Europe in the late twenties and who came back during the mid-thirties to be appointed to senior positions in the army and the bureaucracy, this group also included men from all corners of the Ottoman world, Albanians, Circassians, Georgians, Moreans, Anatolians and Istanbullites. These men came to Egypt with their families seeking employment and entered the Pasha's service both in his civil bureaucracy and his army and navy, gradually becoming members of the new elite centered around Mehmed Ali and his family.[52] But again, as enthusiastic as they might have been in their new posts they were often at odds with their fellow officers with whom they had nothing in common except the desire and willingness to appease the Pasha and members of his family. In the middle of battle the officers would encourage their soldiers to fight telling them not to take heed of the approaching danger and writing in their reports (which they knew quite well would be sent to the Pasha in Cairo), "What do you think we came here for except to sacrifice our souls for the sake of our lord."[53]

48 Sham 2/64, on 10 B 1247/15 December 1831.

49 Sham 2/41, on 3 B 1247/8 December 1831.

50 Sham 5/142, on 23 L 1247/26 March 1832.

51 Sham 7/3, on 1 M 1248/31 May 1832. Contemporary observers also commented that "the officers compose by far the worst class of the Egyptian army"; Scott, *Rambles in Egypt*, II, p. 227.

52 Hunter, *Egypt*, pp. 22–7; al-Sayyid Marsot, *Egypt*, pp. 75–99.

53 This was the lieutenant-colonel of the 8th Infantry Regiment, Mehmed Ağa, encouraging his men in a minor skirmish against some of ʿAbdallah Pasha's soldiers who came out of the castle during the siege of Acre, Sham 2/64, on 12 B 1247/17

The officer corps of Mehmed Ali's army was thus characterized by an odd mixture of their members; and their failure to create a working *esprit de corps* was offset only by Ibrahim Pasha's strong and decisive leadership. Realizing that they were profit-seekers and unwieldy he was constantly complaining of their impetuous behavior to his father in Cairo. In one stormy letter to his father's chief secretary, Sami Bey, the *baş-muʿavin*, he described the officers of the 9th Cavalry Regiment as "Turks with mixed ancestries [who were] nothing but drunkards and rascals (*çapkın*)." He suggested getting rid of them all and replacing them with natives.[54] Occasionally personal, unprofessional rivalries would break out in open conflict and Ibrahim would rush to defuse the situation. At the very start of the Syrian campaign, for example, and just after the army had departed from Ṣālḥiyya a big fight broke out between Saleh Bey, Colonel of the 3rd Cavalry Regiment, and Süleyman Bey (i.e. Colonel Sèves – he had not yet acquired the title of Pasha) who was heading an infantry regiment. The fight seems to have been about how to secure the transportation of the army and its equipment: whether to hire camels from the bedouins or to depend completely on government camels.[55] Whatever its cause the dispute was a serious one and news about it reached Mehmed Ali in Cairo who wrote to Ibrahim asking him to investigate the matter immediately. Ibrahim reprimanded Saleh Bey so heavily that he told his father that he doubted that a court martial would have been that harsh. The reason he went so far, he explained, was that Saleh Bey was a stubborn, thick-headed man (*kafası kalın*). Ibrahim did not have very kind words to say about Süleyman Bey either. He said that since he was originally French, he is known be rude and quick tempered.[56]

Later on, and during the course of the Syrian war, Ibrahim came to develop a very smooth working relationship with Süleyman Pasha. However, he was well aware that in general his officers were not as reliable as his soldiers and that his presence was crucial for the cohesiveness of the entire officer corps. He therefore dealt very firmly with any attempt to challenge his authority. An example might show how careful he was in stressing his authority in the army, particularly among his senior officers. At the height of the Syrian war and after

December 1831. See also Osman Nureddin's letter in which he says "Day and night we do our best to fulfill the Khedival wishes"; Sham 1/35, on 24 C 1247/30 November 1831.

54 Sham 31/79, on 4 S 1251/1 June 1835. It seems that by "natives" he meant Syrians since he was writing this letter from Syria and was referring to people he could raise and train from there.

55 For the details of the dispute, see Sham 1/27, on 30 Ca 1247/6 November 1831.

56 Sham 2/62, on 15 B 1247/20 December 1831.

capturing Damascus, Ibrahim Pasha issued orders to Brigadier Ahmed Bey Istanbullu to march from Damascus to Tripoli and to stay there until further notice. Ahmed Bey, however, disobeyed orders and initiated a march towards Ibrahim Pasha's camp. When Ibrahim heard about this he ordered a court martial to be convened at once "because we do not have beys or princes [in the army], and whoever has his leg slipping (*ayağı kayan*) is immediately led to the court for his case to be reviewed there." Ibrahim wrote to Abbas Pasha asking him to convene a court martial immediately, and sure enough his nephew was soon presiding over one that was composed of six brigadiers, four colonels and a lieutenant-colonel. The military tribunal found Ahmed Bey guilty of violating military laws in times of war and sentenced him to five months' imprisonment in the Liman of Alexandria. Because of the army's need for such a senior officer and owing to the "delicacy of the situation," however, Ibrahim Pasha reduced the sentence to only thirty-one days' imprisonment. Furthermore, it soon became clear why the original harsh sentence was passed in the first place: Ahmed Bey had dared to send his daily reports directly to the War Department in Egypt rather than sending them to Ibrahim Pasha first, thus appearing to ignore and circumvent the authority of Ibrahim Pasha. It was this action rather than the alleged disobeying of orders that prompted Ibrahim Pasha to humiliate the officer since he "pretended that I am not Serasker [i.e. Commander-in-Chief]."[57]

As watchful as Ibrahim was of his commanders, he could not, of course, control the activities of every officer in the army. One problem was particularly difficult: nepotism in promotions. Given the very nature of the army, however, it is not surprising to find nepotism at work whether in cases of appointments, promotions, or exemptions from punishments. Bearing in mind the composition of the officer corps of the army and in particular appointments to the senior positions, nepotism appears to have been an essential element in the army and not a mere aberration to be corrected. As early as 1823 when the first regiments were being formed, complaints about irregularities and inconsistencies in promotion were being reported.[58] In 1838 Mehmed Bey, a colonel in the artillery corps, promoted a certain soldier – who had been studying in the School of Accountants – from student to chief

[57] This account is gathered from the following four documents, all in Sham, box 10: doc. 58, on 8 Ra 1248/5 August 1832; doc. 81, on 10 Ra 1248/7 August 1832; doc. 86, on 11 Ra 1248/8 August 1832, and doc. 96, on 12 Ra 1248/9 August 1832. This is the same Ahmed Bey we saw at the beginning of the chapter.

[58] S/1/48/1/55 on 3 S 1239/9 October 1823.

instructor to second lieutenant. When Mehmed Ali heard about this, he sent a letter to Kani Bey who had been promoted to become Deputy Director of the War Department and asked him how Mehmed Bey could do this knowing that the student had committed many crimes before and had been previously sentenced to stay a private for life (*kaydıhayatla nefer kayd*). He was answered that the colonel had not been aware of this. The Pasha refuted this allegation saying that the student's papers clearly showed his previous record and that this promotion could not have been done except with prior agreement between the student and the colonel.[59]

NCOs were also constantly presenting petitions to the authorities about irregularities in promotion. In 1836, for example, a certain second lieutenant in Ahmed Pasha Menilikli's Guardia Regiment presented a petition directly to the Pasha saying that he had graduated from the Giza School of Cavalry among a class of forty students. Since then his colleagues had been distributed among the various regiments and promoted to higher ranks, some having even been promoted to the ranks of captain and major, while he remained a second lieutenant for six years. The reason, he said, was that his major, Ahmed Efendi, the first Major of the Guardia Regiment, "does not like me very much [*lays bayni wa baynahu maḥabba zayida*]. The major [he added] holds drinking parties every night in his tent and invites the captains of his battalion who back him up in front of his colonel [*yaṣīr baynahum rabiṭa bi'annahum uṣaddiquhu ʿind miralay*]. In return, the major promotes these members of his entourage (*hamshariyatahu*)." He concluded by saying that the same was being done by Brigadier Selim Bey. Significantly, in his response to this petition, Mehmed Ali did not order an investigation into the behavior of the senior officers whose names were mentioned by the petitioner; he only ordered the Deputy Director of the War Department to investigate the matter and "please" the man if he had a case, and "silence" him, if he did not.[60]

The problem in fact lay deeper than addressing a particular grievance or correcting a minor mistake. If these senior officers had been appointed to their positions mostly on the strength of their personal relationship to Mehmed Ali or some member of his household, why should they not do the same thing themselves and appoint or promote some of their own friends or members of their families?

59 Awamir lil-Jihadiyya 1/211, on 26 Z 1253/1 March 1838.
60 Both the petition and Mehmed Ali's response are in Awamir lil-Jihadiyya 1/94, on 12 M 1252/29 April 1836.

The sinews of power

If this is how things looked liked in the sanguinary fields of battle, the situation was not much different in the dimly lit offices of the bureaucracy. As well-knit as the military elite of the army might have been, between the strategic planning mind of Mehmed Ali and the insightful command of Ibrahim Pasha, on the one hand, and the fighting soldiers in the fields, on the other hand, lay hundreds, if not thousands, of bureaucrats, clerks and scribes. It was these meticulous officials and bookkeepers "with ink-stained hands rather than bloody arms"[61] who helped lubricate Mehmed Ali's military machine and it was that bureaucracy that sustained the army and enabled it to wage its numerous victorious battles.

Sustaining an army of around 130,000 men on a more or less constant war footing was no easy task, though. The problems encountered in keeping this army well fed, adequately clothed, and regularly paid were as significant as collecting the peasants from the villages and turning them into disciplined soldiers. This massive task demanded the build-up of state power to an extent unprecedented in Egyptian history and an encroachment by the state on people's lives in a way previously unparalleled. It entailed levying higher rates of taxation to enable the government to pay the soldiers and officers more or less punctually, requisitioning foodstuffs and sending them to the troops on the front and in the camps hundreds of miles away from home, manufacturing uniforms for the troops and finding men and women who were capable of working in the various factories that were geared to military production. In addition, it meant securing horses, mules, cows and oxen that were for the most part the motive force of these factories. Attention had also to be given to such logistical considerations as policing the passage of more and more troops to the battle areas (which by the mid-1830s had covered wide areas of the far-flung Ottoman Empire), establishing a proper communication network that would guarantee the delivery of these various requisitions to the troops, as well as sustaining an efficient postal system, which an army of that size necessitated. Of more importance, the modern army necessitated the founding of a modern medical system that would be capable of treating the wounded in battle, preventing diseases from spreading among the soldiers in the highly crowded camps and barracks, and finally of treating the officers and soldiers from the diseases that they were constantly afflicted by. In short, the importance of Mehmed Ali's army lies not only in its size or

[61] John Brewer, *The Sinews of Power: War, Money and the English State, 1688–1783* (London: Unwin Hyman, 1989), p. xvi.

in the fact that it relied on what appears to have been universal conscription, but also in the economic–bureaucratic structure that supported and sustained it. Without an analysis of the working of this war machine no clear understanding of the performance of this army would be complete.

On the face of it, Mehmed Ali seems to have seen the connection between his fighting force and a strong economic base. Both he and Ibrahim Pasha took care, for example, that their soldiers were regularly paid and well provided for and that they were not allowed to live off the land they marched through. Plunder and booty were strictly forbidden.[62] Orders were issued attempting to send pay, food and other supplies to different army units, wherever they were.[63] This is one of the most important features that distinguished Mehmed Ali's army from previous armies: whereas soldiers in previous armies were left to their own devices, Mehmed Ali's army depended on the modern state structure that had been founded primarily to support it. However, in spite of these orders, the pay of the soldiers was continually several months in arrears,[64] and the soldiers were often complaining and causing disturbances and sometimes rising in open rebellion against their commanding officers.[65] In one incident, troops sent to Cyprus to subdue a rebellion themselves revolted against Mehmed Ali and his government on the island; the Pasha wrote them an open order to be read aloud in front of them warning them of the consequences. He said, "I know that you still have not received a fifteen-month pay in arrears since you were in the Hijaz, and another fifteen-to-twenty-month pay since you were in the Sudan . . . You have to know, however, that you are not alone in this respect and that other troops in the Morea and in Crete also have their pay in arrears." He then warned them that if they did not end their rebellion, he would send troops by sea to deal with them and would write to the Sadrazam asking him to block their way to

62 There are numerous letters and decrees forbidding and punishing these practices. See, for example, S/1/48/1/398 on 9 Ra 1240/2 November 1824 stopping these practices in the Sudan; S/1/48/1/84 on 7 R 1239/11 December 1823 (Cyprus); S/1/50/4/316 on 2 B 1239/3 March 1824 (Crete); S/5/51/3/22 on 22 M 1248/22 June 1832 (Syria).

63 See, for example, S/1/48/2/316 on 22 C 1241/5 December 1825 concerning the pay of the troops in Morea.

64 Barker, *Syria and Egypt*, II, p. 60; Driault, *L'Egypte et l'Europe*, IV, p. 131; Rivlin, *Agricultural Policy*, pp. 202–3.

65 See, for example, the case of the rebellion by troops in Upper Egypt in April 1827, in which they attacked, killed and then mutilated the body of their commander, Abdin Cashef. Although it seems that there were other reasons for this rebellion, Salt is no doubt that it was at least sparked off by delays in pay; FO 78/160, Salt, dispatches of 13, 22 and 22 April 1827.

the north in case they fled.[66] Even during the Syrian campaign, which was arguably the best organized campaign, Ibrahim was writing to his father urging him to send the pay of the troops regularly since the revenue he had been able to raise from Syria was not enough to meet the various expenses of the campaign and "the men are left penniless in these strange lands (*şimdi asker bu gurbette parasız kaldı*)."[67] This was the case not only with soldiers' pay; army physicians and instructors were also complaining that their salaries were six months in arrears. When once they refused to accept a two-month pay out of the six-month pay that they were owed, Mehmed Ali wrote to Osman Nureddin, the Chief of Staff, telling him to try to convince them to be more patient.[68]

Feeding the army was considerably more complicated than paying the troops, if only because of the logistical problems involved. The same discrepancy between the authorities' blueprints and their actual implementation by the bureaucracy existed in the case of requisitioning food for the troops as in that of sending them their monthly pay. When the Pasha dispatched one of his earliest regiments to the Hijaz to quell the ʿAsīrī revolt in 1823 he soon realized that their monthly pay would not be enough for their subsistence and that his new troops had to be fed by their units and not be allowed to live off the land as the old troops used to do. "Although these new troops are well trained and follow known and fixed regulations," he told his nephew, Ahmed Pasha Yeğen, who was then governor of Mecca, "their pay is only 15 piasters and hence they will not be able to subsist in the way the old infantry soldiers used to do. It has been decided, therefore, that their food rations be sent with the army and distributed to them daily."[69] However, in implementing these orders of the Pasha enormous problems were encountered. Sea captains ordered to deliver the army's supplies of food and military equipment from the Egyptian ports of Suez and Quṣair to the Arabian port of Jedda complained of low pay and refused to undertake the job.[70] The amount of food sent to Arabia, when it did arrive, was discovered to be insufficient and it was suspected that the sea captains might have been stealing from it. Since on being loaded in Quṣair, however, it was not weighed, it was impossible to ask them to make good the difference.[71]

Supplying bread and meat are probably the best examples of the

[66] This was when he was still fighting alongside the Sadrazam against the Greek rebels. S/5/51/1/137 and 139, both on 22 N 1242/20 April 1827.
[67] Sham 11/74, on 9 R 1248/5 September 1832.
[68] S/1/48/2/414 on 21 M 1242/25 August 1826.
[69] S/1/50/4/156 on 6 Z 1238/14 August 1823.
[70] S/1/50/4/592 and 593 both on 29 Ra 1240/22 November 1824.
[71] S/1/48/1/149 on 20 Ca 1239/24 November 1823.

authorities' frustrated attempts to feed the soldiers properly and of the logistical problems encountered in making sure that these essential food supplies reached the soldiers regularly and in good condition. The military journals of the army in Syria are full of administrative orders attempting to supply bread (usually *peksimet*, i.e. hard, dried biscuits) and meat to the soldiers in various localities and, in particular, those on the march so that they would not attack peasants' lands on their way.[72] However, in actual fact, these orders were very difficult to implement. The bread issued to the soldiers was often either rotten or improperly cooked, and Ibrahim Pasha had to order an investigation into why it was constantly inedible and black in color.[73] Earlier in Arabia the situation was not much better. In response to repeated complaints that the warehouses in Jedda were empty, Mehmed Ali wrote to the governor of Mecca insisting that enough food supplies had already been sent and it could not be true as was claimed by his officials there that the supplies had already been used up.[74] It was later discovered that these warehouses were unsuitable for storing food and that in consequence a lot of the *peksimet* sent had gone bad and "entered the state of that which has a name but no body (*ismi var cismi yok*)."[75] The problems of inadequate storage conditions, bad quality of food and untimely deliveries to the army in Arabia continued to irk the authorities which could not find proper ways to keep the army well fed. When Mehmed Bey, the Colonel of the 2nd Infantry Regiment stationed in Hijaz, complained about these problems, Mehmed Ali answered him by saying that he had had enough of his complaints and that the governor should be satisfied with whatever was sent to him.[76] More than ten years later the governor who replaced him was still inundated with complaints by officials about the quality of food which they insisted was inedible. He answered them by saying that there was nothing he could do since it was the Pasha in Egypt who had to decide on matters like this. He therefore sent the Pasha a sample of the food that was given to the soldiers so that he could see it for himself. He was not deterred by the fact that it would have taken weeks before his

72 See, for example, Vehid Efendi's report in Sham, 8/105 on 13 M 1248/13 June 1832. But see also Sham 9/81, on 15 S 1248/15 July 1832 in which the same scribe reports that during a twelve-hour march a number of soldiers died of thirst.

73 Sham 11/44, on 5 R 1248/1 September 1832.

74 S/1/48/1/66 on 4 Ra 1239/8 November 1823.

75 Katkhoda 1/60, on 27 R 1239/1 January 1824. It seems that the investigation mentioned in S/1/47/7/273 on 24 Ra 1241/7 November 1825, which was to look into the reason for some 22,000 *qintārs* of biscuits going rotten, was a follow-up of that incident.

76 S/1/48/2/70 on 21 Za 1240/8 July 1825.

shipment was received by the Pasha in Cairo, and that in itself would have made the bread even worse.[77]

Meat was another item that the authorities were desperate to make sure that the soldiers receive in good condition. In principle, besides properly baked bread, rice, lentils and beans,[78] soldiers were supposed to be given meat once every five days.[79] The scribes accompanying the army in Syria repeatedly wrote in their journals how every effort was taken to ensure that meat was supplied to the army. Usually this was done by ordering local governors to buy animals from the farmers at "just prices."[80] However, and in spite of these measures, there were repeated complaints that meat was not delivered to the soldiers on time. An investigation into the condition of the troops in Tripoli conducted by Colonel Yusuf Bey revealed that the soldiers there were left with no food for three days.[81] The Infantry School in Hankah, near Cairo, received no rice or meat for such a long time that the director had to go to the market and buy food with his own money.[82] When the Department of Civil Affairs (the *Divan-ı Hidiv*) heard that the students in a certain military school in Cairo had received meat only once a month the head of the *Divan* wrote to the master of the school and reprimanded him strongly telling him that if the Pasha found out about this, he would be punished "together with every one of us."[83] Soldiers, finding themselves penniless, forbidden to live off the land and, in addition, inadequately fed by their own army, sometimes had to report their commanding officers to higher authorities. In a certain case seven soldiers of a sappers' regiment were left with no food for three days. When they went to their captain to complain he forced them to lie on the floor and gave every one of them four lashes with the cane. They decided to bring their case before a court martial which imprisoned the officer in question for ten days.[84]

Clothing the army was another task that caused enormous problems for the authorities in their attempt to meet the Pasha's targets. Right from the early days of the army Mehmed Ali had decided that like the modern armies of Europe, his soldiers were to be clad in standardized uniforms and his officers were to be dressed in fine, even extravagant

77 Hijaz 4/52, on 21 M 1254/17 April 1838.
78 Clot Bey, *'Ajāla*, p. 7.
79 This stipulation also applied to naval soldiers. Dhawat 2/95, on 7 Z 1241/13 July 1826.
80 Sham 9/31, on 5 S 1248/3 July 1832. For an example of such orders see Sham 2/50, on 4 B 1247/27 November 1832.
81 Sham 2/95, on 2 Ş 1247/6 January 1832.
82 S/1/48/4/435 on 19 Za 1249/10 April 1834.
83 Divan-ı Hidiv, register no. 737, doc. 439, on 13 B 1243/30 January 1828.
84 Sham 3/98, on 6 Ş 1247/10 January 1832. It is obvious from the names of the soldiers that they were all Egyptian Arabs, while the officer (Badr Ağa) was most likely a Turk.

costumes.[85] Initially some soft cloth (*bafta*) was chosen, but seeing that it would not withstand the tough exercises of the soldiers, broadcloth was chosen instead[86] and orders were sent to provincial governors to collect such cloth from the fellahin.[87] A foreign craftsman was invited to start a broadcloth industry in the country, and to guarantee him a regular supply of wool all the sheep in the country were to be registered,[88] and eventually the trade monopolized by the Pasha.[89] Later on it was decided to build cloth factories with the main intention of supplying the army with its cloth needs.[90] In addition to producing the army's uniforms domestically, the Pasha also issued orders for the manufacture of fezzes[91] and shoes.[92] Before the departure of the various campaigns the Pasha used to write to the directors of the various manufacturing establishments as well as to the various army administrators in an attempt to make sure that the uniforms and equipment of the soldiers were sent with them,[93] and he also decided that, as a matter of principle, the soldiers should be issued a new set of uniform every two years.[94]

However, in spite of these ambitious policies of the Pasha and the various decrees he issued whilst attempting to put them into action, there were enormous obstacles in implementation and rarely did things happen exactly as planned. The factories were always given short notice to fulfill the requirements of the army and were constantly late in

85 A colonel's costume was reported to cost 60,000 piastres; see David Nicolle, "Nizam – Egypt's army in the nineteenth century," Pt. I, *The Army Quarterly and Defence Journal* 108 (1978), p. 70. For an idea of the design of the officers' uniforms see S/1/50/2/367 on 22 Z 1237/11 November 1822; 'Abdel Raḥmān Zakī, *Malābis al-Jaysh al-Miṣrī fī 'Ahd Muḥammad 'Alī al-Kabīr* [Uniforms of the Egyptian Army During the Reign of Mehmed Ali the Great] (Cairo: al-Maṭba'a al-Amīriyya, 1949); Bowring, "Report on Egypt," p. 51; Clot Bey, *Aperçu*, II, pp. 223–4; Scott, *Rambles in Egypt*, II, pp. 223–5. For diagrams see Weygand, *Histoire militaire* I, pl. no. 77, and II, pls. nos. 107, 108 and 125.

86 S/1/50/2/174 on 25 C 1237/20 March 1822.

87 S/1/50/2/268 on 8 N 1237/30 May 1822.

88 S/1/50/5/127 on 10 Ca 1239/12 January 1824.

89 S/1/50/5/154 on 26 Ca 1239/28 January 1824. For the cultivation of special dyes see S/1/50/5/185 on 3 B 1239/6 March 1824.

90 S/1/47/7/297 on 26 R 1241/9 December 1825. The cloth produced was not only for the manufacture of uniforms; it was also intended to make sails for the navy's ships (see S/1/48/2/50 on 11 Za 1240/28 June 1825 and S/1/48/2/107 on 9 M 1241/24 August 1825) as well as tents for the army (see S/1/47/7/436 on 9 Ş 1241/19 March 1826).

91 The order establishing the fez factory in Fuwwa is in S/1/47/7/56 on 9 N 1240/27 April 1825. For a description of the factory, see St. John, *Egypt*, I, pp. 84–5.

92 Katkhoda 1/58, on 26 Ra 1239/1 December 1823. For a description of the tannery in Rosetta, see Scott, *Rambles in Egypt*, I, p. 64.

93 When additional troops were sent to Syria, for example, their uniforms were ordered to be prepared and sent with them: Sham 3/118, on 19 Ş 1247/22 January 1832.

94 Awamir lil-Jihadiyya 1/229, on 22 Ca 1257/13 July 1841.

supplying them.[95] Although the Pasha considered that the local production of fezzes should take first priority and insisted that they should not be imported,[96] he found, during an unexpected visit to one of the frigates of his navy, the sailors wearing French headpieces. The factory in Fuwwa was said to have an abundant supply of them but, Motoş Bey, the head of the navy, who was accompanying the Pasha, said that he had not received any fezzes from the factory in question.[97] Moreover, those that the factory did produce were sometimes discovered to be the wrong size and moth-eaten and had to be returned.[98] This in spite of the fact that the fez factory was supposed to be one of the Pasha's best industrial enterprises.[99]

The cloth factories also very often produced defective uniforms and Ibrahim Pasha repeatedly complained to Edhem Bey, the Inspector of Munitions, about the quality of uniforms supplied to the army and told him that "military matters are not to be compared to other matters."[100] The quality of footwear was another matter about which Ibrahim complained.[101] In a certain incident 10,000 pairs of shoes were made in Egypt and promptly sent to the army in Syria only for it to be discovered that they were all so small as to fit only children's feet![102]

Moreover, besides the bad quality of supplies sent to the army, there were also constant complaints of untimely deliveries. In the summer of 1832, for example, when it started to become obvious that the troops might have to spend the winter in Syria and that they were not equipped to face the cold weather, Ibrahim Pasha wrote to the authorities in Egypt requesting the dispatch of proper winter clothes.[103] By December, however, the clothes had still not arrived and the soldiers had to use carpets as coats to protect them from the cold Anatolian winter that they were not accustomed to,[104] and Mehmed Ali was still writing

95 See for example Mehmed Ali's sarcastic letter to his deputy reprimanding him for completing only one-third of the uniforms (36,000 in all) in half the time he was allotted; Katkhoda 1/72, on 21 Ca 1239/14 January 1824.
96 S/1/47/7/62 on 11 N 1240/29 April 1825.
97 Dhawat 2/56, on 18 Z 1244/21 June 1829. Bowring says that the factory was producing ten to twelve dozen a day, although it had the capacity of producing more; Bowring, "Report on Egypt," p. 42.
98 Awamir lil-Jihadiyya 1/83, on 27 N 1251/17 January 1836.
99 St. John, *Egypt*, I, p. 84.
100 S/1/48/4/206 on 14 Ş 1249/3 July 1833. This is the same Edhem Bey who eventually headed the Schools Department from 1839 to 1848.
101 Sham 2/95, on 2 Ş 1247/6 January 1832; Sham 10/55, on 7 Ra 1248/5 August 1832; and Sham 10/62, on 8 Ra 1248/6 August 1832.
102 S/5/51/2/151 on 19 Z 1247/20 May 1832.
103 Sham 10/125, on 16 Ra 1248/14 August 1832; Sham 10/199, on 22 Ra 1248/20 August 1832.
104 Sham 15/175, on 15 B 1248/9 December 1832.

to the Director of the War Department urging him to send the winter clothes that his son had been requesting since the previous summer.[105] In the event, and because of inadequate clothing, some soldiers could not stand the cold and had to be declared medically unfit for service.[106] Even well into the Egyptian occupation the army was still suffering from late delivery of clothes: in December 1834 the 20th Infantry Regiment had been repeatedly asking for its uniforms to be delivered and the soldiers were "left almost naked" (*neferat . . . pek cıplak kalmıştır*).[107] Moreover, and in spite of repeated orders not to send army units without their equipment, regiments were often ordered to be dispatched to their destinations without having "any of their equipment ready." On the very same day of the departure of the army to Syria the 10th Infantry Regiment still had no uniforms and "none of the necessary equipment of the 12th Infantry Regiment had arrived."[108] After the battle of Konia a number of cavalrymen were sent to Anatolia to fill the gaps of the 5th Regiment stationed there. They arrived, however, with neither horses nor saddles. Instead of waiting for their equipment to arrive from Egypt, Ibrahim Yeğen decided to collect between five and ten horses from each tribe in the area as a tax.[109] On arriving in Syria, the 3rd Cavalry Regiment was discovered to have been sent without its uniforms. Ibrahim Pasha wrote to the Director of the War Department telling him that whereas the main responsibility of this lay with the brigadier and the colonel and other senior officers of the regiment he, too, was not blameless. Anticipating that the Director would answer saying that he could not issue such military equipment without having a receipt in exchange, he told him that if he was so concerned about proper proceedings, he should have forged a receipt and sent it to himself "so as to keep your books tidy." He added that such silly bureaucratic excuses should not stand in the way of the execution of those important orders.[110]

These might have been silly excuses for Ibrahim; they were hardly so for the hundreds and thousands of scribes and bureaucrats who had to fulfill these orders. Their daily routine was spent attempting to meet some impossible targets of the Pasha, his son or some senior official. A provincial governor, for example, was ordered to collect 350 *qintārs*[111] of ghee from his province. He was only able to collect 100 *qintārs* and

[105] S/1/48/4/111 on 21 Ş 1248/14 January 1833.
[106] S/1/48/4/199 on 5 S 1249/24 June 1833.
[107] Sham 29/263, on 9 Ş 1250/11 December 1834.
[108] Awamir lil-Jihadiyya 1/22, on 25 Ca 1247/2 November 1831.
[109] Sham 18/193, on 26 N 1248/17 February 1833.
[110] Sham 2/88, on 29 B 1247/31 December 1831.
[111] 1 *qintār* was approx. 100 lbs; Rivlin, *Agricultural Policy*, p. 366.

said in his letter to the Pasha that asking more from the fellahin would result in widespread famine and wholesale absconding. Mehmed Ali did not accept such excuses and merely repeated his order to the official.[112] Moreover, these officials often had to fulfill some order by the Pasha only to discover that it was wrongly issued in the first place: a zero was once missed in an order for a quantity of coal supplied to the army and, of course, the Pasha had to immediately issue another order rectifying his first one.[113] Even if the targets were reasonable and consistent, this did not mean that the orders were executed without difficulties. A missing order would cause unnecessary delays, but the officials in charge would still hesitate to act without documents lest they be accused of corruption.[114] Efficient as the postal system appears to have been, keeping the Pasha in touch with his troops in Syria or the Hijaz hundreds of miles away, different government departments in Cairo would sometimes find difficulty in communicating with each other, even though they might have been located across the same street in Cairo; and "missing letters" were always referred to for not fulfilling orders.[115]

The best example of the inefficiency of the army bureaucracy is probably provided by the different letters issued by Nazif Efendi, the Commissary-General of the army during the early months of the Syrian campaign. In one of the reports sent routinely to the *Divan Efendisi* (Ibrahim Pasha's Aide-de-Camp) he wrote

> I have managed today to ship the artillery equipment that I have here [in the army HQ] to where it was needed by loading it on board small boats with the help of Motoş Bey. I still have sixty crates containing the miners' equipment and a further sixty crates containing seven-pound howitzers (*obüs*), thirty wooden boards for cannon bases, and eight light-cannon wheels . . . I was going to send this equipment tomorrow with Hafiz Efendi, the artillery lieutenant who is in charge of this equipment here. But he refused to transport it saying that the army has no need for these things [which he mentions again in the same order and with the same details]. Motoş Bey was witness to that. I am afraid, therefore, if I send this equipment, it will not be needed. Motoş Bey suggested

112 S/1/47/8/453 on 11 Ş 1241/21 March 1826; S/1/47/8/467 on 13 Ş 1241/23 March 1826.

113 Awamir lil-Jihadiyya 1/19, on 21 R 1247/29 September 1831.

114 Awamir lil-Jihadiyya 1/175, on 25 N 1253/24 November 1837. This case concerns the Director of the Livestock Department who refused to supply a number of horses requested by the official in charge of securing horses for the army because the latter did not have the proper documents.

115 See the correspondence between Mehmed Ali, Ibrahim Pasha, the Director of the War Department, and the Inspector of Munitions (the *baş cephanci*) concerning the non-delivery of different kinds of bombs to the army in Syria in the following documents: S/5/51/2/164 on 21 Z 1247/22 May 1832; S/5/51/2/166 on 22 Z 1247/23 May 1832 and S/5/51/2/176 on 28 Z 1247/29 May,1832.

that I write to Your Excellency asking whether I should send it or not. I am therefore asking you for permission to send these things.

The *Divan Efendisi* answered him saying that Ibrahim Pasha said that he should send these equipment only if he received a receipt ordering him to do so. Then the *Divan Efendisi* commented that it took Nazif Efendi eleven lines to state his simple question and adds that Ibrahim Pasha was wondering "whatever happened to Nazif Efendi? When he was in Egypt he used to complain about lengthy, detailed letters. I wonder where he got this chatty attitude from?" In response, Nazif Efendi wrote back to the *Divan Efendisi* saying, "I have received your letter in which you requested that I be brief and concise in my letters. I wish to draw Your Excellency's attention, however, to the fact that my original letter was eleven lines long and your response was fifteen lines long. In the future I promise to be brief, although I know that to fulfill the tasks diligently one needs to go through the details properly and to do that in a meticulous and thorough manner."[116]

Nazif Efendi continued to have problems in meeting Ibrahim Pasha's orders, however. When he received orders to unload a shipment of bread, for example, he said that he had been doing his best to fulfill this task until it started to rain. Knowing that rain would cause the bread to get wet, he ordered the unloading process to be stopped. "They took no heed of my warning, though, and I am now writing this to free myself of responsibility later when I am asked about the wet bread."[117] His efforts were not much appreciated by his superiors, nevertheless, who continued to press him to be more prompt in executing orders issued to him. Shortly afterwards when he said that he was doing his best to unload the barley from the ships lying off shore to deliver it immediately to the army kitchens, Ibrahim Pasha apparently had had it with him: he told him that if did not get the barley out of the ships, he, Ibrahim Pasha, would get the guts out of his belly.[118] In this respect Nazif Efendi was a typical bureaucrat who seemed to have been torn by the pressing need to execute orders promptly and at all cost while at the same time paying scrupulous attention to details and proper regulations in order not to be blamed later on. When he was ordered to supply the officers with bread, rice and ghee he asked if he should charge them for the price of the sacks and urns in which these foodstuffs were put. He explained that he was asking this question because he knew that in the future he would be

[116] All this is in the army journal in Sham 2/54, letters dated 7 and 8 B 1247/12 and 13 December 1831.

[117] Sham 2/95, events of 1 Ş 1247/5 January 1832.

[118] Sham 2/98, on 4 Ş 1247/8 January 1832.

asked for everything and if there was a shortage, he would have to pay for it from his own pocket. "This in addition to being reprimanded heavily in spite of being constantly worn out doing my best to fulfill orders issued to me."[119] Ibrahim Pasha could not stand the view of an expert whose only claim to be one was his ability to explain why things could *not* be done rather than execute his duties professionally and efficiently. In the event Nazif Efendi was sacked[120] and sent back to Egypt.[121]

Cracks in the edifice of order

The various cases of bureaucratic complications and logistical difficulties mentioned above are only some examples of wider problems that characterized the every-day working of such a huge army as that of Mehmed Ali. The aim of producing these cases is to contrast the image of the army as a consistent structure that functioned in a machine-like manner as argued in the last chapter with the more blurred picture that this chapter has attempted to present. By reading the records of the courts martial and the daily journals of the army, the image that comes across is one that is considerably less impressive than that of the machine-like structure that was presented in the last chapter. The aim of painting this picture that is full of fractures and inconsistencies is not to argue that the Pasha utterly failed in founding a functioning fighting machine or that the victories that Ibrahim secured in the various battles he waged against the Ottomans were exaggerated. In other words, the aim is not to argue that this picture, blurred as it is, takes precedence over that presented in the last chapter, since it approaches more closely the every-day functioning of the army. For as was argued in the last chapter the blueprints, the training manuals, and the military laws that were put down to organize the army were based on the assumption that men's bodies and minds could indeed be thoroughly manipulated and controlled. The point, though, is that no picture of the every-day working of the army can be complete by looking only at these manuals and one has to supplement their impressive picture with other accounts of the ceaseless attempts to make the army function in that neat, machine-like manner.

If the intention of mentioning these inconsistencies in policies, these logistical problems and bureaucratic complications is not to refute the picture presented in the last chapter but to complement it, it is also

119 Sham 2/95, events of 29 B 1247/3 January 1832.
120 Sham 8/191 bis, on 5 M 1248/4 June 1832.
121 Sham 10/65, on 9 Ra 1248/6 August 1832.

important to stress that these were not unique features of Mehmed Ali's army since, for example, compared to contemporary European armies, his was a hastily prepared and badly copied army. In other words, these problems were not characteristic of attempts at "importing the European army," the assumption being that this latter did not suffer from these problems.[122] For even if one assumes that Mehmed Ali was mainly borrowing from the French, Napoleon's army was not as well supplied and properly organized as those studies that concentrate on the Emperor's military genius would like us to believe. A recent study of Napoleon's *Grande Armée* finds that a lot of its campaigns were highly improvised, with corruption, looting, arrears in pay and low morale hitting it and affecting its performance years before the disastrous Russian campaign of 1812.[123] Furthermore, the French had themselves borrowed from the Prussians the famous Frederickian discipline and harsh order. But again, the Prussian army was never as well governed as its admirers in the eighteenth century assumed it to be, and Frederick's iron-fist disciplinary methods could not effectively eliminate desertion that in some crucial moments threatened to make the army melt away.[124] The process of borrowing goes even further: Frederick, in devising his military system, was influenced (ultimately) by Maurice of Nassau, Prince of Orange (1567–1625), who perfected army drill to create the modern Leviathan that fascinated him. Yet Maurice of Nassau looked to ancient Rome for his model,[125] and Rome of course looked to Greece for inspiration. Here, however, the borrowing ends since the Greeks, as is well known, were inspired by the gods.

The point to be made regarding this seemingly endless process of borrowing of military models by "great men" is that there is nothing peculiar about an "oriental prince" borrowing from the "West." The process of simplification and abstraction, of idealizing the situation of the army that is taken as a model goes on at all levels of the "borrowing" process regardless of who is doing it. At every stage there is the belief that the model had indeed been implemented in a pristine, neat fashion in an earlier time and that what is needed is to try to recreate this past as well as to adapt the model to suit the new reality.

122 For a good example of such an argument, see David B. Ralston, *Importing the European Army: The Introduction of European Military Techniques and Institutions into the Extra-European World, 1600–1914* (Chicago: University of Chicago Press, 1990).

123 John Elting, *Swords Around a Throne: Napoleon's Grande Armée* (London: The Free Press, 1988).

124 R. R. Palmer, "Frederick the Great, Guibert, Bülow: From dynastic to national war," in Peter Paret, ed., *Makers of Modern Strategy: From Machiavelli to the Nuclear Age*, (Oxford: Clarendon Press, 1990), p. 98.

125 McNeill, *Pursuit of Power*, p. 128.

This chapter has argued that in thinking about ways of organizing his army Mehmed Ali saw no problem in borrowing both from the French and from the Ottomans and in fusing together both models to suit his interests and capabilities. He showed the same flexibility when it came to adapting what he borrowed to his own needs. It is this flexible approach that accounts for much of the discrepancy between the laws, regulations, and blueprints, on the one hand, and their implementation and execution, on the other. Rather than taking them as fixed rules not to be deviated from, the Pasha and his senior officials approached them only as guidelines to be applied as well as possible, which they also felt had to be contravened if they were faced with some pressing factors. This chapter showed what some of these pressing factors might have been. As much as the Pasha would have liked his army to function in a machine-like manner, he himself was under pressing time and financial constraints that forced him to compromise some of the impressive laws he was passing. Moreover, he had a limited pool of experts to draw upon in putting these regulations in practice. Finally, he was limited by his need to create a loyal elite, a consideration that forced him to turn a blind eye on some of the "extra-legal" measures that some members of this elite were taking and that undermined the machine-like manner in which the army was supposed to have functioned. His son, Ibrahim Pasha, faced similar pressing constraints. In his need to create a reliable officer corps he resorted to appointing men who were often incompetent and whom he had to keep a watchful eye on. As reliable as his soldiers were in battle, securing for him his most important military achievements, his officers, although remaining mostly loyal to him and his father, were corrupt, incompetent and often at odds with each other.

Finally, the huge bureaucracy that managed to sustain this army on its various campaigns encountered considerable problems. Because the Pasha was very unrealistic in the demands he placed on his bureaucracy, the thousands of scribes and bureaucrats who were fulfilling his demands could not cope with what was asked of them. For a bureaucracy still in its infancy, sustaining an army of over 100,000 men scattered over wide areas of the Ottoman Empire was a daunting task that was not made any easier by the Pasha's impossible targets and unrealistic deadlines.

The other reason for highlighting the various bureaucratic problems and logistical obstacles that the army suffered from is to draw attention to the fact that behind the discrepancy – between the neat and precise picture of the army presented in the last chapter and the more complicated one presented in this one – is the different kind of sources used in both chapters. For whereas the previous chapter had relied mostly on the military laws and the training manuals printed at the Būlāq Press, this chapter found the army journals and specifically the records of the courts martial very useful. The intention of using these latter sources was not to argue that the training manual and the military law present a simplistic picture of the army to be replaced by the more complicated and more realistic one offered by the record of the court martial. For the records of the court martial like the reports of the daily checks on the soldiers are in fact applications of these laws and blueprints.

The point to be made, therefore, about relying only on blueprints and official programs to detect and highlight the logic of the new forms of power (as Mitchell and Foucault argue), is that these sources are bound to present too monolithic a picture of this power that impresses us with its logic and consistency. What this chapter attempted to do is to unveil this charade of power to see it for what it really was: offering an impressive façade, it is true, but a façade nevertheless. And one that is full of cracks at that. To rely solely on these sources, therefore, is to overstate the consistency of these new forms of power. This is so not only as mentioned above because there is bound to be considerable difference between the plan and its execution, but also because even on the textual level, even before seeing how the army applied these blueprints, these texts were not as tidy and neat as is often assumed. They are full of gaps, omissions, moments of silence and embarrassing inconsistencies that are often brushed aside in the attempt to produce the logic of these texts. A couple of examples might help illustrate the point.

The *Qānūn al-Dākhiliyya* that was referred to in the last chapter to depict the duties and responsibilities of the soldiers and officers in each battalion appears on paper as an impressive, consistent and, hence, powerful text. It is printed in a neat and tidy manner, giving detailed instructions for each man in the battalion regarding his daily tasks, whom to report to, and how to punctuate his daily life with these numerous tasks. However, there were two different versions of this manual, one in Arabic and the other in Turkish. Both were supposed to be exact translations of an original French manual;[126] a crucial difference, though, was that the Arabic version was considerably shorter than the Turkish one: whereas the Turkish version starts on page 1 with Article 1 dealing with the duties and responsibilities of the colonel of the regiment, the Arabic version starts on page 1 with Article 147 specifying the duties and responsibilities of the adjutant-major. The reason for the

126 al-Shayyāl says that it was translated from the French but could not identify the author; al-Shayyāl, *Tarīkh al-Tarjama*, Appendix 2, item 161.

different versions is that, as will be shown in chapter 6, senior ranks in the army as well as in the civilian bureaucracy were reserved for members of the Egyptian–Ottoman elite who spoke Turkish as a *sine qua non* of membership in that elite. Hence, there was no need to print a complete version of the manual for Arabic-speaking officers since there could be no hope for them to be promoted to these higher ranks, and therefore no need to spell out the duties of these higher ranks in the copies of the manuals handed to them. This crucial omission, this important moment of silence in the text itself, is a reflection of a tension in the society which found its way in the text. In spite of its pretense to be complete and thorough, leaving no small matter in the daily lives of the soldiers untouched, by being itself incomplete, the law in its physical form betrays its own logic.

This example is useful because it shows that relying only on laws, manuals and official pronouncements to approach the reality of a certain historical period is useful insofar as it portrays what the officials had in mind and what their tools in shaping society might have been. Whether reality was shaped by these tools in the neat and exact manner that they envisaged is another point altogether, not only because there was bound to be a discrepancy between the textual plan and its implementation, but also because this differentiation between tool and reality, between the text and its context is an arbitrary one. As was shown above the text itself could not be viewed in isolation of its social context, in spite of its attempts at portraying itself as a detached, primordial and abstract writ.

Another example might help illustrate the problems of relying only on the blueprints and the letters of the Pasha in writing the history of Egypt in his reign. As said in chapter 2 above, the impressive nature of the Pasha's bureaucracy is reflected in its very documents which appear to be following the orders of the Pasha regarding how to organize the administration. A law passed in 1844 organizing the internal structure of the civilian bureaucracy explicitly stated that the pages of the various registers had to be clean and tidy. "The pages of the register have to be stamped and numbered. Writing has to be continuous with no blank pages in the middle. It has to be clear and legible, without any crossings-out or corrections."[127] The clean, blank page which was sequentially numbered and neatly bound in a register was a symbol of the new power of the state: self-assured, rational, and consistent. Scribbling and scrawling in government registers, like losing them, were considered a crime, an affront to the authority of the state. For the most

[127] *al-Lāiʾḥa*, p. 22.

part this is how the registers of Mehmed Ali's government look. Occasionally, however, we come across a case of a mistake, an omission, a word that is crossed out, that betrays the very logic of the text and through which a deeper reality comes across challenging the very image that the bureaucracy had striven to maintain of itself.

For example, after the battle of Ḥomṣ on 9 July 1832 against the Ottoman army a large number of Ottoman soldiers were captured by the Egyptians. Also captured and taken prisoner was the chief scribe (*muhasebetci*) of the "Istanbullite regular army" who was ordered to compile a list of the soldiers and officers captured, all 1,791 of them. When the report was handed in to his captors Mehmed Munib, the Aide-de-Camp of Ibrahim Pasha (his *Divan Efendisi*), could not accept it because, he said, it was wrongly titled. At the top of the list the Ottoman official had written *Asakir-i Mansuremiz Alaylar*: "The Regiments of our Victorious Soldiers." This was supposed to allude to the official title of the new *nizami* army that Sultan Mahmud II had founded in 1826, *Muallem Asakir-i Mansure-i Muhammadiye,* "The Trained Victorious Soldiers of Muhammad." Nevertheless, Mehmed Munib would not allow the word *Mansure*, Victorious, to be used, and ordered the Ottoman scribe to use the word *Makhure*, Crushed, instead! Stunned, the scribe had to make sure that he had not misheard what Mehmed Munib had told him. "Do you mean I cross out *Mansure* and right *Makhure* instead?" he asked "with extreme unease." At this moment the Chief Financial Supervisor of the Egyptian administration in Syria, Hanna Bahari, intervened in an attempt to ease the tension. He suggested to Mehmed Munib that the Ottoman scribe did not mean that the Ottoman army was victorious; only its soldiers were, "since now they have joined our army." Munib Efendi still could not approve the title and said that it would be accepted if the scribe would write *Asakir-i Mansure-i Neferat,* "The [Companies of the] *Privates* of the Victorious Soldiers." To this Hanna Bahari "could find no answer." In the end the original words of the Ottoman scribe were recorded, but they were crossed out and Mehmed Munib's suggestion was written above in the following manner:

Asakir-i Makhuremiz Enferden . . .
~~*Asakir-i Mansuremiz Alaylarından*~~[128]

What is interesting in this case is that it shows that in spite of the explicit regulations of the Pasha that the registers of the bureaucracy be kept clean, with no scribbling or scrawling, the chief scribe of the army

128 Sham 9/158, on 25 S 1248/25 July 1832.

saw clearly that he was facing a situation that dictated his violation of this order. What he was faced with was a scribe of a rival army which was defeated, and crushed, but still claimed to be victorious. Mehmed Munib's witnessing of the act of recording the list of POWs, what for him was tantamount to an act of official surrender, had to be unambiguous, clear in its recognition of the defeat that Ibrahim had inflicted on the Ottomans, even if this implied referring to the Ottoman army by using a title that was different from its official one. The act of crossing out these three key terms and jotting his own words above them was, therefore, symbolic of Ibrahim Pasha's military might and that of his father behind him vis-à-vis the Sultan and his pashas[129] in Istanbul.

The tension apparent in this act of defacing and disfiguring an official text was not only caused by two competing scribes with different systems of inscription, though. Like the case of the incomplete training manual mentioned above this tension that is already manifest in the text is symptomatic of deeper tensions in society. For Mehmed Munib could have asked for the Ottoman scribe's words to be simply replaced by his; rather, he kept the Ottoman scribe's words and crossed them out and then wrote his words above. This, arguably, is a reflection of the ambivalence that the scribes in Mehmed Ali's service and especially those in the army felt when referring to the defeats inflicted on the Ottoman army, the army of the "Defender of the Faith," the "Protector of the Two Holy Shrines," as the Ottoman Sultan was known. We have already seen Mehmed Ali being ambivalent himself regarding his act of rebellion against his master in Istanbul. It is true that Ibrahim, and probably his men in the army, too, did not have so many scruples and were keen on asserting their victories in a clear, unambiguous way. Nevertheless, it has to be remembered that the battle of Ḥomṣ was the first real encounter in open field between Ibrahim and the Ottomans. (The siege of Acre, although it took place two months earlier, was, firstly, a siege and not an open battle, secondly, it lasted for an entire six-month period, and, thirdly, was not fought by any Imperial forces dispatched from Istanbul the way the Ottomans fought in Ḥomṣ.) Referring to the Ottoman defeats was an embarrassing matter for the officials in Mehmed Ali's administration. There is also the added tension embedded in the term "The Crushed Soldiers" since it implies "The Crushed Soldiers of Muhammad," something that Mehmed Munib obviously tried to hide by putting the possessive suffix "*miz*"

129 The battle of Ḥomṣ was known in Egypt as the "Battle of the Pashas' defeat" owing to the fact that the Ottoman army was led by different commanders, all high-ranking officials in the Sultan's service; Zakī, *al-Tārīkh al-Ḥarbī*, p. 415.

after the word "*makhure*" to try, firstly, to apply the defeat inflicted to the Sultan's own army and, secondly, to avoid implying that it was the Prophet Muhammad's soldiers that were defeated!

Conclusion

Like the case of the incomplete printed military regulations, this case is interesting because it draws our attention to the problems inherent in writing the history of nineteenth-century Egypt using the official pronouncements of Mehmed Ali or the various blueprints, laws and regulations that were passed during his time. As Mitchell has cleverly shown in his *Colonising Egypt* and as the previous chapter has attempted to make clear, these were impressive texts and do carry within themselves an important inherent element of power. Nevertheless, behind the neat, clean façade of these impressive texts lay a much more complicated reality. The tension inherent in the text is not only based, as this chapter has attempted to show, on the discrepancy that separates it from the reality it tries to regulate; that text is itself a reflection of this reality, in spite of its pretence to the contrary, in spite of its presumed primordial, detached nature. Even before seeing how the soldiers might have reacted to the power of the modern state, the texts which annunciate that power, the laws, blueprints and government regulations, are themselves *already* compromised and "contaminated" by the reality they set out to organize, regulate and "inscribe." Although these laws and official pronouncements claim to represent reality in what Mitchell called an "enframed" manner, a representation of something as profound as the very concept of order, progress or rationality, they appear as if they themselves have been inscribed upon by that "debased" reality.

In short, the point to be made is that no matter how impressive certain texts appear to be, they still do not write themselves: they are a reflection of the vested interests of a certain group of people who are trying to hide these interests behind some idea of universal truth or abstract writ and couch it in some consistent, impressive language. This chapter has attempted to go beyond this impressive language of Mehmed Ali's bureaucracy. It argued that, besides coming very close to expressing in a nearly pristine manner an ideal order for managing society at large, the Pasha's army also reflected, in the way its highest echelons functioned, the social and economic conditions of Egyptian society. The following chapter completes the picture, as it were, and sees how the men at the lowest echelons of the military hierarchy, the soldiers, understood and reacted to this new order.

5 Behind the lines: daily life in the camps

In February 1832 Islam Ağa, the adjutant-major of the 13th Infantry Regiment, died in the army hospital in Acre. On his death bed, he asked a friend of his, Hüseyin Ağa, the lieutenant-colonel of the 8th Infantry Regiment, to take charge of his funeral. He specifically requested him to sell his belongings, buy him a shroud and have a shaykh "recite the Koran on his soul." Taking this to be his friend's will, Hüseyin Ağa sold the property of his deceased friend so that he could meet the expenses of the funeral. Before the funeral had been conducted, however, the military headquarters in Syria intervened asking Mehmed Bey, the colonel of the 13th Infantry Regiment, to confiscate the deceased man's property and sell it and hand in the money to the *divan*, since all his belongings, it was claimed, were *miri* money, i.e. public property. When he was informed about this, Hüseyin Ağa presented a petition to Ibrahim Pasha citing in it the reasons for his actions and requesting permission to fulfill his friend's will. Ibrahim Pasha referred the petition to Ibrahim Yeğen. Ibrahim Yeğen "gave no answer."[1]

Seven months later the colonel of the 8th Regiment died of hepatitis also in the hospital in Acre.[2] Five days before he died Ala Eddin Ağa gave his eighteen-year-old servant five *kise*s (2,500 piasters) against a stamped certificate and in the presence of various witnesses. When informed about this the *divan* doubted the authenticity of the certificate and laid claim on the money saying that the property of dead soldiers and officers should revert to the army. Seeing that the boy had a stamped certificate, however, the *divan* decided to deal with the issue through the local religious judge (*qāḍī*) who said that according to the *sharī'a* it was illegal to make a will that exceeded one-third of the value of the deceased's property. The case was more complicated than that, moreover, since it was also discovered that besides cash, Ala Eddin Ağa had also left the boy his horse. The *divan*, however, decided to

1 Sham 2/65, on 11 N 1247/13 February 1832.

2 The health conditions in Acre after it had fallen were appalling; 1, 525 men died, most of them of malaria and hepatitis: Sham 18/184, on 25 N 1248/16 February 1833.

confiscate two-thirds of the cash and to take the horse to deliver it to the cavalry, which was in short supply of horses. To add to the young lad's grievance he himself was to be conscripted into the army. He then presented a petition to Ibrahim Pasha saying in it that he was a freed slave of Ala Eddin Ağa and would like to go to Cairo to serve his master's young children. Again, "he was silenced and was given no answer" (*sükut olunup cevap verilmedi*).[3]

". . . no prayers nor bells"[4]

The silence with which the authorities met these two petitions represents a more general silence about the dead and how to treat them. So far every chapter of this book has opened with a scene, an anecdote or a spectacle that set the tone for the chapter to follow. This chapter, however, opens with an *absence* of a scene, a scene that one would expect, but is found missing. Given the two cases of death mentioned above and given that the last chapter opened with a scene of battle, this chapter should have opened with a scene of a funeral. However, in all the thousands of documents about Mehmed Ali's army and his various campaigns there is not a single description of a funeral either of an officer or of a soldier. As illustrated by the example of the two petitions mentioned above, highlighting the absence of the funeral, the hundreds and thousands of men who died in Mehmed Ali's various campaigns received no dignified burial and the only concern of the authorities was that prompt notification be given about dates of death so as to cut salaries that were sometimes delivered to the men's families back in Egypt.[5] As far as the authorities were concerned a dead man, officer or soldier, was only a name to be crossed off the army registers and payrolls.[6] More importantly, and as shown in the two cases mentioned above, the authorities were also concerned to have the deceased man's belongings, claiming that they were *miri* property and had to revert to the government.[7]

3 Sham 11/107, on 12 R 1248/9 September 1832.
4 Wilfred Owen, "Anthem for Doomed Youth," in *The Collected Poems of Wilfred Owen* (New York: New Directions, 1965), p. 44.
5 See for example the case of the widow who was asked to return thirty-five months' pay that she received as her dead husband's salary on the grounds that her husband had died since then but the army authorities were not informed in time to stop delivering to her her husband's pay; Awamir lil-Jihadiyya 1/219, on 24 S 1254/20 May 1838.
6 See article 178 of *Qānūn al-Dākhiliyya*, pp. 16–17. For the text of the order from the War Department in Cairo to the various regiments' scribes to cross off the names of the dead, see Sham 7/52, on 8 M 1248/8 June 1832.
7 There are various records to this effect; see, for example, Sham 2/43, on 3 N 1247/8 December 1831; and Diwan al-Muʿawana 1/2116, on 12 Ca 1248/7 October 1832.

Apart from these "bookish" concerns of the authorities the dead in Mehmed Ali's wars receive no attention. The thousands of men who died in the barren deserts of Arabia, in the hot lands of Sudan, in the cold steppes of Anatolia, and in the deep blue seas of the Mediterranean figure only accidentally in the contemporary documents. Commemorating the dead was not something that the authorities were particularly concerned about. Not only are the documents devoid of accounts of funerals, whether of soldiers or officers, but we also do not have any reference to war cemeteries or war memorials. As the two petitions mentioned above reveal, the officers, let alone the soldiers, were apprehensive that even after their death they were not going to be treated with dignity by the authorities and they had to arrange for their own funerals out of their own money – or what they thought was their own money until the authorities intervened, laying claim to that as well. One's "inscription" in the Pasha's registers was not to end with one's death.

The difficulty of writing the history of the men who lost their lives in Mehmed Ali's campaigns and of their comrades who survived them is not only due to the absence of headstones in beautiful garden cemeteries, however. The fellahin of Egypt, who made up the overwhelming majority of Mehmed Ali's fighting force and certainly represented the bulk of the casualties, were illiterate and did not leave us written testimonies of what it was like to fight in the Pasha's armies; they had no Graves, Owen, Remarque or Sassoon among them to speak on their behalf and to tell us how it must have felt to confront the horrors and fears, the tension and bloody heaps, of the battlefield "Where God seems not to care."[8]

This chapter does not attempt to tell the story of this lost generation. It opens with the silence of the authorities in dealing with death, not in order to fill this vacuum, to speak on these soldiers' behalf, but in an attempt to pose an important question. Having seen in the last chapter how badly fed, irregularly paid and improperly clothed the soldiers were, and, in addition, having seen how they lacked the opportunity of a dignified burial, why then did these men keep on fighting? Judging from the record these men not only kept on fighting for Mehmed Ali and his elite but did so with spectacular success. Was coercion the only thing that kept them fighting? And if coercion can provide an explanation of how they were sent to the killing fields, can this also be an adequate explanation of how well they fared once the actual fighting began?

The task, one has to admit, is not an easy one, not only because of the

[8] "Greater Love," in Owen, *Collected Poems*, p. 41.

scarcity of source material describing the soldiers' feelings and emotions during these tense times but also because the question is generally a difficult one to deal with regarding any battle and any army. Facing the closeness of death when all his senses are stretched literally to the limit, when obeying an order often meant dragging "their feet / Sore on the alleys cobbled with their brothers,"[9] what, it should be asked, impels the soldier to obey orders, march onto the enemy and gallantly "engage with him" and pour out "that red / Sweet wine of youth"?[10]

One possible answer is to argue that the soldiers could not physically leave the battle site because they were prevented from doing so. In almost all descriptions of Ibrahim's distribution of his forces in battles, we always see the irregular cavalry forces standing on guard at the rear of the army. These might have functioned as reserve troops that Ibrahim kept there in time of need. Given the traditional role that bedouins played in Mehmed Ali's army, however, it seems equally plausible to argue that they were placed there to catch any deserters from the Egyptian side. When the actual battle started a large number of soldiers felt trapped not only between their ever watchful sentries behind them and the enemy ahead, but also between the strong urge to flee and desert the army altogether, on the one hand, an urge that was never really effectively quenched, and, on the other hand, the obligation to obey orders and "engage with the enemy" in a courageous, "manly" way. And unless one uncritically believes accounts of nationalist historians arguing that Mehmed Ali's troops were willing to give up their lives for the sake of "Egypt," these men had still not lost their instinct of self-preservation that kept them human in spite of years of training and indoctrination. "Placed in intolerable and unprecedented circumstances of fear and stress, deprived of their sense of control, and expected to react with . . . unnatural 'courage'"[11] a lot of these men could not continue fighting, broke down, and reacted in a manner that recalls the behavior of many British soldiers in the Great War of 1914–18.

Shell shock and home-sickness

On the face of it the Syrian campaign of 1831–40 and the First World War of 1914–18 are so different in nature and distant in time that the

[9] "Insensibility," in *Ibid.*, p. 37.

[10] Rupert Brooke, "The Dead," in *The Collected Poems of Rupert Brooke* (London: Papermac, 1992), p. 314.

[11] Elaine Showalter, "Rivers and Sassoon: The inscription of male gender anxieties," in Margaret R. Higonnet, Jane Jenson, Sonya Michel and Margaret C. Weitz, eds., *Behind the Lines: Gender and the Two World Wars* (New Haven: Yale University Press, 1987), p. 64.

comparison between them becomes nearly untenable. For one thing, the Great War was fought between European powers in the twentieth century and the Syrian campaign was an inter-Ottoman military conflict that took place nearly a century earlier. The tactics employed, the weapons used, and the intensity of the battles of both wars make them look radically different. One was a campaign of swift movement, where thousands of troops marched over hundreds of miles in short spans of time; the other was a war of trenches, of countless abortive attacks, and of millions of troops "entrenched" in their positions for years on end. In addition, the causes of the wars and the quality of the military leadership make comparison even harder. In contrast to the remarkable imagination, the sly wit, and the insightful character of Ibrahim Pasha, Sir Douglas Haig, the commander of the British forces in the Great War, was lacking in "wit and invention . . . [in addition to being] stubborn, self-righteous, inflexible, intolerant . . . quite humourless . . . provincial [and] bullheaded."[12]

Be that as it may, as far as both wars were experienced by the soldiers who did the fighting and not by the commanders who drove them to their deaths there are significant similarities between them that make comparison worthwhile. In both wars there was an underlying current of discontent with the war, of "pacifism," to use a modern term, a feeling that the war was futile, purposeless and unnecessary. In spite of the subsequent attempts to write such "pacifist" tendencies out of the official narratives of both wars, the record shows that in addition to their reactions to the horror, anguish, fear and panic of the actual combat situation the men often broke down and refused to continue with the slaughter. During the Great War such cases were referred to as "shell shock"; by 1916 such cases had accounted for 40 percent of the total casualties in the combat zones.[13] W. H. R. Rivers, the noted anthropologist and clinical psychologist who treated numerous cases of "shell shock" during the war, concluded that the "quantity of neurotic symptoms correlated not with the intensity of battle, the length of an individual's service, or his emotional disposition, but with the degree of

[12] Paul Fussell, *The Great War and Modern Memory* (Oxford: Oxford University Press, 1975), p. 12. Fussell goes on to say of Haig that "he was the perfect commander for an enterprise committed to endless abortive assaulting. Indeed one powerful legacy of Haig's performance is the conviction among the imaginative and intelligent today of the unredeemable defectiveness of all civil and military leaders. Haig could be said to have established the paradigm." Although modern Egyptian and British leaders seem to follow the paradigm, Ibrahim, unlike Haig, could not be said to have established it.

[13] Showalter, "Rivers and Sassoon," p. 63. For an insightful and fuller analysis of shell shock, see also Elaine Showalter, *The Female Malady: Women, Madness, and English Culture* (New York: Pantheon, 1985), chapter 7, "Male hysteria: W. H. R. Rivers and the lessons of shell shock."

his immobility."[14] In the Syrian war it was during the prolonged siege of Acre (early December 1831 to late May of the following year) that thousands of Egyptian troops were feeling vulnerable, sitting immobile as they did in the sappers' trenches that they were digging to approach the walls of the fortress and falling prey to the shells that were being fired from the defiant city. It was then that the men started showing signs that could only be read as "shell shock" and resembled the experiences of the British soldiers eighty years later.

In one incident during that siege a soldier was killed by the shells fired from the fortress. On seeing his body his comrades panicked, left the battle scene together, and headed back to the relative security of the trenches. Their captain also deserted his position and went all the way back to the army camp to inform his commander of the incident. Four days later these men were court martialled. The captain was told that his reasons for deserting his position were not accepted since it was ridiculous to go and inform the commander of every soldier who died. The soldiers were also told that their actions were unmanly and cowardly, and violated the law which said that "if a certain soldier dies and in order to prevent fear spreading his body should be promptly hidden from his colleagues."[15] In another incident during the same siege, a soldier threw himself on the ground in an attempt to escape the shrapnel of the cannon balls fired from the castle. Unfortunately for the poor soldier, Ibrahim Pasha was passing by and happened to witness his behavior which he considered unbecoming to a soldier. He summoned the soldier in question and ordered all the men in the vicinity ("one or two companies") to spit on his face because he dared to show his fear.[16]

What was of concern to Ibrahim Pasha, besides the implicit challenge that such acts pose to the very concept of "manliness," was the possible effects they might have on general morale and discipline: an army whose men crack up and desert on the first opportunity is no army at all. Severe punishments faced those who dared to violate military laws governing the actual combat situation as well as those who transgressed general cultural norms defining "manly" behavior. But "law" alone was not enough, and occasionally "medicine" was resorted to in dealing with other cases of "unmanly" behavior. One such was the feelings of home-sickness that a lot of soldiers fell prey to often immediately after being conscripted.

[14] Eric Leed, *No Man's Land: Combat and Identity in World War I* (Cambridge: Cambridge University Press, 1979), p. 183.

[15] Sham 2/71, on 17 B 1247/22 December 1831. For another similar case see Sham 3/102 *bis*, on 12 S 1247/16 January 1832.

[16] Sham 2/64, on 10 B 1247/15 December 1831.

Anxious about their families left behind and about their lands whose productivity was certainly affected, many men found it extremely painful to be forced to leave their villages for destinations mysterious to them and for a period of unknown duration. And it was not uncommon for the men, on finally returning to their villages, to "find the wives and daughters, whom they, perhaps, loved and cherished, irremediably lost: many families are thus entirely broken up."[17] English travelers could not understand this attachment that the fellahin had to their villages and often saw it as a pathetic case of home-sickness from which they should be cured. "To us Englishmen," one of them wrote, "it appears almost incredible that young men of from eighteen to twenty-five years of age should regard as hardship the being obliged to leave home."[18] Similarly Dr. Bowring on visiting the troops in Syria found "the numbers of persons who pined to death, sinking under the influence of this unmedicable malady . . . very considerable."[19] When he discussed the matter with the physician of the camp, the doctor told him, " 'I cannot keep them alive . . . when they begin to think and talk of home.' And long before they die [Dr. Bowring adds,] they sink into a listless, careless inanity . . ."[20]

Faced with a near epidemic outbreak of "home-sickness" Clot Bey, the Chief Physician of the army, felt it necessary to refer to it in a booklet that he wrote for young army doctors "so that they can consult it at ease without having to refer to other larger tomes."[21] In it he gives special instructions to the officers and doctors telling them how to deal with home-sickness among the soldiers.

Home-sickness [*al-ishtiyāq ila al-waṭan*] is a disease that often afflicts the new soldiers after leaving their homes, families and things familiar to them. This leads them to depression, melancholy, soreness, tiredness and sometimes to death. Therefore, they have to be kept occupied as much as possible and to be promised their imminent return home . . . As much as possible soldiers have to be kept in a happy, content state and their officers have to be ordered to be gentle with them . . . and to make them believe that the dangers they are about to encounter are not grave.[22]

In that sense Mehmed Ali's soldiers, like all soldiers facing any battle, were caught between the devil and the deep blue sea. Before the tense few hours of battle they were confronted with the prospect of meeting the enemy with all the feelings of fear and horror that fighting entailed. Behind them were the memories of home, of fields left unattended, of deserted families, of wives and loved ones abandoned, left to their luck.

17 St. John, *Egypt*, II, p. 176. 18 Scott, *Rambles in Egypt*, II, p. 218.
19 Bowring, "Report on Egypt," p. 5. 20 *Ibid.*, p. 6.
21 Clot Bey, *al-ʿAjāla*, p. 1. 22 *Ibid.*, pp. 10–11.

Leaving the battle scene to return home was impossible since guards and sentries were always looking over them. When the battle started the tension heightened: to do nothing and to stay still or to fall back to the relative security of the reserve lines was always risky, since this carried with it the certainty of being court martialled. Being trapped in this manner, the soldiers had nothing better to do than obey the orders issued to them in the form of command signals and shouts from their officers. An example from the battle of Konia might make this clear. During a minor counter-attack by the Ottomans the Egyptians lost all order and the whole 1st Cavalry Brigade was thrown into confusion. Here is the testimony of one of the majors.

When the Guardia Regiment started to engage with the enemy both our colonel and our lieutenant-colonel gave orders to assume the line formation. I did not hear the Brigadier give this order. Before we had assumed the new formation however both the brigadier and the colonel gave the orders to attack so we attacked but our left wing started to retreat and the whole brigade got muddled with itself (*liva beraberine karışdı*). The standard bearer was wounded and the officers were forcing the soldiers to return by forcing them around with their swords (*zabitan kılıçlar ile askeri cevirdi*). We then gathered our battalions, separated them from each other and put them in order . . . The trumpeters then gave the signal to deploy in column and we soon took that formation.[23]

If ever the Egyptian army could be said to have been superior to its Ottoman adversary, it was in situations like this when it was not the courage, honor or high morale that came to the rescue, but the constant drilling and repetitious training that induced the soldiers to recognize in the midst of the hubbub and clamor of the battle the familiar sight of a banner or the decipherable sound of a trumpet that signified something meaningful to them. These signals, banners and command shouts seemed to give the illusion of order in such tense moments. During the taxing hours of battle soldiers had no choice but to obey commands, not only because not obeying them brought with it the likelihood of punishment but also because disregarding them seemed to bring death closer still. The soldier stood to benefit personally from obeying orders during the decisive hours of battle since these orders gave at least a semblance of order and organization.[24]

But how does the soldier behave, not during, but before and after battle? If he was conditioned to behave during battles as the training manuals portrayed him, i.e. as a soul-less, machine-like being, did he also behave likewise even after the immediate danger of death had

[23] Sham 23/73, on 2 S 1249/21 June 1833, fos. 8–9.

[24] On the effect of the drills on the performance of soldiers on the battlefield for eighteenth-century European armies, see McNeill, *Pursuit of Power*, pp. 132–3.

receded? To answer this question we have to move from "battle pieces" to accounts of the daily lives of the soldiers in their barracks and training camps; we have to go behind the lines where the soldiers prepared for battles or recuperated from them. It is by studying the lives of the soldiers in the relative security of the barracks and military camps that a true assessment of how successful the authorities were in transforming the peasant into a disciplined soldier can be made.

The image we have from the various training manuals and military laws reviewed in chapter 3 leaves one with the impression that the barracks, training camps, naval hospitals, and military schools were heavily guarded, tightly controlled, and closely watched. Like the various orders of Mehmed Ali reviewed in the last chapter, however, the laws governing these institutions were not applied without difficulties and invariably there was a considerable discrepancy between how the training manuals wanted the soldier to behave in the military camp and how in fact he spent his daily life. An example might make this discrepancy clear.

On roaming the camp of the 8th Infantry Regiment a certain captain found an outsider in the quarters of his company. He asked him where he was from, and the stranger answered that he was a fellah from Egypt who had been visiting a relative of his, a sergeant-major in the same company, and had been staying with him for fifteen days. This was at the height of the siege of Acre when the entire army was supposed to be on high alert and when civilians, Egyptians or not, were forcibly refused entry to the camp unless they carried a stamped certificate stating explicitly the reason for and nature of their visit. Alarmed, the captain summoned one of his lieutenants to order the sergeant-major in question to ask his friend to leave the camp, since, as he said, "there is no business for strangers here (*barrani adamın işi yoktur*)." When later it was discovered that the fellah was still on the premises, the captain summoned the fellah again and asked him why he had still not left. The fellah answered that he had nothing to do in the camp but had come to see his relative and now that this had been done he would be moving out. The captain then threatened him that if he did not leave at once, he would arrest him and have him beaten. When the sergeant-major heard this he went to the captain and complained of the way his friend was being treated. He explained that he and the fellah were from the same village and added that he would not order his friend out unless there were a ship available and ready to take him back to Egypt. The captain then arrested the fellah and beat him. In addition, he also arrested the sergeant-major and had him imprisoned. While in prison, and from behind bars, the sergeant-major shouted at his captain that it was only because the captain had recently been moved from another company that they could not get along together and that if they had been serving together in the same company, all this could have been avoided, and "I would have been accepted by you (*senin yanında makbul olurdum*)."[25]

This one case is significant for a number of reasons. First, it undermines the impression one gets from reading the military laws which organized the daily lives of the soldiers in the barracks. In spite of the sentry officers, the soldiers guarding the gates and fences of the camps, the bedouin forces roaming the vicinities of the camps, and the stipulation that all visitors be forbidden from entering such exclusive areas, this fellah not only succeeded in penetrating these supposedly insurmountable barriers but continued to live undetected with his friend for fifteen days. The presumably impermeable boundaries that were erected by the various laws, decrees and manuals were in fact constantly negotiated and crossed by the soldiers during their daily lives in the camps, a fact poignantly illustrated by the ability of the soldier to shout back at his officer from behind bars.

Second, it shows that in spite of years of training, of being subjected to a strict system of surveillance and control and in spite of continuous drills and exercises, the sergeant-major in question did not show signs that all this had had any significant effect on the way he was supposed to think and act – i.e. as a soldier and not as a fellah/civilian. Having come across a fellow villager, it was natural for him to extend him an invitation to stay with him on the camp and he could not see why his commanding officers were so harsh and inhospitable to his visitor. When his friend was arrested he could not see why he was being reprimanded and punished. His body might seem to have been closely controlled, but his heart and mind appeared to still belong to a different world, that of civilian life back in the nostalgically remote lands of Egypt.

Third, it throws doubt on the nature of the soldier–officer relationship, a relationship that is defined in the training manuals and in the different military laws as a hierarchical and clearly defined one. When he was caught and put in jail the only reason he could give for his captain's "odd" behavior was that they had not known each other personally; if they had, this whole issue could have been avoided.[26] Again years of training and indoctrination seem not to have had any

[25] Sham 3/125, on 20 S 1247/24 January 1832.

[26] It is not clear why this captain had been moved from his company in the first place. It is possible that he had recently been promoted to that rank, since newly promoted captains were moved from their original companies lest they were disobeyed by their subordinates, their former peers; for a case in which this is explicitly explained, see Sham 2/88, on 22 B 1247/27 December 1831.

significant impact on the manner in which the soldiers thought about and felt towards their officers.

This chapter, having failed to take its lead from a funeral scene, follows on from this scene of "life behind the bars." It is interested in the men at the lowest echelons of the military hierarchy – the soldiers – and specifically seeks to contrast the impressive and monolithic picture of the army as portrayed in the training manuals and the various military laws with accounts of the daily lives of the soldiers in the camps and barracks. It attempts to understand how these seemingly beneficial regulations and orderly manuals were actually applied, and to elaborate further on the reasons for the discrepancy that invariably existed between these model orders and regulations and the way they were performed. Since this chapter is interested in soldiers and their understanding of, and reactions to, the programs and blueprints that were set down to manage their bodies, one particular aspect of their lives in the camps is analyzed, namely their health, which the authorities, in their constant fear and worry of spread of disease, kept a diligent eye on. Here the manuals and regulations that the following argument takes as its point of departure are not training ones, but medical and hygiene blueprints and regulations that aimed not to turn the new recruit into a well-disciplined soldier, but into a healthy, clean man.

The piercing medical gaze

Besides feeding, clothing and training the troops, the authorities paid considerable attention to the state of physical health and general hygiene of the conscripts. Mehmed Ali appears to have realized that to have a healthy body of troops care had to be given to the general health situation of the population at large. His concern with medical matters was not limited to the troops but included "students in state schools, workers in state industries, and urban and rural communities related to any government activity."[27] The Pasha is often described as opening hospitals, sending students to Europe to study medicine, ordering the vaccination of the population against smallpox, and instituting quarantines around major ports and cities in an attempt to control the spread of contagious diseases, mainly cholera and the plague. His measures to design a modern military and civilian public health program is seen as one of his greatest achievements that laid the basis for the creation of a modern medical profession in Egypt and which

[27] Kuhnke, *Lives at Risk*, p. 134.

"helped get rid of the clouds of ignorance that have been hovering over the country for centuries."[28]

Examples abound of the Pasha's health concerns. As early as 1819 he ordered his deputy to institute a program of vaccination against smallpox throughout the country.[29] This must have been prompted by the exceedingly heavy toll it took on the population: Clot Bey says that on his arrival in Egypt in 1825 smallpox was "cruelly ravaging the country. Every year it killed no fewer than fifty to sixty thousand children,"[30] making it alone responsible for increasing the infant mortality rate by 40 or 50 per thousand, in turn raising the overall annual death rate to something between 3 and 4 per thousand.[31] In 1824 the Pasha requested M. Drovetti, the French Consul-General, to secure a number of doctors from France who would administer a wide vaccination program in the countryside. Three such doctors arrived in Egypt and started to vaccinate the fellahin against smallpox in various provinces in Lower Egypt.[32] A year later they were sent to Middle Egypt to extend vaccination there.[33] After Clot Bey's arrival and his taking over the entire health establishment[34] vaccination was extended all over the country, and in 1834 he wrote a treatise that was translated into Arabic and printed in the Būlāq Press concerning how vaccination was to be performed by the various doctors and the village barbers and how it should be recorded in registers specially prepared for that purpose.[35] As a result of these efforts, by the late 1840s the Azbakiyya Hospital in Cairo was vaccinating children at the rate of 600 per month.[36]

Besides being hit by smallpox, Egypt was repeatedly visited during the first half of the nineteenth century by two other deadly diseases, cholera and the plague, which prompted the authorities to take serious

[28] ʿAbdel-Karīm, *Tārīkh al-Taʿlīm*, p. 266.
[29] Sāmī, ed., *Taqwīm al-Nīl*, II, p. 278, letter dated 5 Ca 1234/2 March 1819.
[30] Clot Bey, *Mémoires*, p. 156.
[31] Panzac, "Population of Egypt," p. 18.
[32] S/1/50/5/413 and Katkhoda 1/101, both on 26 Za 1239/24 July 1824. Each was given a salary of 500 piasters a month: S/1/50/5/419 on 29 Za 1239/27 July 1824.
[33] S/1/47/8/216 on 27 M 1241/12 September 1825.
[34] In his *Mémoires* (p. 157) Clot Bey claims that it was only thanks to him that vaccination was introduced in Egypt. It is obvious from the above-mentioned accounts that this was not the case.
[35] A. B. Clot Bey, *Mabḥath Taʿlīmī fī Taṭʿīm al-Judarī* [An Educational Treatise in Smallpox Vaccination], trans. Aḥmad Ḥasan al-Rashīdī (Cairo: Būlāq, 1843). This is the only copy I could find. al-Shayyāl says that the 1843 edition was in fact the third edition and that the first one appeared in 1250/1834; al-Shayyāl, *Tārīkh al-Tarjama*, p. 106.
[36] Kuhnke, *Lives at Risk*, p. 116. The Azbakiyya Hospital was founded in 1837 and functioned as a hospital for civilians. It was there that most of the children in Cairo were sent to be vaccinated against smallpox; see Diwan Taftish Sihhat Maṣr: M/5/1 p. 6, letter no. 5, on 19 Za 1266/26 September 1850; Clot Bey, *Mémoires*, p. 316.

action to limit their impact on the population.[37] In 1812 the Pasha's Italian physicians suggested that he should restrict the entry of ships coming from Istanbul which had been hit by the plague that year.[38] The following year after plague had spread in different parts of Lower Egypt, having presumably hit Alexandria first, the Pasha expressed his desire to establish a lazaretto in Alexandria to quarantine passengers and sailors from ships arriving from plague-stricken areas.[39] In 1828 he ordered Müharrem Bey, his son-in-law who was governor of Alexandria, to consult with the foreign consuls in the city to draft quarantine regulations and enforce them in the rapidly expanding port city.[40] Besides Alexandria, quarantines were imposed on the ports of Damietta in 1829 and Rosetta in 1831.[41] Eventually, and facing the alarming outbreak of cholera in 1831, an international quarantine board was established in Alexandria composed of the different foreign consuls in the city, the first such attempt at international disease control.[42]

However, it was the narrower concern for the health and hygiene of the soldiers that attracted most of the Pasha's attention and that of his chief medical advisors. The concentration of large numbers of men in the military schools, training camps and, of course, in the field camps along the different warring fronts, brought with it the possibility of widespread disease which could have posed serious threats to a country whose manpower was already drained by the Pasha's insatiable needs. As in his attempt to control smallpox, the plague and cholera, the Pasha learned his lesson the hard way. In the early months of the disastrous Sudan campaign the army that he sent down there lost 600 men who fell dead of various diseases. Owing to the lack of doctors, medicine and qualified medical personnel the number of dead in September 1821 rose to 600 in addition to 2,000 men who had fallen prey to various diseases. The following month the number of dead rose even further to 1,500: this in an army of three thousand troops.[43] Even after that army had managed to secure 20,000 black slaves and to send them down the Nile to Egypt, these unfortunate people could not survive the trip and were falling "like sheep with the rot" prompting the Pasha, as we saw in chapter 2 above, to ask Boghus Bey, his Armenian advisor for foreign

37 For the pattern of their visitations see Panzac, "Population of Egypt," pp. 18–9 and Kuhnke, *Lives at Risk*, pp. 49–91.

38 Kuhnke, *Lives at Risk*, p. 94.

39 al-Jabartī, *'Ajā'ib al-Āthār*, IV, pp. 175, 177 (events of Rabī' al-Thānī, 1228, and Jumādī al-Thānī, 1228); Panzac, "Population of Egypt," p. 19.

40 Sāmī, ed., *Taqwīm al-Nīl*, II, p. 334, letter dated 12 N 1243/28 March 1828.

41 Kuhnke, *Lives at Risk*, p. 94.

42 *Ibid.*

43 Frédéric Cailliaud, *Voyage a Méroé, au Fleuve Blanc, au-delà de Fâzoql* (Paris: L'Imprimerie Royale, 1826), II, pp. 313, 316.

affairs, to fetch him some American doctors who might be useful in treating the slaves. The Morean campaign was similarly ill equipped, with doctors and medical supplies often sent after the departure of the military units they were supposed to serve,[44] and when these medical supplies were finally received, they were often found to be defective.[45]

When he set out to found his new *nizami* army the Pasha could not afford to lose men in that most costly way. In that respect it was Dr. Clot Bey who proved most useful for him. One of the earliest accomplishments of Clot Bey[46] was to build two permanent military hospitals, one for the army and the other for the navy, near areas of high troop concentration. In 1827 the military hospital of Abū-Zaʿbal was built near the Jihad Abad training camp in Hankah in northern Cairo,[47] and in Alexandria the Maḥmūdiyya Hospital was constructed to serve 26,000 soldiers and 11,000 laborers employed in the infamous Liman.[48]

These two hospitals were reputed to be impressive medical institutions conforming "to the pattern of hospital-affiliated training centers that had become the norm in France and England by 1830."[49] Besides being a military hospital, the Abū-Zaʿbal hospital (later to be known after its new location, Qaṣr al-ʿAinī) also functioned as a medical school. On graduation, the students, mostly Arabic-speaking Egyptians, were appointed as military doctors and attached to the various infantry and cavalry regiments thus forming the nucleus of the new military medical corps. On the eve of the Syrian campaign the blueprint creating this corps was put down by Clot Bey and approved by the Pasha in consultation with his chief physician, the Italian Gaetani Bey, and members of the War Department. It was decided that each infantry regiment was to have one European doctor supervising three Egyptian ones. The cavalry regiments were to have one European doctor in addition to two Egyptian ones. Those Egyptian doctors were to be given the rank of second lieutenant. All doctors were to be under the supervision of their respective colonels and brigadiers without these latter, however, interfering in their professional work. The regulations proceeded to give such details as the position of the tents of the various

44 S/1/48/2/93 on 22 Z 1240/8 August 1825.

45 S/1/48/1/392 on 14 S 1240/8 October 1824.

46 He was given the title of Bey only in 1831 in recognition of his efforts in controlling the cholera epidemic of that year; Kuhnke, *Lives at Risk*, p. 42.

47 The order establishing it is in *Vekayi-i Mısıriyye*, issue no. 8, on 14 Ş 1244/17 February 1829, quoted in Sāmī, ed., *Taqwīm al-Nīl*, II, p. 326. For a map depicting the position of the hospital in relation to the camp, see Clot Bey, *Mémoires*, pl. III.

48 Kuhnke, *Lives at Risk*, p. 136. For a short description of the hospital ten years after its foundation, see Bowring, "Report on Egypt," pp. 55–6.

49 Kuhnke, *Lives at Risk*, p. 33.

doctors in respect to those of senior officers in the regiments and the brigades.[50]

Impressive as all these measures might appear, we do not know how they were actually implemented nor how they were received by the soldiers. As far as the civilian population is concerned, very little is known about the response to the new and unprecedented ways in which people's daily lives were managed by the medical establishment that the Pasha created in Egypt. A recent book on the history of the introduction of modern medicine in Egypt in the nineteenth century, for example, failed to take account of the reaction of the average Egyptian to such novel practices as vaccination, post-mortems and/or autopsy. It also lacked any information about the every-day functioning of the numerous health offices (*makātib al-siḥḥa*) which were established in Cairo in the late 1840s. Moreover, it paid no attention to the functioning of the various field hospitals that were founded in the different localities in Syria in spite of these being the first medical institutions that the earliest Egyptian medical students were employed in. In addition, by limiting itself to the performance of the School of Medicine (attached to Qaṣr al-ʿAinī hospital) and uncritically accepting Clot Bey's testimony about the performance of that school and indeed about the whole medical establishment, it becomes inevitable to argue that the school was "more than another academic institution; [that] it played a central role in the creation of a medical profession in Egypt, and [that it] thereby came to represent a center of civilization that was to have an enlightening effect on the country as a whole."[51]

What follows is an attempt to assess the degree to which the different medical establishments faithfully followed the blueprints that were set down mostly by Clot Bey to organize them. Again the intention is not only to highlight the difference between the simplistic picture drawn in

50 Sāmī, ed., *Taqwīm al-Nīl*, II, pp. 383–4, quoting the *Vekayi-i Mısıriyye*, issue no. 309, on 18 Ca 1247/25 October 1831. Sāmī does not mention who drafted the blueprint; he only says that the Pasha had a consultation about it with Dr. Gaetani and the War Department. For a critical comment on Clot Bey's claims that it was thanks to him that a military medical corps was established, see Kuhnke, *Lives at Risk*, p. 188 n. 9.

51 Sonbol, *Medical Profession in Egypt*, p. 21. Sonbol's main source throughout her book is the works of Clot Bey, a man who could not be judged to have offered an objective account of the hospital, to say the least. In addition, Sonbol did not consult any of Clot Bey's Arabic treatises printed in Būlāq. His French ones were aimed at a Western audience to improve the image of his patron in Europe. For the "propagandistic" character of his work, see Heyworth-Dunne, *Education*, p. 122. On the actual performance of the Qaṣr al-ʿAinī school and how Mehmet Ali and Clot Bey "staged" visits by European tourists to it, see Khaled Fahmy, "Women, medicine and power in nineteenth-century Egypt," in Lila Abu Lughod, ed., *Remaking Women: Feminism and Modernity in the Middle East* (Princeton: Princeton University Press, 1998) (forthcoming).

the blueprint with the more complicated account of the daily workings of the medical establishments, but also to understand something about the social and intellectual context of these medical blueprints: who wrote them, what scientific ideas informed them, what interests they served, etc. Furthermore, particular attention is given both to the reaction of the soldiers to having their bodies so minutely scrutinized and to the performance of the regimental field hospitals in Syria, which more than the remote hospital of Qaṣr al-ʿAinī bore the brunt of caring for the soldiers' health during the Syrian campaign.

Syphilis and scabies

The difficulties encountered by the health authorities in controlling the spread of disease among the soldiery, as well as providing them with some medical services, were caused in the first place by the serious structural problems that were endemic to the entire medical establishment, and that were most clearly seen in the military field hospitals. To analyze the nature of these problems, and to try and understand their underlying causes, it is probably useful to look closely at how the health authorities attempted to deal with two ailments that raised particular problems, namely scabies (*uyuz*) and syphilis (*frengi*).[52] There are a number of reasons for choosing these two diseases. First, and most obviously, these were diseases that the authorities themselves were very concerned about both because of their high incidence and because they required a long period of treatment which meant significantly reducing the strength of the fighting force.[53] Second, they were both diseases whose detection necessitated close and regular examination of the soldiers' bodies, especially since soldiers often lied to the authorities rather than admit that they had contracted one of these diseases. This close medical scrutiny prompted the resistance of the soldiers to the authorities in general and also exposed the inadequate medical knowledge of the Egyptians doctors in dealing with these diseases. Third, being highly contagious, they required strict segregation of the afflicted, as well as some basic sanitary conditions for treatment, conditions that were often unmet by the regimental field hospitals that

52 Although strictly meaning syphilis, *frengi* seems to have been used to refer to a variety of venereal diseases. At the same time, syphilis was also referred to as *mubārak* and "goats' disease"; Clot Bey, *Aperçu*, II, p. 370.

53 This was also true of the students in the various schools. See, for example, Clot Bey's letters to the Schools Department regarding the 305 students from the Mubtadayan school and the 104 students from the Translation School who had to be sent to Qaṣr al-ʿAinī hospital for treatment and would thus miss a large number of school days: S/3/122/2 p. 182, letter no. 189, dated 17 C 1263/2 June 1847.

were erected in various parts of Syria. Fourth, and most importantly, dealing with syphilis necessitated a rigid control of the men's sexual behavior, something which, in turn, required a strict segregation from the outside world which often proved difficult to enforce.

Early in 1826 the Pasha wrote to his agent in Istanbul asking him to find a doctor capable of dealing with scabies and venereal diseases since, as he said, "although we have doctors who are adept in dealing with a variety of diseases, we lack doctors knowledgeable about treating these two ailments."[54] It is not clear if any of these doctors were actually sent from Istanbul; nor is it clear, assuming they were in fact sent, if they accompanied the army on its Syrian campaign. If they did accompany the army, then it is obvious that they were not very successful in dealing with these two particular ailments. A couple of months after the outbreak of the Syrian campaign scabies and syphilis were high on the list of diseases prevalent among the soldiers.[55] The hospitals in Syria could not cope with their rapidly increasing numbers and many of the patients had to be sent back to Egypt for treatment.[56] During a particular medical examination, the number of patients afflicted with syphilis was equal to the number of all other patients put together.[57] Recognizing the seriousness of the situation Mehmed Ali had to order his nephew, Ahmed Pasha Yeğen, to supervise checking the soldiers himself.[58] Eventually, and as evidence that these two ailments received particular attention, the pre-printed daily reports of the hospitals in Syria had separate entries for them in which the director of the hospital simply filled in the number of syphilitic and scabietic soldiers.[59]

The young doctors who had recently graduated from the Abū-Zaʿbal hospital faced enormous difficulties in the near-epidemic proportions of these two diseases. At the outbreak of the Syrian campaign the Abū-Zaʿbal school was still in its formative years and was suffering from managerial, financial and technical problems which seriously undermined its performance and greatly affected the level of competence of its early graduates.[60]

54 S/1/50/6/493, on 11 R 1242/12 November 1826.

55 *Vekayi-i Mısıriyye*, issue no. 334, on 29 December 1831, quoted in Kuhnke, *Lives at Risk*, p. 135.

56 See Sham 1/27, on 20 C 1247/26 November 1831, for sending patients to the Abū-Zaʿbal hospital, and Sham 2/54, on 7 B 1247/12 December 1831, and Sham 2/88, on 23 B 1247/28 December 1831, for sending them to the hospital in Alexandria. In all these cases patients were transported by ship.

57 Sham 3/101, on 10 Ş 1247/14 January 1832.

58 S/5/51/2/62 on 30 L 1247/1 April 1832.

59 For examples of these pre-printed reports, see Sham 7/78, on 11 M 1248/11 June 1832, and Sham 10/150, on 17 Ra 1248/14 August 1832.

60 Kuhnke, *Lives at Risk*, pp. 37–40.

Two particular problems seem to have tainted the performance of the school. The first concerned the language to be used as a medium of instruction and the second related to the time spent in the school before graduation. While the Pasha and the chief physician of his army, Clot Bey, resorted to the logical choice of recruiting graduates of al-Azhar since this formed the only pool of young literate men in the country, these men certainly had no knowledge of French or any other foreign language. At the same time, most of the doctors who were employed in teaching in the school had no knowledge of Arabic. To surmount this problem, a number of translators were assigned to each lecturer and asked to translate the lecture while it was being delivered.

> It was a most curious situation; a hundred Egyptian students from al-Azhar who knew only Arabic and who had never received any training but in Arabic grammar, Koranic Exegesis, Fikh, etc. gathered together in order to be trained in medical and scientific subjects of which they had not the slightest idea by a number of European teachers who did not know the language of their students and who themselves were not homogenous [four being French, three Italians, a Spaniard], a Piedmontese and . . . a Bavarian.[61]

This weird system invited all kinds of problems. On one occasion, for example, a certain translator, Shaykh Harrāwī, objected to having to translate some of Clot Bey's lectures because he disagreed with the doctor's opinions. Clot Bey wrote to Mehmed Ali, who in turn wrote to the Deputy Director of the War Department telling him that he was surprised that the Health Council had not reprimanded the Shaykh strongly enough. He then said that the Shaykh should be written a strong letter telling him to mind his own business and not to interfere in Clot Bey's lectures "since he is a translator no more."[62]

Eventually this problem was surmounted. On his return from Paris Shaykh Rifāʿa al-Ṭahṭāwī was intended to be attached to the School of Medicine in Abū-Zaʿbal and to have twenty students working with him on translating medical books from French into Arabic and to compile a French–Arabic dictionary.[63] When it was deemed more suitable to employ Shaykh Rifāʿa elsewhere, the first batch of graduates of the

61 Heyworth-Dunne, *Education*, pp. 126–7. It was obvious even during that time that this system of teaching had serious problems; see Clot Bey's response to contemporary criticisms in his *Aperçu*, II, pp. 428–37.

62 Sāmī, ed., *Taqwīm al-Nīl*, II, p. 451, letters dated 7 and 11 C 1251/30 September and 4 October 1835. Shaykh Harrāwī, however, was not a mere translator; he was the head of the Muristan school that functioned as a preparatory school for the Medical School. On his life and activities, see al-Shayyāl, *Tārīkh al-Tarjama*, pp. 175–7, and ʿAbdel-Karīm, *Tārīkh al-Taʿlīm*, pp. 289–91.

63 "Extrait d'une lettre adressée par M. Le Cheykh Refah, ancien élève de la mission égyptienne en France, à M. Jomard, membre de l'Institut," *Journal Asiatique*, IIe série, 8 (1831), p. 534.

Medical School were themselves employed to teach another generation of students, and this time instruction was conducted in Arabic. In due time Arabic lexicons were compiled and medical books were translated and even written in Arabic.[64] Eventually the entire process of medical education was Arabized.[65] These measures, however, because of their very nature, needed time to come to fruition, and during the Syrian campaign the language problems encountered in instruction were reflected in the low standard of the early graduates.

More important than the language problems was the habit of appointing the early graduates of the Abū-Zaʿbal School as regimental doctors and attaching them to the army in Syria before they had received enough training in the school. Time constraints meant that these students were discharged from school and sent to field service before they had completed their proper training courses. On being sent to active duty they "neglected the medical books they had studied and never went back to consult them. Since they knew that they no longer had to sit for exams, they had no recourse to these books . . . They thus forgot whatever they had learned."[66] Occasionally, having been proven to be unqualified to deal with the various cases they had to face in Syria, these young graduates were charged with incompetence and sent back to Egypt to finish their studies.[67]

Faced with a near epidemic of scabies and syphilis, and having unqualified doctors to deal with them, Clot Bey wrote a special treatise about the subject.[68] Translated into Arabic and printed in the Army Press, the treatise took the form of a personal letter from the chief physician of the army to each regimental doctor. This treatise is significant because it shows the alarming spread of these diseases, something that necessitated the intervention of the chief physician of the army himself. It started by saying that "it has lately been reported that a large number of soldiers had been afflicted with scabies and syphilis, which are highly contagious. It is feared that if no strong and effective measures are taken, they will spread even further."[69] More significant is the tone in which the treatise was written. It was not

[64] al-Shayyāl lists fifty-six books in medical and veterinary science that were translated during Mehmed Ali's reign alone, being exceeded in number only by military books (sixty-four); al-Shayyāl, *Tārīkh al-Tarjama*, p. 38 of the Appendix.

[65] ʿAbdel-Karīm, *Tārīkh al-Taʿlīm*, pp. 269–70.

[66] ʿAbdel-Karīm, *Tārīkh al-Taʿlīm*, p. 267, quoting a report dated 2 Ra 1256/4 May 1840 which was addressed by the European doctors to Ibrahim Pasha and concerned the appalling performance of the Abū-Zaʿbal graduates. See also the letter sent from the Health Council to the Schools Department about the importance of keeping oneself abreast of the latest developments in medical knowledge by reading new books: S/3/122/4 p. 70, letter no. 78, on 14 M 1264/24 December 1847.

[67] Kuhnke, *Lives at Risk*, p. 39.

[68] Clot Bey, *Risāla*.

[69] *Ibid.*, p. 1.

enough for the head of the military medical establishment to say that particular care should be given to treating these two ailments; he also had to write in detail how the physical check-up was to be conducted, and how the patients were to be isolated, treated and regularly examined to make sure that they were cured. Given the low level of competence of the regimental doctors, Clot Bey had to write the book as a manual describing in very simplistic language how to conduct the check-ups so that any doctor with the most basic knowledge of medicine would be able to follow it using a minimum degree of discretion.[70]

Although the low level of competence of the new doctors might have been a serious problem, the main difficulty in dealing with scabies and syphilis lay in the appalling condition of the army hospitals in Syria that militated against a healthy, sanitary environment, an obvious essential condition for preventing the spread of disease. It was one thing for Clot Bey or the medical authorities in Cairo to stipulate that soldiers were to be segregated and regularly examined, it was another thing for this segregation and these examinations to be carried out as planned.

Lack of funds seems to have been one of the principal reasons for the dilapidated condition of the army hospitals in Syria as well as those in Egypt, and Clot Bey was in the habit of writing bitter letters to the War Department complaining about the insufficiency of medicine and food issued to the hospitals. "I do not understand," he said in one such letter, "why there is always a readiness not only to belittle the [entire] medical service but also to abolish [things] related to it . . . [This in spite of the fact] that the medical regulations used in the various hospitals in Egypt stipulate the expenditure of only one-twentieth of what hospitals in Europe spend."[71] In that respect the Chief Physician of the army sometimes had the backing of the Pasha; more often, however, the Pasha in his typical thrifty manner would require him to make do with what was available. For example, when it was brought to his attention that students in the School of Medicine were issued with small uniforms that did not fit them, he characteristically answered that "each person has to extend his legs as much as could be covered by his trousers."[72]

Another example of this stinginess had to do with what appears to have been a trivial matter, but one which was central for the performance of the medical establishment and the subject of a voluminous correspondence, namely, the quality of surgical bandages used to dress wounds. In spite of having a special book translated and

[70] See below for a description of the *Risāla*.
[71] S/3/122/2, pp. 72–3, letter no. 150, on 12 M 1263/1 January 1847.
[72] Madaris 1/49, on 22 N 1251/1 January 1837.

printed in the Būlāq Press on that subject,[73] doctors were constantly complaining about the bandages that were issued to them.[74] In one letter Clot Bey wrote in desperation complaining of the quality of the bandages in Qaṣr al-ʿAinī hospital.

Since the quality of bandages is considered to be one of the key issues in surgery, we have conducted an examination of these bandages used in the hospital and found that they are very bad indeed. They were coarse and dirty, contaminating the wounds that they are supposed to dress . . . [Then he gives his explanation for this situation:] An order has been issued from the War Department to the Director of the Central Depot of Medicine to hand in used and semi-used [*niṣf istiʿmāl*] cloth to the Chief Pharmacist accompanied by a stamped receipt. The Chief Pharmacist is then supposed to hand the cloth to the Chief Surgeon also accompanied by a receipt. The Chief Surgeon, in turn, is then to hand in the cloth to the Director of the Hospital who would then distribute it among the patients to make the bandages themselves. He is then supposed to collect them from the patients. In this manner the bandages would have already changed hands four times. This is against the Hospital regulations that should not be violated.[75]

Another area in which the problem of lack of funds manifested itself was the quality of food issued to the military hospitals. In spite of Clot Bey's explicit regulations that soldiers should be fed clean, well-cooked food and to have a healthy diet,[76] the soldiers in Qaṣr al-ʿAinī hospital were constantly complaining of bad food and this was a regular complaint throughout the hospital's history during Mehmed Ali's reign. When in 1836, for example, an examination was conducted on the conditions of the Ṭura and Qaṣr al-ʿAinī hospitals in Cairo, it was discovered, among other things, that both hospitals were issuing less meat to their patients than was stipulated by the regulations. When the report was sent to Mehmed Ali he forwarded it to the War Department to take the necessary steps to alleviate the problems. The Deputy Director of the War Department returned the report to the Pasha, however, claiming that this was not the War Department's business but that of the Health Council. The Pasha refused to accept this pretext, and insisted that the War Department deal with the complaints.[77] Two years later, when the Pasha saw for himself the appalling condition of the hospitals in Cairo, he wrote to both Clot Bey and the Deputy

[73] Ibrāhīm al-Nabarāwī trans., *al-Arbiṭa al-Jirāḥiyya* [Surgical Bandages] (Cairo: Būlāq, 1839).

[74] See, for example, S/3/122/2, p. 87, letter no. 65, on 4 S 1263/22 January 1847.

[75] S/3/122/2, pp. 73–4, letter no. 152, on 12 M 1263/1 January 1847. The Central Depot of Medicine, *Isbitaliat al-ʿUmūm*, appears to have been a central chemical storehouse from which medicine was issued on demand to the various hospitals and pharmacies.

[76] Clot Bey, *ʿAjāla*, p. 7.

[77] Awamir lil-Jihadiyya 1/100, on 18 Ra 1252/4 July 1836.

Director of the War Department urging them to co-ordinate their efforts in improving the conditions of the hospitals.[78]

Nevertheless, eight years later Clot Bey was still writing to the War Department complaining of the quality of food in Qaṣr al-ʿAinī hospital. In an extensive report he wrote that the

> food of both officers and soldiers is the same and is composed of: rice, broiled meat, and bread that is most often of bad quality . . . [Moreover,] the patients' food, according to medical regulations, should not be composed of rice and meat, but they should occasionally be offered chicken, pigeons, eggs, milk, fish, vegetables, and fruit, in addition to other items ordered by the doctors as stipulated in the Hospital Regulations that have been translated into Turkish and approved by Khedival Order. Accordingly, we hope that attention and revision be given to improving the above-mentioned hospital especially since this will not only be an act of mercy to the poor patients, but also [this will be important] for the fame of this hospital, since all notable European tourists [make it a point to] visit it [while touring the country].[79]

More than ten years later doctors were still complaining of the quality of food issued to the patients and saying that meat in particular was "causing diseases to the patients rather than helping them in their convalescence."[80]

Given this problem of lack of funds it should not be surprising to discover that the hospitals in Cairo, let alone the regimental ones in Syria, were not particularly hygienic. When Selim Bey, the Colonel of the Guardia Regiment, went on an investigative tour of the barracks of his regiment in Syria, he found the whole place stinking deplorably.[81] This, he discovered, was caused by the fact that no one was assigned to clean the bathrooms and that the rooms where the wounded were kept smelt foul because their occupants were still wearing blood-stained clothes. On visiting the hospital he found more than 200 patients with scabies sleeping on the floor because their mattresses were not filled with straw.[82] When the nurses were asked why the mattresses were empty, they answered that they could not do all the jobs themselves and that they had no workers to help them.[83]

78 Dhawat 5/78, on 12 Ra 1254/5 June 1838.

79 S/3/122/2, p. 65, letter no. 136, on 4 M 1263/23 December 1846.

80 S/3/122/8, p. 15, letter no. 105, on 4 Ş 1276/26 February 1860.

81 Among the various complaints about the performance of the hospitals in Cairo were those concerning their smell, a stagnant, stinking smell "known as the smell of the Muristan [the hospital smell]": S/3/122/5 p. 28, letter no. 10, dated 29 L 1264/28 September 1848.

82 Clot Bey was complaining of the same thing in relation to the Qaṣr al-ʿAinī hospital in Cairo: "The mattresses and pillows are filled with rotting hay instead of cotton as the regulations stipulate": S/3/122/2 p. 65, letter no. 136, on 4 M 1263/23 December 1846.

83 Sham 2/71, on 17 B 1247/23 December 1831.

In a revealing letter, Munib Efendi, Ibrahim Pasha's Aide-de-Camp, wrote to Ahmed Bey, the Governor of Damascus, complaining about the problems of securing a sufficient number of these servants (*hizmetkar*). He said that although the army hospitals in Syria were arranged according to European regulations (*Avrupa kanunu üzere*) which stipulated appointing one servant per twelve patients (and one per six patients if they were segregated), he admitted that these regulations could not be carried out. The main reason was lack of funds. He elaborated by saying that there was no problem in appointing barbers for the patients, since these could always be secured from the soldiers of the regiment at large. The problem, he explained, was securing servants to cook and clean the hospitals. These had to be hired from the local population, something that obviously cost money. To cut down on expenses, he suggested the appointment of some of the "semi-disabled" (*yarım sakatlar*) as servants. Since these might not be able to walk, he soon realized, animals would have to be hired to transport them to their jobs, something that would entail more, and not less, expense. After waffling on in this manner, Munib Efendi was at a loss over what to do.[84]

The hospitals in Syria were also suffering from being overcrowded with patients and understaffed by doctors. An investigation was once conducted into the performance of the hospital in Acre. Munib Efendi conducted the investigation himself and cleared the hospital's director of responsibility. The problem, his report said, was that the hospital was overcrowded and the doctors could not cope with the number of patients they were receiving every day. At that particular time it had over 300 inmates and was expecting forty-five more patients that day. This large number made it impossible to order the patients to have their regular baths, something that the patients afflicted with scabies had to do as part of their treatment. The other problem, Munib Efendi added in his report, was that the doctors had no control over the patients, who were constantly going out to the markets and no one could stop them.[85]

When contrasted with Clot Bey's regulations, these accounts of the way the regimental field hospitals in Syria functioned show the enormous gap separating model from reality that so characterizes the entire reign of Mehmed Ali, and not only his health policy. As seen above, the regimental hospitals were underfunded, overcrowded, lacked qualified doctors capable of dealing with the health problems of an army at war and, above all, suffered from all the problems that were

84 Sham 11/107, on 12 R 1248/8 September 1832. On the *yarım sakatlar*, see the next chapter.

85 Sham 9/32, on 6 S 1248/4 July 1832.

characteristic of other establishments of the Pasha, namely corruption and inefficiency.

Having seen the scale of the problems pertaining to the health and hygiene of the soldiers in Syria it is now possible to explain the problems that the authorities faced in their attempts to deal with the two diseases that we are concerned with, scabies and syphilis. As far as the spread of scabies was concerned, one reason seems to have been the overcrowded nature of the barracks and camps.[86] More importantly, the logistical and bureaucratic problems reviewed in the last chapter meant that, as was seen above, the soldiers were rarely issued new uniforms and that they had to stay in their old, often dirty ones for a long time. When Hassan Efendi, the adjutant-major of the 8th Infantry Regiment, received orders to investigate the appearance and uniforms of his soldiers he found most of them in direct violation of the regulations. In a report he sent to his major he said that their uniforms have worn out and "hardly anything is left of the shoes on their feet and a lot of them walk bare-foot in the markets."[87] A general investigation (*yoklama*) was ordered into the appearance and discipline of all the soldiers in various regiments in Syria. Its findings are interesting enough to justify quoting extensively from them.

> Concerning the soldiers of the 13th Regiment in Jaffa . . . Their new footwear was two months overdue and we found some of the soldiers barefoot . . . Their fezzes were old and their new ones three months overdue. Their kits and the straps of their rifles were dirty and have not been cleaned since they left Cairo . . . The patients in the hospital there had no one to look after them day or night and there were no officers [to supervise them].
>
> Concerning the soldiers in Ḥaifa . . . We found their bodies, their weapons, and their belongings dirty and unclean (*wiskha lam naẓīfa*). They were disorderly and doing whatever pleased them (*mashiyīn min gheir tartīb ʿala keifhum*). The patients in the hospital were sleeping on the floor with no mattresses and nothing but a carpet. Their places were absolutely dirty (*maḥallāthum wiskha lam fīhi naẓāfa ʿandahum kulliyyan*). When we asked to see the director, we could not find him, and when he came back from the market, he said that he had written various letters about the mattresses [but had not been answered] . . .
>
> Concerning the soldiers of the 4th Battalion of the 18th Regiment . . . We found them wearing their [ceremonial] broadcloth uniforms. When we asked their lieutenant why his soldiers were wearing their broadcloth uniforms day and night, he said that they had not been issued either with flax or woollen uniforms and they had no choice but to do so. This is something against the regulations . . .

[86] There seems to have been a shortage of soldiers' lodgings and, in one case, some houses belonging to St. Jacob's church in Jerusalem were seized to house the soldiers; S/5/47/1/150 on 29 Z 1249/9 May 1834.

[87] Sham 3/43, on 25 Ş 1247/29 January 1832.

Concerning the artillery soldiers in Acre . . . Some of them were sitting in the sun with no tents and sleeping on the ground with no mattresses . . . They had their food on the fences and were making the fence dirty and stinking . . . Their ammunition was lying in the sun and their tents were thrown against the fence without being put up . . . The [other] soldiers were roaming the markets as they wish. This is all against the Laws of the Military (*Qānūn al-Jihādiyya*).[88]

If these were the conditions in which the soldiers lived, it is no wonder that they easily fell prey to scabies. And seeing how overcrowded, badly equipped and inefficiently run the hospitals were, then it should not be difficult to see why the authorities found it difficult to control the spread of disease to other unaffected soldiers.

Compared to scabies, dealing with syphilis presented much more formidable problems. Detecting and treating syphilis necessitated a much closer scrutiny of soldiers' bodies. The first article of Clot Bey's *Risāla*, written specifically for the treatment of syphilis and scabies, went as follows.

On receiving this letter you must conduct an examination of all the men whose health you are required to look after, officers, NCOs and soldiers. Those afflicted with one of those two diseases [i.e. scabies and syphilis] have to be set aside, and particular care has to be given to those afflicted with syphilis. You have to check their genitalia and their mouths. This examination is to be conducted once every week.[89]

The treatise proceeded to tell the regimental doctors how precisely to examine the bodies of the soldiers, how to prepare a special ointment for treatment and finally how to apply this ointment on the soldiers' genitalia.[90]

During these medical inspections the soldiers found their bodies minutely examined and closely inspected as reflected in the following typical report about one such inspection conducted by the doctor of the Guardia Regiment and ordered by Ibrahim Pasha.

At eight o'clock on Thursday 3rd of Şaban 1247 [7 January 1832] on investigating the soldiers of the eight companies of the 1st Battalion of the Guardia Regiment, no disease was discovered among the musicians of the companies (*musikicilerde hasta yoktur*). Their tents were also found clean and warm. However, the sergeant-major of the 5th Company had hurt the thumb of his left hand while pulling a cannon. It was also discovered that a thorn had penetrated the skin between the fourth and little toes of the right foot of the fifth corporal of the same company causing an inflammation . . . One of the soldiers

[88] Sham 9/116, on 20 S 1248/19 July 1832. This lengthy report is in an interesting Arabic vernacular with its own queer spelling system and local idiomatic expression. I have preferred, therefore, to transliterate it as one would transliterate colloquial Egyptian, as opposed to classical, Arabic.

[89] Clot Bey, *Risāla*, p. 2. [90] *Ibid.*, Arts. 3–8, pp. 2–5.

of the 1st Company of the 2nd Battalion of the same regiment had the skin of his right ankle scratched as a result of his [tight] shoe rubbing against it . . . On seeing signs of syphilis in the mouth of the sixth corporal of the 7th Company of the 3rd Battalion of the same regiment his major was ordered to send him to the [field] hospital . . .[91]

Despite the benefits of routine medical examinations, there does not seem to have been any effort to convince the men of them or to enlist their support. Soldiers resented being so minutely examined by the doctors and often lied about their physical condition in order to avoid being sent to the field hospitals. For example, a general medical examination was once conducted on the soldiers of the 12th Infantry Regiment in Syria. The European doctors found that twelve men were infected with syphilis and 210 with scabies. None of them was sent to the hospital and they were still living side by side with the regiment at large. When the Egyptian doctors were asked why the sick had not been interned in the hospital as the regulations stipulated, they answered that whenever they asked them, the soldiers denied being afflicted with any diseases.[92] On inspecting the army hospital in Haifa Mursi Ağa, the adjutant-major of the 10th Infantry Regiment, found it in an unkempt, messy condition. Contrary to the regulations, those afflicted with syphilis ("about twenty") were not segregated but were found mingling with other patients and with the wounded. When he asked the director why these men had not been set aside as the regulations stipulated, Mursi Ağa received the answer that he did not have enough room to do so, and that neither Nazif Bey, the Commissary-General of the army, nor Abdallah Bey, the Governor of Ḥaifa, had given him enough assistance in that respect.[93]

At the same time soldiers, and occasionally officers, often feigned sickness to avoid being sent to the front and to have a pretext for staying in the relative security of the field hospital.[94] Cadets in military school sometimes acted similarly; on being sent to the hospital it would soon be noticed that they had not lost their appetite and that "each one of them was eating as much as four."[95] Officers who were discovered to have been cheating in this manner were discharged from service

[91] Sham 3/115, on 7 Ş 1247/11 January 1832.
[92] *ibid.*
[93] Sham 8/125, on 19 M 1248/19 June 1832.
[94] Sham 2/71, on 18 B 1247/23 December 1831; Sham 2/95, on 2 Ş 1247/6 January 1832.
[95] This was the case with three students from the School of Cavalry who were sent to Qaṣr al-ʿAinī for treatment. When they were found out, the proposed treatment was "four to five hours daily shooting exercises . . . Our best opinion is that they are suitable for infantry service": S/3/122/2 p. 145, letter no. 163 dated 13 Ca 1263/29 April 1847. Later, in 1861, soldiers feigning illness were sent to the Liman. See the case of the

altogether, sent to the Liman of Alexandria, and were stripped of their medals and uniforms.[96]

This resistance to the self-declared right of the medical authorities to scrutinize bodies in the search for any signs of disease was to be seen not only amongst soldiers in the camps but was also encountered by the authorities in Qaṣr al-ʿAinī hospital in Cairo whose patients were not spared this minute, often humiliating inspection. The following is Flaubert's description of the syphilis ward in the hospital that he visited while touring Egypt in 1849:

> . . . Kasr el-ʿAini hospital. Well maintained. The work of Clot Bey – his hand is still to be seen. Pretty cases of syphilis . . . Several have it in the arse. At a sign from the doctor, they all stood up on their beds (it was like army drill) and opened their anuses with their fingers to show their chancres. Enormous infundibula . . .[97]

Given this humiliating treatment it is not surprising to read about soldiers in that particular ward resisting treatment[98] and sometimes physically fighting the authorities. In one incident the patients went on the rampage in the hospital taking the glass out of the window frames and urinating on the floor and in the drinking water containers. Since most of them were young and "able-bodied" and since they "were not afflicted with diseases that would prevent their doctors from treating them harshly," it was suggested that they be punished with "severe bodily penalties . . . because reprimanding them has not worked so far."[99]

The resistance of the soldiers to these regular medical check-ups was mirrored in the larger society by the civilians' resistance to vaccination. What appears to have been a policy which intended their own benefit and well-being, vaccination was seen by peasants and city folk alike as yet another way of marking their children for conscription.[100] The authorities appear to have made no effort to overcome their expected

corporal ʿAwaḍ Ibrāhīm who rubbed garlic on his genitalia hoping to induce symptoms of syphilis: M/14/2 p. 65, letter dated 23 N 1277/6 March 1861.

96 Sham 9/22, on 8 S 1248/7 July 1832.

97 Gustave Flaubert, *Flaubert in Egypt, A Sensibility on Tour,* trans. and ed. Francis Steegmuller (Boston and Toronto: Little, Brown and Co., 1972), p. 65. It is not known how crowded the ward was at the time of Flaubert's visit. Eight years later, however, it had 1, 400 patients; see S/3/122/6, pp. 8–9, letter no. 39, dated 5 B 1273/1 March 1857.

98 See, for example, the case of the syphilitic cavalry soldier whose treatment had taken several weeks owing to his refusing it, S/3/122/4, p. 27, letter no. 144 dated 7 Z 1273/ 29 July 1857.

99 S/3/122/7, p. 4, letter no. 14, dated 14 Ca 1274/1 January 1858. These were all patients in the syphilis and dermatology ward.

100 Clot Bey, *Mémoires*, p. 157.

resistance by enlisting the support of the village shaykhs or the shaykhs of the quarters, for example. The villagers did everything possible to resist vaccinating their sons; they fled from the doctors, hid their sons,[101] attacked the barber-vaccinators,[102] bribed the local officials to leave their children unmarked,[103] and forged vaccination certificates.[104]

The reaction to the imposition of quarantines was no different. Seeing this as another abrupt intervention in their lives, soldiers attempted to evade the quarantines by all means. After spending nearly two years in Syria and being excited about going back home, soldiers disembarking at Damietta were asked to stay on board their ships for the duration of the quarantine. When they staged a minor mutiny in which the captain of the ship as well as the sentries were beaten by the soldiers,[105] a battalion had to be sent from Cairo to assist the quarantine officials to restore order in the port.[106] Quarantines imposed around certain camps in Syria were also difficult to maintain. In one incident, even after soldiers were warned that if they attempted to break through the quarantine they would be shot,[107] they still dared to break the rules and eventually a trench was dug around the camp to force the soldiers to comply with the regulations.[108]

Life behind the lines

After dealing in some detail with the problems facing the authorities in their attempts to *cure* the soldiers, namely the conditions of hospitals, the unqualified doctors, the unco-ordinated attempts of the bureaucracy in Cairo and the resistance of the patients themselves, what needs to be done now, by way of contrast, is to understand the causes behind the apparent failure to *prevent* diseases from spreading among soldiers. However successful the regimental doctors were in treating syphilis, the real problem lay in the authorities' attempts to prevent the diseases in the first place. This obviously entailed a strict system of control of the soldiers' sexual lives and a strong prohibition on women entering the camps or barracks,[109] something that the authorities singularly failed to

101 Hamont, *L'Egypte*, I, pp. 507–9; Kuhnke, *Lives at Risk*, pp. 116–17.
102 S/3/122/2, p. 194, letter no. 155, on 1 B 1263/15 June 1847.
103 See the case of the eighty-five doctors who accepted bribes from the locals to forge vaccination certificates for them: S/3/122/2, pp. 61–3, letters 11–96, all dated 26 Ca 1263/13 May 1847.
104 M/5/1, p. 79, letter no. 79, on 27 C 1267/30 April 1850.
105 S/1/48/4/311 on 22 Ş 1249/5 January 1834.
106 S/1/48/4/350 on 7 L 1249/17 February 1834.
107 Sham 9/106, on 18 S 1248/17 July 1832.
108 Sham 9/113, on 19 S 1248/18 July 1832.
109 *Qānūn al-Dākhiliyya*, Art. 273, p. 52.

Plate 6 "Encampment of Ibrahim Pasha, near Jaffa"

do. As said in chapter 3 above, as long as the regiments were still in Egypt, the families of the soldiers were allowed to join them and to follow them from camp to camp, but for health reasons this practice had to be stopped. Forbidding the soldiers from having access to their wives proved to be difficult to enforce, however, and some of the women disguised themselves as men and followed their husbands all the way to Syria.[110] When the authorities insisted on forbidding the wives from accompanying their husbands, the men grumbled strongly "and in order to counteract the feeling of despondency as far as possible, the wives, concubines, and parents of the conscripts have been allowed to accompany them."[111]

By giving way to the soldiers' needs on that front Mehmed Ali proved to be more flexible and pragmatic than the contemporary British naval commanders who were aiming at a moral standard "altogether too high for the people with whom it dealt . . . [especially by insisting on] the whole illogical system of indiscriminate pressing with its corollary of not

[110] Sham 1/27, on 4 C 1247/10 November 1831.

[111] The request of the soldiers to have their families brought was relayed to the Pasha in S/1/48/4/250 on 2 Ca 1249/17 September 1833, and his answer is in S/1/48/4/255 on 15 Ca 1249/30 September 1833. The quotation is from Bowring, "Report on Egypt," p. 6.

allowing the men shore-leave when in port."[112] Allowing women to join their husbands in Syria, however, created hygiene problems which certainly contributed to the spread of syphilis and other venereal diseases among the soldiery and which the authorities now found difficult to address.

In the second section of his *Risāla* Clot Bey, in a characteristically simplistic and didactic manner, set out a method that he thought would be effective in controlling the spread of syphilis through prevention rather than cure. It had to do primarily with the health condition of the women's lodgings and their bodies. He said that the wives of the soldiers of each regiment were to be divided into four sections. Each of these sections was to be composed of the wives of the soldiers of each battalion within the regiment. They had to be set aside and examined by the wives of the doctors in charge of the men of the corresponding battalion.[113] The doctors had to teach their wives how to detect signs of syphilis in the women they were to examine and the "women doctors" had to report to their husbands their findings after each examination, which was to be conducted every Thursday. More importantly, the soldiers were ordered not to allow into the camps any women except their wives "even if these women are their mothers or sisters since this will increase the financial burden of the soldiers, in addition to contributing further to the spread of diseases."[114] Finally, the lodgings of these women had to be regularly cleaned and this process had to be supervised by the colonel of the regiment himself. In addition, their lodgings had to be built "along two neat parallel lines with a wide street separating them and they have to be above the ground by a standardized height. In this manner disease could be stopped from spreading."[115]

Judging from the performance of the regimental doctors, it is doubtful that their wives, who had not received any medical training whatsoever, could have been more successful than their husbands in treating these sensitive diseases. Furthermore, seeing how unhygienic and dirty the field hospitals were, it is also doubtful if the soldiers' barracks, let alone the lodgings of their wives, were as healthy and properly built as Clot Bey desired them to be. But even if they were, there still was another considerable problem to deal with, namely the uncontrolled encounter not with the wives, but with women from outside the camps, and specifically prostitutes.

There is some evidence to suggest that prostitution in big cities in

112 Michael Lewis, *The Social History of the Navy, 1793–1815* (London: George Allen and Unwin, 1960), p. 282.

113 Clot Bey, *Risāla*, Section 2, Art. 1, p. 6.

114 *Ibid.*, Art. 4, p. 6.

115 *Ibid.*, Art. 11, p. 8.

Egypt and Syria was on the rise during the first half of the nineteenth century. This occurred not so much because of any sudden appearance of vice, as represented in a person such as *al-ʿalmeh* Kuchuk Hanim[116] on her divan, or because of a sudden increase in the number of *khawals*[117] dancing in the streets in their female dresses. Nor is it, as Clot Bey opined, because of the high rise in the rate of divorce or the "voluptuous temperament of Egyptian women."[118] Rather, it was caused by the unprecedented social mobility, with thousands of men moving around from camp to camp and from city to city and also with thousands of women left behind by their husbands, fathers and brothers. "Numbers of young wives thus abandoned are compelled by starvation, or to prevent their children from perishing to join the almé [i.e. prostitution], all whose profligate habits they must soon acquire."[119] In March 1833, during a visit to Banī Suwayf in Middle Egypt, St. John described what was most probably a typical scene.

> On reaching [the town] unusual bustle and activity were observable in the streets . . . The cause was soon discovered: Ahmed Pasha [Yeğen], with a division of the Egyptian army, had just arrived from the Hedjaz,[120] and the soldiers . . . were spreading themselves through the city, snatching in haste the coarse pleasures within their reach. All the dancing girls, singers and musicians were consequently employed, and we found the caravanserai so entirely occupied by this military rabble, that not a single apartment could be obtained.[121]

Until that time prostitution had been, strictly speaking, a legal profession[122] and a tax was even levied on this "trade" which Mehmed Ali's government was keen on collecting.[123] In May 1834, however, the Department of Civil Affairs (Divan-ı Hidiv) debated the matter and decided to abolish the tax and ban the whole trade from the city of Cairo. The shaykhs of the quarters were ordered to compile lists of the brothels in the quarters and of the prostitutes working there. The brothels were to be shut down and the prostitutes warned that on being

116 The famous "public dancer" immortalized by Flaubert in his travel notes to Egypt; see Flaubert, *Egypt*, pp. 113–20.

117 These were male dancers who impersonated women in their appearance and behavior. They often danced in the streets, before houses and in the courtyards of certain mansions on various occasions; Edward W. Lane, *An Account of the Manners and Customs of the Modern Egyptians* (London: Ward, Lock, 1890), pp. 351, 467.

118 Clot Bey, *Aperçu*, I, p. 336. 119 St. John, *Egypt*, II, p. 176.

120 He had recently been appointed as War Director and must have come to Egypt to assume his new post.

121 St. John, *Egypt*, II, p. 265.

122 Raymond says that in the eighteenth century prostitutes in Cairo were organized as a guild; André Raymond, *Artisans et commerçants au Caire au XVIIIe siècle* (Damascus: Institut français, 1973–74), II, p. 527.

123 Tucker, *Women*, p. 150.

caught practicing their trade they would be given fifty lashes of the whip, to be doubled if caught a second time.[124]

Tucker attributes this sudden prohibition to public pressure led by the *ʿulamāʾ* which convinced the Pasha to ban all prostitution in Cairo, "thereby assuaging public opinion and adding another feather to his cap of reform."[125] This could hardly be the reason why Mehmed Ali gave up a considerable source of government revenue.[126] For one thing Mehmed Ali could not have been so keen to assuage the *ʿulamāʾ* and he could, and did, disregard their opinion on various other occasions. It is significant, for example, that during the deliberations that were held in the Department of Civil Affairs concerning the abolition of the tax, it was suggested that the punishment stipulated in the Islamic religious law be applied to prostitutes. In the event it was decided on the punishment mentioned above and it was the civil administrators, not the shaykhs, who were to execute these punishments.

That prostitutes were considered a menace more to discipline and health than to morals and good manners is also clear from the fact that they were prohibited from practicing their trade only in big cities and around the camps. When Flaubert visited Egypt in 1849–50 he knew that no prostitutes could easily be found in Cairo, that they had moved on to Upper Egypt and that "good brothels no longer exist[ed] in Cairo."[127] This ban on prostitution in Cairo was largely imposed for fear of its effect on soldiers' health and their discipline. As lenient as the Pasha might have been in allowing the soldiers to bring their wives to live with them in Syria, no concessions were given in allowing them to solicit the services of prostitutes. This was true both for European officers "whoever they might be,"[128] and for Turkish-speaking officers.[129]

124 S/2/32/5/72 on 18 M 1250/28 May 1834. A couple of months later it was decreed that "beautiful female domestic servants" had to be employed only through official, authorized offices (*makātib takhdīm maẓbūṭa*); S/2/32/5/104 on 1 R 1250/7 August 1834.

125 Tucker, *Women*, p. 152.

126 Clot Bey says that this amounted to 60, 000 francs in 1833; *Aperçu*, II, pp. 208–9. St. John, moreover, says that the revenue from this tax increased nearly ten-fold from 1821 to 1830; St. John, *Egypt*, II, pp. 468–9.

127 Flaubert, *Egypt*, p. 83. However, he did find the "soldiers' prostitutes, who let themselves be taken . . . in exchange for a few *paras*" along the aqueduct in Cairo; *ibid.*, p. 76. Clot Bey says that in spite of the public ban, prostitutes still practiced in Cairo albeit in hiding; *Aperçu*, I, p. 336.

128 S/1/48/4/594 on 20 Ca 1250/24 September 1834. This case concerned two European officers, a pharmacist and a cartographer, who had "a dancer and a singer" in their tents at night. The Pasha's language in this letter is particularly harsh and categorical in forbidding prostitutes from living near army camps.

129 Awamir lil-Jihadiyya 1/10, on 6 S 1246/27 July 1830. This case concerned a certain Osman Ağa who had taken a twenty-four–hour leave but returned five days later. On

Apart from the threat to the health of the soldiers and officers, prostitutes were also banned from the vicinities of camps and barracks because a lot of them on entering the camps brought with them liquor with all that that entailed in terms of threat to the discipline of the troops and to public order. For example, when the wagoneer (*arabaci*) Derviş and the sapper (*baltaci*) Osman were punished by seventy-five and 150 lashes of the whip, respectively, it was more for the disturbances they had caused after getting drunk than for being caught in a brothel.[130] Many cases concerning the undisciplined behavior of soldiers in Syrian cities were due to the soldiers getting drunk in the taverns and taking to the streets, "abusing the old and the young and the Christian population with no reason."[131] Taverns (*meyhaneler*) were thus banned as forcefully as brothels, although it was difficult to separate the one from the other. But again, and as was the case with brothels, the ban was not categorical; it was only the taverns in close proximity to the camps that were ordered to be shut down. When a foreigner opened a tavern near a mosque in Acre he was *politely* asked to close it down and to move it to the Frankish quarter.[132] This might have been due to the fact that he dared to open his tavern near a mosque. But the fact that he was still allowed to open it in a more distant place means that the authorities were not that concerned with matters of public morality or decency. In any case, and as proof that Mehmed Ali's administration in Syria was not so keen on the outright prohibition of taverns, Şerif Pasha, the governor-general of Syria, was ordered by the Pasha to compile a list of the revenue accrued by all taverns in the province.[133]

Impermeable boundaries?

The real problem underlying the authorities' attempt to control the soldiers' encounters with prostitutes lay in the fact that, in spite of all the regulations reviewed in this and previous chapters aiming at forbidding the soldiers from mingling with the local population and at

investigation he was discovered to have spent his time in a brothel. He was expelled from service altogether.

130 Sham 3/119, on 16 Ş 1247/20 January 1832.

131 See for example the investigation report mentioned above (note 88): Sham 9/116, on 20 S 1248/19 July 1832. See also, for a report giving the same picture, Sham 8/130, on 20 M 1248/19 June 1832.

132 Sham 8/184, on 28 M 1248/27 June 1832.

133 S/5/47/1/124 on 7 Z 1249/17 April, 1834. See also Ibrahim's letter to his father's Chief Secretary, Sami Bey, requesting some officials from Cairo who would be able to tax the taverns properly since a lot of the potential revenue, he said, was not being tapped; Sham 20/511, on 25 Z 1250/24 April 1835.

creating formidable boundaries around the barracks and training camps, the men continued to filter through to the surrounding areas. Although the military and health authorities wanted to have tight control over the soldiers' bodies, a control that is graphically represented by the policy of segregation and internment in the camps, the soldiers were always crossing the supposedly insurmountable boundaries enclosing their camps. These simple acts of negotiating and crossing boundaries, even though they were not as dramatic as desertion (which will be dealt with in the next chapter), were still quite alarming, for they undermined the whole logic of the modern army, a logic that saw the best way of disciplining and training an army in isolating it from the wider society and in drawing sharp distinctions between civilian and military lives.

There are various examples that show the discrepancy between the impressive picture portrayed by such internment devices as the *tezkere*, for example, and the actual performance of the soldiers on the camps. For instance, on visiting the local market in Acre, Vehid Efendi, Ibrahim Yeğen's scribe, saw Egyptian soldiers roaming in the market, abusing the local population and insulting the shopkeepers. One of these shopkeepers approached him and complained bitterly of the behavior of the troops. He told him that they had never been so humiliated and insulted before, and that even the irregular troops of the previous Ottoman vali, Derviş Pasha, had been behaving better, adding that "when we heard that Ibrahim Pasha was arriving at the head of a formidable regular army we were relieved, thinking that you will comfort us (*rahat edeceğiniz deyerek*)."[134]

Besides going to the neighboring towns and cities in search of pleasure, the other main reason for the soldiers to go there was to buy and sell goods. There is the case, for example, of a certain private, Ali by name, who took a rifle and a carpet from a colleague's tent and then went to the market to sell the carpet and exchange the rifle for a pair of shoes. (According to the law he was supposed to be imprisoned; instead he was given 300 lashes of the whip.)[135] After the fall of Acre, the soldiers pillaged the whole city and sold their booty in the local market.[136] Their activities could not be controlled and Munib Efendi had to write in his report that "their officers are either unable to control them or are turning a blind eye to what is happening. This is certainly

134 Sham 3/131, on 21 Ş 1247/25 January 1832.

135 Sham 3/128, on 21 Ş 1247/25 January 1832. See also the case of another soldier who stole gunpowder and sold it in the market at Jaffa; Sham 3/116, on 16 Ş 1247/20 January 1832.

136 Sham 8/109, on 16 M 1248/15 June 1832.

against the regulations and might turn the locals against us."[137] When Ibrahim Pasha was informed about how unruly the city had become, and that "the soldiers are behaving like senior officers," he wrote a stern letter to the colonel in charge of the city warning him of the consequences if he did not restore discipline.[138]

Who is to guard the guards?

Although this problem of the uncontrolled mingling of the soldiers with the civilian population at large was encountered by the military authorities in various lands that Mehmed Ali's army fought in, it was particularly noticeable in Syria. Unlike the barren deserts of Arabia or the Sudan, Syria was a rich province dotted with big towns and cities offering all kinds of attractions for the soldiers to leave the camps and have a taste of the civilian life they must have missed. And unlike Morea or the Mediterranean islands that Mehmed Ali sent troops to, Syria was also an Arabic-speaking province, a fact that allowed the soldiers to mix with the local population for all the reasons mentioned above. And this at a time when, as was said in the last chapter, life in the camps, in terms of food, clothing, pay or lodgings, was not particularly pleasant.

There were thus enough pull and push factors to induce the soldiers to cross camp boundaries and mingle with the local population nearby. Obviously this was something that the authorities had expected, and the various blueprints, laws, manuals and official pronouncements of Mehmed Ali, or Clot Bey for that matter, had intended to create a strict regime of internment which aimed at preventing such undisciplined activities. This chapter, however, attempted to contrast the impressive picture presented in previous chapters that comes across from reading these blueprints with the more mundane accounts of the actual performance of the soldiers in the camps. To explain the reasons behind the authorities' failure to prevent the spread of syphilis, one area was highlighted, namely the encounter with women and especially with prostitutes.[139] For this encounter to be controlled a diligent watch had to be kept on the gates and boundaries of the camps. The duty of

137 Sham 8/120, on 17 M 1248/16 June 1832.

138 Sham 8/130, on 20 M 1248/19 June 1832. See also Yitzhak Hofman, "The administration of Syria and Palestine under Egyptian rule (1831–40)," in *Studies on Palestine During the Ottoman Period*, ed. by Moshe Ma'oz (Jerusalem: The Hebrew University, 1975), p. 311 n. 3.

139 Obviously this was not something specific to Mehmed Ali's army; venereal diseases have always been thought to spread most effectively through armies. On Napoleon's army's encounter with syphilis while in Egypt and elsewhere, see Elting, *Napoleon's Grande Armée*, p. 294.

executing Clot Bey's strict regulations preventing prostitutes from ever approaching the camps[140] lay squarely on the shoulders of sentries guarding the gates of the camps.

Ironically, it was invariably these very same sentries whom the authorities had problems controlling and it was the guards themselves who often violated the law. The guards controlling the camp in Tyre, for example, forced the local merchants to give them half their loads or else they would not allow them in.[141] After the fall of Acre it was the guards who, more than the soldiers, attacked the local population[142] and robbed the merchants.[143] When their attacks on the local merchants could not be stopped, the merchants refused to supply the castle with food altogether.[144] The general investigation report (*yoklama*) mentioned above was very apprehensive about the way the guards in particular were behaving. "The guards [in Ḥaifa] were sitting in the sun . . . not asking anyone anything, he who wants to enter [the camp], enters, and he who wants to get out, gets out. This is against the regulations that they [are supposed to] follow. All this is due to the soldiers not caring about what happens." The guards appointed to the hospital in the city were not preventing the patients from leaving the hospital and going to the market. In Acre "the soldiers are roaming the city as they wish (*ʿala keifhum*) against the regulations, and the guards are not doing anything to stop them. This is the reality (*hukm al wāqiʿ*) that we saw of the soldiers in Acre."[145]

This discrepancy between "*hukm al-wāqiʿ*" (reality) and "*al-qānūn*" (the law, the regulations) was also to be seen in the performance of the guards inside the camps. On passing in front of the camp jail one summer night, Colonel Ayup of the 11th Regiment could not find the guard who was supposed to watch over the jail. Looking for him, he found that he had gathered some of his friends together and they were chatting, laughing and telling stories in the middle of the night.[146] During one cold December night some soldiers lit a camp fire and sat around it chatting and joking. The fire was close to the ammunition dump, however, and could have blown up the whole camp. When the guard on duty was asked why he did not forbid the soldiers from lighting their fire at such close proximity to the ammunition dump, he claimed

140 Art. 5 of the second section of Clot Bey's *Risāla* forbade prostitutes from entering the camps or dwelling near them.
141 Sham 9/95, on 9 S 1248/8 July 1832.
142 Sham 7/75, on 11 M 1248/10 June 1832.
143 Sham 8/109, on 16 M 1248/15 June 1832.
144 Sham 9/59, on 11 S 1248/10 July 1832.
145 Sham 9/116, on 20 S 1248/19 July 1832.
146 He was sentenced to eleven days in the jail; Sham 11/8, on 2 R 1248/29 August 1832.

not to have seen them. On another rainy night, two soldiers who were appointed as guards on Abbas Pasha's tent left their site and went for shelter in the stable.[147] Soldiers left on guard duties for long periods without enough sleep could not help falling asleep.[148] During the bombardment of the castle of Acre a certain soldier, Ibrahim by name, was left with a number of his colleagues to act as sentries overnight guarding the cannon bases that shelled the city during daytime. On making his regular round, their commanding officer, a certain Hassan Ağa, found Ibrahim asleep. He attempted to take his rifle to show it to *his* commanding officer to prove that the soldier was asleep while on duty. The guard woke up, however, when he felt his rifle being taken from him. When the captain insisted on taking the rifle, the guard hit him in the face, knocking out some of his teeth.[149]

Conclusion

This chapter opened with an account of death, of how officers and soldiers attempted to confront it, and of how the authorities avoided dealing with it in a manner that could be remotely described as respectful to the dead. It attempted to explain how the soldiers in the Pasha's army were able to confront the fatal dangers of the battlefield with such success but, admittedly, was unable to offer any explanation other than to argue that years of training might have had their impact on how the soldier behaved in battle: obeying orders issued from commanders he did not know, orders that were heard from afar and carrying, if executed, the close possibility of his own death. It was argued, however, that this is not a good criterion to measure how well disciplined the soldiers were: under stress soldiers might, indeed, behave in the manner in which the authorities attempted to train them. To see how well disciplined soldiers were we have to look at them in more relaxed times and to follow their lives as much as possible not on the fields of pitched battles, but in the relative security of the camps. One particular aspect of their lives was highlighted, namely their health and general hygiene.

It is here that we come to focusing on problems that characterized Mehmed Ali's military authorities and indeed his entire reign: impressive blueprints and programs that gave stunning spectacles of order,

147 They were each given fifty lashes of the whip in front of their regiment; Sham 3/106, on 12 Ş 1247/16 January 1832. For the delay in supplying rain-protecting coats (*kukuleteler*) see Sham 3/101, on 10 Ş 1247/14 January 1832.

148 Sham 1/35, on 26 C 1247/3 December 1831. This is case of a guard who fell asleep while on duty because he had not slept for two consecutive nights.

149 The soldier was sentenced to seven days in jail; Sham 2/54, on 5 B 1247/10 December 1831.

but which floundered at the first attempt at implementation. Besides the usual problems that were mentioned in the previous chapters that related to lack of funds, cumbersome bureaucratic regulations, unrealistic demands by the Pasha, and internal divisions among the elite itself (represented by the problems that Clot Bey had with the War Department), this chapter touched on the issue of resistance by the soldiers to the authorities' regulations and concluded with the apparently trivial, but crucial problems that the authorities had with guards and sentries. Passing laws that forbade prostitutes from ever entering or approaching military camps, issuing regulations that prevented soldiers from having access to the outside world, printing *tezkere*s that soldiers had to have on them if they left military precincts – all were impressive innovations that characterized Mehmed Ali's regime. Impressive as they might be, however, they did not guarantee that the Pasha's will went fulfilled. Inasmuch as modern laws, regulations and disciplinary devices might create a framework which, as Mitchell would say, appear prior to things in themselves, "conjuring up . . . the prior abstractions of progress, reason, law, discipline . . . and order,"[150] the fact remains that these devices still do not execute themselves; they needed an agency to come to life, in spite of their pretence at autonomy and self-enunciation. And as was seen with the case of the sentries and guards who were expected to execute the laws and regulations aiming at creating ideas of "inside" and "outside," these agencies were often behaving in a manner that was not particularly representative of any abstract notions of "progress, reason, law, discipline . . . [or] order."

Having opened this chapter with two moments of silence on the part of the authorities regarding death, let me then close it on an arguably more positive note: two accounts of marriage by an official and a soldier that went contrary to the authorities' wish to interfere in this aspect, as in all others, of the soldiers' and officers' lives.

The first case concerned the governor of Ṣafad after it fell to Mehmed Ali's control: the governor was suspected of forcing a local muleteer (*katırcı*) to divorce his wife to allow him to marry her himself. On investigation it was discovered that the muleteer had two wives, that they were constantly fighting with each other and that in fact they had come to the governor to help them with their husband. The governor told the muleteer that he was too poor to keep two women and that he had to divorce one of them. After they left, the governor sent a special messenger to one of the women telling her that if her husband divorced

[150] Mitchell, *Colonising Egypt*, p. 179.

her, he would be willing to marry her himself. When the muleteer got to know about this, he took it to be the governor's wish and divorced his wife in court after writing a testimony (*hüccet*) saying that he did so voluntarily. When Munib Efendi heard about the case, however, he reprimanded the governor politely and told him that since he was a high-ranking Egyptian official (*cenab-ı şerifiniz devlet-i mısıriyyenin ümerasından madud olub*), and although he was not, strictly speaking, a military man, he should have sought permission from the military authorities to get married.[151] In response, the governor said, "I have been married a number of times while I was in Egypt, and never before was I asked for a permit. It did not occur to me that I needed one now."[152] The fact that he took no heed of the authorities' opinion on what he regarded to be a private matter and, moreover, the apparent abuse of his position, is an example not only of how difficult it was for the authorities to control the activities of its senior officials, but more generally, of the discrepancy between *al-qānūn* (the law, the regulations) and *ḥukm al-wāqiʿ* (reality) that is characteristic of Mehmed Ali's rule.

The second case concerns a soldier, ʿAlī Khalīl by name, who was wounded and sent to hospital to be nursed there. While hospitalized he met a Christian Syrian girl and fell in love with her. After she had agreed to convert to Islam, they decided to get married. His colonel, however, refused to allow the marriage to take place saying that "all the activities and stillnesses (*harekat ve sekenat*)" of the soldiers should be approved by their officers and the soldiers should keep themselves busy only with their weapons. On hearing this the soldier heedlessly and without asking permission (*hodbehot bila istizan*) left the camp. The colonel said that he thought that that was against regulations.[153] That a woman could be found in an army hospital, that a soldier fell in love with her and decided to marry her and that his colonel could not stop him from doing so attest to the fact that the authorities had as much difficulty in controlling "all the activities and stillnesses of the soldiers" as they had with keeping an eye on the behavior of the senior officials.

As tightly as the authorities wanted to control the activities of the

151 Those of Mehmed Ali's mamluks who by the time of the Syrian campaign had been promoted to the ranks of major, adjutant-major and captains and who had not yet got married still needed the approval of the Pasha to get married; he would ask to see the "registers of their behavior (*sicil ahlakları*)" before giving his consent; S/1/48/4/221 on 3 Ra 1249/21 July 1833.

152 Sham 9/113, on 17 S 1248/16 July 1832.

153 Sham 8/130, on 20 M 1248/19 June 1832. The cool, laid-back attitude of this soldier is similar to the manner in which a senior officer responded when giving testimony in a court martial in which he was charged for violating the law because he shouted during battle: "I did not know that one is not to raise one's voice during fighting." Sham 1/35, on 23 C 1247/1 December 1831.

soldiers, reality spoke differently. The training manual might have portrayed the soldier as a robot with every gesture, every glance meticulously controlled and vigilantly manipulated. Judging from the accounts of the battles, however, it appears that soldiers were full of the all-too-human emotions of love, hate, jealousy, pride and fear of death. And reading the accounts of their daily lives on the camps, it does appear that the authorities failed in capturing their bodies, let alone in imprinting on their minds that this was indeed their army.

Could it be argued, however, that given time this was exactly how the soldiers came to think of the army, i.e. that it was "ours" rather than "theirs"? This and the previous chapters have shown the authorities attempting to capture the fellahin's bodies and minds, and the fellahin, on the other hand, resisting these manipulative attempts of the state. Yet, was there no positive incentive that induced the fellahin to join the army out of their own accord, or, having joined it, to think about it in some positive way? The following chapter deals with this question, namely, the possibility that soldiers might have thought of it as a national army fighting for their own country.

6 Mehmed Ali's army and the Egyptian nation

One of the things that Mehmed Ali was concerned about when he took the first steps in creating his conscript army in Egypt was the design and shape of its flags.[1] After the soldiers had been trained and their officers appointed and after the entire regiment had been prepared to be dispatched to its destination, a festive ceremony was held in which the banner was delivered by the Pasha in person to the colonel of the regiment, thus officially marking the birth of a new regiment. On such occasions the Pasha is said to have given the following speech:

This banner is the symbol of victory, of pride, of life and of faith . . . Make sure it does not fall while there is still a breath of life left in any one of you. If it does fall – God forbid – then let the spot on which it falls be the spot on which you die.[2]

In one of their earliest assignments, these first regiments appear to have obeyed the Pasha's commands literally. In a joint naval and land attack on a spot near Mesolonghi in the Morean peninsula the new troops of the Pasha were fighting side by side with other Ottoman troops of the Sultan dispatched from Crete and Anatolia.

When the infidels saw these troops approaching from the sea-side they fired their cannons and their guns like rain on the believers' heads, who in spite of this, kept on advancing towards the shore heedless of the danger befalling them. When they nearly reached the shore, however, the Cretan soldiers as well as the Anatolian ones stopped advancing and only the [Egyptian] *nizami* troops were proceeding giving up their lives for the sake of the faith and the [Ottoman] State . . . During the advance of the *nizami* troops, however, the standard-bearer of the 20th Battalion could not advance because of difficulties in walking in the mud. He was then approached by Hamza Ağa, the major of the same battalion, who took the banner from him . . . Shortly afterwards his adjutant-major approached him and insisted on carrying the banner himself . . . and marched a few yards with it before being hit by a bullet fired by the infidels. Seeing this, one of the *evlad-ı Arab* [lit. sons of Arabs] lieutenants rushed to his side and

[1] S/1/50/2/405 on 12 S 1238/29 October 1822.

[2] ʿAbdel-Raḥmān Zakī, *al-Aʿlām wa Shārāt al-Mulk fī Wādī al-Nīl* [Flags and Royal Insignia in the Nile valley] (Cairo: Dār al-Maʿārif, 1948), p. 40.

Plate 7 "The speech at the flag"

took the banner from him, but was soon hit himself and the banner was taken by a corporal who was also hit and killed on the spot. Then one of the sergeants took the banner but was hit by various bullets in different parts of his body. A soldier rushed to carry the banner but was also soon hit by bullets and the banner was then carried by one of the corporals, Hüseyin the namesake of the Martyr of Kerbela.[3] When the Serasker, Ibrahim Pasha, saw that the signs of defeat were spreading among his troops he shouted at them saying, "I am not one of those who turn their backs on fighting when the going gets tough. Look at me and see my forehead stained with blood and sand." He then pulled his sword from its sheath, dismounted from his horse, and marched forward through the water until he was submerged up to his neck . . . On seeing this, the soldiers were filled with faith and courage and soon followed their commander depending on no one but God who said in His Book, "It was incumbent upon Us to assist the believers."[4]

It appears from the behavior of the soldiers in this particular incident and specifically from the courage and valor with which they were following and defending the banner that they were implementing the

[3] A reference to Imam Hussain, the grandson of the Prophet, who was killed together with his followers near Karbalā', Iraq, in AD 680.

[4] Bahr Barra 10/100, on 3 Ş 1241/13 March 1826.

Pasha's orders to defend the flag, "the symbol of victory [and] . . . pride," at whatever cost. It is not known what was inscribed on the banners at this particular battle; in other battles, however, the flags and banners carried during the actual fighting as well as the medals cast to commemorate the subsequent victories were decorated with Mehmed Ali's name and nothing else. It has often been argued that it was during the first half of the nineteenth century and mostly by being allowed to carry weapons and to defend their own country that the fellahin of Egypt came to think of themselves as Egyptians first and foremost. Given the fact that most banners of Mehmed Ali's battalions had his name on them, would it be more accurate to argue that this was the Pasha's personal army fighting what were in essence his own wars and not those of "Egypt," and that the men who fought in them conceived of it as such, i.e. as a personal not a national army?

And if this were indeed the case, can one argue that the soldiers, in spite of knowing that they were fighting the Pasha's own wars, still managed to produce all the victories that they did? Was there at least an attempt on the part of the Pasha and his authorities to sell these wars, so to speak, to the soldiers as their own wars? As the example mentioned above shows, the language used both to incite the soldiers to fight and to describe their performance afterwards was often a religious language. Referring to the Egyptian fighters as the "believers," to the enemy as the "infidels," quoting from the Quran, and citing particular episodes from Islamic history, all show that defending the faith, rather than the *patrie*, was, in this case, the prime concern of officers and soldiers alike. In the Morean war, when the enemy was composed of the Christian Greek subjects who had rebelled against the authority of the Ottoman Sultan, this could very well have been the case. However, the situation was essentially different during the Syrian campaign, when the enemy was nothing other than the army of the Ottoman Sultan, the Defender of the Faith and Protector of the two Holy Cities of Mecca and Medina. Using religious language to incite the soldiers to fight the *Asakir-i Mansure-yi Muhammadiyye* (The Victorious Soldiers of Muhammad), as the new Ottoman army was called after 1826, would not have been appropriate. How then did the men think when they were fighting not the Greek rebels but the Ottoman Sultan?

This obviously is a difficult question since, as has been said in the previous chapter, the overwhelming majority of these soldiers were illiterate and have not left us written records of how they might have conceived of the army and of their role in it. Nevertheless, this is an important question and one that needs to be raised if the nature of that army, and indeed of the Pasha's regime in general, is ever to be assessed.

This chapter is mostly concerned with this question, namely, the alleged national character of the army. It attempts to address it by closely studying the ideas and sentiments of Ibrahim Pasha as the Commander-in-Chief whose views regarding the army, the nature of the wars it waged, and the character of its adversaries are said to have differed from those of his father. In addition to alluding to Ibrahim's character and his sentiments, this chapter deals with the officer corps that Ibrahim headed which we have seen to have been formed of a motley group of disparate factions. Finally, the chapter tries to come as close as possible to the thoughts and feelings of the soldiers regarding the army and serving in it. Although it casts doubt on the traditional view that saw the army as giving the opportunity for the men to "discover" their true identity as Egyptians and to be able to "call Egypt their own," the chapter tries to see if it is possible to argue that, nevertheless, whilst lacking strong nationalistic feelings, joining the colors was still a "colorful" experience, as it were, that allowed the soldiers to take pride in their uniform, for example, or that gave them the opportunity to foster links with each other that marked them off from the rest of the population and which in due time would have made them proud of belonging to an institution that cared for and looked after them.

No full analysis of the nature of this army and of the wars it was fighting in could be complete if we do not study the views and sentiments of one key player in this whole equation, the Pasha himself. Since these are important and complicated in and of themselves, I will be dealing with the Pasha and his thoughts in the following chapter.

The "Turkish" officers

As Mehmed Ali's son and Commander-in-Chief of his army, the sentiments of Ibrahim Pasha toward the Turks and the Ottoman Empire have been the subject of a lot of speculation. It is claimed that unlike his father, Ibrahim could not see himself as a Turk or an Ottoman; he "identified with Arabs, spoke Arabic and admired the Arabs where he despised the Ottomans and Turks."[5] He used to say that his Turkish officers were good for nothing, "smoke[d] all day and [had] people to wash their hands."[6] When he was heard expressing similar views, one of his Arab soldiers asked him how he could say such things given the fact that he was a Turk himself. "I am not a Turk," he replied. "I came as a mere child to Egypt, and since then the Egyptian sun has changed my

[5] al-Sayyid Marsot, *Egypt*, p. 229.
[6] FO 78/431 no. 70, on 21 February 1841, quoted in Temperley, *Near East*, p. 29.

blood and made me wholly Arab."[7] It has been claimed that this feeling of "outright animosity and contempt for [the Ottomans], their government and their military character" might have had its origins in a year he spent when a teenager as a hostage in Istanbul.[8]

We have already seen Ibrahim forcefully expressing these sentiments against the Ottomans during the Morean campaign, and the record shows that his contempt for them only grew stronger in the course of the Syrian war. After the Sultan had decided to strip him and his father of their titles, he wrote to Mehmed Ali telling him that he was very pleased that that sign of slavery (*bendelik*) had been removed and that "we have been relieved of this burden" (*bu gaileden halas olduk*). He added that the fame and glory that they would accomplish would make the Ottomans envious and think of restoring their titles to them; this time, he said, he would not accept them.[9] On another occasion, he wrote to his father telling him that he was thanking God because "the independence of our family and the freedom of Egypt (*Mısır'ın serbesti*) are gradually being realized."[10] Sentiments like these that Ibrahim often expressed to his father prompted some historians to argue that it is Ibrahim rather than his father who "certainly deserves the place of honor in the history of nationalism in the Arab East."[11]

Ibrahim, however, does not appear to have had any illusions as to the dynastic nature of the struggle between his *family* and the Ottomans. After each military victory he accomplished in the Syrian campaign he wrote to the various notables ordering them to pray for the health and happiness of "our father, the vali of Egypt."[12] When he thought that the Ottomans were spreading rumors about him and his father in their *Vekayi*, he ordered a scribe to write down his version of events and to send it to Acre to be translated there into French so as to dispatch it to Europe. On receiving these orders, Vehid Efendi, Ibrahim Yeğen's scribe, suggested that it might not be the right moment to do so considering that fighting was at its peak; Ibrahim answered angrily, "These matters will be written in history books, and a hundred years from now it will be said that Mehmed Ali did this and

7 Douin, ed., *Boislecomte*, p. 249. For discussions about this difference between father and son, see Dodwell, *Founder of Modern Egypt*, pp. 256–8 and Rustum, *Origins*, pp. 93–6.
8 al-Sayyid Marsot, *Egypt*, p. 81. For his departure to Istanbul together with the Grand Admiral and Musa Pasha who was supposed to replace Mehmed Ali as vali of Egypt, see al-Jabartī, *ʿAjāʾib al-Āthār*, IV, pp. 19–20 (events of Rajab, 1221).
9 Sham 7/8, on 1 M 1248/31 May 1832.
10 Sham 10/257, on 29 Ra 1248/26 August 1832.
11 Rustum, *Origins*, p. 96.
12 Rustum, ed., *Uṣūl*, II, pp. 16, 21, 28, 56.

that. Is this not so, you animal?"[13] Like his father, Ibrahim was also ordering medals to be cast with the words "Mehmed Ali" inscribed on them. But whereas his father was honoring senior officers and officials in his administration by such medals, Ibrahim had them given to soldiers who distinguished themselves on the battlefield.[14]

Ibrahim might have felt that it was thanks to his Egyptian soldiers that he was able to achieve the victories he accomplished, or that his insightful command was instrumental in securing them. He knew too well, however, that it was to his father's ability to raise and maintain such a large army that he was ultimately thankful.[15] During the siege of Acre he had secret negotiations with ʿAbdallah Pasha's deputy who came out of the castle to negotiate with him.

> He then said that they had a lot of ammunition [Ibrahim wrote to his father about the failed negotiations.] I answered him by saying "We are speaking about friendship, so why refer to ammunition? However, mentioning ammunition, do you think we care about how much you have, when we receive from Egypt 1,200 ship-loads of ammunition annually? Your case is like someone who has a lot of food when another man with an iron fist comes along and grabs all the food he has."

Then he told him that although they had been able to withstand Napoleon's siege thirty years earlier, they had no chance of succeeding this time, since he was much better prepared than Napoleon and his army had been. He added that if 200,000 shells were fired, "the price of each being three piasters, the total will be 1,200 *kise*s, which is nothing for Mehmed Ali Pasha."[16]

Similarly, Ibrahim might have felt closer to his Egyptian subjects than his father did; still he had no illusions that they were his slaves fighting for the fame and glory of his family. When his father first opened the subject of conscripting men from Syria to join his army, he replied saying that he did not see it fit to do so in that year. Nor did he approve of his father's coming to Syria to supervise the process. He explained that "the problems we are facing in Egypt due to conscripting our subjects (*reayamız*) are not over yet, in spite of the fact that Egypt is in

[13] Sham 9/122, on 21 S 1248/20 July 1832. The refutation was eventually published in *Vekayi-i Mısriyye*, issue no. 416, on 16 Ra 1248/13 August 1832.

[14] Sham 18/198, on 27 N 1248/18 February 1833. One side was to have the Pasha's name on it and the other the name of the battle being commemorated.

[15] See the interesting letter in which he boasts about being a commander of an army engaging in battles in which 260 cannons and more than 60,000 guns were being fired. His father reminded him that it was he who had supplied him with these cannons and rifles in the first place: S/5/47/2/160 on 6 Ca 1255/18 July 1839.

[16] Sham 3/100, on 10 Ş 1247/14 January 1832.

our possession and its inhabitants are but our common slaves (*Mısır mülkümüz ve ahalisi bayağı memlukümüz iken*)."[17]

The characterization of an army as a national institution, however, cannot be done solely by analyzing the sentiments and personality of its commander-in-chief, as crucial as these surely are. No matter how "liberal" or "enlightened" one wishes to judge Ibrahim, the performance of the army was much more influenced by the composition of the officer corps and by the problematic relationship that existed between officers and their men. Naturally, any army is bound to have serious problems between the officers issuing the commands and the men doing all the dirty work, problems that emanate from the social and economic backgrounds of both groups.[18] Yet, in addition to these problems, Mehmed Ali's army also had an important point of tension that had its origins in the ethnic and linguistic differences between officers and soldiers.

When he first conceived of founding a conscript army in his province, the Pasha's plan was to appoint Turkish-speaking officers to lead and command the Arabic-speaking fellah conscripts. The idea was to appoint his personal mamluks (*gulam ağalar*) to high positions, and Turkish-speaking officers (*Türk askerler*) to lower ranks, while the fellah conscripts would make up the soldiery.[19] Eventually, mamluks and "Turks" fused together into one group and it became difficult to differentiate between them. The main distinction, however, was between soldiers and officers: soldiers were Arabic-speaking, while officers spoke Turkish.

This linguistic basis for differentiating between officers and soldiers was characteristic of the civil bureaucracy as well. Members of the high echelons of the bureaucracy and the "aristocracy" at large were Turkish-speaking, people from all over the Ottoman world who had come to Egypt seeking employment in the Pasha's administration and, depending on their connections, would be given a position in the civil service.[20] Indeed, the "meanest man who [spoke] Turkish [was] *ipso facto* considered as belonging to a caste high above the indigenous

[17] Sham 11/73, on 9 R 1248/5 September 1832.

[18] On this aspect, see Keegan, *Face of Battle*, pp. 224–5, 321–2.

[19] S/1/48/1/3/ on 13 L 1238/23 June 1823.

[20] For a *huge* number of such requests to be appointed to the civil service see, for example, Divan-ı Hidiv, 1/261–361, dated Şaban 1244–Sefer 1245/February–July 1829. All are presented in Turkish and all petitioners have Ottoman names, e.g. Maraşlı, Alanialı, etc. See also the interesting example of the petition of Nazif Bey, the chatty Commissary-General, requesting to have his family brought from Istanbul and asking the Pasha himself for financial facilities to help settling them in Egypt; Sham 2/91, on 1 Ş 1247/5 January 1832.

inhabitant."[21] Lower down on the administrative scale Arabic was more common, giving rise to a duality in administrative language that often caused considerable confusion and ambiguity.[22]

Membership in the higher echelons of the society, the elite, was not only based on linguistic differences. Belonging to what has been termed the "Ottoman–Egyptian elite," while necessitating knowledge of Turkish, also meant "shar[ing] the values and heritage of Ottoman culture . . . [being] mostly, but not exclusively, Muslim . . . [coming] from various parts of the [Ottoman] Empire . . . [and sharing certain ideas about] dress, etiquette or manners and customs, and . . . verbal forms of entertainment."[23] The boundaries separating core members of this "Ottoman–Egyptian elite" from those outside this privileged group, however, were not water-tight and, given time, individuals within that group started to learn Arabic, took Cairo, rather than Istanbul, to be their main dwelling place, and came to identify more and more with Egypt as their country. At the same time, those outside the group, anxious to improve their lot, started to learn Turkish, intermarried with elite members and gradually assumed more and more of "Ottoman" manners and etiquette. Indeed the history of Egypt in the nineteenth century, and especially the second half of it, can be seen precisely as showing this tendency to cross and transgress these boundaries.

During the first half of the century, however, and especially in the military, these boundaries were much more difficult to cross. The Pasha clearly had in mind the idea of creating a conscript army in which the soldiers would be firmly dominated by their officers. He once told a distinguished French visitor, "I have not done in Egypt except what the British are doing in India; they have an army composed of Indians and ruled by British officers, and I have an army composed of Arabs ruled by Turkish officers . . . The Turk makes a better officer, since he knows that he is entitled to rule, while the Arab feels that the Turk is better than him in that respect." He added, however, that he was determined to forbid these Turkish-speaking immigrants from legally acquiring land in Egypt and "from becoming proprietors and creating for themselves a personal leverage over the population."[24]

As a rule Egyptians, referred to as *evlad-ı Arab*, were not allowed to be promoted beyond the rank of *yüzabşı* (captain) and very few of them

[21] Bowring, "Report on Egypt," p. 7.

[22] ʿAbdel-Samīʿ al-Harrāwī, *Lughat al-Idāra al-ʿĀmma fī Miṣr fī al-Qarn al-Tāsiʿ ʿAshr* [The Language of Public Administration in Egypt During the 19th Century] (Cairo: n.p., 1963), pp. 314–20.

[23] Toledano, *State and Society*, p. 16.

[24] Douin, ed., *Boislecomte*, pp. 110–11.

were even promoted to that rank in the first place.[25] As for the ranks of *mülazim evvel* and *mülazim sani* (lieutenant and second-lieutenant, respectively), half of them had to be "Turks" and the other half "Arabs."[26] Before signing the orders promoting men to these ranks, Ibrahim Pasha had to inquire if the nominees were from "those who can be promoted to these ranks, since it is against the rules to have more than four Arab lieutenants per battalion."[27] Nominations for promotions to upper ranks, on the other hand, usually stated the place of birth of the candidate, to make it clear that he was a "Turk."[28] Otherwise, it would be stated clearly that the candidate was a mamluk.[29] These guidelines were strictly followed and Mehmed Ali insisted that his son not promote "Arabs" to senior ranks even if he was in short supply of "Turkish" officers. During the Morean campaign Ibrahim was urging his father to send him Turkish officers (*evlad-ı Türk*) since he was forbidden from replacing dead or wounded officers by "Egyptian" ones that he had with him in Morea.[30]

Being a Turk, that is, speaking Turkish and having one's origins in Anatolia, Istanbul, Albania, or other parts of the Ottoman world, was therefore enough for a man to be considered a candidate for a senior position in Mehmed Ali's army[31] even if he had originally been caught as a POW! After the defeat of the Ottoman army in the various battles in Syria, a considerable number of officers and soldiers were taken prisoner. They were given three choices: either to agree to go back to their countries (but via Alexandria so as not to join the Ottoman army again), to join the Egyptian army by enlisting at the HQ in Acre, or to be sent to join one of the schools in Cairo.[32] Eventually an entire regiment was formed from prisoners captured after the Ottoman army was defeated.[33] More significantly, a number of the men taken prisoner

25 *Ibid.*, p. 100. For an example of a "Turk" (in this case a Circassian) promoted to that rank, see Sham 7/15, on 2 M 1248/1 June 1832.

26 Sham 23/1, on 1 M 1249/21 May 1833.

27 Sham 2/88, on 22 B 1247/27 December 1831.

28 A special council (*divan*) would be convened of senior and middle-ranking officers of the nominee's regiment. The nomination would then be presented to Ibrahim Pasha for approval, who, in turn, forwarded it, signed and sealed, to Ibrahim Yeğen for implementation. See, e.g., Sham 2/95, on 29 B 1247/3 January 1832.

29 Sham 11/33, on 4 R 1248/31 August 1832.

30 Bahr Barra 10/10, on 5 M 1241/20 August 1825.

31 For the same prerequisites for joining the civil service, see Ḥilmī A. Shalabī, *al-Muwaẓẓaffūn fī Miṣr fī ʿAṣr Muḥammad ʿAlī* [Public Employees in Egypt During the Reign of Mehmed Ali] (Cairo: General Egyptian Book Organization, 1989), pp. 29, 63.

32 Sham 9/138, on 22 S 1248/21 July 1832; Sham 10/14, on 3 Ra 1248/31 July 1832; Sham 11/17, R 1248/13 September 1832. For the 130 soldiers who were actually sent by boat to Alexandria to join the schools there, see S/1/48/4/13 on 23 R 1248/19 September 1832.

33 Sham 16/18, on 2 Ş 1248/25 December 1832.

were appointed as officers in the Egyptian army. Aref Bey, one of the officers in the Ottoman army, for example, was taken prisoner at the battle of Konia and was appointed as colonel to a newly formed regiment, created out of Turkish prisoners captured in the same battle.[34] Other prisoners were appointed as lieutenants and captains over the soldiers who had captured them: the main criterion qualifying them for these positions was their Turkish identity. This caused much resentment among the soldiers who complained, "Why do we sacrifice our lives and put ourselves in danger to capture these men only to find them appointed as our officers ruling over us?"[35] Neither Mehmed Ali nor Ibrahim found any problems with this practice, although Ibrahim, being closer to the soldiers and more sensitive to their sentiments, might have been more apprehensive than his father about it.[36] As far as both men were concerned, these were *evlad-ı Türk* who were more entitled and capable than "Arabs" to be appointed as officers.

These basic and essential differences between officers and soldiers caused considerable tension between the two groups. Interestingly, communicating in different languages did not in itself create serious problems. As was shown in chapter 3 command shouts and signals were given in Turkish. These need not have been understood linguistically; indeed the soldiers were *not* supposed to think of their meaning. They were intended to function as signals inducing the soldiers to perform a given act without hesitating to think of their meaning. It was in the daily encounters on the camps, however, that the tension between the two groups manifested itself. This tension was essentially due to the fact that the officers did not appreciate the efforts of their men, nor deal with them respectfully. A certain captain, Derviş Ağa by name, once asked a soldier (his servant, *hizmetkar*, as he called him) to fetch him a water bottle. When the soldier brought him an empty one, he shouted at him, cursing his faith, and beating him on the back of his neck. When he was court-martialled he said defiantly, "If you want to punish me for insulting a fifteen-piaster fellah, then go ahead. As far as I am concerned, the fellah is not worth more than this."[37] When a certain regiment was dispatched to Damietta and paraded through the city, a Turkish official there publicly cursed the days in which the "blind fellahin" had been made soldiers. He added that they would never be as

34 S/1/48/4/107 on 18 Ş 1248/11 January 1833.
35 Sham 11/105, on 12 R 1248/8 September 1832.
36 Ibrahim wrote to his father wondering if it was right to conscript Turkish soldiers in large numbers to serve alongside the fellah soldiers: Sham 11/116, on 13 R 1248/9 September 1832.
37 He was sentenced to five days in jail; Sham 2/88, on 21 B 1247/26 December 1831.

good as Turkish ones.[38] Some officers cheated their soldiers, selling them goods at ten times their price on the market "until they were left penniless."[39] The habit of insulting and abusing soldiers was so widespread that Ibrahim had to write and distribute a general pamphlet to all the regiments in Syria reminding the officers that it was due primarily to the "bravery and zeal" of the soldiers that the army was victorious in its numerous battles. He ordered them not to abuse or insult their soldiers and to send them to a court martial (*divan*) to be tried there according to the laws, rather than take the law into their own hands. He warned the officers that whoever was found violating these orders would be expelled from service altogether.[40]

In spite of this clear and stern warning, however, it proved difficult to force the officers to treat the soldiers respectfully and complaints about such bad treatment would not stop.[41] Even if one believes that Ibrahim's sympathies were with his Arabic-speaking soldiers, the problems he had with his officers that were highlighted in chapter 4 (above) were deeply ingrained in the army and were much more formidable than could be solved by his kind-heartedness or his ostensibly liberal ideas. In other words, when push came to shove Ibrahim knew where his true interests lay: with his father and the mamluk–Turkish elite that formed the heart of the officer corps. This comes through clearly from the following letter in which he was responding to a letter from his father implicitly blaming him for lax discipline which Mehmed Ali thought had caused disturbances in Syria to go out of control.[42] Ibrahim responded by saying that, in effect, he could not be more strict for he was faced with the possibility of officers defecting and with the likelihood of a massive mutiny by the soldiers. The matter, it seemed, concerned harsh penalties that were needed to maintain discipline and his belief that they might be counter-productive.

> These severe punishments are not unknown to me and I saw them in Morea. [Back then] in one incident [one senior officer] whipped more than sixty men in one day with his own hands including an officer with the rank of adjutant-major. In another incident Süleyman Pasha [Sèves] lowered one officer from the rank of adjutant-major all the way to second lieutenant. Time will only tell what the effect of this policy will be on the defection of officers [to the Ottomans]. Of course, injustices and misapplication of the law are inevitable. Be that as it may,

38 Sāmī, ed., *Taqwīm al-Nīl*, II, p. 348, letter dated 12 M 1245/14 July 1829.
39 Sham 1/11, on 21 Ca 1247/28 October 1831.
40 Sham 15/146, on 23 B 1248/17 December 1832.
41 See, for example, Sham 23/47, on 19 M 1249/9 June 1833.
42 This is a reference to the serious rebellion that broke out against the Pasha's rule in Syria in the first months of 1834 and which took Ibrahim more than a year to subdue; see Asad J. Rustum, ed., *The Royal Archives of Egypt and the Disturbances in Palestine, 1834* (Beirut: The American Press, 1938).

however, everyone knows that those who commit injustice are officers and those on whom injustice is committed are soldiers . . . If the men lose their patience, things can go completely out of our hands, and then neither Your Highness, nor your humble slave, author of these lines, will be able to do anything about it. If these were some fellahin from the villages, we would have expected them to bear up with this system. Since they are [not peasants, however, but] soldiers, we have to think of the dangers if they lose their patience.[43]

In that sense Ibrahim was faced with the usual problems confronting a commander of any of the European armies that preceded the rise of the modern nation-state: a mercenary officer corps that was on the "job market" seeking employment in the expanding armies of this or that prince or king and a disgruntled peasantry which had been conscripted by force but which had not yet been fooled into thinking that it was their own interest that they were fighting for. Force and lucrative pay were the only way to keep such armies intact. It follows that too little pay might push the officers to defect and seek another career opportunity elsewhere, and too much force in imposing discipline might incite the soldiers to open rebellion.

In spite of these problems Ibrahim could not afford to do away with the ethno-linguistic distinction between officers and soldiers since this was an important cementing element that kept the army together, albeit by force. Retaining this ethno-linguistic distinction was not without its own problems since the officers felt, not without reason, that the regime so heavily depended on them that they could get away with nearly anything. Ibrahim or his father might have reprimanded this or that officer for mistreating the soldiers; ultimately, however, the very fabric of the army depended on the need to control the fellah conscripts by appointing ethnically different officers to command them. Whatever his true sentiments might have been regarding the qualities of the "Arabs" vs. "Turks" under his rule, Mehmed Ali knew that it was only by appointing Turkish-speaking officers that it was possible to prevent the fellah conscripts from turning against him and his ruling family. The Pasha knew too well that if "Arabs" were allowed to assume leadership positions, whether in the army or the civilian administration, they would challenge the very basis of his power, *viz.* the Turkish–mamluk coalition that he had so laboriously formed.[44]

Of equal importance was the fact that both father and son saw senior positions in the army as rewards to be personally given to particular individuals who were flocking to their service from different corners of

[43] Sham 31/140, on 27 S 1251/25 June 1835.

[44] Douin, ed., *Boislecomte*, p. 104; Cattaui, ed., *Mohamed Aly*, II, Pt. 2, p. 352; Hunter, *Egypt*, pp. 22–3.

the Ottoman Empire. Besides prisoners of war, a number of senior officers in the Ottoman army approached Mehmed Ali requesting employment in his army.[45] These were received with dignity, and medals and ceremonial uniforms were issued to them.[46] However, as much as Mehmed Ali and his son were offering lucrative employment opportunities to potential defectors from the Ottoman army, if they were not careful with the manner in which they treated their own officers they stood the danger of losing them again to the Sultan's service. This comes across clearly in a letter Ibrahim sent to his father answering an earlier letter in which Mehmed Ali was asking for his son's opinion regarding the promotion of a senior officer, Menilikli Ahmed Pasha, the second brigadier of the elite Guardia Regiment. Specifically, Mehmed Ali was asking his son what the reaction of other officers would be if Ahmed Pasha was promoted to the newly introduced rank of *Mirmiran*, and whether Mehmed Bey, another brigadier, would get jealous and defect to the Ottomans. In response, Ibrahim said that he trusted Mehmed Bey to be totally devoted to "our Sublime Family" and did not think that the brigadier was contemplating defection since he had tested him previously and on all occasions Mehmed Bey had shown himself to be genuinely dismayed at the repeated defections of other officers to the "opposing side." However, he suggested that to save themselves any problems, Mehmed Bey should be promoted to the same rank as his colleague Ahmed Pasha.[47]

In short, the composition of the officer corps in the Pasha's army was problematic, to say the least, and both father and son were well aware of its precarious nature. The officers, rather than thinking of themselves as serving in a national army, were behaving as mercenary officers who moved from one patron to the other depending on who paid better. Joining the "Egyptian" army for them meant joining the force of an Ottoman pasha who had a better organized and better paid army than the Sultan. It was an army that was fighting the Ottoman Sultan, it is true, but that fight was not an example of a national struggle of a people against their foreign oppressor. It could even be said that, as far as these officers were concerned, the "other" was more the fellah soldiers that they were commanding than the Ottoman army they were fighting. It was not completely unusual, for example, to find two brothers fighting in the two opposing armies.[48] Having previously served in the Sultan's

[45] See, for example, S/1/48/4/5 on 13 Ca 1248/8 October 1832; S/1/48/4/100 on 1 Ş 1248/24 December 1832; S/1/48/4/112 on 16 January 1833; and S/1/48/4/298 on 18 B 1249/2 December 1833.

[46] Sham 11/10, on 2 R 1248/29 August 1832.

[47] Sham 30/468, on 24 Za 1250/24 March 1835.

[48] This was the case of Ismail Bey, a major in "Istanbul's" army, and Selim Bey, the

army, or at least being familiar with the world that it represented, the Ottoman world, the officers in the Pasha's army were closer to the officers and soldiers of the army they were fighting against than to the soldiers of the army they were fighting in, soldiers who spoke a different language, came from a completely different social and economic background and believed in a different set of cultural and moral values.

The fellah soldiers

If this was how the officers behaved towards their soldiers and if they did not view the struggles that they were engaged in as national struggles against an enemy that was gradually conceived of as the "other," how then did the soldiers themselves think of the army at large and their role in it in particular? None of the battles that these men were about to fight in were ever portrayed to them as national battles, i.e. battles in which the word "Egypt" as meaning a nation-state was referred to. Instead, to incite them to fight or to encourage them to excel in training, reference was made either to religion or to their superior training and better organization. When the earliest conscripts were being trained in Aswan, Mehmed Ali wrote to Mehmed Bey, head of the military school there, telling him that soldiers had to recite the *Fātiḥa* (the first chapter of the Quran) every day before training.[49] When the soldiers misbehaved and when examples of undisciplined behavior were reported to the Pasha, he would write to them an order reminding them that Jihad was a religious duty and quoting extensively from the Quran verses stressing the importance of discipline and obeying orders.[50] Furthermore, the official name by which the new army was known in Egypt was *Cihadiye-i Mısıriyye*, i.e. the Jihadiyya of Egypt, a name that had more religious than nationalistic connotations.[51] As we saw at the beginning of this

brigadier of the Guardia Regiments in the "Egyptian" army. When he found out that his brother was serving in the "enemy's" army, Ismail switched sides and joined the Pasha's forces: Sham 9/189, on 29 S 1248/28 July 1832. Equally interesting is the fact that most of the spy and reconnaissance reports in northern Syria were carried out by officers who were familiar with the region and who had previously been in the Sultan's service; see, for example, the report written by the chief accountant of the 19th Cavalry Regiment who was originally from Diarbakır. The report is attched to Ahmed Menilikli's report to Ibrahim Pasha in Sham 30/517, on 27 Z 1250/27 April 1835.

49 S/1/50/2/379 on 14 M 1238/2 October 1822.

50 Bahr Barra 16/96, no date given.

51 Sham 15/146, on 23 B 1248/17 November 1832. See also Khalīl ibn Aḥmad al-Rajabī, *Fī Sha'n al-Wazīr Muḥammed 'Alī* [Regarding the Vizier Mehmed Ali]. Unpublished MS dated AH 1238/AD 1822–3, Cairo, Dār al-Kutub no. 585 Tārīkh (partially translated and edited by Husam N. Shakhshir, unpublished MA thesis, American University in Cairo, 1985), fo. 3a. This whole work is written to refute the arguments that the new army contradicted the teachings of Islam.

chapter, Mehmed Ali could afford to evoke religious feelings and use religious language to incite his soldiers to fight when he was sending his army to the Hijaz or to the Morea. The situation was essentially different, however, when the fight against the Ottoman Sultan started. During the Syrian campaign the enemy was no other than the Sultan of the Muslims, and the Protector of the Two Holy Shrines himself. In that case, as was shown during the storming of the fortress of Acre, it was the superiority of their training and their organization that the soldiers were referred to in order to encourage them before battle started. The soldiers themselves had no doubt in their minds that they were fighting for Mehmed Ali. When soldiers in Aleppo received news of the victory in Ḥomṣ, they shouted together "God saves our master" (*Allah yunṣur afandīnā*).[52]

If the language that was used to refer to the army was not a national language, could it be argued that the soldiers, nevertheless, saw the army as a national army, i.e. an army that was fighting for the defense or the glory of the fatherland? Having seen how badly treated they were and how remote they were from the Pasha and what he stood for, can one still present an argument that within that particular institution the soldiers had the opportunity to participate in an experience that would distinguish them from their fellow Egyptians in a positive manner? Could it be said that the army, although not intended to create such feeling, might have created it unwittingly? Can one say, for example, that the soldiers eventually came to feel proud of belonging to an institution that cared for them, an institution in which they were better paid than they could have been otherwise? Apart from the grandiose nationalistic slogans (or the absence of them) can one say, as a further example, that joining the colors was a special experience because of, for example, the colorful uniforms, regular pay, or assured pension, practices that might have made the soldiers feel distinguished from their fellow fellahin and that could have induced in them some feeling of pride in belonging to such an institution?

The answer to all these questions is "no." The way the army functioned as an institution could not have allowed the soldiers to think of it in a proud manner. Not only were they badly treated by their officers, but they also soon realized that even in law they were discriminated against. Ibrahim might have been against the degrading treatment of the soldiers by their officers, but he was even stricter about

[52] Sham 9/143, on 23 S 1248/23 July 1832. Munib Efendi, author of this report, comments that since it was strange that the soldiers did so voluntarily, he decided to mention it. I transliterated the shout in Arabic since he reproduces it in Arabic in his otherwise Turkish report.

the principle that no officers were to be punished by being beaten in front of the men: only soldiers were to be punished that way.[53] The soldiers were also much less regularly paid than their officers.[54] Moreover, the difference in pay between their salaries and that of their senior officers was phenomenal: the ratio of the soldier's salary to that of a colonel in the Sultan's army was 1:60; in the Egyptian army it was over 1:500.[55] It has also been seen in chapter 4 how ill equipped the soldiers were in terms of their uniforms. Here again they were discriminated against. The uniforms they were issued were worn out not only because the new ones were overdue, but also because the Pasha occasionally insisted that if insufficient funds were to force him to cut expenses, then it would be the soldiers and not the officers who would bear the brunt of the cuts. When the soldiers in the Sudan were to be issued new uniforms to celebrate the Islamic feast of al-Aḍḥa, Mehmed Ali saw it fit to send new uniforms only to the officers "so as to be distinguished from the soldiers."[56] In short, service in the army was an ever-present reminder to the soldiers of the injustice and misery that were reigning all over the country during Mehmed Ali's rule.

The "fallen"

The clearest example of how that particular institution, the army, did not care for its members was in how the disabled were treated. After being treated for their wounds, the *sakat* (lit., the fallen), as the disabled were referred to, were checked by the *hakimbaşı*, the chief doctor of the hospital. Those who were found not to be completely disabled and who were still capable of bearing arms would be designated as *yarım sakat*, i.e. half-disabled, and would be retained in the army.[57] When enough of those half-disabled soldiers had been so designated they would be grouped together to form a battalion and a *sakat* officer would be appointed as their commander.[58] Alternatively, they were appointed within military units, not in fighting positions, but as, e.g, trumpeters or drummers.[59] When the army had no need for them but they could still

53 Sham 2/64, on 10 B 1247/15 December 1831.
54 Nada Tomiche, "Notes sur la hiérarchie sociale en Egypte à l'époque de Mohammad 'Ali," in P. M. Holt, ed., *Political and Social Change in Modern Egypt* (London: Oxford University Press, 1968), p. 252.
55 See the table of salaries in Douin, ed., *Boislecomte*, p. 114; Bowring, "Report on Egypt," pp. 50–1, 195.
56 S/1/48/4/388 on 25 L 1249/8 March 1834.
57 Sham 9/13, on 29 M 1248/28 June 1832.
58 Sham 11/48, on 6 R 1248/2 September 1832, and Sham 11/58, on 7 R 1248/3 September 1832.
59 Sham 11/197, on 20 R 1248/16 September 1832.

be used for other jobs, they were not released or sent back to their villages, but were formed in companies, had a "half-disabled" officer appointed as a commander and assigned to perform various tasks.[60] These might be to assist in guard duties,[61] in repairing and fortifying buildings,[62] or as servants in military hospitals.[63]

On the other hand, those who received serious wounds and were of no use whatsoever to the army were designated by the chief physician as disabled, given a certificate to the effect that they were unfit for military service, and sent to Egypt by ship.[64] According to an order from the Pasha those *sakat* were entitled to a monthly salary.[65] However, judging from the number of petitions requesting a pension, it does not seem that this order was strictly adhered to.[66] Some of the petitioners felt betrayed by the army which they had spent their whole life serving, as the case of a certain soldier named ʿAbdallah shows. He said in his petition that he had fought against the Wahhabis in Arabia, with Ismail Pasha in the Sudan, and then in both Crete and Morea. He was then wounded and released from service. He said, however, that he could not work and had a lot of children and was thus requesting the Pasha to give him a regular pension.[67] Another soldier was declared *sakat* and given an exemption after losing an eye. In spite of having an exemption certificate, however, he was asked to join the army again. He presented a petition to Mehmed Ali in person asking for his "merciful consideration of my blindness."[68] On receipt of such petitions, the Pasha would pass them to the Deputy Director of the War Department to find a solution for those disabled men "who are bothering us with their petitions" (*bizleri taciz etmişler*).[69]

The "fallen" in Mehmed Ali's army were people who had spent their whole lives serving the Pasha and on being disabled as a result of fighting in his army would not be rewarded or treated with dignity. As far as the authorities were concerned, these people would be "utilized" to the limit, and once they lost their utility they would then be

60 Sham 9/201, on 29 S 1248/28 July 1832 and S/1/48/4/569 on 15 R 1250/21 August 1834.
61 S/1/48/4/559 on 7 R 1250/13 August 1834.
62 Sham 9/113, on 19 S 1248/18 July 1832 and Sham 11/23 on 3 R 1248/30 August 1832.
63 Awamir lil-Jihadiyya 1/21, on 22 Ca 1247/29 October 1831.
64 These usually were men who had lost both limbs; Sham 8/157, on 23 M 1248/23 June 1832, and Sham 9/44, on 8 S 1248/7 July 1832,
65 Sāmī, ed., *Taqwīm al-Nīl*, II, p. 335, letter dated 3 L 1243/18 April 1828.
66 See, for example, Awamir lil-Jihadiyya box no. 1, documents no. 33 on 21 M 1248/20 June 1832; no. 74 on 25 Ş 1251/17 December 1835; and no. 92 on 25 Z 1251/13 April 1836.
67 Awamir lil-Jihadiyya 1/55, on 2 Ca 1249/17 September 1833.
68 Awamir lil-Jihadiyya 1/82, on 23 N 1251/13 January 1836.
69 Awamir lil-Jihadiyya 1/4, on 3 Z 1244/6 May 1826.

discharged from service since they would then become a burden on the finances of their units.[70]

Serving in Mehmed Ali's army was, therefore, a dreadful experience. The Pasha's army was an army which the soldiers were dragged into against their wishes and with minimal use of persuasion. It was an army that they were conscripted to practically for life and in which they were forced to fight wars that made little or no sense to them. It was an army in which they were continuously humiliated and in which the conditions of camp life were appalling. They were insulted, abused and humiliated by an officer corps that was ethnically, linguistically and socially different and with which they had very little in common. They were, moreover, poorly fed, poorly clothed and poorly paid. It was an army that did not recognize the sacrifice given by those who were wounded while serving in it. Above all, and as was shown in the previous chapter, it was an army that did not respect its dead.

The deserters

If that was the case, why then did these men continue to fight? If it is true that life in the camps was so intolerable, why did these thousands and thousands of men put up with it? The answer is that they did not. The soldiers fighting in Mehmed Ali's army deserted when they were given the slightest opportunity. They fled from the camps[71] and during marches.[72] They escaped from military hospitals,[73] from military ships,[74] from military schools,[75] and from military establishments.[76] Not only soldiers, but NCOs also fled.[77] More significantly the guards themselves fled[78] and the elite regiments, the Guardia Regiments, that

70 The same situation obtained in the civil service. For example, a scribe who lost his sight as a result of years of hard work in the bureaucracy was also designated as a *sakat* and also was not entitled to a pension. He would be dismissed as soon as he went completely blind. See Shalabī, *al-Muwaẓẓaffūn*, pp. 25–6.

71 S/1/48/1/411 on 29 Ra 1240/22 November 1824.

72 Sham 10/189 bis, on 21 Ra 1248/19 August 1832.

73 S/1/48/1/375 on 7 M 1240/1 September 1824.

74 S/1/48/2/224 on 17 Ra 1241/31 October 1825; Sham 2/64, on 11 B 1247/16 December 1831. In the second of these reports the soldiers who escaped while disembarking were later found and said they dared to escape because they could not stand their captain who was beating them with and without a reason.

75 Sāmī, ed., *Taqwīm al-Nīl*, II, p. 453, letter dated 7 B 1251/30 October 1835.

76 Awamir lil-Jihadiyya 1/27, on 4 Ş 1247/8 January 1832 and Awamir lil-Jihadiyya 1/137, on 2 Ş 1253/1 November 1837.

77 S/1/48/1/349 on 6 Za 1239/3 July 1824 (two lieutenants and three second-lieutenants); Sham 1/35, on 27 C 1247/4 December 1831 (a corporal and a sergeant); Sham 11/91 and 95, both on 11 R 1248/7 September 1832 (a captain); and Awamir lil-Jihadiyya 1/242, on 1 Ra 1259/1 April 1843 (a second-lieutenant).

78 Sham 1/27, on 26 Ca 1246/3 November 1831.

were created to catch deserters, among other things, were rampant with desertion themselves.[79]

Desertion was not a matter of individual isolated cases that the authorities succeeded in limiting and controlling; it was a phenomenon that continued to irk the authorities because of its frequency and magnitude, as attested to by the fact that the regiments' scribes were given pre-printed tables with "*noksan*," i.e. missing, as one of their standard headings.[80] Seeing these reports, both Mehmed Ali and his son were alarmed at the scale of the problem. Ibrahim rejected the officers' claim that it was the increased duties of the soldiers that prompted them to desert. He said that this was a mere pretext and that desertion was more due to the laxity and carelessness of the officers.[81] His father was of a similar opinion. He wrote to the Director of his War Department telling him that he had seen reports of the various regiments and that all suffered from desertion. There was, however, one exception, the 18th Infantry Regiment, which he took to be proof that desertion could be prevented. He therefore suggested that the colonels of the other regiments be court martialled.[82]

Having succeeded in escaping from their units, where did these men go? One obvious place was to go back to their villages. After the registers had been checked and the villages of these deserters identified, however, an order would be issued to the governor of the province in which these villages lay.[83] The order would give the names and descriptions of the deserters; the shaykh of the village would be fined fifty piasters for every deserter found in his village as well as receiving 100 stripes of the whip.[84] Spies (*baṣṣāṣīn*) were also sent roaming the countryside searching for deserters.[85] Otherwise, deserters left for Cairo in the hope that they would not be be found since it was supposedly more difficult to spot strangers there.[86] To curb this practice, the Director of the War Department would write orders to quarter and street shaykhs to keep an eye open for all deserters who might have found refuge in the city.[87]

79 Sham 9/106, on 16 S 1248/15 July 1832; S/5/47/1/346 on 17 Ca 1250/21 September 1834.
80 See, for example, Sham 10/129, on 16 Ra 1248/13 August 1832. In this case 128 men out of a battalion of 521 were missing.
81 Sham 10/63, on 9 Ra 1248/6 August 1832.
82 Awamir lil-Jihadiyya 1/35, on 27 M 1248/26 June 1832.
83 Rivlin, *Agricultural Policy*, pp. 90–1.
84 Dhawat 5/113, on 3 Ra 1246/22 August 1830.
85 S/1/48/4/549 on 2 B 1250/4 November 1834.
86 S/1/48/1/343 on 4 Za 1239/1 July 1824; Sham 2/71, on 17 B 1247/22 December 1831.
87 Divan-ı Hidiv 2/273, on 17 Ca 1250/21 September 1834.

This was also one of the important functions of the Cairo Police (*Zabtiyyat Mişr*).[88]

Finding it difficult to go back to their villages or to disappear in the anonymity of Cairo, some soldiers attempted to leave Egypt altogether, although even that proved difficult since the bedouins were always on the look-out for any soldiers who succeeded in escaping from their camps.[89] In spite of this strict surveillance, however, some soldiers managed to escape to the Hijaz and the Pasha had to write to his nephew, Ahmed Pasha Yeğen, to ask him to catch all deserters who sought refuge there.[90] When it was discovered that some soldiers were posing as pilgrims to escape to Arabia,[91] all pilgrims were ordered to have a stamped certificate stating their names, the names of their villages and their physical descriptions.[92] Finally, when one of the Egyptian officials that the Pasha had sent to France told the Pasha that he had found a number of deserters in Paris (!), Mehmed Ali desperately admitted that desertion was impossible to stop, but that did not mean that nothing could be done about it and he urged senior officers to have a discussion about ways of limiting desertion from their regiments.[93]

Besides ordering the shaykhs to capture any deserters who might have taken refuge in their villages, and threatening them that they would be whipped if they did not comply,[94] Mehmed Ali also threatened his own officers "for any negligence that [they] showed in that respect." He said that any officer from whose unit a deserter fled had to find a replacement himself. Otherwise, if he failed, a percentage of his salary would be deducted.[95] Furthermore, it was decreed that deserters who had decided voluntarily to return to their units would be pardoned; otherwise on being caught they would each receive 500 stripes of the whip.[96] In another desperate attempt to control desertion people who caught deserters were rewarded with fifty piasters for each soldier they caught.[97] Yet, the Pasha knew quite well that responsibility for catching

88 See, for example, L/2/1/1/14 on 21 Za 1260/3 December 1844.
89 S/1/48/1/331 on 22 L 1239/21 June 1824.
90 S/1/48/4/92 on 6 B 1249/19 November 1833.
91 S/1/50/5/130 on 14 Ca 1239/18 November 1823.
92 S/1/47/8/353 on 28 C 1241/7 February 1826.
93 Dhawat 5/208, on 27 M 1251/26 May 1835. Neither the nature nor the purpose of the official's visit are stated. His name was given as Mehmed Emin Efendi.
94 S/1/47/14/442 on 2 Ş 1244/7 February 1829.
95 That was for officers from colonel to captain; officers from the rank of captain to that of corporal would be beaten: Awamir lil-Jihadiyya 1/36, on 28 M 1248/27 June 1832. For an Arabic translation, see Sāmī, ed., *Taqwīm al-Nīl*, II, pp. 397–8.
96 Sham 11/171, on 18 R 1248/14 September 1832. Four deserters who were caught were punished in that way: Sham 11/210, on 21 R 1248/17 September 1832.
97 Sham 2/71, on 15 B 1247/20 December 1831.

deserters ultimately rested with the local and provincial officials whom he warned that if they were not strict in that respect, he would forget their previous services and would beat them up himself.[98]

In spite of all these orders and decrees, in spite of the heavy surveillance that they were under, and in spite of the drastic punishments inflicted upon those who were caught, the fellahin were deserting in a steady stream and nothing that the authorities did was effective in stopping them from doing so. During the early years of the Syrian campaign it was difficult to know exactly how many men went missing from their units at any one time; the roll-calls gave estimates as low as 10 percent and as high as 25 percent of the size of any one regiment.[99] Six years into the campaign, however, Mehmed Ali received a report which was most alarming regarding deserters. It said that as many as 60,000 men had gone missing from the army in addition to 20,000 from the navy![100] Bearing in mind that the army could not have been larger than 130,000, this means that for every two conscripts, one soldier managed to desert.

The size and scale of desertion is more eloquent that any allegations by nationalist historians regarding how the population of Egypt thought of the Pasha's army and his regime in general. The scale and regularity of desertion was the most striking testimony to the fellahin's willingness to resist a regime they found oppressive, intolerant and inhuman. There is something almost splendid about defying Mehmed Ali and his authorities in that way and at that level. Desertion and the authorities' frustration with it show how much Mehmed Ali's policies found no echo in the fellahin's minds and souls. The Pasha might have created an elaborate machinery to conscript and train the fellahin. He managed to aggregate their forces and organize them along European lines and to fight his wars with them successfully. But just as he managed to create what appeared as a disciplined soldiery, the fellahin, through desertion, asserted their power to disrupt his machinery and to contest his wish to subjugate them.

As alarming as the issue of desertion was to the authorities, it was not the only way that the fellahin showed their dissatisfaction with the Pasha's army and with serving in it. They also developed more subtle and cunning techniques to evade the service. One way was to make

98 S/1/47/8/351 on 26 C 1241/6 February 1826.

99 This is based on information from the *yevmiyyet*, i.e. journals of the regiments. See, e.g., that of the 13th Infantry Regiment in which more than 25% of the soldiers were missing: Sham 23/70, on 1 M 1249/21 May 1833; and that of the 12th Infantry Regiment in which 13% were missing: Sham 10/69, on 9 Ra 1248/6 August 1832.

100 Maʿiyya Saniyya, Mulakhkhaṣāt Awāmir Mustakhraja min al-Dafātir, Box 3, Booklet 28, Order dated 8 M 1253/14 April 1837.

cross tattoos on their arms to try to convince the conscripting officers that they were Copts and hence should be exempted from the *tertip*.[101] Mehmed Ali wrote to Nazif Bey, who had recently been appointed in charge of conscription after losing his job as Commissary-General,[102] telling him not to be taken in by this trick and to conscript all healthy men who could be found, whether they claimed to be Copts or not.

The self-maimed

More seriously, many fellahin went as far as maiming themselves in the hope that they might be declared medically unfit for service in the army. Initially, the most common way of maiming was to remove the front teeth in order to be deemed incapable of loading the muskets. However, when Mehmed Ali was informed that a lot of men in Upper Egypt had resorted to this habit, he said that since the training manuals did not specify which teeth should be used in loading the musket, these men could use other teeth and should therefore be conscripted.[103]

Other ways of maiming were more dangerous and resulted in serious bodily harm. One such method resorted to by the fellahin was to blind themselves by putting rat poison in their eyes. On hearing about such terrible practice, Mehmed Ali wrote to the governors forbidding the spice merchants from selling rat poison altogether. As for those unfortunates who had actually used it, they were sentenced to life imprisonment in the Liman of Alexandria.[104] In one case a woman gouged out the eyes of two men, one a soldier who had deserted from the army, and the other her son (who might have been asked to join the army himself). On being informed about this case, the Pasha ordered her to be drowned in the Nile, the deserter to be sent to the Liman of Alexandria, and the son to be pardoned.[105] In an attempt to prevent those who assisted the men in maiming themselves, usually their wives or mothers, an order was issued to hang these women at the entrances of their villages so "as to be an example to others."[106] When the maimed were of no practical use to the army, they were consistently sent

[101] S/1/48/4/365 on 14 L 1249/23 February 1834.
[102] S/1/48/4/321 on 3 N 1249/17 December 1833.
[103] S/1/48/4/648 on 18 C 1250/23 October 1834.
[104] Sāmī, ed., *Taqwīm al-Nīl*, II, p. 362, letter dated 17 Ş 1245/11 January 1830.
[105] *Ibid.*, p. 365, letter dated 13 Za 1245/6 May 1830. See also the case of the mother who chopped off the finger of her son who had been released from one of the Pasha's schools but was asked to return. She was given 200 lashes; S/6/2/1/5, p. 52, on 7 L 1264/6 September 1848.
[106] S/1/48/3/235 on 7 B 1243/25 January 1828.

to the Liman in Alexandria to serve there for life.[107] Otherwise if it were judged that they would be useful in other government establishments, then they would be sent there. For example, when workers were demanded for a new powder-magazine Mehmed Ali ordered 120 of those who had maimed themselves, either by gouging out an eye or by chopping off a finger, to be sent to work in his new establishment.[108]

A clear message was being delivered to the Pasha and his military authorities: the fellahin resented his army and were going to extreme lengths to resist serving in it. In response, the Pasha was sending back an equally clear message to anyone who might be thinking of mutilating himself to evade conscription: he would still be taken for the service – if not for the army, then for any of the Pasha's projects. In short, it proved extremely difficult to evade the army for it seems that there was a stubborn determination on the part of the Pasha that the mutilated would not escape conscription. When all methods failed in preventing the fellahin from stopping the terrible practice of mutilation, the authorities went ahead with drafting the maimed all the same. On visiting Asyout in 1834 St. John described a scene where "there was a whole regiment which had been composed of mutilated conscripts, every one of whom had either lost an eye, a finger, or the front teeth."[109]

Ultimately, Egyptians, seeing that life had become so unbearable under the new "enlightened" regime of Mehmed Ali because of corvée, taxation, monopolies, imprisonment and, above all, conscription, decided that even if they could bear these atrocities themselves, there was no reason why they should see their own children subjected to the same fate. Thus a new method of resistance developed which reflected the Egyptians' utter despair: they simply refused to marry and have children. In 1828 Mehmed Ali wrote to the Director of his War Department, Mahmud Bey, telling him that a lot of fellahin were abstaining from marriage in order to avoid seeing their children being subjected to these various government demands, e.g. taxation and imprisonment. He therefore ordered him to suggest means to issue orders to the shaykhs that would meet government demands and at the same time pacify the fellahin and discourage them from this habit, since "the prosperity of the country depends on increasing its population."[110]

One of the main reasons behind the fellahin's hatred of conscription was that it was not limited by any fixed period of time in spite of the

107 S/1/48/4/365 on 14 L 1249/23 February 1834; Awamir lil-Jihadiyya 1/159, on 11 N 1253/10 December 1837.

108 Awamir lil-Jihadiyya 1/150, on 5 N 1253/4 December 1837.

109 St. John, *Egypt*, II, p. 175; see also Bowring, "Report on Egypt," p. 52.

110 S/1/48/3/235 on 7 B 1243/25 January 1828.

Pasha's initial order to have it limited to three years.[111] When Ibrahim Pasha realized this – after more than ten years of active conscription, during which time the countryside had been drained of its male population – he wrote to his father suggesting that they limit the service to a fixed period. He explained:

> It is natural for any sane person to resist conscription, since conscription and captivity are [practically] the same. No conscript would ever have the hope of saying "I will be conscripted for a fixed period, then I will be discharged and live the remaining years of my life [outside the army]." Men have the right to think likewise since we do not discharge men unless they receive serious wounds in their hands, legs, eyes or heads; that is, they are not discharged unless they are good neither for the army nor [any other] service. This is why we face resistance in conscripting them.[112]

After thinking about it, Mehmed Ali saw the logic of his son's suggestion and wrote back telling him that he had decided to limit the period to fifteen years! Ibrahim said that he was going to announce this good news to the soldiers thinking that this showed how merciful and benevolent the Pasha was.[113] On second thoughts, however, his father said that this way they would lose a lot of men and suggested that this new system be applied only to the new conscripts and that those already in service be treated as if they had spent five years already.[114]

Given this mentality it was natural for the male population of Egypt to hate the army into which they were dragged by Mehmed Ali's military machine and to seize every opportunity to evade it whenever and wherever they could. Nothing can be further from the truth than al-Rāfʿī's allegation that the fellahin eventually saw that "military life was more comfortable than their village life [which, in fact, is not saying much], and even became proud of it."[115] In all the numerous cases about conscripting the male population of Egypt into Mehmed Ali's army there was only a single instance of a man voluntarily requesting to join the army. He had been released and allowed to go back to his village, then some time later came back saying that he had heard from some pilgrims that his village had been deserted and that none of his relatives or friends had remained behind.[116] This could hardly be viewed as a positive reason for joining the army that Mehmed Ali founded, the "prime pillar of Egyptian independence."[117]

Yet is it plausible to argue that the spectacular victories which that

111 See chapter 2 above. 112 Sham 30/510, on 25 Z 1250/25 April 1835.
113 Sham 31/6, on 7 M 1251/5 May 1835.
114 Sham 31/62, on 28 M 1251/27 May 1835.
115 al-Rāfʿī, *ʿAṣr Muhammad ʿAlī*, p. 331.
116 S/1/48/4/407 on 3 Za 1249/14 March 1834.
117 al-Rāfʿī, *ʿAṣr Muhammad ʿAlī*, p. 321.

army secured were accomplished by peasants who were dragged in it completely against their wishes? Lacking the positive incentive of fighting in defense of the fatherland, and at the same time being prevented from looting and pillaging the lands they conquered, how then can one account for the successive victories that these soldiers were able to secure? In an attempt to answer this important question the following section compares the Pasha's army with that of Napoelon, an army on whose example it was partly modeled and one which shows that it is possible for a disgruntled peasantry which had been pressed into military service to produce successive victories for its commanders. This is followed by a comparison with the Sultan's own army – which was Mehmed Ali's most formidable adversary – a comparison that is intended to show how Ibrahim's victories were not that hard to come by in the first place.

The Pasha's *Cihadiye* and the Emperor's *Grande Armée*

As the French Revolution was approaching, an already existing feeling of common citizenship was gaining more ground while a common psychology was diffusing among all Frenchmen. "France was becoming a *nation* or a *patrie* and ceasing to be a mere *royaume*."[118] As far as the military was concerned more and more people were gradually allowing themselves "to trust to something other than Prussian discipline for getting apt performance out of the troops . . . Were soldiers not also *men*? And who should fight better for his regiment, king or country than a man and a patriot who could feel loyalty and affection and who could fight for motives of love and belief, rather than from routine, roughness, and fear?"[119]

This romantic account of the French army at the time of the Revolution overlooks the important fact that desertion and other means of resistance to conscription were as central characteristics of that army as they were of Mehmed Ali's. Apart from the single spectacular response to the Legislative Assembly's call to arms to defend *la patrie* after the initiation of hostilities against Austria and Prussia in 1792,[120] resistance to conscription was rampant right from the beginning of systematic conscription in 1798.[121] During Napoleon's disastrous Russian campaign "pillaging, indiscipline and desertion soon became

118 M. S. Anderson, *War and Society*, pp. 200–1.

119 Geoffrey Best, *War and Society in Revolutionary Europe, 1770–1870* (London: Fontana, 1982), p. 52.

120 John Gerard Gallaher, "Recruitment in the district of Poitiers: 1793," *French Historical Studies*, 3 (Fall, 1963), p. 247.

121 Eugen Weber, *Peasants into Frenchmen* (London: Chatto and Windus, 1977), p. 292;

rife on an unprecedented scale."[122] Two years later, in 1814, resistance to conscription was so high that only one-eighth of those who were supposed to report to the army depots saw active service.[123] This high level of desertion might have been due to the prolonged wars that the Emperor was waging and his "insatiable appetite for conquest [which] did nothing to dispel traditional distrust of the recruiting-sergeant."[124] However, it is wrong to assume that resistance to serving in the army reached alarming proportions only after 1812. A study conducted about the scale of desertion during the nineteen-month period from December 1804, to July 1806, a period that witnessed the peak of Napoleon's popularity, estimates that the number of men who deserted from all over France was around 800 per month, i.e. 9,600 a year. If draft-dodgers (i.e., those who evaded being conscripted in the first place) are accounted for this figure reaches 15,000. These were alarming figures for the authorities, but nothing that they did "had the desired effect of completely and finally solving difficulties resulting from this opposition [to conscription]".[125] Even before the advent of Napoleon, and during the early years of the Revolution, desertion amounted to 2 percent of the total strength of the regiments, a figure which "rose considerably whenever the threat of war loomed."[126] In spite of all attempts by the revolutionary authorities to curb desertion and other means of resistance to conscription "the problem of disobedience and the connivance of parents, officials, and entire communities remained a serious rebuke to a state which claimed to control the persons of its citizens."[127]

The claim that the French Revolution "had transformed the ethos and size of the French army, and had based it spiritually and physically at the heart of the nation" might be correct. It might also be true to argue that with the outbreak of the Revolutionary Wars, "the army assumed simultaneously the defense both of France and of the new order, and that in consequence all three – army, nation, and Revolution – were identified together."[128] This, however, does not mean that the French peasants accepted service in the colors without hesitation.

R. C. Cobb, *The Police and the People: French Popular Protest, 1789–1820* (Oxford: Oxford University Press, 1970), pp. 96–7, 207.

122 F. M. H. Markham, *Napoleon and the Awakening of Europe* (London: English Universities Press, 1954), p. 128.

123 *Ibid.*, p. 142. 124 Forrest, *Conscripts and Deserters*, p. 7.

125 Eric A. Arnold, Jr., "Some observations on the French opposition to Napoleonic conscription, 1804–1806," *French Historical Studies*, 4 (1966), pp. 461–2.

126 Alan Forrest, *Soldiers of the French Revolution* (London: Duke University Press, 1990), p. 35.

127 *Ibid.*, p. 187.

128 Hew Strachan, *European Armies and the Conduct of War* (London: George Allen and Unwin, 1983), p. 40.

Indeed, "for many Frenchmen the service demanded by the government quickly assumed the guise of a new and unwelcome *corvée*, a tax in blood to a distant and impersonal master, imposed in the name of a national cause that they understood only in the dimmest terms."[129] "Nationalism, the dream of 'la grande nation' so dear to the historians of the First Empire, had little appeal to those who were called on to fight in its name."[130]

The French peasant, then, like the Egyptian peasant was an unwilling conscript fighting for a distant and impersonal leader whom he could neither comprehend nor sympathize with. Both were reacting to despots who had ambivalent feeling towards the men they led. Like Mehmed Ali, Napoleon knew too well that his glory could only be built on the sacrifices of his men, and for this he was grateful to them. But also like him, he had the sense of self-importance and contempt for human life (life of the poor peasant, that is,) that is characteristic of Great Men in the battlefield and which allowed him to say in a letter to Metternich in 1813, "Un homme comme moi ne regarde pas à un million de morts."[131] The men, for their part, had no ambivalence towards their despotic leaders and saw service in their respective armies not as an honorable duty owed to a larger community but as a heavy tribute exacted by an oppressive and distant regime.

If the comparison between the two armies shows that in both of them the distance was great between the poor, oppressed soldiers and their alien, impersonal despot, there is, however, a crucial difference between the two armies. This concerned the type of people who lay between the soldiers and their distant sovereign, *viz.* the officers. Napoleon was successful in bringing together members of the old nobility *and* the new, rising bourgeoisie and in making a more-or-less homogenous officer corps that was loyal to his person. "The corps of officers was to be a melting-pot in which people who belonged to the 'two Frances,' so to speak, would be reconciled. Sitting together in the military schools and, even more, fighting at the front against the enemy, they would learn to respect one another."[132] More importantly, they would try to sell the idea of nationalism, as it were, to their soldiers, convincing them that in giving up their lives in defense of the Emperor, they would in fact be defending the nation as represented in him. In these schools they would be taught that the "courageous soldier was one who worshiped honor and was ready to sacrifice [his

129 Forrest, *Conscripts and Deserters*, p. 4. 130 *Ibid.*, p. 19.
131 Quoted in *ibid.*, p. 19.
132 Jean-Paul Bertaud, "Napoleon's officers," *Past and Present*, 112 (1986), p. 94.

life] . . . for the sake of the community."[133] Judging from the record, it does not seem that the officers succeeded in convincing the soldiers that what they were fighting for was the nation. It was only towards the end of the nineteenth century that the soldiers came to think that what they were doing was fighting for their *patrie*; only in the 1890s is there "persuasive evidence that the army was no longer 'theirs' but 'ours' . . . At least for a while, the army could become what its enthusiasts hoped for: the school of the fatherland."[134] This was possible not only because the soldiers believed this to be the case, but more importantly, because their officers, since their Great Emperor's time, had been convinced strongly enough of this themselves and were then able to pass on this feeling to their subordinates.

In that respect Mehmed Ali's army was different. Two crucial features characterized his officers. Like Napoleon's, they were loyal to their master, owing him allegiance and devotion, and strove to appease him and his family. However, unlike the Emperor's officers, they were not from or of the country they were defending. Being themselves newcomers to Egypt, the officers in Mehmed Ali's army had no roots in the country that they were supposedly fighting for and the ethnic and linguistic differences that separated them from their soldiers made any attempt to convince the soldiers of any nationalistic argument nearly impossible. The officers could not attempt to "sell the idea of nationalism" to their soldiers, not only because they spoke different languages, and communication with their soldiers was kept to the absolute minimum, but also, and above all, because they themselves did not believe that they were fighting for the nation. It took at least two or three generations for the Turkish-speaking officer corps to settle in Egypt and to start to think of Egypt as their country. By that time, however, resentment among the lower ranking Arabic-speaking officers was high and eventually led to open rebellion.

As early as the mid-1830s, when John Bowring visited Egypt, the resentment of Egyptians, in the full sense of the term, against their Turkish-speaking rulers was starting to become obvious, mainly in the army. "An Arab soldier of the last generation was wholly at the mercy of his Turkish officer; it is so no longer . . . [T]he whole character of the population is undergoing a silent but obvious change. The Egyptian element is gradually replacing the Turkish . . ."[135] By the late 1870s this "Egyptian element" had acquired enough self-consciousness such that it "dared to acknowledge its own exis-

133 *Ibid.*, p. 95. 134 Weber, *Frenchmen*, p. 298.
135 Bowring, "Report on Egypt," pp. 8–9.

tence,"[136] and to express itself in open rebellion. The 'Urābī Revolution of 1881–2, in addition to being a revolution by various sectors of the urban and rural population against European dual control, was also a revolt of these estranged Arabic-speaking fellah officers against their Turkish-speaking superiors.[137] This domination was represented most clearly by the system, initially put down fifty years earlier by Mehmed Ali and Ibrahim Pasha, whereby only Turkish-speaking officers were allowed to be promoted to high ranks in the army as well as in the civilian bureaucracy. The "Egypt for the Egyptians" slogan of the 'Urābī Revolt, therefore, represents this rising sense of Egyptian nationalism that was directed partly against the Turkish domination, a domination that was a central feature of Mehmed Ali's army and which was best represented in the figure of the Pasha himself.

In that respect, the main difference between the Pasha's army and that of Napoleon is that whereas the former preceded the national bourgeois revolution, the latter succeeded it. It is this difference that accounts for the fact that when fighting for "Egypt" the soldiers in Mehmed Ali's army were marching under banners with the Pasha's name inscribed on them, while the French soldiers, when fighting what were essentially Napoleon's wars and not those of the Revolution, did so under the tricolored standards of the Revolution. "Thousands of young Frenchmen might seek to avoid serving beneath [the army's] standards. But as long as the standards were tricolored, as long as they proclaimed Liberty, Equality, Fraternity, those who still cared could console themselves with the belief that the Revolution [still] lived."[138] This pretense of fighting a national war was not even attempted as a consolation for sending thousands and thousands of Egyptian men to their deaths for the glory of Mehmed Ali and his family.

It could be argued, however, that Mehmed Ali's army was instrumental in propagating the idea of Egyptian nationalism, albeit unwittingly. It did this not because the Pasha, his son, or any of their chief military commanders thought of the various wars they waged as "national"; the dynastic aspect of these successive military confrontations, as was shown above, was clear to all to see, and Ibrahim, in spite of his often-quoted "Egyptian" sentiments, had no doubts about it. At the same time, the fellah-soldiers never questioned the fact that they were fighting for the Pasha and his family. To judge from the record,

136 Charles Wendell, *The Evolution of the Egyptian National Image, From its Origins to Ahmad Lutfi al-Sayyid* (Berkeley: University of California Press, 1972), p. 133.

137 Juan Cole, *Colonialism and Revolution in the Middle East: Social and Cultural Origins of Egypt's 'Urabi Movement* (Princeton: Princeton University Press, 1993), pp. 235–41.

138 Keegan, *Face of Battle*, p. 178.

"selling" the battles against the Sultan to the men as being necessary to the defense of the "fatherland," important for protecting the "Faith," or upholding their pride and dignity was not even attempted.

Nevertheless, the army did unwittingly contribute to the rise of Egyptian nationalism by homogenizing the experience of tens of thousands of Egyptians over a period that exceeded twenty years by instilling in them the feeling of hatred of the "Ottomans," and thus helped in their collective "imagination" of the nation.[139] This creation of the "other" that wars are singularly successful at doing was operational in Mehmed Ali's army not in directing the men's sentiments of animosity against the army of the Greek rebels, or the Wahhabi brigands, let alone the army of the Ottoman Sultan, but against their own Turkish-speaking officers. These feelings of animosity towards the "Ottoman" eventually came to fruition two or three generations later when the frustrated leaders of these fellah-soldiers, the middle-ranking, Arabic-speaking officers, broke out in open rebellion together with other disgruntled members of Egyptian society against Turco-Circassian domination.

These developments, however, needed time to come to the surface and during the Pasha's reign their manifestations were hardly perceptible. Yet, their seeds had already been sown, giving rise to an inherent paradox of the Pasha's army and of his entire military career, namely, the absence of legitimacy for his incessant expansionist military activities. For while using a religious argument to justify fighting against a state that claimed to be upholding the Faith for five centuries could not have sold very well, at the same time using an argument based on ethnicity, as nationalist arguments necessarily do, would have been counter-productive for the Pasha, his household, and his entire elite, the very same elite that was leading their ethnically different soldiers in the various wars.

The Pasha's *Cihadiye* and the Sultan's *Asaker-i Mansure*

Lacking this essential ingredient for their militaristic exploits, namely, a legitimate excuse, however vaguely defined it might be, how then can one explain the successive victories that Ibrahim and his men snatched from the Ottomans? Furthermore, having argued that the soldiers were not well paid, that they were not allowed to loot and pillage the countries they were fighting in, and that at the same time they lacked the positive incentive of thinking that they were fighting for the glory of

[139] Benedict Anderson, *Imagined Communities: Reflections of the Origins of Nationalism* (London: Verso, 1983).

the fatherland, how can one explain the fact that they still managed to accomplish these successive victories? Comparing the Egyptian Pasha's army to that of the Sultan against which it fought most of its battles might provide an answer for this intriguing question.

On the face of it, the military reforms of both Mehmed Ali and Sultan Mahmud II look strikingly similar. Both men were influenced by the *nizam-i cedid* army that Sultan Selim III established prior to his deposition in 1807. Both also realized that to start introducing new tactics and drills in their respective domains, they had to get rid of the traditional military castes that saw the introduction of such new techniques as a direct threat to their privileged positions. Mehmed Ali thus got rid of the Mamluks in the infamous massacre of the Citadel in 1811, and Mahmud got rid of the Janissaries in 1826, to pave the way for the introduction of new drills. Furthermore, they seem to have realized that the new European states had gone a long way towards monopolizing the means of violence and enhancing the deadly capacity of their armies, and in that field, the field of military reform, both Cairo and Istanbul had lagged behind. They seem to have understood that without borrowing from the Europeans and seeking their assistance in founding their new armies, their reforms would be seriously undermined. In that manner both Pasha and Sultan sought the assistance of various European military advisors, the most famous of whom were Süleyman Pasha (Colonel Sèves) and Lieutenant (later Field Marshal) Helmuth von Moltke.

These apparent similarities, however, are misleading since they conceal far more important differences in the way both armies functioned – differences in the performances of both armies, and in particular of their respective officer corps, that account for most of the spectacular defeats of the Ottomans by Mehmed Ali's army.

The Pasha's officers might have had different origins and social backgrounds from the men they led. They also might have formed conflicting factions and cliques. They were, however, extremely loyal to the Pasha and to members of his family. The stipulation that no *evlad-ı Arab* be promoted to senior ranks might have created a rift between soldiers and officers and weakened the link that the officers might have had with the land on which they were serving: that stipulation, however, was crucial for the creation of a loyal officer corps. By inviting "Ottomans" to be employed in his service, by opening schools in which young men from various parts of the Ottoman world were given subsidized and sometimes even free education, by employing these men in his bureaucracy and army and by further promoting those people up to the higher ranks of the military, Mehmed Ali succeeded in founding an elite which was deeply dependent on the Pasha and firmly loyal to him.

Similarly, the Europeans who flocked to Egypt seeking to work for the Pasha were given terms of employment that compared very favorably with any other that they might have sought. Differences in religion did not prevent them from rising in the military and civilian hierarchy and accordingly they received some of the highest salaries that the Pasha was offering. These included not only Süleyman Pasha, who by the early 1830s had become the second-in-command in the army after Ibrahim Pasha, but also Engineer Cerisy who constructed the new arsenal for Mehmed Ali in Alexandria, M. Planat, Director of the Staff College,[140] Col. Seguera, the head of the Artillery School, Clot Bey, the head of the military medical establishment, and numerous other Europeans.

Moreover, the army that the Pasha established benefited from a remarkable working relationship between Mehmed Ali and his son, Ibrahim Pasha. Occasionally tensions would surface between father and son, but on the whole and for the best part of the Pasha's rule the relationship between these two remarkable men was amicable, and it allowed Mehmed Ali to devote his energy to the exploitation of the province's manpower to enhance agricultural and commercial revenues, while leaving for his son the task of exploiting the services of the male population for the military.

Above all, the army that the Pasha founded in Egypt was fortunate enough to have Ibrahim Pasha as its commander. There is no doubt that Ibrahim made one of the best military commanders in the history of the Ottoman Empire and that most of the victories that his army achieved were a direct result of his perceptive and insightful command. This expertise expressed itself not only in his skillful deployment of troops before battle,[141] but also in his adept choice of terrain, his ability to engage the enemy at the right time,[142] and his seizing the advantages he had over his adversary and forcing the enemy to give battle at *his* own opportune moment and at a spot of his choosing.[143] Commenting on the battles of 1832 that Ibrahim waged against the Ottomans in Syria and Asia Minor, a contemporary French military observer said that "the campaign of 1832 was highly honorable to Ibrahim Pasha, and I believe all intelligent military men will admit that it is not open to criticism, having been conducted with prudence, sagacity, and vigour . . ."[144]

140 See his *Histoire de la régénération de l'Egypte*, pp. 40–1, for the positions of Frenchmen in the Pasha's service.

141 Marshal Marmont, *Turkish Empire*, pp. 248–9 (on the battle of Ḥomṣ).

142 *Ibid.*, p. 251 (for the battle of Bilan).

143 Levy, "The officer corps," p. 26 (for the battle of Nezib).

144 Marshal Marmont, *Turkish Empire*, p. 262.

The Ottoman army with which Sultan Mahmud replaced the Janissaries was a complete contrast to all this. Although the act of getting rid of the Janissaries was important, it was neither as decisive nor as successful as Mehmed Ali's massacre of the Mamluks in 1811. Unlike the Mamluks who had succeeded in secluding and isolating themselves from the population of Egypt for centuries,[145] the Janissaries had, by the time Mahmud managed to get rid of them, penetrated Ottoman society and "branched out from the military to penetrate and overlap other social strata."[146] Getting rid of them, therefore, was not as "neat" an operation as massacring the Mamluks. Moreover, the Janissaries were fulfilling tasks other than purely military ones, the most important of which was keeping the peace and security in the capital, Istanbul. Abolishing that most prestigious of military castes within the Empire left the capital defenseless in the face of possible riots. Unlike the situation of Mehmed Ali whose massacre of the Mamluks helped him restore security and order in Cairo and in Egypt at large, the Sultan, by getting rid of the Janissaries, felt even more insecure in his own capital. That sense of insecurity limited his course of action in his attempt to spread his reforms over wider segments of his army.[147]

Furthermore, when the Sultan decided to seek the assistance of Europeans in helping him create his new *Mansure* army, these were employed only as advisors or instructors and none of them was allowed to assume posts even half as important as that of Süleyman Pasha in Egypt. Whether because of religious reasons, or the sense of pride and jealousy with which the Ottomans regarded their military past, when Europeans were employed in Sultan Mahmud's new army every effort was made to ensure, as an official directive put it, that "foreign officers will not gain influence and independence. Thus they shall have authority only in matters of training, and in all matters of command, discipline, and the like they shall operate only through . . . Ottoman officers."[148] This inferior position of the Europeans who were employed in the new army was also reflected in the low salaries that they were paid: whereas Süleyman Pasha was said to receive a monthly salary of 17,500 piasters, his compatriot, Gaillard, who was Sultan Mahmud's chief infantry instructor, received less than one-tenth that amount.[149]

Another major problem that affected the performance of Sultan

145 David Ayalon, "The Muslim city and the Mamluk military aristocracy," *Proceedings of the Israel Academy of Science and Humanities*, 2 (1967), pp. 322–5.
146 Levy, "The officer corps," p. 23.
147 Temperley, *Near East*, p. 56; Levy, "The officer corps," p. 21.
148 *Baş Vekalet Arşivi* (Archives of the Prime Minister's Office, Istanbul); *Hatt-ı Hümayunlar* collection, 48338A; quoted in Levy, "The officer corps," p. 23.
149 *Ibid.*, p. 24.

Mahmud's army was the training and composition of his officer corps. Shortly after the Sultan got rid of the Janissaries, and in order to create a new nucleus for his officer corps, he founded the Battalion of the *Ağas* of the Court's Inner Service (the *Enderun-i Hümayun Ağavatı*) in which young slaves from the Sultan's own household, as well as from those of important notables and officials in the Empire, were enrolled. This unit, in effect the first modern Ottoman officer training institution, was, however, a battle-ground for intrigues and feuds among many dignitaries who tried to ensure that their sons would find a place in it. Dissatisfied with its performance, the Sultan finally abolished it in May 1830, only four years after it had been created.[150] The lack of well-trained officers to lead the Sultan's new army was felt more desperately after the successive defeats at the hands of Ibrahim's army in 1831–2, and a new school for cadets had to be opened. In 1834, therefore, the School for Military Science (*Mekteb-i Ulum-u Harbiye*) was opened, although initial problems arising from opposition by leading dignitaries, as well as lack of funds, books, qualified teachers and a place suitable for instruction, all meant that the school came into real existence only in October 1837. Even then its curriculum was limited to such traditional subjects as reading, writing, arithmetic, Arabic, and military tactics.[151]

Viewed in the light of these differences, it is not the least surprising that Sultan Mahmud's army suffered successive defeat at the hands of Mehmed Ali's army. On the face of it, it would seem that the main reason behind these humiliating defeats was that, whereas Mehmed Ali started to build his new army and train it along European lines in 1820, the Sultan did this six years later. There are, however, much more important reasons for the contrasting performances of the two armies. First, there was the important factor that the *Mansure* army of the Sultan lacked a commander of the caliber of Ibrahim Pasha. Second, although the army of the Sultan had been able to secure the services of some European advisors, these were neither authorized nor trusted enough to be given high positions in the army; this at a time when Süleyman Pasha had been able to rise up in the military hierarchy until he became second-in-command after Ibrahim Pasha. Third, the Ottoman army never witnessed anything like the superb working relationship between Mehmed Ali, Ibrahim Pasha and Süleyman Pasha; instead, it was a battle-ground for intrigues and internal fights among various officials. A significant factor in the defeat of the Ottoman army in the battle of Ḥomṣ, for example, was the fact that the Serasker, Husrev Pasha, was jealous of the authority of Hüseyin Pasha, who was

150 *Ibid.*, pp. 27–9. 151 *Ibid.*, pp. 32–6.

appointed as Commander-in-Chief of the army that was to fight Ibrahim Pasha. To curb his influence, Husrev had Mehmed Pasha, one of his protégés, appointed to Hüseyin's staff as second-in-command although the two men could neither work together nor agree on common tactics.[152] Fourth, by the time of the initiation of hostilities between Mehmed Ali and the Sultan, the Pasha's new military schools had managed to train officers who were capable of leading his army to successive victories, at a time when the Sultan was still tampering with the remnants of his old system. The officers graduating from Mehmed Ali's schools might have been discharged earlier than they should have been, and only a few of them ever managed to finish studying the proper curriculum set for the school; yet, by comparison, they were better trained and more loyal than the Sultan's officers.

In more than one way, therefore, the victories that Ibrahim managed to secure in his illustrious career were as much due to the innate qualities of his army as to the shortcomings of his adversaries and in particular, the Ottomans. For as Marshal Marmont put it in the mid-1830s, "doubtless it was advantageous to Ibrahim to be opposed to troops who are incapable of manoeuvring, and whose invariable practice it is either to await the advantage of their enemy or to rush forward to attack without either system or order."[153]

The battle of Nezib (24 June 1839) illustrates very clearly how these differences between the two armies can explain the various defeats of the Ottomans by Mehmed Ali's army. Throughout the second half of 1838 and the early part of 1839 Sultan Mahmud was more determined than ever to settle accounts with his rebellious vassal and to have back the lands he had acquired against his wishes. He thus sent his Minister of Foreign Affairs, Mustafa Raşid Pasha, to Europe to secure the backing of Europe in any confrontation with Mehmed Ali. His mission was not successful, however, since Britain, the most important player among the Powers, agreed to back the Sultan only if Mehmed Ali declared himself independent.[154]

The Sultan's policy was therefore based on the principle of avoiding direct confrontation with Ibrahim Pasha's army and of seeking instead to threaten Syria by land and sea so as to provoke an uprising among the inhabitants there. This policy was based on erroneous and misleading information sent by Hafiz Pasha, Commander-in-Chief of forces in Anatolia, who pointed to the imminence of an uprising against Mehmed

152 *Ibid.*, pp. 37–8; Cadalvène and Barrault, *La Guerre de Méhémet-Ali*, pp. 98–100.

153 Marshal Marmont, *Turkish Empire*, p. 262.

154 Temperley, *Near East*, pp. 98–9. For further information on Raşid Pasha, see chapter 7 below.

Ali's rule in Syria.[155] The Sultan amassed a sizeable force composed of local Turkish and Kurdish tribesmen from southern Anatolia whose mere presence was hoped to spark such a revolt. In the event, the Syrians were too cowed by Ibrahim's troops to revolt against Egyptian rule.[156] After a brief period of hesitation and indecision, however, Mehmed Ali finally decided that he could not accept this blatant act from the Ottomans and was not deterred by European calls for restraint. He thus ordered his son to advance against Hafiz Pasha's troops and to proceed to capture Orfa and Diyarbakır after routing the Ottoman army and not to wait for any further commands from him, since "the pot has overflown and there is no need any longer for the spoon."[157]

The actual performance of the Ottoman army showed how ill-prepared and badly led it was, and that thirteen years of military reforms initiated by Mahmud could not stand the first serious test posed to it. As opposed to the superb logistical preparations of Ibrahim Pasha[158] and the admirable division of labor between him and his best general, Süleyman Pasha,[159] that eventually allowed Ibrahim's army to assume an impressive formation at the start of the battle,[160] the Ottoman army had a divided leadership, had lost the initiative it had had, and was already tired even before the battle had started.

On more than one occasion Hafiz had a chance to disrupt Ibrahim Pasha's movements in preparation for the battle.[161] Instead, his troops "took up battle positions in such a slow and disorganized manner [and] had to be maintained in combat positions for three days and nights while Ibrahim maneuvered in the area."[162] Furthermore, and against the advice of von Moltke who was sent by the Sultan to assist him, Hafiz Pasha ordered his troops to leave their fortified positions and to venture out in open country, which is precisely what Ibrahim wanted them to do. This he did in compliance with the suggestion of his *'ulamā'* who first advised him against fighting on a Friday and then deemed it shameful to sit behind the entrenchment and instead urged him to advance against the adversary in the open.[163] Even after committing these grave mistakes, Hafiz could have still salvaged the situation, especially since at one crucial moment Ibrahim's army was lacking in

[155] Levy, "The officer corps," p. 37. [156] Shaw and Shaw, *History*, II, p. 50.
[157] S/5/47/2/124 on 28 Ra 1255/10 June 1839.
[158] Zakī, *al-Tārīkh al-Ḥarbī*, pp. 462–73 [159] *Ibid.*, pp. 467, 470.
[160] For a map showing Ibrahim's distribution of forces see Driault, *L'Egypte et l'Europe*, I, pp. 88–9.
[161] Zakī, *al-Tārīkh al-Ḥarbī*, pp. 469–70. [162] Levy, "The officer corps," p. 26.
[163] Enver Z. Karal, *Osmanlı Tarihi* [History of the Ottomans] (Ankara: Türk Tarih Kurumu Basımevi, 1983), V, p. 141; Temperley, *Near East*, p. 104; Shaw and Shaw, *History*, p. 50.

ammunition. However, he missed that opportunity and, again disregarding von Moltke's advice, refused to order the advance of an unbroken column and kept himself busy with stopping the chaotic retreat of his own troops. The result of this extremely incompetent leadership was disastrous for, in von Moltke's description of the battle, "the army of Hafiz Pasha has ceased to exist . . . The Turks threw down their arms and abandoned their artillery and ammunition, flying in every direction."[164] In the event the Ottomans lost all their guns and up to 10,000 prisoners were captured by Ibrahim Pasha.

This last victory of Ibrahim's was made possible by his insightful and clever command, by the assistance that Süleyman Pasha gave him, by his well-trained soldiers and loyal officers who had been hardened and tried in an army that had had a short but successful history, and above all by the infrastructure that was built to feed and supply the army. Of equal importance, however, this victory was made possible by the Ottomans' own dismal performance. As opposed to Ibrahim, Hafiz was without previous battlefield experience.[165] He was inflexible, indecisive and stubborn, refusing to accept the advice of his capable Prussian advisor, von Moltke. His army was ill-trained, his officers' loyalty was in doubt and above all the directives and instructions he was receiving from Istanbul were contradictory and confusing.

By comparing the performance of Mehmed Ali's army to those of Napoleon and Sultan Mahmud II it is possible to come up with suggestions as to how the Pasha's army was capable of accomplishing these spectacular victories in spite of the fact that its soldiers were drafted into it against their wishes and used every means at their disposal to resist it. While to argue, as most contemporary observers did, that "the Turkish defeat in the conflict with Muhammed Ali [was due] primarily to the inadequacies of the Ottoman military leadership"[166] might be to stress the point too forcibly, it remains true that Ottoman incompetence and timid military reform contributed significantly to Ibrahim's victories, and that had the Ottomans been more successful in managing their own armies, Ibrahim Pasha's career and, indeed, that of his father would seem much less impressive.

Conclusion

This chapter has attempted to challenge the received wisdom that the Pasha, by founding his army and conscripting Egyptians into it, was

164 Quoted in Temperley, *Near East*, pp. 104–5.
165 Karal, *Osmanlı Tarihi*, p. 141.
166 This was the opinion of British, French and Prussian observers; see Levy, "The officer corps," p. 38.

trying to gain independence for Egypt as meaning a nation-state. While it is acknowledged that the Pasha himself was Turkish-speaking and that he might not have seen his army or his policies in general in an Egyptian nationalistic light, it is sometimes claimed that, nevertheless, he and "his new administration inevitably put Egypt on the path of independent statehood and self-recognition as having a separate identity from other Muslims and Ottomans . . . [and that] without his efforts it might have taken Egyptians much longer to be able to call Egypt their own."[167] We have yet to deal with the Pasha's own personal feelings towards and thoughts about Egypt; in this chapter we questioned the effect of the army on Egyptian nationalism by looking at Ibrahim Pasha's policies towards his Arabic-speaking soldiers, by investigating the composition of the officer corps and the relationship between soldiers and officers, and finally by trying to sketch the reaction of the men to the brutal regime of the Pasha that they came to experience and confront in a very physical way.

One of the main arguments that nationalist historians have put forward to prove that the army was indeed a national army in spite of the Turkish ethnicity of its founder is that of how different his son was in this respect. Ibrahim, it is alleged, was closer to his Egyptian soldiers and never identified himself as an Ottoman. Be that as it may, what this chapter has argued is that Ibrahim had no doubt in his mind regarding the nature of the wars that his army was fighting. As far as he was concerned these were wars that he waged in the name of his father and for the sake of his family. More important than Ibrahim's sentiments, though, was the very composition of the officer corps that he was leading which, as this chapter has tried to show, was ethnically, linguistically and culturally different from the soldiery. Like their leader, the officers in the Pasha's army had no doubt that they were serving the Pasha and his family and had no sympathies in common with the men they were commanding. With their origins in different parts of the Ottoman world and having come to Egypt to seek employment in the Pasha's army and bureaucracy, they tied their own destinies to that of the household they were fighting for. Like Ibrahim Pasha they, too, thought of the army as a dynastic army fighting the Pasha's own wars, wars that they stood to benefit from since the army that was successful in those wars could give them a better, more lucrative employment and, arguably, a better and more prestigious social status in the new province they settled in, Egypt.

As far as the fellah-soldiers were concerned, the allegation that this

[167] al-Sayyid Marsot, *Egypt*, p. 264.

was their army, and that they were fighting for their own sake, would have been the most ludicrous claim they would have heard. For them, nothing could have been further from the truth. The soldiers came to see the army as the most detestable aspect of the Pasha's already hated regime. They were dragged to serve in it practically for their entire lives, often never to see their families again. During their life-long period of conscription they were ridiculed, beaten and humiliated by their Turkish-speaking officers. They saw the army as an institution that came to represent to them in the most concrete and direct way the atrocious, inhuman and dreadful policies of Mehmed Ali. Seeing it in this light, they spared no means at their disposal to express their true sentiments of disgust and hatred to the regime that made them pay with their blood and lives for the glory of Mehmed Ali and his family. They might not have left us written records to let us know what their sentiments were towards the army and the Pasha. But they have made their feelings known by much more eloquent means: through desertion and maiming they showed that they would use every means to evade an institution that came to represent to them in a very real way all the brutalities of the Pasha's regime.

So how then can we understand the Pasha's army and the nature of the various wars it waged in its long and colorful history? If the men who fought in this army did not think of it as "theirs" and if the officers who led them to their deaths did not think that they were doing so for the sake of delivering "Egypt" from foreign oppression, in what light then can we view this army? The following chapter deals with this question.

7 The Egyptian Vali, the Ottoman Pashas and the British Lord

In 1836, and at the height of his career, Mehmed Ali is reported to have received a letter from one of his officials informing him that a number of workers had been imprisoned in the "factory" they were working in. The Pasha answered the official sternly telling him not to treat the fellahin in that brutal way.

> Did I not tell you before [he reprimanded him], that the sources of my benefaction [lit. *awliā' ni'matī*] are two: Sultan Mahmud and the fellah. The reason I am repeating this to you is to urge you not to treat the fellah as your enemy . . . [since] our honor and glory and all we receive and give is due to the fellah and his efforts.[1]

Amīn Sāmī highlights this letter by printing it in boldface, to stress the theme that runs throughout his book, that the Pasha was indeed the humane, enlightened reformer who had nothing but the well-being of his people in mind. As such, the letter could easily be dismissed as an hagiographical account of Mehmed Ali's rule that finds its origins in the words of the Pasha himself. The letter should be taken seriously, however, since it shows the Pasha playing with words in a characteristic way that betrays his own ambivalent feelings towards his Egyptian subjects and his Ottoman adversaries. For when he says that both the Sultan and the fellah were his *awliā' al-ni'am*, i.e. his benefactors, the Pasha is echoing here his own title: he was known in Egypt as *wali al-ni'am*, the Benefactor. Any contemporary would have seen the pun used here as a thinly disguised attempt at ridiculing both the fellah and the Sultan, for it was precisely these two "persons" whom the Pasha ridiculed, each in a different way. Let us give the Pasha the benefit of the doubt, though, and argue that he did mean what he said. In that case, and given the fact that he practically enslaved the fellah and repeatedly and ferociously fought the Sultan, the letter shows the ambiguity of feelings towards both his nominal sovereign and his fellah

[1] Sāmī, ed., *Taqwīm al-Nīl*, II, p. 474, letter dated 29 C 1252/11 October 1836.

subjects, an ambivalence that characterized his rule and was behind all his major decisions.

This chapter attempts to view developments from the Pasha's perspective and tries to understand the nature of this ambivalence that he felt towards both his *awliā' al-ni'am*, the fellah and the Sultan, i.e. Egypt and the Ottoman Empire. In addition, this chapter is interested in analyzing the nature and the aims of the wars that the Pasha fought against the Ottoman Sultan. These wars, in particular, are usually highlighted to argue that Europe, and specifically Great Britain, by backing the Sultan in his fight against his Egyptian vali, dismantled Mehmed Ali's "empire," weakened Egypt and placed its power and progress under a weighty vassalage.[2] Seen from a modern, nationalist perspective that takes "Egypt" to refer to an undivided entity capable of sovereignty and autonomy, this may well be the case. However, what is asked below is how these struggles would look if viewed from an Ottoman perspective and placed in their original nineteenth-century context. In other words, is it possible to view the wars that the Pasha waged during his illustrious career, and specifically against Sultan Mahmud II, not as wars of independence as is often claimed but as an example of an inter-Ottoman rivalry, or even a civil war within the Ottoman Empire?

Let us begin with the Pasha's own apparently confused feelings about what he set out to accomplish. We have already referred to Mehmed Ali's ambivalent feelings towards the Ottoman Empire and his position as a nominal vassal within it, an ambivalence that shaped his outlook and policies towards Istanbul and the viziers there. To recapitulate, the Pasha was torn between two feelings. On the one hand, he was familiar with the Ottoman world: he was knowledgeable about the Empire's past, well informed about developments in its capital and knew which options were available to decision-makers there and, moreover, he believed that he had a role to play in shaping its future. More importantly, his culture, his manners, and his language were all "Ottoman" in the sense that they were more connected to, and influenced by, the Turkish centre of the Empire than its Arabic-speaking provinces, of one of which he was governor. On the other hand, he also disdained and was disgusted by the way the Empire was run and came to realize, especially when he was repeatedly called upon to help the Sultan out of his troubles, that the Empire was not run in the most efficient way. As was shown in chapter 1, this feeling was especially exacerbated during the Morean campaign when the eventual confronta-

2 See, for a good example, al-Rāf'ī, *'Aṣr Muḥammad 'Alī*, pp. 285–9.

tion with the Sultan was becoming more likely, a confrontation that finally surfaced during the Syrian conflict.

This conviction of the inefficiency and feebleness of the Ottoman administration was due not only to a difference in temperament between him and the Ottoman officials or to variations in the style of governing. There was essentially a qualitative difference between the Sultan's and the Pasha's views of what a government was supposed to be and how it was supposed to function. The way Mehmed Ali organized the government of his province, Egypt, and the manner in which he reaped its potential wealth immediately threw into high relief the inefficiency and corruption of the central government in Istanbul. The developments and innovations that the Pasha introduced in Egypt were not only unprecedented in the Ottoman Empire; they also ushered in a new conception of government which was essentially *interventionist* rather than merely *preservationist* in nature. The new bureaucracy, the modern schooling system, the health system and above all the new model army that the Pasha founded in Egypt all pushed the realms of government into unchartered waters seldom navigated by an Ottoman government before. Looked at from this perspective, the reforms of Mehmed Ali were closer to those of Mahmud II than to those of Selim III. While both sultans were trying hard to arrest the decline of the Empire basically by having tighter control over the provincial economic and administrative activities, Mahmud went much further than his predecessor in extending the aggressive hand of the government to control his subjects' lives both in the central lands as well as in the provinces. In doing so he was certainly inspired by his vali's "experiments" in Egypt. Since coming to power more or less at the same time and for nearly two decades both Sultan and vali had "compatible, even complementary policies in regards the establishment of strict, efficient administrative control over the empire's revenues."[3] Indeed, the Sultan stood to benefit from the Pasha's services in dealing with the Wahhabi unrest, in the extension of control over the Sudan, in attempting to subdue the Greek revolt, and, above all, in his better organization of Egypt itself.

The problem, however, was that although the Pasha might have thought that he was rejuvenating the Empire by showing the officials in Istanbul how to run it,[4] by the late 1820s he had practically managed to create in Egypt another center of power. For while Cairo commanded a smaller proportion of the overall revenue of the Empire, it was being

3 Byron Cannon, *Politics of Law and the Courts in Nineteenth-Century Egypt* (Salt Lake City: University of Utah Press, 1988), p. 12.

4 On this claim, see Rustum, *Origins*, pp. 33–46.

turned into a more efficient and vibrant centre which diverted more and more resources away from Istanbul. It was this ability of Mehmed Ali's government to extract more revenue and to mobilize the resources of his province that enabled him to invade Syria. Seen in this light, the Syrian campaign, therefore, while highlighting the inefficiency and cumbersome nature of Ottoman reform to date, pointed out the way as shown by Mehmed Ali of how affairs of state could be better organized. It is in this respect that Mehmed Ali could have been sincere (as sincere as he could be, that is) in saying that he was interested in reforming and rejuvenating the Ottoman Empire. He had done it in Egypt, so why should not his reforms be copied in the central lands of the Empire? Yet the manner he chose to show the Ottoman officials the folly of their ways, namely by going to war with them, underscores the problems he had in justifying his own actions while still remaining within the Ottoman fold.

The Pasha's feelings towards Egypt were equally problematic. On the one hand, he knew that Egypt was not simply another province within the Ottoman Empire. He was aware that whatever he was successful in achieving during his long career was possible not because he was a docile, obedient vali of the Ottoman Sultan. Rather, he was clearly conscious that his fame and prestige within the Ottoman world was based on his being the vali of Egypt, a wealthy province in the Empire that he had managed to organize in an efficient manner and whose enormous potential wealth he had realized.[5] He also knew that his prestige in the Ottoman world rested on his ability to control and rule that particular province properly and efficiently. In a letter to Ibrahim he once complained of the enormous wage bill that he had to face each year because of the ever-increasing duties that his government was undertaking. He added, however, that "Egypt's ability to pay all these salaries increases its reputation and its honor."[6] When an Ottoman spy was captured during the early days of the Syrian campaign, Mehmed Ali wrote to his son: he said he should show him around the camps and tell him, "You have now known how much the Egyptian officers and soldiers are paid and have seen the degree of comfort and freedom they enjoy. Now go and report this to your Istanbullite colleagues who live in misery and shame and you will have served your faith properly."[7] Just after the fall of Acre the Pasha wrote a general letter to his men to

[5] For an example of his views of how rich Egypt has been through history and how much richer it still could be "since its lands can be cultivated up to four times a year," see Sāmī, ed., *Taqwīm al-Nīl*, II, pp. 525–6, letter dated 4 C 1259/3 June 1843.

[6] S/5/51/2/90 on 17 Za 1247/18 April 1832.

[7] S/5/51/2/92 on 18 Za 1247/19 April 1832.

congratulate them for their "courage and chivalry . . . From now on we want you to show the same qualities . . . towards any one who wants to harm the Egyptian lands [lit. *al-diyār al-Miṣriyya*], lands which have enhanced our position and increased our reputation."[8]

On the other hand, the Pasha harbored very negative views towards the population of Egypt. He despised the fellahin and could not respect them except as a source of cheap and hardworking manpower. He once ordered a certain legal code to be translated from a European language so that it could be applied in Egypt. He told the translator, however, not to copy the European model blindly, since the law suited the "Europeans [who are] enlightened and civilized people. Our people, however are like wild beasts [*vahşlar*] for whom obviously this law will not be suitable."[9] On another occasion he said that "the inhabitants of our province, Egypt, are of three kinds. The first does not care except about themselves. The second, although they can be loyal and kind, are devoid of any sense of discretion. The third are in the same position as animals."[10]

Yet, he obviously knew that it was these "animals" who were the source of his wealth and good fortune. Moreover, they were cheap and docile for the most part. When he imported two steamships from Britain, the British technicians and workers manning them caused a lot of problems, basically because they were expensive, "stubborn and unreliable." The Pasha then thought of appointing a couple of Egyptian men as assistants to the British workers to learn from them the job so that he could get rid of them eventually.[11]

The Pasha's opinions about his Egyptian subjects are probably best shown by reviewing the rationale behind his educational policies. In spite of the fact that the Pasha is often praised for spreading education, opening one school after the other, sending students to Europe and founding a modern press and the first regular newspaper in the East, he still had strong reservations regarding educating the masses. In a letter to his son, Ibrahim, answering his request to open new schools and to admit more native Egyptians, the Pasha said that he had no intention of spreading education among the masses in Egypt. He told his son to look at what happened to European monarchs when they attempted to educate their poor. He added that he should satisfy himself with educating a limited number of people who could assume key positions

[8] Rustum, ed., *Uṣūl*, II, p. 13, letter dated 21 M 1248/20 June 1832.

[9] S/1/48/4/204 on 11 S 1249/30 June 1833. For a very distorted translation of this letter see Sāmī, ed., *Taqwīm al-Nīl*, II, p. 413, where he has the Pasha simply say that there was no need to fetch the (original) text from Europe "since it is unsuitable."

[10] S/5/51/2/57 on 5 L 1247/8 March 1832.

[11] S/1/48/2/183 on 11 S 1241/25 September 1825.

in his administration and give up ideas about generalizing education.[12] Even after founding these schools he was displeased because they were mostly full of Arabic-speaking Egyptian students. He wrote to Ibrahim while he was in Anatolia at the height of the war against the Ottomans telling him to try to attract (*rıza ile alınıp*) some Turks from areas around Adana, Maraş and Orfa and send them to schools in Egypt.[13]

In short, Mehmed Ali's position vis-à-vis the Ottoman Sultan, on the one hand, and the fellah subjects, on the other, is very similar to that of a feudal lord. Above him loomed the authority of the Sultan, an authority that resembled that of a feudal overlord above that of his vassals and an authority that Mehmed Ali could, and did, challenge. Similarly, the Pasha viewed Egypt as his own personal fief. "Our lord, the *Wali al-Niʿam*," a report published in the *Vakayi-i Mısıriyye* proclaimed, "is so dedicated to the welfare of the country . . . that he aims at viewing all Egyptian lands (*al-aqālīm al-Miṣriyya kāffatan*) as his own personal domain (*kadāʾiratihi al-khāṣṣa*), and to have all who live on it, young or old, grow up in his grace as his own children."[14] Given his inherently contradictory position vis-à-vis both the Sultan in Istanbul and the Egyptian population, Mehmed Ali had nothing to resort to but his own self and his own name to legitimate his rule. When in 1826 he decided on a design for his army's flags, an important symbol of power, the Pasha chose one that was similar to that used by Sultan Mahmud II,[15] and to mark his insignia of power in a manner that would distinguish them from those of his nominal ruler, he had nothing to resort to except his own name. To honor the two regiments which were particularly brave during the siege of Acre, the Pasha ordered two flags to be handed to the regiments' colonels, with the words "Mehmed Ali" inscribed on them.[16] Similarly, to commemorate the fall of Acre a medal was cast with his name inscribed on it in precious stones.[17] In 1836 he ordered the head of his navy to hang wooden plaques inscribed with his name in the cabins of every line-of-battle ship.[18] Most telling is the answer he gave to Ibrahim when the latter had reached Kütahia, a day's marching distance from Istanbul,

12 S/1/51/7/277 on 29 Z 1251/19 March 1836.
13 S/5/47/2/263 on 19 Ş 1255/28 October 1839.
14 *Vekayi-i Mısıriyye*, issue no. 3, 29 C 1244/6 January 1829; quoted in Ṣubḥī, *Tārīkh al-Ḥayāh al-Niyābiyya*, V, p. 14. Ṣubḥī quotes from the Arabic version of the *Vekayi*.
15 Like the Ottoman flag Mehmed Ali's flags were red in color; see S/1/47/7/350 on 25 N 1239/25 May 1824. The only difference was in the shape of the stars on the flag: whereas the Ottoman star had six points, the Egyptian one had only five; Zakī, *al-Aʿlām*, p. 40.
16 Sāmī, ed., *Taqwīm al-Nīl*, II, pp. 404–5, letter dated 21 R 1248/17 September 1832.
17 *Ibid.*, p. 397, letter dated 22 M 1248/21 June 1832.
18 *Ibid.*, p. 473, letter dated 16 C 1252/28 September 1836.

and when his victorious son was pleading with him to press for independence. In response to these repeated pleas, and finding no plausible excuses to legitimate his rebellion against the Sultan, Mehmed Ali replied saying, "My Mehmed Ali-ness is enough for me."[19]

It would be erroneous therefore to argue that when the Pasha decided to officially ask for independence from the Ottoman Empire in May 1838 he was acting on behalf of the Egyptian population and expressing their sentiments, sentiments that made them see themselves as different and distinct from other subjects of the Ottoman Sultan. What prompted the Pasha to make this bold move, rather, was his desire to secure his efforts in Egypt to his family and his sons after him. As John Campbell, the British Consul-General in 1838, said "he cannot . . . ever permit all [the] establishments [that he founded in Egypt over thirty years] to revert to the Porte and be lost at his death, and that he should have the pang of feeling that all his labours should merely have been for the Porte which would allow them to go to ruin, whilst his own family and children would be exposed to want and perhaps even to be put to death."[20] These were the reasons he put to the British government for his asking for independence from the Ottoman Empire. There is nothing here or elsewhere in the contemporary documents to show that he had any illusions about the nature of his struggle with the Sultan. That struggle was a dynastic one and it was conceived of as such by him and his contemporaries.

The wars that the Pasha fought, and in particular those that were waged against the Ottoman Sultan, could not therefore be viewed as wars of national independence, aimed at liberating the Egyptians from the "Turkish yoke," nor could they be compared to those that the Greeks fought against the Sultan. Not only would the thousands of fellahin who made up the bulk of his fighting force have found this claim difficult to believe, but also the Pasha himself could think of these wars only along dynastic lines. He repeatedly said that what he was seeking to do was to foil the intrigues directed against "our family,"[21] and hoped for nothing more than to "strengthen the foundations of my dynasty,"[22] and to "carve a place for my family and my dynasty's families in history to be remembered in four or five centuries' time."[23]

19 Sham 31/7, on 7 M 1251/5 May 1835. On Mehmed Ali's reluctance to use any titles or attach any prefixes to his name, see FO 78/147, Salt, 24 September 1826.

20 FO. 78/342, Campbell, 25 May 1838; quoted in Dodwell, *Founder of Modern Egypt*, p. 171.

21 S/5/51/2/10 on 2 Ca 1248/27 September 1832.

22 S/5/47/2/16 on 30 Ş 1251/20 December 1835.

23 S/5/47/2/160 on 6 Ca 1255/18 July 1839.

The Pasha and his foes

If one sees Mehmed Ali as a governor of an Ottoman province who was constantly concerned about his position within the Empire and was anxious about the future of his family after his death, as he himself certainly was, then the person who appears as the Pasha's nemesis whom he spent all his life fighting was not Sultan Mahmud, not even Lord Palmerston, the British Foreign Secretary (to whom we will turn shortly), but Mehmed Husrev Pasha, his old enemy whom he first encountered in 1801 and who since then had been appointed as governor of various provinces in Anatolia and Rumelia, as Grand Admiral of the Ottoman navy, who eventually became Grand Vizier more than once in his long career of public service. In fact, the careers and mentalities of both men appear remarkably similar: both were keen, yet distant, observers of the European scene; both were interested in military reform; and both were concerned about the fate of the Empire and eager to help defend it. But whereas Mehmed Ali succeeded in making Egypt into his own fief and in exploiting it for himself and his family while at the same time thinking that he was thus offering a model of how the Empire could be reformed, Husrev was much less fortunate. He never had a wealthy province like Mehmed Ali's on which to try out on a small scale his ideas of how to rejuvenate the Empire, and while being a protégé of reform-minded officials, he was never as successful as the Egyptian Pasha was in putting his ideas of military refom into practice, this in spite of occupying very senior posts in the Empire's military and civilian administration during his long and active career. While there were many obstacles that stood in Husrev's way of implementing his ideas, one of the most important was Mehmed Ali himself. This feeling of animosity was heartily reciprocated since the Egyptian Pasha was convinced that Husrev was leading a faction in Istanbul that was determined to thwart his efforts and to deny him the fruits of his various military victories over the Sultan's armies.[24]

Their story together starts in 1801 when they independently joined an Ottoman naval force that the Sultan dispatched to Egypt to help British troops evict Napoleon's *Armée d'Orient* from the wealthy province.[25] The force was headed by Küçük Hüseyin Pasha, a close friend of Sultan Selim who was appointed as Grand Admiral in 1792

[24] The following account, besides relying on the sources mentioned below, is also based on Halil İnalçık, "Husrev Paşa," in *İslam Ansiklopedisi* (Istanbul: Milli Eğitim Basımevi, 1950), V, pt. 1, pp. 609–16.

[25] A land force was also dispatched by the Sultan headed by the Grand Vizier himself; for how it was perceived and judged by contemporary British officers, see Macksey, *British Victory*, pp. 21–2, 24–6, and 178–9.

and who was a strong supporter of naval reform.[26] Since Husrev was himself a protégé of the Grand Admiral, he was appointed as his lieutenant and joined him on his expedition to Egypt.[27] For his part, Mehmed Ali was appointed as second-in-command of a force of 300 troops of Albanian origin that was headed by a certain Tahir Pasha.[28] After the British had managed to evict the French from Egypt, it was natural for Istanbul to appoint the most senior Ottoman official in the campaign as governor of Egypt in recognition of his efforts in collaborating with the British in their military activities. Since both the Grand Vizier and the Grand Admiral had earlier left for Istanbul, Husrev was the Sultan's best choice and he was soon appointed as vali of Egypt. In that way Husrev found himself with a wealthy province to rule in the name of the Sultan and he began to try out his ideas of military reform. He did not have much time to do so, however; soon after he was confirmed as vali the Albanian troops under Tahir revolted and forced him to flee for his life to Damietta. Tahir himself was then assassinated, apparently at the hand of some of Mehmed Ali's men, and in time Mehmed Ali turned against Husrev, took him prisoner and eventually had him deported from Egypt. Two years later Mehmed Ali was himself confirmed as vali of the prized province. Thus, through trickery and deception Mehmed Ali managed to deny Husrev his precious prize and instead snatched it for himself. Their deep-seated mutual hostility can be said to have started from that early time and it continued throughout their long lives.[29]

After being appointed to other posts including that of Governor of Bosnia during the Serbian revolt of 1806 and later as vali of Erzurum during the Kurdish rebellion (1818), Husrev was finally appointed as Grand Admiral of the Ottoman navy during the Greek war (December 1822). While he managed to construct a fleet of small vessels capable of maneuvering in the shallow waters of the Aegean and was thus successful in cutting the lines of communication of the Greek rebels, he could not reap the rewards of his innovative moves because of the appearance of Mehmed Ali's son, Ibrahim, on the theater of operations. We have already seen how much Husrev's position as Grand Admiral

[26] Shaw, *Between Old and New*, pp. 87–8, 155. Marsot, misreading Sabry (*L'Empire égyptien*, p. 24), says that it was Husrev who headed the Ottoman Navy; al-Sayyid Marsot, *Egypt*, p. 31.

[27] Shaw, *Between Old and New*, p. 274. For Küçük Hüseyin's arrival in Abū Qīr in March 1801, see al-Jabartī, *'Ajā'ib al-Āthār*, III, p. 154 (events of Dhū'l-Qi'da, 1215), and Walsh, *Campaign in Egypt*, pp. 108, 111.

[28] For a description of this force, see Macksey, *British Victory*, p. 155.

[29] al-Jabartī, *'Ajā'ib al-Āthār*, III, pp. 249–51; Shaw, *Between Old and New*, pp. 274, 286–7; Ghorbal, *Egyptian Question*, pp. 207–8, 211. Mehmed Ali died at the age of eighty in 1849, while Husrev died six years later in 1855 aged more than ninety.

was resented by Mehmed Ali since he was believed to have been interfering in the activities of his son. After months of trying to work together, Ibrahim wrote to his father's agent in Istanbul, Najib Efendi, informing him that there was little chance of the success of the joint efforts of the Egyptian and Ottoman naval forces since their commands were not unified. He added that they could not be unified or co-ordinated, however, because of the "old and well-entrenched hatred that Husrev has towards our family."[30] In the event, and as we saw in chapter 1 above, Husrev was removed from the command of the Ottoman navy as a result of Mehmed Ali's pressure, adding yet another grudge to those that Husrev held against his old enemy.

Shortly afterwards and soon after the formation of Mahmud's new *nizami* army, the *Asaker-i Mansure-yi Muhammadiyye*, Husrev was appointed as Serasker and began to introduce military refoms in a way that resembled those that Mehmed Ali had been introducing in Egypt, although on a smaller scale. He continued to occupy that position until the outbreak of the Syrian war. It was Husrev's personal former slave and protégé, Mehmed Raşid Pasha, whom Ibrahim captured in Konia only a few months after Raşid had been appointed as Grand Vizer at Husrev's insistence. Given Husrev's influence in the capital, his easy access to the Sultan and his ability to affect matters in the Palace, Mehmed Ali and Nagib Efendi felt that his personal presence there damaged their interests. After the conclusion of the truce of Kütahia (March 1833) whereby Ibrahim was named as governor of the Syrian provinces, while Mehmed Ali was reinstated in his position as vali of Egypt, Husrev continued to be seen by Mehmed Ali as his main obstacle in Istanbul.

The truce of Kütahia, it has to be remembered, was not a permanent settlement; it was an agreement that neither Sultan nor vali put their signatures to and, moreover, its terms were to be renewed each year, giving Mehmed Ali the feeling that he had still not guaranteed for his family the secure future he was striving for. In addition, Mehmed Ali was required to pay an annual tribute to Istanbul, the amount of which was one of the most contentious issues in the years between 1833 and 1839: while the Sultan was claiming significant arrears, the Pasha refused to pay them. This issue became more acrimonious since the Pasha was convinced that the presence of Husrev as Serasker in Istanbul and his proximity to the Sultan made Mahmud particularly susceptible to his intrigues. The Pasha attempted, therefore, to impress upon the Sultan that as long as his old enemy continued to be present in the

30 Bahr Barra 9/36, on 25 M 1240/20 September 1824.

Divan, there would always be problems between Sultan and vali. He therefore proposed that "if the Sultan would only consent to remove [Husrev] from his councils, he [i.e. Mehmed Ali] would not only pay the tribute regularly . . ., but he would also pay a great part of what the Sultan demanded as arrears."[31]

The rivalry between the two old men had its final showdown immediately after the battle of Nezib (24 June 1839). As we have seen, the battle resulted in an astounding victory for Ibrahim. A week later and before news of the disaster reached him, Sultan Mahmud died and was succeeded to the throne by his sixteen-year old son, Abdul-Mecid. In the panic that followed in Istanbul the Grand Admiral, Ahmed Fevzi Pasha, instead of co-ordinating his efforts with those of the Serasker, as had been planned, and effecting a popular uprising among the Syrian population against Mehmed Ali's rule there, decided to head for Alexandria not to bombard it but to hand the entire Ottoman fleet to Mehmed Ali.[32] Thus in little less than a month the Ottoman Empire lost its Sultan, its army, and its navy and Mehmed Ali was left as the single most powerful man in the Empire. He had under his command a powerful army that had so far been victorious in all the major battles it had fought. He also had in Alexandria a combined Ottoman–Egyptian fleet that was capable of establishing effective control over the waters of the eastern Mediterranean and which was an important bargaining card to use in the coming negotiations with Istanbul. Mehmed Ali thus thought that the scene was set for him to appear on center stage in the capital and to dictate to the young Sultan and his defenseless Porte his conditions of "peace": recognition as independent ruler of all the lands he had seized and for this recognition to be passed on to his children after his death.

However, instead of finding himself being invited to Istanbul to accept these terms graciously, he discovered to his greatest dismay that his old enemy, Husrev Pasha, had literally seized power in Istanbul: during Mahmud's funeral he had snatched the imperial seals and appointed himself as Grand Vizier.[33] Immediately after being informed of Husrev's dramatic *coup de force* and his "appointment" to the Grand

[31] FO 78/245, Campbell, 10 May 1834; quoted in Dodwell, *Founder of Modern Egypt*, p. 155.

[32] He did this when he thought that Husrev was going to hand over the fleet to the Russians and that they were together going to attack Mehmed Ali. For Mehmed Ali's letter to Ahmed Fevzi warning him of Husrev's intrigues and the likelihood of surrendering the fleet to the Russians and "inviting him to Alexandria to discuss matters," see S/5/47/2/150 on 27 R 1255/11 July 1839.

[33] News of this reached Mehmed Ali on 10 July 1839: S/5/47/2/148 on 26 R 1255/10 July 1839.

Vizirate, Mehmed Ali started a ferocious campaign to have him deposed. On 16 August he sent a letter to the new Serasker, Halil Pasha, urging him to depose Husrev.[34] The following day he wrote a letter to the Valide Sultan, the Sultan's mother, to the same effect.[35] This was followed by a stern letter to Husrev himself warning him that if he did not resign, then the bloodshed would not be stopped.[36] Other letters and circulars were also sent to various senior, and not so senior, officals in Istanbul, all pressing for Husrev's dismissal.[37]

Husrev, however, was not dismissed; on the contrary, he was stubborn and himself asked his old rival to give up all his possessions and be satisfied with the pashalık of Egypt alone. When Mehmed Ali received these "peace offers" he wrote to his old enemy wondering what would force him to accept such terms when he had earlier refused better ones offered by Mahmud. He again repeated his demand to Husrev to resign and told him that if he was concerned about his livelihood after retirement, then he, Mehmed Ali, promised to meet all his expenses and those of his household, no matter how large these might be. He even invited him to retire with him in the Hijaz where, he explained, he had built himself two residences, a winter one in Mecca and a summer one in Ṭāʾif where they could both retire in peace, devote their time to prayer and meditation, and preserve good and illustrious names for themselves in history books![38]

What prevented their age-old rivalry from being resolved in this happy and blissful manner was not the stubbornness of Husrev, who, as much as he hated Mehmed Ali, would not have been able to stand this formidable pressure. It was, rather, the unified position that Europe took for the first time in the rivalry between the Sultan and the Egyptian vali: at five in the morning of the very same day that Husrev was to reply to Mehmed Ali's demands (27 July 1839) the representatives of the five European powers (Great Britain, France, Prussia, Austria and Russia) handed the Grand Vizier a collective note asking the Porte "to suspend any final determination [of the Eastern Question] without their concurrence."[39] This gave Husrev the breathing space he needed, and with a unified Europe behind him, which denied Mehmed Ali the

[34] S/5/47/2/181 on 5 Ca 1255/16 August 1839.

[35] S/5/47/2/182 on 6 Ca 1255/17 August 1839.

[36] S/5/47/2/190 on 15 Ca 1255/26 August 1839.

[37] See, for example, the circular to twenty-four dignitaries, court officials and provincial governors in S/5/47/2/189 on 13 Ca 1255/24 August 1839.

[38] S/5/47/2/208 on 5 C 1255/16 August 1839.

[39] For the text of the "Note," see J. C. Hurewitz, *The Middle East and North Africa in World Politics: A Documentary Record.* Volume. I: *European Expansion, 1535–1914* (New Haven: Yale University Press, 1975), p. 268.

French assistance he was counting on, he not only rejected the vali's demands for his own resignation, but repeated *his* demands that the vali hand back areas he had occupied and return the Ottoman fleet that had defected to Alexandria. In the event, and mainly because of British pressure, Mehmed Ali was forced to comply.

Not before putting up a strong and hopeless resistance, though.[40] On 7 August 1839 the young Sultan dispatched Munib Efendi, Mehmed Ali's new agent in Istanbul, with a clear and stern message to Cairo telling the Pasha that the matter was now not in his or Husrev's hands but was being decided by the European representatives in Istanbul.[41] Ten days later the British and French Consuls-General in Cairo met with the Pasha and told him that if he did not comply, then he stood a chance of having both the British and French fleets "arriving" at Alexandria. To this he responded by saying that he would block the port of the city with an iron chain, summon his troops from Arabia, and order Ibrahim to march on to Anatolia. Campbell told him that this would be fatal and if he did proceed with such a plan, then he would have to fight the Russians, not the Turks. The Pasha was still adamant and said that if the Powers wanted blood to be shed, then blood he would shed.[42]

Finally, in desperation, and when it became clear that the European powers were not bluffing, he wrote to Ibrahim on 23 August and confided in him what he suspected most: a Russian–British agreement to split the Ottoman Empire, whereby Russia would occupy Istanbul and Britain Egypt. He added that if his suspicions were not correct and if the European powers were sincere in what they said, then it would mean that they would force him to withdraw his troops from Syria and Arabia to prevent the partition of the Empire.[43] Given these two bleak alternatives, he said, there was no choice for him but to fight. "And if you [i.e. Ibrahim] think that it would not be wise to fight the Europeans and that we have no chance of defeating them, then I will have to agree

[40] Besides using sources cited below, the following account is also based on Temperley, *Near East*, chs. 3–5; Dodwell, *Founder of Modern Egypt*, ch. 6, al-Rāfʿī, *ʿAṣr Muḥammad ʿAlī*, chs. 8–9 and Sabry, *L'Empire égyptien*, chs. 10–12.

[41] S/5/47/2/173 on 25 Ca 1255/7 August 1839.

[42] S/5/47/2/177 on 5 C 1255/16 August 1839. See also the following letter (no. 178, dated on the same day) addressed to Husrev in which he reiterated his demands for his resignation and for Syria to be legally granted to him.

[43] During the Morean war he wrote to Nagib Efendi in Istanbul telling him "although I may be well versed in European mercantile affairs, I am ignorant when it comes to its political situation" (Bahr Barra 12/7, on 14 Ra 1243/6 October 1827). To contemplate that Britain might be agreeing with Russia on the partition of the Ottoman Empire shows that he was still as ignorant of the European "political situation" in 1839 as he had been fifteen years earlier.

with you. But not all things are to be conducted rationally, and occasionally one has to face matters that are contrary to rational and political calculations by trusting in Fate as destined by God, and depend on His mercy and His Prophet's intercession."[44]

True to his word, and riding a false sense of elation, he ordered his son not to withdraw from Syria or to pull back any forces from any other provinces. And for an entire year there was a tense deadlock of the "Eastern Question": the Pasha would not withdraw his troops nor return the navy to the Sultan and, at the same time, the Sultan would not grant Mehmed Ali the much desired recognition of independence. In response to the Pasha's intransigent position, Palmerston convened a Convention in London in July 1840, "The Convention for the Pacification of the Levant," to which all the major European powers (this time, however, France declined to join the Concert of Europe) were invited; this gave the Pasha an ultimatum to withdraw from Syria, Adana, Crete and Arabia.[45] When he still refused to comply, a British force landed in Beirut in September and forced Ibrahim to withdraw to Egypt. By December the Pasha had no choice but to accept the conditions laid down by the British-led European powers. Finally, on 1 June 1841, the Sultan issued a firman naming Mehmed Ali as governor of Egypt for life and granting his male descendants the hereditary rights of the governorship of Egypt. In addition, though, the firman stipulated that the Pasha reduce the size of his army to 18,000 troops in peace-time. Moreover, the Sultan added that "all the Treaties concluded and to be concluded between my Sublime Porte and the friendly Powers shall be completely executed in the Province of Egypt likewise."[46]

This last stipulation was the most significant for it clearly referred to the Balta Liman Commercial Convention that had been signed in 1838 between the Sublime Porte and the British Empire. In that Convention the Ottoman Empire's import and export duties were fixed, the level of internal duties was drastically reduced and, most importantly, monopolies within all the provinces of the Ottoman Empire were banned.[47] Having effectively stripped the Pasha of his army which formed a significant outlet for his locally produced commodities, forced him to withdraw from Syria, Crete and Arabia, and coerced him to abolish internal monopolies, Britain, it is argued, succeeded in ruining

[44] S/5/47/2/212 on 12 C 1255/23 August 1839. Contrast this remark with his own rational and sober calculation before the Navarino disaster: see note 95 in chapter 1.

[45] For the text of the Convention's resolutions, see Hurewitz, *Middle East*, pp. 271–5.

[46] For the text of the firman, see *ibid.*, pp. 276–8.

[47] See *ibid.*, pp. 265–6, for the text of the Convention.

Mehmed Ali's commercial and industrial enterprises and thus aborted one of the most impressive development projects outside of Europe.[48] Since these crucial events are often presented in a manner that shows European malice towards Egypt which prevented her from gaining full independence,[49] it is necessary to discuss this issue and in particular Britain's reasons for opposing Mehmed Ali.

It is often asserted that the reason why Britain opposed Mehmed Ali was because the "industrialization" policy which he was introducing in Egypt threatened British economic interests in the area. The Pasha was considered a menace for Britain and her economic interests because he attempted to produce more and more commodities locally, had a "textile industry [that] was growing, and [through monopolizing trade] dominated the potential markets that Britain coveted."[50] Realizing that her economic interests would be harmed by his policies, Britain was determined to frustrate them. She was given such an opportunity when the Porte agreed to sign the Balta Liman Convention of 1838 banning monopolies throughout the Empire, and was specifically aimed at the Pasha's monopolies that barred British goods from the areas under his control and at the same time allowed him to have the protection needed to defend his nascent industry. As a result of the Convention "his attempts at economic self-sufficiency and industrialization were to be arrested, and in their place he was assured of a permanent influx of foreign capital and foreign goods, which would indubitably deprive the country of any financial and economic independence."[51]

This, however, is to misread British interests in the Middle East in the nineteeth century and her entire foreign policy during the crucial decades of the 1830s and 1840s. There is no doubt that Britain opposed Mehmed Ali strongly and resolutely and that this animosity was best represented by Lord Palmerston, the Foreign Secretary for most of the 1830s (1830–4, 1835–41, and later 1846–51) who took a strong personal dislike to the Pasha. It is also true that in his fight against Mehmed Ali Palmerston wanted to abolish his monopolies and that the Balta Liman Convention was categorical in its insistence on banning all commercial monopolies throughout the Empire. Yet British hostility and Palmerston's personal animosity could not have been caused only by any perceived threat posed by the nascent Egyptian industry to the mighty British manufactures. For at the peak of the Pasha's "industriali-

48 For this argument see Batou, "Muhammad-ʿAli's Egypt"; and al-Sayyid Marsot, *Egypt*, pp. 238–57.

49 al-Rāfʿī, *ʿAṣr Muḥammad ʿAlī*, pp. 286ff.

50 al-Sayyid Marsot, *Egypt*, p. 237.

51 *Ibid.*, p. 247. For a similar argument, see Fahmy, *Revolution*; and al-Rāfiʿī, *ʿAṣr Muḥammad ʿAlī*.

Plate 8 "Henry-John Temple, Viscount Palmerston"

zation" schemes the country had no more than seven or eight steam engines, most of the power of the thirty-odd "industrial" establishments being supplied by the workers themselves.[52] (St. John in his tour of the country in the 1830s said that "the mills are in ruins, and immense heaps of machinery, no longer employed, are covered with rust, and

52 For a discussion of the Pasha's interest in "industrialization," see Roger Owen, *The Middle East and the World Economy, 1800–1914* (London: Tauris, 1993), pp. 69–76.

mouldering to decay."[53]) Nor was Britain concerned about Mehmed Ali closing off the Egyptian market to British goods for, as Marsot states, the Pasha "tried to woo British friendship by promising all manner of facilities to British trade."[54] Partly as a result of this assistance the value of British exports to Egypt increased from £49,377 in 1827 to £237,444 in 1840, while its exports of cotton textiles, supposedly the one item that the Pasha's "factories" were most efficient at producing, increased from £27,939 to £179,328 over the same period.[55]

That some of the country's products were processed locally rather than exported in a raw form to British factories must have been irksome to Palmerston. He might also have been affronted by the Pasha's "illiberal" policies of conscription, corvée and high taxation.[56] Palmerston, however, was concerned above all about the dangers that the Pasha's territorial expansion were causing to Istanbul. These military activities, Palmerston rightly believed, were pushing Istanbul to seek assistance from the Russians who were only too eager to provide the Sultan with all the help he needed, thus giving them the perfect opportunity to interfere in Ottoman affairs. It was the prospect of Russia's increased influence in Istanbul and its southward expansion towards India rather than any loss of actual or potential markets in the eastern Mediterranean that inflamed Palmerston's feelings against Mehmed Ali's monopoly policies. For it was precisely the system of monopolies that the Pasha had introduced, Palmerston again rightly thought, that allowed the Pasha to syphon profits accrued from the agricultural and commercial sectors to the military, thus enabling him to build a powerful army and a formidable navy that he then used to threaten the Sultan's dominions. Ultimately Palmerston's greatest concern was for British possessions in Asia; his greatest fear was that Russia might interfere there. In other words, what was at stake was the British market in Asia rather than the much smaller ones in the eastern Mediterranean. Both London and Bombay viewed Mehmed Ali as causing a grave threat to these important markets by his giving the Russians the opportunity and the pretext to encroach onto Ottoman lands, and possibly to do away with the Ottoman Empire altogether.

[53] St. John, *Egypt*, II, p. 421. One should be careful in reading St. John, though, since in this particular respect he was, as a matter of principle, against introducing the "manufacturing system" in Egypt.

[54] al-Sayyid Marsot, *Egypt*, p. 237.

[55] Owen, *The Middle East*, tables 3.6 and 3.7, p. 85. All figures are annual averages.

[56] Being a landlord himself Palmerston was enraged by the Pasha's "land reform" policies in Crete where there was an attempt to redistribute land to the poor peasants to enhance productivity. For Palmerston's views on this, see Jasper Ridley, *Lord Palmerston* (London: Constable, 1970), p. 211.

Palmerston's motto of "the preservation of the integrity of the Ottoman Empire" was his most effective bulwark against possible Russian aggression and was not a "malicious" act directed at Egypt.[57]

That it was fear of Russia's expansion more than concern over British markets in the eastern Mediterranean that caused Palmerston's alarm at Mehmed Ali's monopolies is further corroborated by following the British Foreign Secretary's policies towards the Pasha from the early months of the first Syrian crisis of 1831–3 to the crucial ones of the second crisis of 1839–41. As mentioned in chapter 1 during the early months of the first crisis the British Foreign Secretary had almost nothing to say, apparently preferring to view the crisis as a purely Ottoman affair. "There is not a single word [from Palmerston] either to Constantinople and Alexandria or to the British ambassadors at Paris, Vienna, and St. Petersburg; hardly any observation can be noticed during 1832 on despatches coming from these centers and touching on the subject of the Syrian war."[58] This has prompted some historians to argue that Palmerston had not made up his mind yet as to which horse to back, as it were, the Sultan or Mehmed Ali.[59] At this crucial time the question in Palmerston's mind was: would British interests be harmed more if Mehmed Ali was opposed by Britain, which would cause him to be swayed even more towards France and therefore increase that country's influence in Egypt, or if he were allowed to get away with his attack on the Sultan, thus jeopardizing the very existence of the Ottoman Empire? Palmerston made up his mind as early as September 1832 that

> if the Sultan is beat his empire may tumble to pieces, and the way in which the fragments may be disposed of may essentially affect the balance of power in Europe; Russia would profit by the scramble, to a degree which might be highly inconvenient to her neighbors. It is true that if we repel Mehemet's advances & the French receive them, and he should hold his ground, French influence will gain strength in Egypt, but after all perhaps that would not do us any great harm till we went to war with France, and then our naval superiority would bring us back the friendship of Mehemet who would not like his navy to be sent to an English port.[60]

57 See his logic spelled out in his famous note to the British ambassador to Vienna on 28 June 1839 reproduced in Hurewitz, *Middle East*, pp. 267–8. For British public opinion that Palmerston was not addressing the "Russian threat" effectively, see Ridley, *Palmerston*, pp. 213–16 and Kenneth Bourne, *Palmerston: The Early Years, 1784–1841* (London: Allen Lane, 1982), pp. 561ff.

58 Vereté, "Palmerston and the Levant Crisis," p. 145.

59 F. S. Rodkey, "The attempts of Briggs and Company to guide British policy in the Levant in the interest of Mehemet Ali Pasha, 1821–1841," *Journal of Modern History*, 5 (1933), p. 338; Temperley, *Near East*, p. 63.

60 Palmerston to Grey, 6 September 1832; quoted in Bourne, *Palmerston*, p. 376.

Five months later whatever hesitation he had earlier had on the relative benefits of supporting Mehmed Ali or the Sultan was gone. He had decided that British interests were certainly to be served if Britain stood by the Sultan.

We ought to tell the Pasha forthwith to retire to Egypt [he wrote to Granville, the Ambassador to Paris] . . . That the possession of Syria must carry with it that of Bagdad, a glance of the map will serve to shew . . . But it is very doubtful whether it could be for the advantage of England that the Sultan should be so weakened and that a new state should be created in Egypt, Syria and Bagdad. It is obvious that so great a defalcation from the territory and resources of the Sultan would render him less able than he is now to resist Russia, and that he would really become her vassal . . . This is by no means what we wish . . ."[61]

Nevertheless, and in spite of this clear position, when in November 1832 the Sultan requested British naval protection to defend Istanbul, Palmerston answered him four months later saying that Britain could not order the dispatch of the required squadron. This he was forced to do not out of lack of conviction, but because his colleagues in the cabinet thought that the navy could not be spared to leave the European theater of operations where it was needed to enforce economic sanctions against Holland.[62] The Sultan therefore was left with no option other than to ask for Russian assistance.[63] Palmerston's worst fears came true: instead of seeing British ships in Istanbul, it was the Russian fleet that was allowed to moor there in February 1833. As if this was not enough Russia and the Ottoman Empire together signed the Hünkar İskelesi Treaty in July which had a secret clause changing the traditional policy of the Porte of excluding all foreign ships from the Sea of Marmara, by excepting Russian ships from that stipulation. When informed about the treaty, Palmerston was enraged not so much about the secret clause as about the stipulation that both signatories consult each other before taking any step regarding foreign affairs. As far as Palmerston was concerned, this meant that "the Russian Ambassador becomes chief Cabinet minister to the Sultan."[64] It was this increased influence of Russia in Ottoman affairs that Palmerston was most apprehensive about. This apprehension was based on his gradual realization that

[61] GD 29 (The Granville Papers in the Gifts and Deposits Collection of the PRO), box 415: Palmerston to Granville, 29 January 1833; quoted in *ibid.*, p. 150.

[62] Temperley, *Near East*, pp. 63–4; Ridley, *Palmerston*, p. 160.

[63] For the cabinet's views, see *ibid.* Years later Palmerston wrote that "There is nothing that has happened since I have been in this office which I regret so much as that tremendous blunder of the English government. But it was not my fault; I tried hard to persuade the Cabinet to let me take the step:" quoted in *ibid.*

[64] *Ibid.*, pp. 160–1. The text of the treaty and the British protest to it is in Hurewitz, *Middle East*, pp. 252–4.

British interests in Europe, which he believed to be best protected by maintaining the existing balance of power, were equally threatened by the Pasha's latest moves as were Britain's interests in Asia which, in turn, he believed to be best protected by strengthening Turkey to function as a buffer between Russia and India. For as Palmerston himself said he did not object, in principle, to Mehmed Ali's gaining independence or to his founding "an Arab kingdom including all the countries of which Arabic is the language. There might be no harm in such a thing in itself; but as it would necessarily imply the dismemberment of Turkey, we could not agree to it."[65]

It was not the Pasha's monopolies policy as such that Palmerston attacked, rather, it was Mehmed Ali's expansionist policy which posed serious challenges to the Sultan's empire, as had been made clear by the Hünkar İskelesi Treaty of July 1833. As far as Britain was concerned this treaty highlighted the failure of the Sultan to fulfill the duties that his empire as a European and an Asiatic one was supposed to perform: the European duty of defending the Straits, and the Asiatic one of checking Russian designs on areas bordering India. By prompting the Russian fleet to dock in Istanbul and by increasing Russian political influence there Mehmed Ali was seen in London and Bombay as giving the Russians the opportunity to undermine the stability of the Ottoman Empire, and so Palmerston believed that Mehmed Ali "might not himself destroy Turkey; [but] he might give Russia the chance to do so later."[66]

It appears that the Pasha was aware of these British fears and that he attempted to allay them by suggesting that Britain join a coalition of forces composed of the Sultan in Istanbul, the Shah of Iran, and himself as an aggrandized Pasha in Cairo who would be allowed to control, in addition to Egypt, Syria and Mesopotamia. Such a coalition of forces, Mehmed Ali argued, would be a strong deterrent against Russian designs in Asia.[67] As early as January 1833, however, Palmerston had already received a report from Henry Ellis, a member of the influential Board of Control of India, strongly arguing against such a scheme. In this report Ellis warned the Foreign Secretary against ignoring the Pasha's expansionary moves and argued that Britain would not have her interests served by allowing the Pasha to delve in Indian affairs. For Ellis was convinced that "the political and commercial interests of Great

65 Palmerston to Temple, 21 March 1833, quoted in Edward Ingram, *The Beginning of the Great Game in Asia, 1828–1834* (Oxford: Clarendon Press, 1979), p. 242.

66 *Ibid.*

67 See his remarks to this effect that were relayed through Campbell to Palmerston in Campbell to Ponsonby, private, 21 August 1834, in same to Palmerston, no. 42, 25 August 1834, FO 78/246; quoted in Ingram, *Great Game*, p. 278.

Britain . . . will be best consulted by having these provinces placed, as they are now, under the Government to whom relations with India, and Persia, are matters of very secondary, rather than primary importance."[68] In other words, Mehmed Ali's suggestion that through this coalition he could better defend Britain's interest against Russia's designs was not to be accepted. It was a risk not worth taking.

From that time onwards and throughout the 1830s Palmerston's hatred of the Pasha intensified. He came to see the Pasha as undertaking actions that could only attract the further interference of Russia in Ottoman affairs. This viewpoint was fueled by the blatantly Russophobic reports that his new ambassador in Istanbul, Ponsonby, was constantly sending him.[69] Furthermore, as Palmerston had predicted, Mehmed Ali spread his influence further east and was threatening British interests in Mesopotamia. By the early 1830s these interests were centered around the exploration of the Euphrates river with a view to checking whether it was navigable. The British parliament had allocated the sum of £20,000 for such a project which a certain Colonel Chesney was to lead. Two steamships were especially constructed (appropriately called the *Tigris* and the *Euphrates*) which were to be shipped in pieces to the Syrian coast and then carried overland from there to be assembled on the Euphrates. The whole project was of considerable importance for British communication with India since it was expected to shorten the distance from Bombay to London and also reduce the time taken to cover the distance. Furthermore, if successful, it would prove that steamships would be able to reach India all year round instead of the eight months per year that they were restricted to by taking the Red Sea route.[70]

However, the problem as far as Palmerston was concerned was that Mehmed Ali was controlling these lands and "while promising aid to the Expedition 'as far as his authority extended,' he actually employed every possible device to thwart the success of the experiment. In this he was largely successful."[71] Protective towards the overland route to India that he already controlled, the Pasha was determined not to have the expedition succeed. In spite of repeated remonstrations from the British

[68] "Henry Ellis Memorandum," reproduced as Appendix I in Kelly, *Britain and the Persian Gulf*, pp. 838–9. See also Ingram, *Great Game*, p. 272.

[69] Ponsonby was ambassador from 1833 to 1841. On his Russophobia, see Temperley, *Near East*, p. 75, where he attributes his initial anti-Russian feelings to his arrival in Istanbul when the Russian fleet was there: "For three months he watched it, expecting every hour to hear its guns firing."

[70] Halford L. Hoskins, *British Routes to India* (London: Longman, 1929), pp. 154–82. See also Chesney's *Reports on the Navigation of the Euphrates* (London, 1833).

[71] Hoskins, *India*, p. 163.

consuls in Syria and Egypt and in spite of presenting the Pasha with a firman from the Sultan himself permitting the expedition to go ahead,[72] Ibrahim Pasha, on orders from his father, did everything possible to obstruct it.[73] "The most astonishing accidents occurred: waggons were overturned, machinery was broken, draft animals were stampeded – all without rime or reason – . . . Very soon it became obvious that an organized system of sabotage was in operation . . ."[74] These moves were not lost on Palmerston: when Samuel Briggs, who was acting as an agent of the Pasha in London, presented a report urging Palmerston to support the Pasha's bid for independence and arguing that the Pasha's rule in Egypt was important for British "valuable possessions in India," Palmerston wrote in the margins to that memorandum "Mehemet Ali controls the Euphrates route."[75]

Not only was Mehmed Ali menacing such important work on the Euphrates, he also had his forces, Palmerston must have thought, all over the Arabian peninsula, an area that was gaining more and more importance for British control of India. Significant improvement in steam ships and the rapid expansion of their use to carry mail and passengers to India led to heated discussion in London in the mid 1830s about who was to pay for the mail steamers: the government or the East India Company. After that issue had been resolved and more and more steamers were making their way regularly up and down the Red Sea, the pressing question was that of finding suitable coaling stations. In that respect Mehmed Ali "was quick to meet British requests for the establishment of coaling depots."[76] Yet Palmerston continued to view the Pasha's military presence in Arabia with suspicion, especially his operations in Yemen. What made matters more

72 See the text of the firman, in Hurewitz, *Middle East*, pp. 258–9.

73 There are various letters between Ibrahim and his father to show how they tried to delay work on the expedition and to confuse the various British officials in matters related to the project. See, for example, S/5/47/1/547 on 14 Z 1250/13 April 1835 from Mehmed Ali to Ibrahim in which he tells him frankly that he does not know what to do about continued British requests for assistance in this matter. His son's reply is in Sham 31/7, on 7 M 1251/5 May 1835. In this letter Ibrahim conjectured that the heavy equipment which he heard the British were downloading on the Mediterranean coast and moving across the desert to the Euphrates was needed to build a military outpost to control Baghdad. Alternatively, he suggested to his father, the British might be interested in simply having a fortress to keep their equipment in. "In this case," he added, " we can suggest that we keep this equipment for them and try to convince them to give up the idea." It appears, therefore, that the political aspect of the whole expedition, that of preventing a confrontation between Mehmed Ali and the Sultan which it was feared would prompt Mahmud to ask again for Russian help (see Ingram, *Great Game*, pp. 292–9), was not entirely lost on Ibrahim and his father.

74 Hoskins, *India*, p. 165. 75 Rodkey, "Briggs," p. 346, n. 31.

76 R. J. Gavin, *Aden Under British Rule, 1839–1967* (New York: Barnes and Noble, 1975), p. 26.

alarming for the Foreign Secretary was a report he received from a British captain, Captain Mackenzie, on the condition of south-west Arabia. His main findings confirmed Palmerston's worst fears: Mackenzie wrote that "Muhammad ʿAli was intent on the conquest of the whole [Arabian] Peninsula, that he had designs on Aden, and once there, would push through the Hadhramawt to overturn the rule of the Imam of Musqat – the only Arab ruler on whom the British could rely."[77]

Besides the reports mentioned so far, namely, the Ellis report on Mehmed Ali's territorial expansion and its effect on British possessions in India, the Chesney report on the navigability of the Euphrates, the consuls' reports on Ibrahim's lack of co-operation with Chesney in his endeavors, and Mackenzies' reports on Mehmed Ali's territorial ambitions in Arabia, Palmerston was constantly fed by Ponsonby's alarming reports about the possibility of an Egyptian–Russian alliance. As a result of all these reports Palmerston became convinced that Mehmed Ali had expanded beyond the permissible. His mini-empire was threatening not only the Sultan's but His (after 1837, Her) Britannic Majesty's. The main beneficiary, Palmerston feared, would be the Czar, Emperor of all the Russias. But Palmerston could not devise a way of containing the Pasha of Egypt within his original pashalık without, at the same time enhancing the power of either the Russians in Istanbul or the French in Cairo. This opportunity presented itself when he read the report that Bowring submitted upon his return from Egypt in 1839 in which he assumed a very positive tone on the vali's policies in Egypt. Besides the tone, however, the one thing that mattered most to Palmerston was Bowring's highlighting the fact that it was the monopolies that enabled the Pasha to finance his military machine.[78] If only the Pasha could be forced to give up his monopolies, Palmerston thought, then his wings could be trimmed and thus India would be saved from the Russian menace. But the only person who could force the Pasha in this matter legally was the Sultan, and the Sultan of course was in no position to do so.

Palmerston finally found his answer in the person of another rival of Mehmed Ali in Istanbul, a man much less known to the old Pasha in Cairo than Husrev was, but much more resourceful and perceptive of the grave condition of the Empire than either old men had ever been. He was a man of a younger generation who did not inherit their personal, mutual grudges and was much better informed about the

[77] *Ibid.*, p. 27. For Memed Ali's forces in Arabia in the 1830s, see Kelly, *Britain and the Persian Gulf*, chs. 7 and 8.

[78] Bowring, "Report on Egypt," pp. 44–5.

Plate 9 "Reschid Pacha"

European scene and about the interests of the main European player, Great Britain, a fact that was to prove decisive for the future of the Ottoman Empire. This was Mustafa Raşid Pasha, later to become Grand Vizier for the exceptionally long period of six years and one of the most original of the so-called Tanzimat men.

In contrast to the pro-Russian Husrev, Mustafa Raşid was decidedly an Anglophile. In 1833 he was actively involved in the negotiations of the peace of Kütahia which followed the Sultan's defeat at the hands of Ibrahim Pasha. Like Palmerston, Raşid was dismayed at the opportunity that this defeat gave the Russians to increase their influence in Istanbul and he was disappointed at the British reluctance to assist the Sultan during the early months of the year. His disappointment at British policy was repeated five years later when he went to London in late 1838 after he had been appointed as Foreign Secretary to secure an alliance with Great Britain against Mehmed Ali to force him out of Syria. In spite of his failure in negotiating an agreement with Palmerston about joint military activities, Raşid Pasha remained convinced that it was only Britain which could curtail the power of the rebellious Pasha and thus stop Istanbul from slipping further in the Russian trap.

During his long stay in London (he returned to Istanbul in August 1839 after Mahmud's death) Raşid realized that although Britain had repeatedly denied the Porte military assistance, Palmerston was not uninterested in limiting the power of the Egyptian Pasha. After initially disagreeing about how best to achieve this, Raşid and Palmerston finally concurred that a new commercial treaty between the Sublime Porte and Great Britain that would ban monopolies in the Sultan's empire would be the sure way of fighting Mehmed Ali. Both men believed, and in this they were soon joined by Ponsonby, Palmerston's ambassador in Istanbul, that demanding that the terms of the treaty be applied to Egypt would weaken Mehmed Ali both politically (by treating his dominions as part of the Ottoman Empire) and economically (by drastically limiting his monopoly revenue). Both Britain and the Sultan would stand to benefit from this: Britain would benefit from a reduction in the Ottoman Empire's dependence on the Russian Tsar because of the lowered risk to its stability; the Sultan from the enforced withdrawal of the Pasha's troops from Syria due to the squeeze on his revenue. After lengthy and difficult negotiations the Balta Liman Treaty was signed which, while reducing the Sultan's own revenue was, Raşid thought, a fair price to be paid if the Empire was to be saved from Mehmed Ali's menace without being caught in the Russian trap.[79]

For his part, Mehmed Ali was aware that his continued existence depended on British support. This support could have been secured if he had confined himself to Egypt; his expansionary policy, however, was necessarily harmful to Britain's interests. This he seems to have realized but it also appears that he had managed to fool himself into thinking

[79] See Frank E. Bailey, *British Policy and the Turkish Reform Movement: A Study in Anglo-Turkish Relations, 1826–1853* (Cambridge, Mass.: Harvard University Press, 1942), pp. 122–6.

that if he were allowed to annex Syria and Mesopotamia in addition to Egypt, he would then be able – together with Persia and the Sultan in Istanbul – to pose a united front that would repulse any Russian move against India. This, as was shown above, Palmerston found to be unnecessary and too risky.

When this card did not succeed, Mehmed Ali tried to impress upon Palmerston that he was the liberal reformer he was looking for and with whom he could do business. He is famously reported to have told Palmerston (through Dr. Bowring): "Do not judge me by the standards of your knowledge. Compare me with the ignorance that is around me . . . I can find very few to understand me and do my bidding . . . I have been almost alone for the greater part of my life."[80] At the height of the second Syrian crisis he had not given up: he was still trying to force Palmerston to take him seriously as a liberal reformer. In June 1840 he told Colonel Hodges, the new British Consul-General, "When I came to Egypt it was really barbarous, utterly barbarous. Barbarous it remains to this day. Still I hope that my labours have rendered its condition somewhat better than it was. You must not however be shocked if you do not find in these countries the civilization which prevails in Europe."[81] Palmerston was not impressed by any of these allegations. He wrote to his ambassador to Paris, "For my part I hate Mehemet Ali, whom I consider as nothing but an ignorant barbarian . . . I look upon his boasted civilization as the arrantest humbug; and I believe that he is as great a tyrant and oppressor as ever made a people wretched."[82] In other words, Palmerston did not judge Mehmed Ali's "reforms" to have gone far enough or to have been genuine enough.

In Mustafa Raşid, on the other hand, Palmerston found the man who could fulfill his dream of imperialism couched in liberal terms: an Ottoman official who was bent on genuine reform but who acknowleged European superiority. It was Raşid after all who had drafted the imperial edict of Gülhane, the main piece of legislation that ushered in the Tanzimat period in earnest and which used a language of liberalism, equality and freedom, a language that Palmerston could understand and deal with. By drafting that imperial edict, Raşid proved himself to be the one person in the capital who could frustrate Mehmed Ali's ambitions. He did this by beating Mehmed Ali at his own game: that of trying to impress the West, especially Great Britain, of how reform-oriented he was. These reforms, Palmerston believed, were necessary if

80 Bowring, "Report on Egypt," p. 146.
81 FO 78/405, Hodges, 18 June 1840; quoted in Dodwell, *Founder of Modern Egypt*, p. 195.
82 Temperley, *Near East*, p. 89.

the Sick Man of Europe, as the Sultan's empire was infamously known, was to regain some of his former strength in order to fight the menacing Russian colossus. The Pasha tried half-heartedly to introduce some of these reforms but his efforts did not go far enough. Mehmed Raşid's did, however.[83]

Conclusion

This chapter has attempted to challenge the popular view by which Mehmed Ali appears as a strong, perceptive reformer who tried to improve the position of Egypt and to deliver her from Ottoman control, and whose efforts were frustrated by European, especially British, opposition. Far from being a champion of Egypt's interests (if by Egypt we mean a modern nation-state) Mehmed Ali was an ambitious governor of an Ottoman province who managed to introduce various reforms in his wealthy province and who was anxious lest the fruits of his labors would not be reaped by his family. As we have seen, the dynastic dimension of his struggle against the Ottoman Sultan was never far from his sight and it could be said that the various wars he waged against the Ottoman Sultan, far from being nationalist, could more appropriately be seen as dynastic struggles within the Empire at best, or a civil war at worst.

This dynastic rivalry was not directed at the Sultan himself, for after all Mehmed Ali's lineage was not so illustrious as to enable him to compete successfully with the House of Osman. Rather, it was at Husrev Pasha that his rivalry was directed. While to reduce all the Pasha's military activities in the second half of his reign to an attempt to frustrate and baffle his old rival would be to stress the point too forcefully, it remains true that Mehmed Ali's struggle against the Ottomans was shaped in no small degree by the age-old hatred of these two old, grumpy men. The irony of course is that the Pasha turned out to have been fighting the wrong man, and the one person who contributed more than any other to his alleged "undoing" was not Husrev but Mustafa Raşid, the man who would later play the reform game, the Tanzimat, much more adeptly.[84]

This chapter has also argued that Britain's opposition to Mehmed Ali's policies was not informed by any perceived threat that his "industrialization" schemes posed to British trade, but that it was his imperialist expansion that was the target and cause of British hostility.

[83] On Raşid's efforts in drafting the Gülhane Edict, see Bailey, *British Policy*, pp. 183–6.

[84] It should be added that Raşid was equally effective in the "undoing" of Husrev Pasha: he had him deposed as a traitor soon after the promulgation of the Gülhane edict.

By expanding far beyond the borders of his province, Mehmed Ali attracted the attention and hostility of Great Britain, who saw in his policies a grave danger to her imperial interests in Asia. It was this perceived danger rather than any threat to losing potential markets in the eastern Mediterranean that attracted British hostility to the Pasha's expansionary policy. By aligning herself with leading men in Istanbul and by presenting Mehmed Ali with a unified European stand, Britain succeeded in averting the danger of partitioning the Ottoman Empire. This she managed to do not only by waving the stick of military confrontation and warning him of serious repercussions if he did not comply, but also by offering him the carrot of legal recognition of himself and his heirs as governors of Egypt. The 1841 settlement of the "Eastern Question," therefore, does not demonstrate any malice against Egypt or its ruler, for if by "Egypt" we mean the people of Egypt as a "nation," then this "Egypt" had nothing to do with the Pasha's wars. And if we mean by "Egypt" its ruler, then he was certainly content with the resolution of the crisis: to have Egypt as his province for himself and for his children after his death is what he had been striving for all his life and this is what he finally achieved at the age of seventy. This was the crowning success of the Pasha's long career and he lived the remaining nine years of his long life basking in it until he literally went mad at the age of eighty.

Conclusion

By studying the army of Mehmed Ali this book has attempted to challenge the powerful Egyptian nationalist discourse on Mehmed Ali Pasha's reign, according to which the Pasha is seen as laying the foundations for a national recovery of Egypt aimed at gaining her independence from the Ottoman Empire. The thousands of Egyptians who served in the Pasha's army, while not seeing themselves *yet* as Egyptians first and foremost, are claimed in this powerful, dominant nationalist discourse to have eventually discovered their true identities and to have seen themselves as Egyptians fighting for the glory of the fatherland. The Pasha's policy of conscription pushed the inherent nationalist feelings of these conscripts to the surface and gave the fellahin a chance to express their true sentiments after centuries of being silenced by Ottoman domination. The three centuries of Ottoman rule, thus, suddenly appear as foreign and oppressive, and Mehmed Ali's greatness is seen as allowing, even if inadvertently, these sentiments to be finally exhibited.

Following this nationalist tradition, al-Rāfʿī, for example, while recognizing that there was a personal dimension in Mehmed Ali's struggle with the Ottoman Sultan, could not but see that "all the wars that Egypt waged during Mehmed Ali's rule paved the way for her independence and enhanced her position among other nations."[1] Marsot, similarly, as we have already seen, concludes her book by insisting that, in spite of not intending to do so, "Muhammad Ali . . . put Egypt on the path of independent statehood and self-recognition as having a separate identity distinct from other Muslims and Ottomans."[2]

This book showed a number of problems with this argument. One such problem with the nationalist argument insofar as it pertains to Mehmed Ali's army was the fact that the soldiers, far from rushing enthusiastically to join the colors and defend the nation, came to view conscription as a heavy tax exacted by an already oppressive and

[1] al-Rāfʿī, *ʿAsr Muḥammad ʿAlī*, p. 117.
[2] al-Sayyid Marsot, *Egypt*, p. 264.

intolerant regime that they found it difficult to sympathize with. The soldiers gradually came to see their own commanding officers and not the enemy they were fighting as the "other." How does the nationalist discourse explain the fact that the Egyptian soldiers resisted serving in the army, allegedly *the* national institution, or that they saw their own officers and not the Ottoman army as the other? In other words, having insisted that the Egyptian nation has always already existed and that "Egypt" refers to a conscious subject acting clearly towards independence, autonomy, sovereignty and dignity, but faced at the same time with the historical fact that the nation was not always manifesting itself in this manner, how then could the nation be forced to exhibit itself and to strive for its own independence and dignity? Herein lies the importance of Mehmed Ali for Egyptian nationalist historiography. He appears literally from nowhere to show Egyptians that they are really Egyptians and to force them, even against their own wishes and contrary to his own intentions, to fight for their own nation. In this sense his foreign origins paradoxically become an asset since they give him the necessary vantage point from which to see clearly with his penetrative gaze the suffering that his people were beseeching him to deliver them from.

If this is why Mehmed Ali is useful for the Egyptian nationalist project, his appeal exceeds it to touch on other nationalisms, too. For the Pasha was equally mesmerizing for European as well as Egyptian historians, and this requires an explanation. The cases of Dodwell and Driault offer good examples. Dodwell was fascinated by the character and policies of the Great Pasha because he found in Mehmed Ali's career an echo of what he believed the British were doing in India. For like the British viceroys in the sub-continent Mehmed Ali "hated disorder and corruption and misgovernment. Like them, he desired freedom in order that a new and better form of government might be framed."[3] Dodwell, therefore, offers a good example of a British historian who had a wonderful topic at hand that allowed him to look back a hundred years and nostalgically write about a time when Britannia could comfortably and uncontestedly rule the waves and when she was still confident that she could carry the "white man's burden." In other words, Dodwell's book is as much a book on British imperial history as it is a study of the Egyptian Pasha.

For their part, French historians saw Mehmed Ali as owing a lot of his greatness to his resemblance to Napoleon. Both men, it is argued, had a dream they wanted to fulfill and both had their dreams frustrated by the British. In his *Mohamed Aly et Napoléon* Driault, in typical

[3] Dodwell, *Founder of Modern Egypt*, pp. 263–4.

romantic manner, accepted both men's self-characterizations: while the great French Emperor saw himself as a descendant of the Caesars, Mehmed Ali was more like a Pharaoh. Both, Driault believed, shared a deep-seated desire to revive a great power and to found an enlightened regime.[4] Driault takes the existence of the French or Egyptian nation as given, nations whose ancient glories were waiting to be rekindled and awakened.

There are therefore various factors that contributed to the positive image that Mehmed Ali has received throughout the ages. Besides his usefulness to nationalist historiography where he is depicted either as a founding father, a liberal legislator, or a romantic hero, the Pasha had the good fortune to have lived till the age of eighty. His long and, as this book has tried to argue, successful career (for only if one accepts the nationalist argument would the Pasha's efforts look thwarted and frustrated) offers numerous episodes and material that historians could chew on. In addition, and as has been shown throughout this book, the Pasha was able to manipulate his various interlocutors and successfully influenced their portrayal of him. Let us visit the "old spider in his den" one last time to see how this successful manipulation was not limited to his contemporary observers but outlived them to influence more recent historians.

Date: 21 November 1832. Location: the Pasha's palace in Alexandria. Players: the Pasha and St. John, a British traveler who wrote one of the most perceptive and accurate books on Egypt and the Pasha's government.

"I understand it is your intention to write a book. Is it so [the Pasha asks his British interlocutor]?"

"Your highness has been rightly informed."

"In that case, I shall be happy to afford you all kinds of facilities. But do you confine your researches, as is the custom, to ruins and other remains of ancient art?"

"On the contrary, my principal object is to obtain an insight into the character of your Highness's government, and the present state of the country."

When I had spoken these words [St. John continues] a remarkable change, I thought, took place in his manner. He seemed more polite than before, but was evidently more grave and thoughtful.

"Ah! Then," he continued after a brief pause, "you do not run about after antiquities; your object is wholly political." . . .

[They then entered into a long discussion about the Pasha's image in Europe and the Ottoman campaign in the Western press to tarnish it].

"I have hitherto been accustomed to reply to words with actions: but since the Sultan lays so much stress on words – on articles of a mere journalist – I also will have my newspaper, which shall be published here at Alexandria." . . .

[4] Edouard Driault, ed., *Mohamed Aly et Napoléon, 1807–1814* (Cairo: Royal Egyptian Geographical Society, 1925), pp. xxxviii–xxxix.

> "No one can doubt that your Highness has acted prudently; for the influence of newspapers is incalculable . . . After all, the opinion of Europe is of consequence."
>
> At this he seemed to start as from as dream [St. John explains]; became fidgety upon his divan; and, making a slight movement towards me, replied in the most animated manner, – "Oh, do not mistake me: I am not indifferent about the judgement which the world may form of me; and of this I will give you a convincing proof. For a long time I have been engaged in composing the history of my life. During every moment which I can snatch from public business, from the affairs of my people, I am attended by a secretary, whose sole employment is to write down what I dictate, in my own words; and to obviate the objections which might be urged against a history of so long a period, composed from recollection, I may remark that nature has endowed me with a very strong memory. I can describe, as if they occurred yesterday, events which took place forty years ago. In consequence, my biography will be very full. It will contain the history of my youth, before my arrival in Egypt. I shall describe the state of this country when I came into it; and all the events of any importance, which happened during my military expeditions in Nubia, Sennar, Kordofan, the Hejaz, and Syria."[5]

St. John did not fall in the trap, however, and his book did *not* proceed chronologically following the Pasha from his childhood to his old age, the narration culminating with his different military adventures. More than a hundred years after his death, though, books are still being written which, having been based on an archival material that had been cleverly selected in the first place, appear as if they had been dictated by the Pasha himself, and in his own words. They proceed with an account of the situation of Egypt before the appearance of the Pasha on its landscape, then proceed chronologically, following him through one after the other of his adventures, and end with his supposedly aborted attempts to gain independence from the Ottoman Empire highlighting Britain's role in frustrating these attempts.[6]

The Pasha and his men

Like St. John's book, this study has tried to avoid the trap of writing Egypt's history in the first half of the nineteenth century as if it were Mehmed Ali's biography. Ideally it would have been better to avoid

[5] St. John, *Egypt*, I, pp. 51–5.

[6] Marsot's book, for example, starts with a chapter entitled "Egypt under the mamluks," which is followed by another with the title "Muhammad Ali the man," then "A country without a master," "Master in his own house," and culminates in a chapter whose heading is "Expansion to what end?" The book ends with two chapters, "The undoing: Muhammad Ali and Palmerston" and "The aftermath": if Mehmed Ali's proposed autobiography had been written, and had it survived, it would hardly have offered a more uncritical account.

referring to him altogether, but that would have given a version of Egypt's history as incomplete as a history of Germany in the 1930s without mention of Hitler. Instead, this book, by concentrating on his army, the key institution around which all his reforms were centered, challenged the nationalist version of Egyptian history that sees in Mehmed Ali a proto-nationalist leader. It argued that the Pasha did not aim to achieve independence for "Egypt," but intended to carve out a small empire for himself and for his children after him. It also argued that Great Britain, who is usually taken to have opposed Mehmed Ali ferociously and to have "prevented Egypt from reaping the fruits of her military victories" was not antagonistic to the Pasha's "reform" policies in Egypt, but was against his empire-building efforts that she saw as challenging and endangering her own possessions in Asia. In addition, it argued that neither the Pasha himself nor his senior military commanders and top advisors including his own son, Ibrahim Pasha, ever thought of this whole exercise as being aimed at achieving the independence of Egypt from Ottoman rule, if by "Egypt" we mean a clearly identified nation-state.

Instead, this book has placed Egypt and the Pasha's long rule within the larger Ottoman world. It argued that not only was Egypt technically and legally an Ottoman province, but that Mehmed Ali and his officials were also "Ottomans": they originated from different parts of the Ottoman Empire, spoke Turkish, were familiar with the history of the Empire and of the dangers that confronted it, and thought of themselves in Ottoman terms, their eyes set on horizons that were essentially those of the Ottoman world. Seen in this light the career of Mehmed Ali appears not as that of a national leader who fought hard to deliver Egypt from the heavy burden of foreign oppression, but as a problematic reformer of the Ottoman Empire who, through the numerous changes he managed to effect in the Egyptian economy and society, showed the administrators in Istanbul an example of how to introduce much-needed reforms in the central lands of the Empire. In so doing, Mehmed Ali was not moved by any desire to improve the lot of the Egyptians, let alone to deliver them from "foreign oppression," but by his constant, pressing desire to make more secure his precarious position as governor of Egypt.

Mehmed Ali was clearly aware that his appointment to that important and lucrative post was made against the Sultan's wish and he was equally aware that first Sultan Selim III and then Sultan Mahmud II had tried to have him removed from Egypt. Realizing that he lacked an effective military force that would enable him to rebuff any attempt by Istanbul to dislodge him forcibly from his wealthy province, he made numerous attempts to found one, culminating in the crucial attempt to create a modern army based on conscripted fellahin in 1820–1. Once he had taken that fateful decision, not only was the efficiency of his administration and its ability to affect and touch the daily lives of the average Egyptians greatly enhanced; his relationship with the Sultan in Istanbul was also radically changed. As was shown above, the crucial turning point came during the Greek war when he first agreed to send some of his newly trained troops to fight alongside the Sultan's forces; after suffering from the major disaster of Navarino in 1827, he seems to have decided not to assist the Sultan any more and to engage in his own military exploits instead, even if these were at the expense of the Sultan himself.

Furthermore, and contrary to the attractive nationalist allegation that Mehmed Ali's efforts were frustrated by Great Britain, this book has attempted to show that his policies in Egypt did in fact benefit Britain: through allowing more and more British goods to find their way to Egyptian markets (albeit through him as sole intermediary), through constantly wooing British officials, and above all through protecting British merchants resident in Egypt and establishing a state of law and order in Egypt that secured British overland communication with India. As was shown above, British hostility to Mehmed Ali was caused by his military expansion that was seen in London and Bombay as threatening British possessions in Asia by giving the Russians a pretext to interfere at their expense in Istanbul. Once this menace had passed, the British were well disposed towards the old Pasha and he was equally well disposed to them, something that the popular *Illustrated London News* was quick to notice. In an article appearing in August 1844 it commented on the possibility of the Pasha's death and on the numerous services he had afforded the British Empire. It said, "Even when we were battering down his forts and beating his troops, the old Pacha escorted the mail-bags and passengers across the desert as if nothing had happened . . . We are glad that Mehmet Ali is . . . smoking his pipe, levying taxes, and abusing his councils in Alexandria."[7]

In short, rather than seeing Mehmed Ali as striving to achieve independence on behalf of the Egyptian nation, and instead of viewing Great Britain as the main obstacle in this endeavor, this book has argued that Mehmed Ali was seeking the establishment of a secure personal rule for himself and his household in Egypt. His efforts in this regard were crowned with success when in 1841 the Sultan, with the acquiescence of Britain, granted him a firman bestowing on him the hereditary rule of Egypt.

[7] *Illustrated London News*, 31 August 1844..

Plate 10 "Egyptian soldier"

Moreover, the main criticism that this book has leveled against the nationalist version of Egyptian history is its assumption that "Egypt" has always had a unified, self-contained, clearly recognizable identity, and that its inhabitants have always realized – through their strong attachment to its soil, and through their conscious links to its history – that they are, and have always been, clearly and exclusively "Egyptians." In other words, the main problem of Egyptian nationalist historiography, like all nationalist historiographies, is the assumption that Egypt is an undivided subject and that the Egyptian nation is a primordial, eternal entity possessing a unified, conscious will potentially capable of autonomy and sovereignty.[8] Studying the army of Egypt in the first half of the nineteenth century, an army that is supposed to have been the national institution *par excellence*, this book found no evidence that this central institution functioned along national lines. Not only did the idea of the army as being a national one never cross anyone's mind from the Pasha all the way down to any of his soldiers, there was not even a pretense at portraying the wars that the men were dying in as national wars waged to defend "Egypt" or to deliver her from foreign tyranny. As such, this book has attempted to show that the nation has been written into existence by nationalist historians and that it is partly an outcome of nationalist historiography and not a given that already existed prior to it.

This book, however, has also argued that "Egypt," as referring to a nation-state, was not simply a result of a semantic shift brought about by the dominant discourse of nationalism. Neither was the birth of the Egyptian nation in the nineteenth century a result only of the modern state's ability to monopolize the means of violence by reorganizing the administrative and military apparatuses so that it could extend its control over wider areas in a permanent manner. The Egyptian nation was brought into being as a result of a multiplicity of practices and discourses that transformed the administration in Cairo from being interested mainly in taxation and in maintaining law and order to a government devising modern techniques of control and using more effective and more subtle ways of manipulating its population. As we have seen throughout this book by concentrating on the Pasha's army, examples of such novel practices were the issuing of *tezkere*s which functioned as identity cards that people had to carry all the time in order for the authorities to be able to catch deserters; regularly checking the bodies of conscripts for signs of diseases that were now treated in newly constructed hospitals; subjecting the bodies of the soldiers to a strict regime whereby all their movements were supposed to be subject to control and surveillance. In the wider society similar practices were instituted that together turned Egypt from a province within the Ottoman Empire into a modern nation-state.

Mehmed Ali's army was instrumental in founding the modern Egyptian nation not by enlightening its soldiers as to their true and hidden identity. It was not by fighting their supposedly foreign enemies that Egyptians came to call Egypt their own. Rather, by relying on thousands of Egyptians to man his army, and at the same time by

[8] For an insightful critique of the remarkably similar Indian nationalist discourse, see Gyan Prakash, "Writing post-Oriental histories of the Third World: Perspectives from Indian historiography," *Comparative Studies in Society and History*, 32 (1990), pp. 383–408.

making sure that none of these *evlad-ı Arab* was to be promoted to senior ranks, the Pasha inadvertently helped to homogenize the experience of these thousands of Egyptians in a manner that was crucial in the founding of their "imagined community." The deeply felt sentiments of injustice, frustration and animosity that the Arabic-speaking soldiers and their junior officers had towards the Turkish-speaking military elite was a powerful ingredient in forging the rising national consciousness and was made even more potent by being echoed in the civilian society at large. For the ethno-linguistic "division of labor" that characterized the Pasha's army was mirrored by a similar one in the civilian administration where the ruling elite remained "Turkish" and where "Arabs" were prevented from being promoted to higher posts.

The Pasha's army was above all crucial for the rise of the modern nation-state of Egypt by introducing practices that together changed the nature of the Egyptian state and its relationship to its "citizens" and completely transformed the very fabric of Egyptian society. By catching its deserters, punishing its criminals, educating its youth, vaccinating its children, silencing its women, interning its insane, and by doing all this in a subtle, "humane" and "rational" manner . . . this is how the Egyptian nation came into being in modern times. It was by a process of violence, silence and exclusion that Egyptians were taught the essential truths of the nation.

Besides challenging that dominant discourse of nationalism, this book also seeks to offer an account of Mehmed Ali's army in a manner that does not reiterate the world view of great generals and romanticizes their military exploits; rather, it has attempted to come as close as possible to the soldiers' perception of the army and their experiences in it. It attempts to deny the Pasha the privilege he has always been given in most books about Egypt in the first half of the nineteenth century: that of dictating his own story. This book started from the conviction that it is much more interesting and useful to write the history of the Egyptian army, or any army for that matter, from the point of view of the people who did the actual fighting and suffered most from its atrocities, rather than from the viewpoint of their commanding officers, watching from a safe distance on horseback. It has therefore attempted to give these soldiers a chance of narrating their own experience and writing their own history.

This, however, was not possible since the men left us no accounts of their own which, if reconstructed, would give them back the voice they have been denied. Furthermore, when these men appear occasionally in contemporary records, they do so as "criminals" who were tried for a "crime" they had committed, as young men whose names had to be registered in the conscription register, or as deserters who had been caught and were then brought in front of a court martial. In these situations the "voice" of the soldier, when it is recorded, appears not as an "authentic," personal voice, but as an already censored one, muzzled by the intimidating circumstances in which it was recorded. The records of the court martial, therefore, that most precious source through which one would expect to get as close as possible to capturing the voice of the illiterate soldier, turn out to be a means of silencing him and of incorporating him within the power structure that he was resisting.

So how can this problem be solved? Being, in effect, shouted at constantly by the Pasha to write at his dictation, and at the same time being denied the real voice of the soldier, how then can an historian write a history of the Pasha's army, a history that gives justice to the soldiers, without at the same time romanticizing them and their acts of defiance? This is the central question of this book and there was a deliberate attempt not to resolve that tension since, as has been shown, the soldiers did resist the army, yet found themselves, nevertheless, winning for the Pasha his great victories. It is this tension, this constant struggle between the Pasha and his men, that is the central theme of this book. Because of its centrality, the very format the book takes is intended to echo this tension: a soldier's story of his service from conscription to desertion flanked by two scenes of the Pasha entertaining his guests. Nevertheless, and as far as the soldier's own story is concerned, this book has attempted to argue that desertion offers a historically more nuanced ending than nationalist versions do with their emphasis on "martyrdom" or "fighting for Egypt's independence." In other words, I find acts of desertion to be a much more eloquent testimony of how Egyptians felt towards the Pasha's regime than all the tomes written on Mehmed Ali's nationalist enterprise.

The army and the modernization of Egypt

Besides writing the history of this constant struggle between Mehmed Ali and his soldiers, this book is also interested in showing how the army, given its centrality, helped to "modernize" Egypt or, as Mitchell has put it, to "colonize" it. This it does by critically presenting the logic of the military machine as depicted in the different laws, regulations and manuals that were issued to regulate various aspects of military life. For these laws and manuals not only affected and shaped military life; they also offered a model of how society in general could be organized, as indeed it was. For example, as we have seen, effective surveillance and policing systems that would enable the military authorities to track down and catch deserters were generalized throughout the country to establish a truly controlled society where individuals and their movements were monitored. In addition, the army's need to screen the conscripts medically, to treat them for disease, and to maintain a healthy environment in the crowded camps and barracks provided the impetus to found a medical school, to institute a country-wide vaccination program, and to make the bodies of the soldiers (and eventually of civilians as well) available to the self-assured medical gaze. Finally, the requirement that the soldiers should not live off the lands they marched through or ended up occupying, and that their food, clothes and equipment should be sent from central depots in Egypt to whichever war front they happened to be stationed at, meant that an efficient administrative system was needed that would ease the functioning of the army, and would also provide a model for the civilian bureaucracy to copy.

As said above, this attempt at representing the underlying logic of the "modern" institutions of power was done by Mitchell in his *Colonising Egypt*, and with the exception of chapter 3 there has been no deliberate attempt to reproduce this logic in its own terms elsewhere in this book. Rather, the aim was to complement the impressive picture of the law that Mitchell provides with the more fractured one of its implementation and to elaborate on the nature of and reasons for the discrepancy between both pictures. Specifically, the aim was to contrast a decree of Mehmed Ali, for example, with the understanding of a petty bureaucrat to whom it was addressed for implementation, to juxtapose a sanitary manual by Clot Bey with the soldiers' resistance to having their bodies so minutely investigated, and to compare a "neat" conscription order with the repeated attempts – sometimes successful, at other times not – of the soldiers to escape their units and desert the army altogether. This contrast of the law with its implementation was not reproduced here to argue that these institutions of power completely failed or that they were practically ignored by the people; rather this juxtaposition was required for two main reasons.

First, given that one of the intentions of this book is to demystify the aura of Mehmed Ali, reproducing the letter of the laws and regulations without stressing the difficulties that were encountered in implementing them would have enhanced, rather than diffused, the Pasha's mystique. Instead, what this book has attempted to do with regards to the premier institution of power in nineteenth-century Egypt is to stress the imperfect, contingent and incomplete nature of these laws and regulations. Seeing how Ibrahim dealt with his officers, for example, was important for the understanding, as attempted in chapter 2, of how these laws and regulations as well as the entire organizational structure of the army were decided upon after a long and tedious process of negotiation and deliberation. In spite of the pretence of the texts which enunciated modern notions of power at presenting themselves as if they were primordial, self-contained and self-perpetuating texts, they were in fact negotiated, amended and refined by conscious agents whose conflicting interests and confused, fractured vision of society were reflected in these very same texts. As we have seen in chapter 4 for example, the training manual, that most powerful of military texts, had an important "moment of silence" that reflected a wider conflict in society, a conflict that existed between the Turkish-speaking officers and their Arabic-speaking subordinates regarding how far these latter could be promoted up the military hierarchy. While bringing to light the problems inherent in *writing* the text was intended to argue that texts do not write themselves, stressing the problems of *reading* the text, on the other hand, served to argue that laws and regulations also do not implement themselves; they need an agency for their verbal content to be translated into tangible reality. As was shown with the apparently trivial example of sentry guards mentioned in chapters 4 and 5 the policy of surveillance that was crucial for the disciplining of the army was never as neatly and unproblematically implemented as Foucault or Mitchell have argued: it was constantly compromised by the activity of the one minor agent who was supposed to carry it through, the sentry guard.

Second, as Mitchell himself acknowledges in the preface to his book, there is a danger of "overstat[ing] the coherence of [the] technologies [of power] . . . disciplines can break down, counteract one another, or overreach."[9] This book has shown precisely how military discipline was constantly breaking down in the Pasha's army, a notion that Mitchell, in spite of his warning, does not stress enough in his book. Since the present book is about the history of the every-day functioning of the army and not only a study of the concept of power that informed it, analyzing the underlying notions of power that helped shape the structure of the army has to be complemented with accounts of how this power was implemented, negotiated, accommodated, and, most importantly, resisted by its supposedly mute objects. Through numerous rebellions and mutinies, and by repeatedly performing small acts of defiance, and, above all, through desertion and countless, tragic acts of self-mutilation, the soldiers showed that they could and did retain for themselves an area from where they could resist power, a territory from

[9] Mitchell, *Colonising Egypt*, p. xi.

which they were able to assert their own wills above a system and a regime that attempted to enslave and dehumanize them. Not that the authorities were helpless in confronting these repeated acts of resistance and defiance; as we have seen, the Pasha and his officials passed numerous decrees to curb the phenomenon of desertion and to punish all acts of insurrection that they found most alarming and undermining to the whole performance of the entire army. Power, in other words, as much as it attempts to silence, to be all-inclusive and to penetrate minds and control bodies, is always constantly negotiated, suspended, and resisted.

This book is not a study of how modern discourses and institutions of power manage to achieve an unprecedented hold over the body through its capture, isolation and surveillance. It is, rather, a study of the dialog that power constantly has with resistance. My main subject is the army that Mehmed Ali managed to found in Egypt in the first half of the nineteenth century, an institution that represented the modern notions of power in as pristine a form as could possibly be found. It argues that it is true that the Pasha and his authorities managed to capture the bodies of tens of thousands of Egyptian men and that it is correct that they succeeded in training them and in aggregating their efforts to form a modern, disciplined army. As a result, the Pasha was capable in his old age of achieving what he had always aspired to, namely, to secure for himself and for his children after his death rule over the rich lands of Egypt, and for the hundred years after his death Egypt was, indeed, ruled by his descendants. Yet the soldiers, by resisting him and his authorities and by undermining his impressive, powerful structure, proved that they were not part of this project, that they were implicated in it against their will, and that they attempted to resist it by all means possible and imaginable. Only if one uncritically believes nationalist accounts of the Pasha and his military machine, could one accept that these soldiers were indeed all the Pasha's men. I have no doubt, however, that he was not their man.

Bibliography

PRIMARY SOURCES

ARCHIVAL MATERIAL

Egyptian National Archives (Dār al-Wathā'iq al-Qawmiyya), Cairo
Sijillāt (Registers)

Sijillāt Dīwān al-Maʿiyya al-Saniyya (registers of the Viceregal Department), designated by the code S/1.

Sijillāt Dīwān Khedewī (registers of the Department of Civil Affairs), designated by the code S/2.

Sijillāt Dīwān al-Jihādiyya, Mashūrat al-Ṭibb (registers of the Health Council, a subdivision of the War Department), designated by the codes S/3/122.

Sijillāt ʿĀbdīn (collection of registers of various departments originally housed in ʿĀbdīn Palace), designated by the code S/5.

Sijillāt al-Waqā'iʿ al-Miṣriyya (photocopies of the original copies of this newspaper), designated by "*Vekayi-i Mısıriyye*."

Sijillāt Dīwān Taftīsh Ṣiḥḥat al-Maḥrūsa – Ṣādir (outgoing letters from the registers of the Department of Health Inspection of Cairo), designated by the code M/5.

Sijillāt Dīwān al-Tarsāna: Dafātir Qayd Asmā' al-Mudhnibīn bi-Līmān Iskandariyya (registers of the Navy Department giving names of the convicts of the Liman of Alexandria), designated by the code M/14.

Maḥāfiẓ (Boxes)

Maḥāfiẓ al-Shām (boxes containing the original documents pertaining to the Syrian campaign), designated by "Sham."

Maḥāfiẓ Baḥr Barra (boxes containing the original letters written to and received from foreign dignitaries), designated by "Bahr Barra."

Maḥāfiẓ al-Hijāz (boxes containing the original documents pertaining to the Arabian campaign), designated by "Hijaz."

Maḥfaẓat Awāmir lil-Jihādiyya (one box containing Mehmed Ali's orders to the *Cihadiye Nazırı*, Director of the War Department), designated by "Awamir lil-Jihadiyya."

Maḥāfiẓ Dhawāt (boxes containing original letters to and from members of Mehmed Ali's family), designated by "Dhawat."

Maḥāfiẓ Dīwān Khedewī (boxes containing original documents issued by the Department of Civil Affairs), designated by "Divan-ı Hidiv."

Maḥāfiẓ Dīwān Katkhoda (boxes containing original documents issued by the Department of the Pasha's First Deputy), designated by "Katkhoda."

Public Record Office, London

FO 78. General Correspondence, Turkey, 1817–58.

OFFICIAL EGYPTIAN PUBLICATIONS

Clot Bey, Antoine B. *al-ʿAjāla al-Ṭibbiyya Fīmā lā Budda Minhu l'Ḥukamāʾ al-Jihādiyya* [A Short Medical Treatise Necessary for Army Doctors] Trans. August Sakākīnī. Cairo: Maṭbaʿat Madrasat al-Ṭibb bi Abī Zaʿbal, 1833.

Mabḥath Taʿlīmī fī Taṭʿīm al-Judarī [An Educational Treatise in Smallpox Vaccination].Trans. Aḥmad Ḥasan al-Rashīdī. Cairo: Būlāq, 1843.

Risāla min Mashūrat al-Ṣiḥḥa ila Ḥukamāʾ al-Jihādiyya [A Treatise from the Health Council to Army Physicians]. Cairo: Maṭbaʿat Dīwān al-Jihādiyya, 1835.

Kanunname-i Bahriye-i Cihadiye [Naval Regulations]. Cairo: Būlāq, AH 1242/AD 1827.

Kanun-u Seferiye [Campaign Regulations]. Cairo: Būlāq, Ramaḍān AH 1258/October 1842.

al-Lāiʾḥa al-Mutaʿalliqa bi-Khadamāt al-Mustakhdimīn wa Mutaʿallaqātiha [The Decree Regarding the Duties of (Public) Employees and its Appendices]. Cairo: Būlāq, AH 1260/AD 1844.

al-Nabarāwī, Ibrāhīm, trans. *al-Arbiṭa al-Jirāḥiyya* [Surgical Bandages]. Cairo: Būlāq, 1839.

Qānūn al-Dākhiliyya. [Regulations for Barracks and Camps]. Cairo: Maṭbaʿat Dīwān al-Jihādiyya, AH 1250/AD 1834–35. (This is the Arabic version. The original Turkish was published in the previous year as *Kanunname-i Dahiliye-i Asaker-i Piyadegân*.)

Taʿlīm al-Nafar wal-Bulok [Training Manual for the Soldier and the Company]. Cairo: Maṭbaʿat Dīwān al-Jihādiyya, 1853. (This is the Arabic translation of *Talimname-i Asaker-i-Piyadegân*. Cairo: Maṭbaʿat Dīwān al-Jihādiyya, AH 1250/AD 1834).

EDITED COLLECTIONS OF STATE PAPERS

Cattaui, René, ed. *Le Règne de Mohamed Aly d'après les archives russes en Egypte*. Four volumes. Cairo: Royal Egyptian Geographical Society, 1931–36.

Douin, Georges, ed. *L'Angleterre et l'Egypte*. Volume II: *La Politique mameluke (1803–1807)*. Cairo: Royal Egyptian Geographical Society, 1928–30.

La Mission du Baron de Boislecomte, L'Egypte et la Syrie en 1833. Cairo: Royal Egyptian Geographical Society, 1927.

Une mission militaire française auprès de Mohamed Aly. Cairo: Royal Egyptian Geographical Society, 1923.

Mohamed Aly et l'expédition d'Alger. Cairo: Royal Egyptian Geographical Society, 1930.

La Première Guerre de Syrie. Two volumes. Cairo: Royal Egyptian Geographical Society, 1931.

Driault, Edouard, ed. *l'Egypte et L'Europe; la crise orientale de 1839–41*. Five volumes. Cairo: Royal Egyptian Geographical Society, 1930–33.

L'Expédition de Crète et de Morée (1823–28). Cairo: Royal Egyptian Geographical Society, 1930.

La Formation de l'empire de Mohamed Ali de l'Arabie au Soudan (1814–23). Cairo: Royal Egyptian Geographical Society, 1927.

Mohamed Aly et Napoléon, 1807–1814. Cairo: Royal Egyptian Geographical Society, 1925.

Jallād, Fīlīb, ed. *Qāmūs al-Idāra wa'l-Qaḍā'* [Dictionary of Administration and Justice]. Four volumes. Alexandria, 1890–92.

al-Qāmūs al-'Āmm lil-Idāra wa'l-Qaḍā' [General Dictionary of Administration and Justice]. Seven volumes. Alexandria, 1900.

Rustum, Asad J., ed. *A Calendar of State Papers from the Royal Archives of Egypt Relating to the Affairs of Syria*. Four volumes. Beirut: The American Press, 1940.

al-Uṣūl al-'Arabiyya li-Tārīkh Sūriyya fī 'Ahd Muḥammad 'Alī Bāshā [Materials for a Corpus of Arabic Documents Relating to the History of Syria Under Mehemet Ali Pasha]. Five volumes. Beirut: The American Press, 1930–34.

Sāmī, Amīn, ed. *Taqwīm al-Nīl* [Chronicle of the Nile]. Volume II: *'Aṣr Muḥammad 'Alī*. [Mehmed Ali's Reign]. Cairo: Dār al-Kutub, 1928.

SECONDARY SOURCES

'Abdel-Karīm, Aḥmad 'Izzat. *Tārīkh al-Ta'līm fī 'Aṣr Muḥammad 'Alī* [History of Education in the Reign of Mehmed Ali]. Cairo: Maṭba'at al-Nahḍa al-Miṣriyya, 1938.

Abū-'Izzeddīn, Sulaymān. *Ibrāhīm Bāshā fī Sūriyya* [Ibrahim Pasha in Syria]. Beirut: al-Maṭba'a al-'Ilmiyya, 1929.

Abu-Lughod, Janet, *Cairo: 1001 Years of the City Victorious*. Princeton: Princeton University Press, 1971.

Aḥmad, Layla 'Abdel-Laṭīf. *Siyāsat Muḥammad 'Alī Izā' al-'Urbān fī Miṣr* [Mehmed Ali's Policy Towards the Bedouins in Egypt]. Cairo: Dār al-Kitāb al-Jāmi'ī, 1986.

Anderson, Benedict. *Imagined Communities: Reflections of the Origins of Nationalism*. London: Verso, 1983.

Anderson, M. S. *War and Society in Europe of the Old Regime, 1618–1789*. Leicester: Leicester University Press, 1988.

Arnold, Eric A., Jr. "Some observations on the French opposition to Napoleonic conscription, 1804–1806." *French Historical Studies* 4 (1966): 452–62.

Ayalon, David. "The Muslim city and the mamluk military aristocracy." *Proceedings of the Israel Academy of Science and Humanities* 2 (1967): 311–29.

'Azabāwī, 'Abdallah M. *'Umad wa Mashāyikh al-Qurā wa Dawruhum fī al-Mujtama' al-Miṣrī fī al-Qarn al-Tāsi' 'Ashr* [Village Mayors and Shaykhs and Their Role in Egyptian Society During the Nineteenth Century]. Cairo: Dār al-Kitāb al-Jāmi'ī, 1984.

Baer, Gabriel. "Urbanization in Egypt, 1820–1907." In W. R. Polk and R. L. Chambers, eds., *Beginnings of Modernization in the Middle East*. Chicago: University of Chicago Press, 1968, pp. 155–69.

Bailey, Frank E. *British Policy and the Turkish Reform Movement: A Study in Anglo-Turkish Relations, 1826–53*. Cambridge, Mass.: Harvard University Press, 1942.

Bakr, ʿAbdel-Wahāb, *al-Dawla al-ʿUthmāniyya wa Miṣr fī al-Nisf al-Thānī min al-Qarn al-Thāmin ʿAshr* [The Ottoman Empire and Egypt since the Second Half of the Eighteenth Century]. Cairo: Dār al-Maʿārif, 1982.

Barakāt, ʿAlī. *Taṭawwur al-Milkiyya al-Zirāʿiyya fī Miṣr, 1813–1914 wa Atharuhu ʿala al-Ḥaraka al-Siyāsiyya* [Development of Agricultural Property in Egypt, 1813–1914 and its Effects on the Political Movement]. Cairo: Dār al-Thaqāfa al-Jadīda, 1977.

Barker, John. *Syria and Egypt Under the Last Five Sultans of Turkey*. Two volumes. London: Samuel Tinsley, 1876.

Batou, Jean. "Muhammad-ʿAli's Egypt, 1805–48: A command economy in the 19th century?" In Jean Batou, ed., *Between Development and Underdevelopment: The Precarious Attempts at Industrialization of the Periphery, 1800–70*. Geneva: Droz, 1991, pp. 181–217.

Bertaud, Jean-Paul. "Napoleon's officers." *Past and Present* 112 (1986): 91–112.

Best, Geoffrey. *War and Society in Revolutionary Europe, 1770–1870*. London: Fontana, 1982.

al-Besumee, Hassanaine. *Egypt Under Mohammad Aly Basha*. London: Smith Elder & Co., 1838.

Bourne, Kenneth. *Palmerston: The Early Years, 1784–1841*. London: Allen Lane, 1982.

Boustany, Saladin, ed. *The Journals of Bonaparte in Egypt*. Ten volumes. Cairo: al-ʿArab Bookshop, n.d.

Bowring, Sir John. "Report on Egypt and Candia." *Parliamentary Papers, Reports from Commissioners* 21 (1840): 1–236.

Brewer, John. *The Sinews of Power: War, Money and the English State,1688–1783*. London: Unwin Hyman, 1989.

Brooke, Rupert. *The Collected Poems of Rupert Brooke*. London: Papermac, 1992.

Cadalvène, E. de, and Barrault, E. *Histoire de la guerre de Méhémed-Ali contre la Porte Ottomane, en Syrie et en Asie Mineure*. Paris, 1837.

Cailliaud, Frédéric. *Voyage a Méroé, au Fleuve Blanc, au-delà de Fâzoql*. Four volumes. Paris: L'Imprimerie Royale, 1826.

Cameron, D. A. *Egypt in the Nineteenth Century*. London: Smith, Elder & Co., 1898.

Cannon, Byron. *Politics of Law and the Courts in Nineteenth-Century Egypt*. Salt Lake City: University of Utah Press, 1988.

Chesney, Francis R. *Reports on the Navigation of the Euphrates*. London, 1833.

Clot Bey, Antoine B. *Aperçu général sur l'Egypte*.Two volumes. Paris: Fortin, Masson, 1840.

Mémoires de A.-B. Clot Bey. Ed. Jacques Tagher. Cairo: Imprimerie de l'Institut Français d'Archéologie Orientale, 1949.

Cobb, R. C. *The Police and the People: French Popular Protest, 1789–1820*. Oxford: Oxford University Press, 1970.

Cole, Juan. *Colonialism and Revolution in the Middle East: Social and Cultural Origins of Egypt's 'Urabi Movement*. Princeton: Princeton University Press, 1993.

Crecelius, Daniel. *The Roots of Modern Egypt: A Study of the Regimes of 'Ali Bey al-Kabir and Muhammad Bey Abu al-Dahab, 1760–1775*. Minneapolis: Bibliotheca Islamica, 1981.

Cuno, Kenneth M. *The Pasha's Peasants: Land, Society and Economy in Lower Egypt, 1740–1858*. Cambridge: Cambridge University Press, 1992.

Dean, Mitchell. *Critical and Effective Histories: Foucault's Methods and Historical Sociology*. London: Routledge, 1994.

Dhikrā al-Baṭal al-Fātiḥ Ibrāhīm Bāshā, 1848–1948 [The Hundredth Anniversary of Ibrahim Pasha the Conqueror, 1848–1948]. Cairo: Royal Egyptian Geographical Society, 1948, rpt. Cairo: Madbūlī, 1990.

Dodwell, Henry Herbert. *The Founder of Modern Egypt; A Study of Muhammed Ali*. Cambridge: The University Press, 1931.

Douin, Georges. *Navarin, le 6 Juillet–20 Octobre, 1827*. Cairo: Royal Egyptian Geographical Society, 1927.

Elting, John. *Swords Around a Throne: Napoleon's Grande Armée*. London: The Free Press, 1988.

Fahmy, Khaled. "Women, medicine and power in nineteenth-century Egypt." In Lila Abu Lughod, ed., *Remaking Women: Feminism and Modernity in the Middle East*. Princeton: Princeton University Press, 1998 (forthcoming).

Fahmy, Mustafa. *La Révolution de l'industrie en Egypte et ses conséquences au 19e siècle*. Leiden: E. J. Brill, 1954.

Flaubert, Gustave. *Flaubert in Egypt, A Sensibility on Tour*, trans. and ed. Francis Steegmuller. Chicago: Academy Chicago Press, 1979.

Forrest, Alan. *Conscripts and Deserters: The Army and French Society During the Revolution and Empire*. Oxford: Oxford University Press, 1989.

Soldiers of the French Revolution. London: Duke University Press, 1990.

Foucault, Michel. *Discipline and Punish: The Birth of the Prison*, trans. Alan Sheridan. New York: Vintage Books, 1979.

The History of Sexuality. Volume I: *An Introduction*. London: Pelican, 1981.

"Two lectures." In *Power/Knowledge: Selected Interviews and Other Writings 1972–1977*. New York: Pantheon, 1980.

Fussell, Paul. *The Great War and Modern Memory*. Oxford: Oxford University Press, 1975.

Gallaher, John Gerard. "Recruitment in the district of Poitiers: 1793." *French Historical Studies* 3 (Fall, 1963): 246–67.

Gavin, R. J. *Aden Under British Rule, 1839–1967*. New York: Barnes and Noble, 1975.

Geertz, Clifford. "Centers, kings, and charisma: Reflections on the symbolics of power." In Sean Wilentz, ed., *Rites of Power: Symbolism, Ritual and Politics Since the Middle Ages*. Philadelphia: University of Pennsylvania Press, 1985.

Ghorbal, Shafik. *The Beginnings of the Egyptian Question and the Rise of Mehemet Ali*. London: Routledge, 1928.

Giddens, Anthony. *The Nation-State and Violence*. Berkeley and Los Angeles: University of California Press, 1985.

Gilbert, Arthur N. "The Regimental Courts Martial in the eighteenth-century British army." *Albion* 8 (1976): 50–66.

Gouin, Edouard. *L'Egypte au XIXe siècle; histoire militaire et politique, anecdotique et pittoresque de Méhémet-Ali, Ibrahim-Pacha, Soliman Pacha (Colonel Sève)*. Paris, 1847.

Halls, J. J. *The Life and Correspondence of Henry Salt*. Two volumes. London: Richard Bentley, 1834.

Ḥamdān, Jamāl. *Shakhṣiyyat Miṣr* [The Identity of Egypt]. Three volumes. Cairo: 'Ālam al-Kutub, 1981.

Hamont, P. N. *L'Egypte sous Méhémet Ali*. Two volumes. Paris: Léauty et Lecvonte, 1843.

al-Harrāwī, 'Abdel-Samī'. *Lughat al-Idāra al-'Āmma fī Miṣr fī al-Qarn al-Tāsi' 'Ashr* [The Language of Public Administration in Egypt During the 19th Century]. Cairo: n.p., 1963.

Heidegger, Martin. "The age of the world picture." In *The Question Concerning Technology and Other Essays*, trans. William Lovitt. New York: Harper and Row, 1977.

Heniker, Sir Frederick. *Notes During a Visit to Egypt, the Oases, Mount Sinai and Jerusalem*. London: Murray, 1823.

Heyd, Uriel. *Studies in Old Ottoman Criminal Law*. Oxford: Oxford University Press, 1976.

Heyworth-Dunne, J. *An Introduction to the History of Education in Modern Egypt*. London: Luzac, 1938.

Hintze, Otto. "Military organization and the organization of the state." In Felix Gilbert, ed., *The Historical Essays of Otto Hintze*. New York, 1975.

Hirschkind, Charles. "'Egypt at the Exhibition': Reflections on the optics of colonialism." *Critique of Anthropology* 11 (1991): 279–98.

Hogg, Edward. *Visit to Alexandria, Damascus and Jerusalem, During the Successful Campaign of Ibrahim Pasha*. Two volumes. London: Saunders and Otley, 1835.

Hoskins, Halford L. *British Routes to India*. London: Longman, 1929.

Howard, Michael. *War and the Nation State*. Oxford: Clarendon Press, 1978.

Hunter, F. Robert. *Egypt Under the Khedives, 1805–79: From Household Government to Modern Bureaucracy*. Pittsburgh: University of Pittsburgh Press, 1984.

Hurewitz, J. C. *The Middle East and North Africa in World Politics: A Documentary Record*. Volume. I: *European Expansion, 1535–1914*. New Haven: Yale University Press, 1975.

Ibn Nujaym, Zayn al-Dīn Ibrāhīm. *al-Baḥr al-Rā'iq*. Cairo: al-Maṭba'a al-'Ilmiyya, n.d.

Illustrated London News, 31 August 1844.

İnalçık, Halil. "Husrev Paşa." In *İslam Ansiklopedisi*. Istanbul: Milli Eğitim Basımevi, 1950.

Ingram, Edward. *The Beginning of the Great Game in Asia, 1828–34*. Oxford: Clarendon Press, 1979.

"Interviews with Mehemet Ali," *Tait's Edinburgh Magazine* 5 (1838): 695–8.

al-Jabartī, 'Abdel-Raḥmān. *'Ajā'ib al-Āthār fi'l-Tarājim wa'l-Akhbār*. Four volumes. Cairo: Būlāq, AH 1297/AD 1880.

Tārīkh Muddat al-Faransīs bi-Miṣr, trans. and ed. S. Moreh. Leiden: E. J. Brill, 1975.

Kafāfī, Ḥussayn. *Muḥammad ʿAli: Ruʾya li-Ḥādithat al-Qalʿa* [Mehmed Ali: A View on the Citadel Incident]. Cairo: General Egyptian Book Organization, 1993.

Karal, Enver Z. *Osmanlı Tarihi* [History of the Ottomans]. Ankara: Türk Tarih Kurumu Basımevi, 1983.

al-Kāsānī, Alāʾ al-Dīn. *Badāʾiʿ al-Ṣanāʾiʿ fī Tartīb al-Sharāʾiʿ*. Cairo: al-Imām, 1972.

Kato, Hiroshi. "Egyptian village community under Muhammad ʿAli's rule: An annotation of 'Qanun al-Filaha.'" *Orient* 16 (1980): 183–222.

Keegan, John. *The Face of Battle*. London: Penguin, 1976.

Kelly, J. B. *Britain and the Persian Gulf, 1795–1880*. Oxford: Clarendon Press, 1968.

Kuhnke, LaVerne. *Lives at Risk: Public Health in Nineteenth-Century Egypt*. Berkeley, University of California Press, 1990.

Lane, Edward. *An Account of the Manners and Customs of the Modern Egyptians*. London: 1842, rpt. London: Ward, Lock, 1890.

Arabic–English Lexicon. London: Williams & Norgate, 1863, rpt. Cambridge: The Islamic Texts Society, 1984.

Laurens, Henry. *L'Expédition d'Egypte, 1798–1801*. Paris: Armand Colin, 1995.

Lawson, Fred H. *The Social Origins of Egyptian Expansionism During the Muhammad ʿAli Period*. New York: Columbia University Press, 1992.

Leed, Eric. *No Man's Land: Combat and Identity in World War I*. Cambridge: Cambridge University Press, 1979.

Levy, Avigdor. "Military reform and the problem of centralization in the Ottoman Empire in the eighteenth century." *Middle Eastern Studies* 18 (1982): 227–49.

"The officer corps in Sultan Mahmud II's New Ottoman Army, 1826–39." *International Journal of Middle East Studies* 2 (1971): 21–39.

Lewis, Michael. *The Navy of Britain*. London: George Allen and Unwin, 1948.

The Social History of the Navy, 1793–1815. London: George Allen and Unwin, 1960.

Lindsay, A. W. C., Lord, *Letters on Egypt, Edom, and the Holy Land*. Two volumes. London: Henry Colborn, 1938.

Lutfi Efendi, Ahmed. *Tarih-i Lutfi* [Lutfi's History]. Eight volumes. Istanbul, 1873–1915.

McCarthy, Justin. "Nineteenth century Egyptian population." *Middle Eastern Studies* 3 (1976): 1–39.

Macksey, Piers. *British Victory in Egypt, 1801*. London: Routledge, 1995.

McNeill, William H. *The Pursuit of Power*. Chicago: University of Chicago Press, 1982.

Madden, Richard R. *Egypt and Mohammed Ali*. London: Hamilton, 1841.

Markham, F. M. H. *Napoleon and the Awakening of Europe*. London: English Universities Press, 1954.

Marshal Marmont, Duc de Raguse, *The Present State of the Turkish Empire*, trans. Colonel Sir Frederic Smith. London: Thomas Harrison, 1854.

Marx, Karl. *The Eighteenth Brumaire of Louis Bonaparte.* New York: International Publishers, 1984.

Measor, H. P. *A Tour in Egypt, Arabia Petræa and the Holy Land in the Years 1841–2.* London: Francis and John Rivington, 1844.

Mengin, Felix. *Histoire de L'Egypte sous le gouvernement de Mohammed-Aly.* Two volumes. Paris: Arthus Bertrand, 1823.

Mitchell, Timothy. *Colonising Egypt.* Cambridge: Cambridge University Press, 1988.

Murray, Charles A. *A Short Memoir of Mohammed Ali.* London: Bernard Quaritch, 1898.

Mustafa Rashid Celebi Efendi. "An explanation of the Nizam-y-Gedid." In William Wilkinson, *An Account of the Principalities of Wallachia and Moldovia, Including Various Political Observations Relating to Them.* London: Longman, 1820, pp. 216–94.

Mutwallī, Aḥmad F., ed. *al-Khiṭṭa al-ʿAskariyya Allati Waḍaʿatha al-Dawla al-ʿUthmāniyya l-Istirdād Miṣr min Qabḍat Muḥammad ʿAli* [The Military Plan Put Down By the Ottomans to Recapture Egypt from Mehmed Ali's Grasp]. Cairo: al-Zahrā', 1991.

Najm, Zayn al-ʿĀbidīn S. "Tasaḥḥub al-fallāḥīn fī ʿaṣr Muḥammad ʿAlī: Asbābuhu wa natā'ijuhu" [The absconding of the peasants in Mehmed Ali's reign: Its causes and effects]. *al-Majalla al-Tārīkhiyya al-Miṣriyya* 36 (1989): 259–316.

Nicolle, David. "Nizam – Egypt's army in the 19th century." *The Army Quarterly and Defence Journal* 108 (1978): 69–78 (Part I) and 177–87 (Part II).

Nubar Pasha. *Mémoires de Nubar Pasha,* ed. Mirrit Botros Ghali. Beirut: Librairie du Liban, 1983.

Owen, E. R. J. *Cotton and the Egyptian Economy, 1820–1914.* Oxford: Clarendon Press, 1969.

The Middle East and the World Economy, 1800–1914. London: Tauris, 1993.

Owen, Wilfred. *The Collected Poems of Wilfred Owen.* New York: New Directions, 1965.

Palmer, R. R. "Frederick the Great, Guibert, Bülow: From dynastic to national war." In Peter Paret, ed., *Makers of Modern Strategy: From Machiavelli to the Nuclear Age.* Oxford: Clarendon Press, 1990, pp. 91–119.

Panzac, Daniel. "The population of Egypt in the nineteenth century." *Asian and African Studies* 21 (1987): 11–32.

Paret, Peter. *Understanding War.* Princeton: Princeton University Press, 1992.

Paton, A. A. *History of the Egyptian Revolution.* Two volumes. London: Trubner, 1863.

Patton, Philip. *Strictures on Naval Discipline.* Edinburgh: Murray and Cochrane, n.d.

Planat, Jules. *Histoire de la régénération de l'Egypte.* Paris: n.p., 1830.

Politis, Athanase G. *L'Hellénisme et l'Egypte moderne.* Two volumes. Paris: Félix Alcan, 1929.

Prakash, Gyan. "Writing post-Oriental Histories of the Third World: Perspectives from Indian historiography." *Comparative Studies in Society and History* 32 (1990): 383–408.

Raḍwān, Abūl-Futūḥ. *Tārīkh Maṭba'at Būlāq* [History of the Būlāq Press]. Cairo: Būlāq, 1953.

al-Rāf'ī, 'Abdel-Raḥmān. *'Aṣr Muḥammad 'Alī* [Mehmet Ali's Reign]. Cairo: Dār al-Ma'ārif, 1989.

al-Rajabī, Khalīl ibn Aḥmad. *Fī Sha'n al-Wazīr Muhammad 'Alī* [Regarding the Vizier Mehmed Ali]. Unpublished MS dated AH 1238/AD 1822–23. Partially trans. and ed. by Husam N. Shakhshir, unpublished MA thesis, American University in Cairo, 1985.

Ralston, David B. *Importing the European Army: The Introduction of European Military Techniques and Institutions into the Extra-European World, 1600–1914*. Chicago: University of Chicago Press, 1990.

Raymond, André. *Artisans et commerçants au Caire au XVIIIe siècle*. Two volumes. Damascus: Institut français, 1973–74.

Ridley, Jasper. *Lord Palmerston*. London: Constable, 1970.

Rif'at, M. A. *The Awakening of Modern Egypt*. London: Longman, 1947.

Rivlin, Helen Anne B. *The Agricultural Policy of Muhammad 'Alī in Egypt*. Cambridge, Mass.: Harvard University Press, 1961.

Rizq, Yūnān Labīb. "al-Jabartī wa'l-shakhṣiyya al-Miṣriyya" [al-Jabartī and the Egyptian identity]. In Aḥmad 'Izzat 'Abdel-Karīm, ed., *'Abdel-Raḥmān al-Jabartī: Dirāsāt wa Buḥūth*. Cairo: General Egyptian Book Organization, 1976.

Rodkey, F. S. "The attempts of Briggs and Company to guide British Policy in the Levant in the Interest of Mehemet Ali Pasha, 1821–41." *Journal of Modern History* 5 (1933): 324–51.

Rose, N. and P. Miller. "Political power beyond the State: problematics of government." *British Journal of Sociology* 43 (1992): 173–205.

Rustum, Asad J. *Notes on Akka and its Defences Under Ibrahim Pasha*. 1926.

The Royal Archives of Egypt and the Disturbances in Palestine, 1834. Beirut: The American Press, 1938.

The Royal Archives of Egypt and the Origins of the Egyptian Expedition to Syria. Beirut: The American Press, 1936.

Rustum, Asad J., ed. *Ḥurūb Ibrāhīm Bāshā fī Sūriyya wa'l-Anāḍūl* [Ibrahim Pasha's Wars in Syria and Anatolia]. Two volumes. Heliopolis: Imprimerie Syrienne, n.d.

Sabry, Mohamed. *L'Empire égyptien sous Mohamed-Ali et la question d'Orient (1811–49)*. Paris: Geuthner, 1930.

St. John, James Augustus. *Egypt and Mohammed-Ali*. Two volumes. London: Longman, 1834.

Sālim, Laṭīfa M. *al-Ḥukm al-Miṣrī fī al-Shām, 1831–41* [Egyptian Rule in Syria, 1831–1841]. Cairo: Madbūlī, 1990.

al-Sayyid Marsot, Afaf Lutfi. *Egypt in the Reign of Muhammad Ali*. Cambridge: Cambridge University Press, 1984.

Scott, C. Rochfort. *Rambles in Egypt and Candia*. Two volumes. London: Henry Colburn, 1837.

Serheng, Ismā'īl. *Ḥaqā'iq al-Akhbār fī Duwal al-Biḥār*. [The True Narrations About Maritime Nations]. Three volumes. Cairo: Būlāq, AH 1316/AD 1898–99.

Shalabī, Ḥilmī A. *al-Muwaẓẓafūn fī Miṣr fī ʿAṣr Muḥammad ʿAlī*. [Public Employees in Egypt During the Reign of Mehmed Ali]. Cairo: General Egyptian Book Organization, 1989.

Shaw, Stanford J. *Between Old and New, The Ottoman Empire Under Sultan Selim III, 1789–1807*. Cambridge, Mass.: Harvard University Press, 1971.

"The established Ottoman army corps under Sultan Selim III (1789–07)." *Der Islam* 40 (1965): 142–84.

"The origins of Ottoman military reform." *Journal of Modern History* 37 (1965): 291–306.

Ottoman Egypt in the Eighteenth Century. Cambridge, Mass.: Harvard University Press, 1962.

Shaw, Stanford J., and Ezel Kural Shaw. *History of the Ottoman Empire and Modern Turkey*. Volume II: *Reform, Revolution and Republic: The Rise of Modern Turkey, 1808–1975*. Cambridge: Cambridge University Press, 1977.

al-Shayyāl, Jamāl al-Dīn. *Tārīkh al-Tarjama wa'l-Ḥaraka al-Thaqāfiyya fī ʿAṣr Muḥammad ʿAlī* [History of Translation and the Cultural Movement During the Reign of Mehmed Ali]. Cairo: n.p., 1951.

al-Shihābī, Ḥaidar. *al-Ghurar al-Ḥisān fī Akhbār Abnāʾ al-Zāmān*, ed. Asad Rustum and Fuʾad al-Bustānī. Beirut: The Catholic Press, 1933.

Showalter, Elaine. *The Female Malady: Women, Madness, and English Culture*. New York: Pantheon, 1985.

"Rivers and Sassoon: The inscription of male gender anxieties." In Margaret R. Higonnet, Jane Jenson, Sonya Michel and Margaret C. Weitz, eds., *Behind the Lines: Gender and the Two World Wars*. New Haven: Yale University Press, 1987.

Shukrī, Muḥammad F. "Baʿtha ʿaskariyya Būlūniyya fī Miṣr fī ʿahd Muḥammad ʿAlī" [A Polish military mission during Mehmed Ali's reign]. *Majallat Kulliyyat al-Ādāb, Fouad I University* 8 (1946): 27–47.

Sonbol, Amira el-Azhary. *The Creation of a Medical Profession in Egypt, 1800–1922*. New York: Syracuse University Press, 1991.

Steppler, G. A. "British military law, discipline, and the conduct of regimental courts martial in the later eighteenth century." *English Historical Review* (October 1987): 859–86.

Strachan, Hew. *European Armies and the Conduct of War*. London: George Allen and Unwin, 1983.

Ṣubḥī, Muḥammad Khalīl. *Tārīkh al-Ḥayāh al-Niyābiyya fī Miṣr min ʿAhd Sākin al-Jinān Muḥammad ʿAlī Bāshā*. [History of Parliamentary Life in Egypt Since the Reign of the Late Mehmed Ali Pasha]. Five volumes. Cairo: Dār al-Kutub, 1939.

al-Ṭahṭāwī, Rifāʿa Rāfiʿ. "Extrait d'une lettre adressée par M. Le Cheykh Refah, ancien élève de la mission égyptienne en France, à M. Jomard, membre de l'Institut." *Journal Asiatique* IIe série 8 (1831): 534–35.

Taymūr, Maḥmūd. "Abū al-Hawl yunājī al-Qāhira" [The Sphinx confides in Cairo]. *al-Hilāl*, 57 (August 1949): 36–41.

Temperley, H. W. V. *England and the Near East: The Crimea*. London: Longman, 1964.

Toledano, Ehud. "Mehmet Ali Paşa or Muhammad Ali Basha? An historiographical appraisal in the wake of a recent book." *Middle Eastern Studies* 21 (1985): 141–59.

State and Society in Mid-Nineteenth-Century Egypt. Cambridge: Cambridge University Press, 1990.

Tomiche, Nada. "Notes sur la hiérarchie sociale en Egypte à l'époque de Mohammad 'Ali." In P. M. Holt, ed., *Political and Social Change in Modern Egypt*. London: Oxford University Press, 1968, pp. 249–63.

Tucker, Judith. *Women in Nineteenth-Century Egypt*. Cambridge: Cambridge University Press, 1985.

Tusun, Prince 'Umar. *al-Tārīkh al-Ḥarbī li-'Aṣr Muḥammad 'Alī al-Kabīr* [Military History of the Reign of Mehmed Ali the Great]. Cairo: Dār al-Ma'ārif, n.d.

'Ubaid, Jamīl. *Qiṣṣat Iḥtilāl Muḥammad 'Alī lil-Yūnān* [The Story of Mehmed Ali's Occupation of Greece]. Cairo: General Egyptian Book Organization, 1990.

Vatikiotis, P. J. *The History of Egypt*. London: Weidenfeld and Nicolson, 1985.

Verdery, Richard N. "The publications of the Buluq Press under Muhammad 'Ali of Egypt." *Journal of the American Oriental Society* 91 (1971): 129–32.

Vereté, M. "Palmerston and the Levant Crisis, 1832." *Journal of Modern History* 24 (June 1952): 143–51.

Waghorn, Thomas. *Egypt in 1837*. London: Smith Elder, 1837.

Walsh, Thomas. *Journal of the Late Campaign in Egypt*. London: Hansard, 1803.

Weber, Eugen. *Peasants into Frenchmen*. London: Chatto and Windus, 1977.

Wendell, Charles. *The Evolution of the Egyptian National Image, From its Origins to Ahmad Lutfi al-Sayyid*. Berkeley: University of California Press, 1972.

Weygand, Maxime. *Histoire militaire de Mohammed Aly et de ses fils*. Two volumes. Paris: Impremeire Nationale, 1936.

Wilde, W. R. *Narrative of a Voyage to Madeira, Teneriffe and Along the Shores of the Mediterranean Including a Visit to Algiers, Egypt, Palestine, etc.* Dublin: William Curry, 1844.

Wilkinson, Sir John Gardner. *Modern Egypt and Thebes*. Two volumes. London: John Murray, 1843.

Wilkinson, Spenser. *Britain at Bay*. London: Constable, 1909.

Wirtschafter, Elise K. "Military justice and social relations in the Prereform army, 1796–1855." *Slavic Review* 44 (1985): 67–82.

Woloch, I. "Napoleonic conscription: state power and civil society." *Past and Present* 111 (1986): 101–29.

Woodhouse, C. M. *The Battle of Navarino*. London: Hodder and Stoughton, 1965.

Zakī, 'Abdel-Raḥmān. *al-A'lām wa Shārāt al-Mulk fī Wādī al-Nīl* [Flags and Royal Insignia in the Nile valley]. (Cairo: Dār al-Ma'ārif, 1948.

"The first and second Syrian campaigns," in *Dhikrā al-Baṭal al-Fātiḥ Ibrāhīm Bāshā, 1848–1948*.

"The governors of the Sudan." *al-Majalla al-Tārīkhiyya al-Miṣriyya* 1 (1948): 428–43.

Malābis al-Jaysh al-Miṣrī fī 'Ahd Muḥammad 'Alī al-Kabīr [Uniforms of the Egyptian Army During the Reign of Mehmed Ali the Great]. Cairo: al-Maṭba'a al-Amīriyya, 1949.

al-Tārīkh al-Ḥarbī li-'Aṣr Muḥammad 'Alī al-Kabīr [Military History of the Reign of Mehmed Ali the Great]. Cairo: Dār al-Ma'ārif, 1950.

Zubaida, Sami. "Exhibitions of power." *Economy and Society* 19 (1990): 359–75.

Index

Arabic ʿ (ʿain) and the prefix "al-" are ignored for the purposes of alphabetization, as are English "and," "his," "in," "of" and "the."